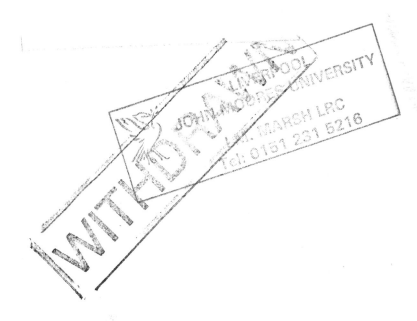

D1134680

FOOD AT WORK

WORKPLACE SOLUTIONS FOR MALNUTRITION, OBESITY AND CHRONIC DISEASES

The author

Christopher Wanjek is a freelance health and science writer based in the United States. He is a frequent contributor to The Washington Post *and popular science magazines, and he is the author of* Bad medicine: misconceptions and misuses revealed. *Mr. Wanjek has a Master of Science in environmental health from Harvard School of Public Health.*

FOOD AT WORK

WORKPLACE SOLUTIONS FOR MALNUTRITION, OBESITY AND CHRONIC DISEASES

Christopher Wanjek

INTERNATIONAL LABOUR OFFICE • GENEVA

Wanjek, C.
Food at work: Workplace solutions for malnutrition, obesity and chronic diseases
Geneva, International Labour Office, 2005

ILO descriptors: provision of meals, food service, occupational health, occupational safety, developed country, developing country. 13.08

ISBN 92-2-117015-2

ILO Cataloguing in Publication Data

The designations employed in ILO publications, which are in conformity with United Nations practice, and the presentation of material therein do not imply the expression of any opinion whatsoever on the part of the International Labour Office concerning the legal status of any country, area or territory or of its authorities, or concerning the delimitation of its frontiers.

The responsibility for opinions expressed in signed articles, studies and other contributions rests solely with their authors, and publication does not constitute an endorsement by the International Labour Office of the opinions expressed in them.

Reference to names of firms and commercial products and processes does not imply their endorsement by the International Labour Office, and any failure to mention a particular firm, commercial product or process is not a sign of disapproval.

ILO publications can be obtained through major booksellers or ILO local offices in many countries, or direct from ILO Publications, International Labour Office, CH-1211 Geneva 22, Switzerland. Catalogues or lists of new publications are available free of charge from the above address or by email: pubvente@ilo.org

Visit our website: www.ilo.org/publns

Typeset by Magheross Graphics, France & Ireland *www.magheross.com*
Printed in Italy   LAS

FOREWORD

The rights to safe drinking water and to freedom from hunger are basic human rights and yet all too often ignored in the context of rights at work. Equally, they are an essential foundation of a productive workforce, and yet also all too often ignored in the context of productivity improvement and enhanced enterprise competitiveness. Measures to ensure a properly fed and healthy workforce are an indispensable element of social protection of workers, and yet frequently absent from programmes to improve working conditions and occupational safety and health. And despite the fact that these concerns are indeed fundamental ones for both employers and workers, they all too rarely feature as topics for social dialogue.

Food at work is therefore inextricably linked to the pillars of the ILO's Decent Work Agenda. It touches not only on questions of nutrition, food safety and food security, although these in themselves are important enough. But it also calls into question other basic issues of working and employment conditions: wages and incomes, since workers – and their families – cannot eat decently if they do not receive an adequate income; working time, since workers cannot eat decently if their meal break is too short, or if their shift requires them to work at times when food is not available; and work-related facilities, since workers' health will be affected both by the quality of what they eat and drink at work and the conditions in which they consume it (such as protection from workplace chemicals and other hazards).

The importance of food at work is reflected in the Millennium Development Goals which set targets of halving, by 2015, the proportion of people who suffer from hunger and those without sustainable access to safe drinking water and basic sanitation. These targets are not only to be met at the workplace, but the workplace is an essential place to make a start. This recognition is not new: food at work was recognized as a building block of social justice in the 1944 Declaration of Philadelphia concerning the aims and purposes of the ILO, which recognized the ILO's obligation "to further among the nations of the world programmes which will achieve: ... the provision of adequate nutrition, housing and facilities for recreation and culture".

This book was conceived as a response to the lack of attention to the issue of food at work. It aims to show not simply why this issue is important – that is rather easily done – but also, and more importantly, what employers, workers and governments can do and what they have done to improve food at work. It is intended as a practical rather than a theoretical contribution. We hope that amongst the many examples of good practice from around the world that are presented here, some will seem useful, relevant and replicable to the readers. These examples, taken from a wide range of countries and enterprises – from multinationals operating in highly industrialized countries to small-scale enterprises in developing countries and countries in transition – show that every business can benefit from improved attention to food at work. They also provide evidence that improvements – whether through improved cafeterias or mess halls, the introduction of meal voucher programmes, working with local vendors and others to improve street foods, or the provision of safe drinking water – are within the reach of any business, even the smallest. Furthermore, they demonstrate the active role that can, and indeed must, be played in this process by workers and their organizations, as well as the role for governments.

François Eyraud, Director
William Salter, Senior Adviser
Conditions of Work and Employment Programme
Social Protection Sector

CONTENTS

FIGURES

TABLES

BOXES

ACKNOWLEDGEMENTS

The author would like to acknowledge the valuable contributions of the following people at all stages of the book: Suzumi Yasutake, Mariano Winograd, Vladimir Usatyuk, Susanne Tøttenborg, K.C. Tang, Vivien Stone, Beatrice Spadacini, Jørgen Schlundt, Marta Senyszyn, William Salter, Chris Rochette, Richard Rinehart, Gerhard Riess, Nathalie Renaudin, Dries Pretorius, James Platner, Robert Pederson, Jane Paul, Sarah O'Brien, Dara Nov, Biplap Nandi, Alice Mwangi, Franklin Muchiri, Gerald Moy, Golam Mowlah, Richa Mittal, Joann Lo, Nathalie Liautaud, Anne Lally, Jutta Kellner, Belay Kassahun, Edín Rolando Pop Juárez, Juan Carlos Hiba, Lyle Hargrove, Thierry Guihard, Elizabeth Goodson, David Gold, Sylvia Fulgencio, Franceen Friefeld, Laurent Fourier, Valentina Forastieri, Kristine Falciola, Patrick Dalban-Moreynas, Edward Croushore, Mabel Chia-Yarrall, Indira Chakravarty, Enrico Casadei, Alexandra Cameron (co-author for parts of Chapter 1), Joannah Caborn, H. Müge Çamligüney, Eric Boulte, Gopal Bhattacharya, Bruno de Benoist, Charlotte Beauchamp, Jacqueline Baroncini, Omara Amuko, and all the company and union representatives who provided information for the case studies.

INTRODUCTION

Why workers' nutrition is important

- Nearly a billion people are undernourished and one billion are overweight or obese; a stark contrast of the haves and have-nots (WHO, 2004a).

- Workplace meal programmes can prevent micronutrient deficiencies and chronic diseases, including obesity. Investments in nutrition are repaid in a reduction of sick days and accidents and an increase in productivity and morale.

- Access to healthy food (and protection from unsafe and unhealthy food and eating arrangements) is as essential as protection from workplace chemicals or noise.

- Adequate nourishment can raise national productivity levels by 20 per cent (WHO, 2003a).

- A 1 per cent kilocalorie (kcal) increase results in a 2.27 per cent increase in general labour productivity (Galenson and Pyatt, 1964).

- Increasing the average daily energy supply to 2,770 kcal per person per day with adequate nutrients in a sample of countries could have increased the average annual GDP growth rate by nearly 1 per cent each year between 1960 and 1990 (Arcand, 2001).

- Iron deficiency affects up to half the world's population, predominantly in the developing world (Stoltzfus, 2001). Low iron levels are associated with weakness, sluggishness and lack of coordination.

- As much as a 30 per cent impairment in physical work capacity and performance is reported in iron-deficient men and women (WHO, 2001, p. 30).

- Micronutrient deficiencies account for a 2–3 per cent loss in GDP in low-income countries; and in South Asia, iron deficiency alone accounts for a loss of US$5 billion in productivity (Ross and Horton, 1998, p. 38).

- Hypoglycaemia, or low blood sugar, which can occur when one skips a meal, can shorten attention span and slow the speed at which humans process information (McAulay et al., 2001).

- Obesity accounts for 2–7 per cent of total health costs in industrialized countries (Kumanyika et al., 2002).

- In the United States, the total cost attributable to obesity calculated for 1995 amounted to US$99.2 billion (Wolf and Colditz, 1998).

- Studies have shown that obese workers are twice as likely as fit workers to miss work (Wolf and Colditz, 1998).

- In 2001, non-communicable diseases contributed to about 46 per cent of the global disease burden and 60 per cent of all deaths worldwide, with cardiovascular disease alone amounting to 30 per cent of deaths (WHO, 2002a, p. 188). The global disease burden from non-communicable diseases is expected to climb to 57 per cent by 2020 (WHO, 2003b, p. 4).

- The diabetes epidemic is particularly acute in the South Pacific, where the percentage of total health-care resources allocated to this disease is 6 per cent in Fiji, 10 per cent in the Federated States of Micronesia, 14 per cent in the Marshall Islands and 14 per cent in the Cook Islands (WHO Regional Office for the Western Pacific, 2003).

Workers' meal programmes are good for workers, good for business and good for the nations.

This book addresses a simple question – how do workers eat while at work? This question, we have found, is not always given much thought. This is strange, as food is the fuel that powers production. One would think that employers, wanting to maximize productivity, would provide their workforce with nourishing food or, at the very least, convenient access to healthy food.

What we have found in researching material for this book is that workplace meal programmes are largely a missed opportunity. It is a salient fact that world-wide nearly a billion people are undernourished while over one billion are overweight. How do we address this catastrophic misappropriation of food resources? The World Health Organization (WHO) and the Food and Agriculture Organization (FAO), among other international bodies, have taken great steps in remedying malnutrition through projects focused on better food supply chains, storage, land management, food fortification, bulk food distribution and education. Our view, in assisting this global aim, is that the workplace should be a locale for meal provision and nutrition education initiatives.

Too often the workplace meal programme is either an afterthought or not even considered by employers. Work, instead of being accommodating, is frequently a hindrance to proper nutrition. Canteens, if they exist, routinely offer an unhealthy and unvaried selection. Vending machines are regularly stocked with unhealthy snacks. Local restaurants can be expensive or in short supply. Street foods can be bacteria laden. Workers sometimes have no time to eat, no place to eat or no money to purchase food. Some workers are unable to consume enough calories to perform the strenuous work expected of them. Agricultural and construction workers often eat in dangerous and insanitary conditions. Mobile workers and day labourers are expected to fend for themselves. Migrant workers, far from home, often find themselves with no access to local markets and no means to store or cook food. Night shift-workers find they have few meal options after hours. Hundreds of millions of workers face an undesirable eating arrangement every day. Many go hungry; many get sick, sooner or later. The result is a staggering blow to productivity and health. Poorer nations, in particular, remain in a cycle of poor nutrition, poor health, low productivity, low wages and no development.

Presented in this book are mostly positive examples of how governments, employers and trade unions are trying to improve the nutritional status of workers. In wealthier nations, where obesity and related non-communicable diseases – cancer, diabetes, cardiovascular disease and kidney problems – are epidemic, we find some employers offering healthier menus or better access to healthier foods, such as on-site farmers' markets. In developing and emerging economies, where hunger and micronutrient deficiencies such as anaemia are epidemic, we find some employers offering free, well-balanced meals or access to safer street foods.

Chapter 1 provides governments, employers and workers with a rationale for embracing a proper workplace meal programme. Governments gain from a well-nourished population through reductions in health costs, through tax revenue from increased work productivity, and – in feeding its children – through the security of future generations of healthy workers. The savings are significant. In Southeast Asia, iron deficiency accounts for a US$5 billion loss in productivity. In wealthier nations, obesity accounts for 2 to 7 per cent of total health costs. In addition to these costs, employers must understand that poor nutrition is tied to absenteeism, sickness, low morale and higher rates of accidents. Obesity, inadequate calories and iron deficiency result in fatigue and lack of dexterity. Employees must understand that their health and thus job security is dependent upon proper nutrition. The workplace can be an instrument for eating well.

Chapter 2 is an overview of nutrition, complemented by Appendices A and B. Chapter 3 demonstrates how the workplace is the logical setting for nutrition intervention. First, nutrition is an occupational health and safety concern. Spoiled food can be as deadly to the workforce as a chemical leak; poor nutrition can be as deadly as a weak ladder rung. Second, workers usually come to the workplace regularly for an extended period, making intervention convenient. Larger enterprises regularly have the means to make some improvement at little cost, such as negotiating with food suppliers for safer, healthier food or providing better shelter to make the meal more restful and enjoyable. Even the smallest enterprises have low-cost options, such as working with local vendors to supply clean water or discount vouchers. Issues raised in this chapter include cost, place, time, comfort, accessibility and gender.

Chapter 4 begins a series of case studies – the heart of this publication. The Chapter 4 case studies concern canteens, a facility where freshly prepared, hot food is served. A proper canteen is a reflection of a well-run enterprise. Canteens require the greatest investment of resources among the meal solutions presented in this book, but examples of inexpensive canteen improvement are also listed here. Canteens are well suited for remote sites, such as mines and factories, where there are no local food options. Some remote sites offer lavish canteens as a means to attract employees, while other sites (particularly in the agricultural sector) offer very basic meals of grain with little meat or vegetables. Notable canteens presented in Chapter 4 include those who: have removed unhealthy foods completely; offer subsidized meals designed to combat specific nutritional deficiencies; made radical improvements at the request of unions or employees; and improved hygiene.

Chapter 5 contains case studies of countries with food and meal vouchers. Vouchers are tickets provided by the employer to the employee, or sometimes their families, for food and meals at selected shops and restaurants. The voucher programme, sanctioned by the government, is common in Europe and South America and is spreading to other regions. The programme offers many benefits: saves employers the cost of maintaining a canteen; helps governments in tax collection, keeping transactions on the books; and revitalizes urban centres with restaurants and shops. The Brazil voucher system has sharply reduced malnutrition and increased productivity. Vouchers work best in densely populated areas with a variety of shops to choose from.

The case studies in Chapter 6 are about mess rooms and kitchenettes – spaces at an office or facility set aside for eating. Mess rooms and kitchenettes usually require less investment than canteens and vouchers. At a minimum, a decent mess room could be a simple room with chairs, tables, protection from the weather and a place to wash before eating. Mess rooms entail little or no cooking and food storage. Employers, for example, can invite a local caterer daily to sell food. Kitchenettes are small rooms with some means to cook or heat food (stove, microwave oven, hotplate, rice cooker), to store food (refrigerator or cupboard) and to wash up. Although simplistic, properly maintained mess rooms and kitchenettes can increase an employee's meal options and provide a high level of comfort and convenience.

In Chapter 7 the case studies describe local vendors: nearby shops, street food vendors, vending machines and office foods for meetings and events. Employers who work with local vendors can improve their employees' meal options. For example, employers can provide street vendors with fresh water, ice chests, stainless steel utensils or any other item that improves food safety, as well as assisting them to receive training on food safety and nutrition. Construction workers usually rely on local vendors. Often this is low-quality food eaten in undesirable conditions, such as on the roadside or on a dirty construction site. Novel programmes presented in this chapter include workplace farmers' markets, the workplace free fruit programme and street food improvement activities.

Chapter 8 extends workplace nutrition to the family. Feeding an adult at work will leave more food at home for the family. Yet some employers can reach out directly to the workers' families. In wealthier nations, the take-home dinner option from the company canteen is growing in popularity among working parents. Some companies distribute food staples in bulk, such as rice, which can curb hunger at home. Other companies run low-cost shops or bakeries with discounted foods for the worker to bring home.

Chapter 9 concerns water. Access to clean drinking water is particularly important for workers in warm climates or performing arduous work. Some workers are drinking more water for health or dietary reasons. Employers have many options in providing clean water. If the municipal water is unsafe or inaccessible, employers can install water coolers or water filtration systems.

Chapters 10, 11 and 12 will help employers make proper nutrition a reality. Chapter 10 lists the many factors that employers need to consider when developing meal options for their employees, such as budget, space, number of employees, nutritional needs and food safety. This is followed by a checklist of specific items and concerns for each food solution presented in this book. Chapter 11 provides a description of useful documents on international standards, policies and programmes. Chapter 12, the conclusion, ties it all together.

In short, this publication demonstrates how good nutrition is good business and a sound investment. Proper nutrition leads to gains in productivity and worker morale, prevention of accidents and premature deaths, and reductions in health-care costs. For the government, employers and workers, proper nutrition at the workplace is a win-win-win proposition.

PART I

NUTRITION AND THE WORKPLACE

1

THE HISTORY AND ECONOMICS OF WORKPLACE NUTRITION

Photo: WHO/P. Virot

"All sorrows are less with bread."

Spanish proverb

Key issues

The price of poor nutrition

- Nearly a billion people are undernourished while over one billion are obese or overweight.

- The cost of cardiovascular disease for the United States in 2002 was US$329.2 billion.[1]

- In India, the cost of lost productivity, illness and death due to malnutrition is US$10–28 billion, or 3–9 per cent of gross domestic product (GDP).

- Iron deficiency accounts for up to a 30 per cent impairment of physical work capacity and performance.

Nutrition as an element of a healthy workplace

- In 1956, the International Labour Conference and various International Labour Organization (ILO) committees adopted the Welfare Facilities Recommendation (No. 102), which specified guidelines for the establishment of canteens, cafeterias, mess rooms and other food facilities.

---

[1] Unless otherwise stated, all currency exchange rates in this book were converted into United States dollars on 5 December 2004, using mid-market rates posted online (consult: http://www.xe.com/ucc/convert.cgi)).

- The workplace, where many adults spend a third of their day, or half their waking hours, is a logical place for health intervention.

- Providing nourishing food to workers, even for a fee, can improve quality of life and work.

The rationale for government

- Governments gain from a well-nourished population through revenue from increased work productivity and reductions in health costs for adults and, by feeding children, through securing future generations of healthy workers.

- In 2001, non-communicable (diet-related) diseases contributed to about 46 per cent of the global disease burden and 60 per cent of all deaths worldwide, with cardiovascular disease alone amounting to 30 per cent of deaths.

- The global burden from non-communicable diseases is expected to climb to 57 per cent by 2020.

- Obesity accounts for 2–7 per cent of total health costs in industrialized countries.

- In Australia, diabetes costs the government health system AUS$1 billion (US$0.78 billion) and may reach AUS$2.3 billion (US$1.8 billion) by 2010.

- Micronutrient deficiencies account for a 2–3 per cent loss in GDP in low-income countries; and in South Asia, iron deficiency accounts for a loss of US$5 billion in productivity.

- Increasing the average daily energy supply to 2,770 kcal per person per day with adequate nutrients in a sample of countries could have increased the average annual GDP growth rate by nearly 1 per cent each year between 1960 and 1990.

The rationale for employers

- Obesity and iron deficiency both result in fatigue and loss in dexterity.

- A 1 per cent kcal increase results in a 2.27 per cent increase in general labour productivity.

- In the United States the annual economic costs of obesity to business for insurance, paid sick leave and other payments are US$12.7 billion.

- In Canada, the cost-effectiveness of workplace health promotion programmes is estimated to be CAN$1.75–6.85 (US$1.50–5.75) for every corporate dollar invested.

The great houses of the Chaco were architectural marvels. Built over a thousand years ago by the indigenous people of what is now New Mexico in the United States, these impressive structures were often five storeys tall with hundreds of rooms, vast open public areas and sophisticated astronomical markers. Unlike other extended earthen buildings around the world, with rooms and units added as needed over the years, the Chaco's great houses were carefully planned from the beginning. They were constructed in the high desert, surrounded by sacred mountains and mesas and often at least 50 kilometres from fertile lands. It is thought that they were used only periodically, for religious and ceremonial purposes. An extensive network of roads connected each site.

Construction of such magnitude required extraordinary coordination of supplies and labour, similar to large projects today. This was no simple feat. The great houses, which took years to complete, were situated in the desert where conditions were not favourable for growing corn, a staple for the Chaco. So how did the workers eat? A recent archaeological excavation of the great houses at Pueblo Bonito, the largest of the sites in the Chaco Canyon, revealed that corn was hauled great distances to feed the workers (Benson et al., 2003). It seems that a thousand years ago, the leaders of Chaco society understood that workers' nutrition was paramount in producing high-quality work.

Workers need nutritious foods to remain healthy and productive. This basic need has remained unchanged through the millennia. Yet with what we now understand about nutritional deficiencies, obesity and non-communicable diseases associated with nutrition, such as cancer and anaemia, the need for proper nourishment is all the more pressing to ensure a healthy population. The workplace, where workers gather day after day, is the logical locale to provide nutritious foods to curb hunger and lower the risk of disease.

This publication is intended to raise awareness of the importance of workers' rest and nutrition, and their potential contribution to workplace initiatives to improve health, safety and productivity. The following pages present a multitude of "food solutions" applicable to a variety of workplaces around the globe and demonstrate that providing nutritious foods to workers is not only economically viable but a profitable business practice. The rationale, summarized in this chapter but expanded in later chapters, is delivered in terms of gains in productivity and worker morale, prevention of accidents and premature deaths, and reductions in health-care costs. Governments gain from a healthy workforce too by virtue of attracting and maintaining businesses, increasing tax revenue and reducing the health and opportunity costs of non-communicable and communicable diseases. For the employer, employee and government, proper nutrition at the workplace is a win-win-win proposition.

1.1   The price of poor nutrition

The world has become increasingly divided between those who are under-nourished and those who are overfed. Nearly a billion people are undernourished while over one billion are overweight or obese – a stark contrast of haves and have-nots (WHO, 2004a). In the first group we find the chronically malnourished, often in poor and developing nations but also in rural and urban pockets of wealthy, industrialized nations. Through a lack of consistent access to food, such people suffer from nutritional deficiencies. The second group has easy access to food, but of the high-calorie, fatty, sugary and salty kind. These people are often in wealthier nations and pockets of poorer, developing nations. Both groups are at risk of non-communicable and communicable diseases. Both groups suffer as a result of lower productivity. And the costs are staggering.

Consider the epidemic of obesity in the United States, where over two-thirds of the adult population are overweight, including over 30 per cent who are obese, according to the United States National Health and Nutrition Examination Survey (NHANES) 1999–2000 (Flegal et al., 2002). In one of several studies, the total cost attributable to obesity calculated for 1995 amounted to US$99.2 billion (Wolf and Colditz, 1998). Direct medical costs accounted for approximately US$51.6 billion and lost productivity approximately US$3.9 billion – reflected in 39.2 million lost work-days, 239 million restricted-activity days, 89.5 million bed-days and 62.6 million physician visits. Conditions attributed to obesity in this analysis include diabetes, coronary heart disease, hypertension, gallbladder disease, several cancers and osteoarthritis. Obese workers were twice as likely to miss work as non-obese workers (Wolf and Colditz, 1998). Other studies have found similar costs. If no action is taken, the problem won't go away. Obesity is largely viewed as an emerging pandemic. Over 15 per cent of American children are overweight, a rate that has risen consistently each year of the last decade, according to the NHANES data referred to earlier (Ogden et al., 2002). Populations in other developed nations, adopting a diet of fatty and sugary processed foods and an increasing level of physical inactivity, are also growing obese. Those in developing countries may be particularly susceptible to obesity when faced with new food choices as a result of experiencing bouts of food shortages in years past that set their metabolisms to survive on minimal calories.

Consider too the cost of iron deficiency, the most common nutritional disorder in the world. As many as four to five billion people, 66–80 per cent of the world's population, may have some level of iron deficiency (WHO, 2003a). Estimates of the extent of iron deficiency anaemia range from two billion (WHO, 2003a) to three billion people (Stoltzfus, 2001). Iron deficiency reduces the work capacity of entire populations, a serious hindrance to economic development.

Common symptoms in adults include sluggishness, low immunity, low endurance and a decrease in work productivity for mental and repetitive tasks. As much as a 30 per cent impairment of physical work capacity and performance is reported in iron-deficient men and women (WHO, 2001, p. 30). For children, iron deficiency can result in learning disabilities, stunted growth and death, thus hampering economic development efforts in future generations. The economic implications of iron deficiency and of the various intervention strategies to combat it suggest that food-based approaches and targeted supplementation are particularly cost-effective. The highest benefit-to-cost ratio comes through food fortification (WHO, 2001, pp. 52–55). Adequate nourishment can raise national productivity levels by 20 per cent (WHO, 2003a). Early ILO research found that a 1 per cent kcal increase resulted in a 2.27 per cent increase in general labour productivity (Galenson and Pyatt, 1964).

1.2 Nutrition as an element of a healthy workplace

The importance of adequate nourishment for general health and work productivity hardly needs emphasis. Since its establishment, the International Labour Organization has been concerned with this topic. Scholarly articles on the subject began to appear in the 1930s, culminating in 1946 with ILO's *Nutrition in industry* (ILO, 1946), a book about feeding workers in large enterprises in Great Britain, Canada, and the United States. In 1956, the International Labour Conference and various ILO committees adopted the Welfare Facilities Recommendation (No. 102), which specified guidelines for the establishment of canteens, cafeterias, mess rooms and other food facilities. The focus has changed somewhat in developed countries since 1956, when the concern was to ensure that workers had enough food, to today where obesity is a major problem in some areas; and there is also greater attention to food safety and education. The guidelines remain especially significant in developing countries where, whether at local- or foreign-owned enterprises, workers too often have poor diets. The workplace is a logical place for health intervention, for workers are usually there most days. Providing nourishing food to workers, even for a fee, can improve quality of life and work, and have positive "trickle down" effects for the family as well. In many cultures where food is in short supply, the adult male in the family is the first to eat and either the children or mothers are last. Food at work or provided by work can increase food availability at home.

The ILO strives for decent work and equates decent work with human dignity. Through its Workers' Health Promotion and Well-being at Work programmes, part of the In Focus Programme on Safety and Health at Work and the Environment, the ILO endeavours to "further among the nations of the world programmes which will achieve ... adequate protection for the life and health of workers in all occupations", as stated in the 1944 Declaration of Philadelphia, Annex to the ILO Constitution, Article III. Moreover, the World Health Organization (WHO) and the ILO share a common definition of occupational health. Occupational health should aim at the promotion and maintenance of the highest degree of physical, mental and social wellbeing of workers in all occupations. It is in this context that the ILO includes nutrition as an element of a healthy workplace, alongside physical exercise, mental health, HIV/AIDS protection and programmes to reduce violence, stress and substance abuse.

1.3   The rationale for government

Governments gain from a well-nourished population through revenue from increased work productivity, through reductions in health costs for adults, and, by feeding its children, through the security of future generations of healthy workers. Of the ten leading risk factors of morbidity – underweight, unsafe sex, high blood pressure, tobacco, alcohol, unsafe water and hygiene, iron deficiency, indoor smoke from fuels, high cholesterol and obesity – five are diet related. Let us first discuss the rationale for addressing non-communicable diseases associated with diet and physical inactivity: obesity, diabetes, cardiovascular disease, stroke, hypertension and certain cancers. The following summary of the cost of chronic diseases is based on an unpublished literature review by Alexandra Cameron for the World Health Organization (WHO), along with other sources.

1.3.1   Obesity and the non-communicable disease epidemic

Non-communicable diseases are on the rise globally, with the greatest increases in incidence rates in developing and transitional countries. In 2001, non-communicable diseases contributed 46 per cent of the global disease burden and 60 per cent of all deaths worldwide, with cardiovascular disease alone amounting to 30 per cent of deaths (WHO, 2002a, p. 188). The global disease burden from non-communicable diseases is expected to climb to 57 per cent by 2020 (WHO/ FAO, 2002, p. 4). Of deaths from non-communicable diseases, 79 per cent occur in the developing world; and by 2020, the WHO estimates that 70 per cent of diabetes deaths, 71 per cent of ischaemic heart disease deaths and 75 per cent of stroke deaths will occur in developing countries (WHO/FAO, 2002, p. 5).

The WHO describes the cost of non-communicable diseases in terms of direct, indirect or intangible costs. Governments are sharply affected by direct costs: medical expenditures for hospitalization, medication, laboratory testing and welfare payments. Indirect costs are spread across government and business: lost productivity from sickness, disability, absenteeism or premature death.

Intangible costs refer to quality of life issues. The costs of diet-related diseases, although not an exact science, have been reported in numerous studies.

Obesity accounts for 2–7 per cent of total health costs in industrialized countries (Kumanyika, 2002). Throughout the 1990s, the British health-care system was burdened with an estimated 525 million to 2.6 billion ECUs (US$700 million to US$3.5 billion) per year as a result of obesity (Eurodiet Project, 2003). This estimate (in the pre-euro currency) includes direct medical costs but not the indirect costs of lost productivity, and thus it is considered an underestimate of true costs. The United States has a much larger problem with obesity. Similar to that estimated in the Wolf and Colditz 1998 analysis, referenced earlier, another study in 2001 found that the direct costs were US$45.8 billion and indirect costs were an additional US$22 billion (Eurodiet Project, 2003). In 2004, the Centers for Disease Control and Prevention (CDC) in the United States co-published a report that found that obesity-attributable medical expenditures in the United States were US$75 billion, and approximately half of these expenditures were financed by Medicare and Medicaid, systems of welfare for senior citizens and low-income people, respectively (Finkelstein, Fiebelkorn and Wang, 2004). In California, which declared a fiscal emergency in December 2003, Medicare costs were US$1.7 billion (out of total costs of US$7.7 billion). In the state of New York, Medicaid costs were US$3.5 billion. The 2001 estimate for annual hospital costs for obese children in the United States was US$127 million, up from US$35 million in 1980 (Wang and Dietz, 2002).

Cardiovascular disease is associated with obesity, and some costs intermingle. The total economic cost of cardiovascular disease for the United States in 2002 was US$329.2 billion, with US$199.5 billion in direct costs, US$30.9 billion for morbidity and US$98.8 billion for mortality (NHLBI, 2002, p. 29). In the United Kingdom the annual cost of heart disease is £7 billion (US$13.6 billion), which includes £2.5 billion in informal care costs and £1.73 billion to the British health-care system for coronary bypass operations, heart transplants and coronary angioplasties (Liu, 2002). Indirect costs of coronary heart disease were twice the direct costs in South Africa and four times the direct costs in Canada and Switzerland (Leeder, 2003).

Diabetes, also associated with overweight and obesity and, more broadly, with diet, accounts for 2.5–15 per cent of national health-care budgets (WHO, 2002b). As reported by the United States Congressional Diabetes Caucus, the cost of diabetes in the United States in 2002 was US$132 billion (Hogan, Dall and Nikolov, 2003). Direct medical expenditures totalled US$91.8 billion and comprised US$23.2 billion for diabetes care, US$24.6 billion for chronic complications attributable to diabetes and US$44.1 billion for excess prevalence of general medical conditions (Hogan, Dall and Nikolov, 2003).

In Australia, diabetes was costing the health system AUS$681 million (US$520 million) (Australian IHW, 2002, p. 108) in the mid-1990s; today it is estimated at AUS$1 billion and may reach AUS$2.3 billion by 2010 (Australian DHA, 2004). In Brazil and Argentina the annual direct costs are estimated at US$3.9 billion and US$800 million, respectively (WHO, 2002b). The diabetes epidemic is particularly acute in the South Pacific, where the percentage of total health-care resources allocated for the disease is 6 per cent in Fiji, 10 per cent in the Federated States of Micronesia, 14 per cent in the Marshall Islands and 14 per cent in the Cook Islands (WHO ROWP, 2003). Health promotion and prevention account for only a small part of the total expenditure.

The governments of developing countries, often consumed by the prevention and treatment of infectious and parasitic diseases, face a serious challenge regarding non-communicable diseases, which are more costly to treat. These diseases are appearing in increasingly younger age groups, in particular in middle-aged men. Deaths from cardiovascular disease among working-age men, aged 35–64, are three to four times more likely in Brazil, China, India, South Africa and Tatarstan (southwest Azerbaijan) compared with the United States (Leeder, 2003). In many emerging economies, a transition is seen from communicable to non-communicable diseases. Diet-related non-communicable diseases in the mid-1990s accounted for 22.6 per cent of heath care costs in China and 13.9 per cent in India (Popkin et al., 2001). In Brazil, cardiovascular disease accounts for 20 per cent of health-care costs. One theory states that the reason the problem is particularly acute in emerging economies is due to the fact that the population cannot handle the swift change in diet. The shift to high-fat, high-protein diets that occurred in the West over 200 years is occurring in developing countries in just over two decades.

1.3.2 The lingering malnutrition problem

The economic impact of malnutrition has been studied for many years and is characterized in detail in presentations from the Food and Agriculture Organization World Food Summit of 1996 and subsequent publications. According to the WHO, malnutrition (literally, bad nourishment) concerns not enough as well as too much food, the wrong types of food, and the body's response to a wide range of infections that result in malabsorption of nutrients or the inability to use nutrients properly to maintain health. Clinically, malnutrition is characterized by inadequate or excess intake of protein, energy, and micronutrients such as vitamins, and the frequent infections and disorders that result. For governments, malnutrition represents a double burden. Macro- and micronutrient deficiencies have an immediate impact on workforce productivity and the health of the nation. These deficiencies also stunt the physical and mental development of children, which plunges nations into a cycle of disease, early mortality and poverty that hinders economic development for generations. Although this book focuses on the adult worker, programmes aimed at feeding workers do affect children in that well-nourished adults are better equipped to feed their children.

Micronutrient deficiencies account for a 2–3 per cent loss in GDP in low-income countries; and in South Asia, iron deficiency alone accounts for a loss of US$5 billion in productivity (Ross and Horton, 1998, p. 38). Iron deficiency is responsible for a 5 per cent loss in productivity for light blue-collar work and a 17 per cent loss for heavy manual labour (Ross and Horton, 1998, p. 26). In Asia, adults moderately stunted from childhood micronutrient deficiencies are 2–6 per cent less productive; and severely stunted adults are 2–9 per cent less productive (Horton, 1999). The WHO has demonstrated that higher rates of stuntedness are intricately tied to lower GDP (WHO, 2000a). In Bangladesh, the estimated annual cost of malnutrition is US$1 billion; the country spends about US$246 million fighting malnutrition and could lose US$22 billion in productivity costs over the next ten years without adequate health investment (World Bank, 2000). In India, the World Bank estimates that the cost of lost productivity, illness and death due to malnutrition is US$10–28 billion, or 3–9 per cent of GDP (Measham and Chatterjee, 1999). Concern about malnutrition is not limited to developing countries. A 2003 report from the Malnutrition Advisory Group found that two million Britons (60 per cent of hospital patients) were malnourished, costing the Government £226 million (US$439 million).

Yet there are economic solutions. One study found that increasing the average daily energy supply to 2,770 kcal per person per day with adequate nutrients in a sample of countries could have increased the average annual GDP growth rate by nearly 1 per cent each year between 1960 and 1990 (Arcand, 2001). Numerous programmes exist around the world, such as food fortification and food distribution initiatives, which have met with moderate success. Over the past 15 years, the Bangladesh Integrated Nutrition Project has reduced the proportion of underweight children by 20 per cent and stunting in children under age 5 by 25 per cent. Workplace initiatives to prevent malnutrition, as the following chapters will detail, are relatively new in comparison.

1.3.3 Savings through diet and exercise

Seemingly small behavioural changes can yield large results. In the United States, researchers have estimated that US$5.6 billion in direct and indirect costs could be saved annually if only 10 per cent of the adult population aged 35 to 74 engaged in walking programmes (Jones and Eaton, 1994). A 1995 study from Ontario found that a 1 per cent increase in physical activity participation rates in this province would result in direct government health savings of CAN$31 million (US$26 million) (Saskatchewan DOH, 2001, p. 68). Similarly, the Conference Board of Canada calculated that treatment costs for heart disease, diabetes and colon cancer would drop by CAN$11.5 million (US$9.6 million) annually if the number of physically active Canadians increased by just 1 per cent (Saskatchewan DOH, 2001, p. 68). In Australia, researchers estimated that a 5 per cent increase in the number of physically active adults would save AUS$36 million (US$28 million) annually in direct health-care costs (Stephenson et al., 2000, p. 41).

Few studies have measured the potential cost savings of a healthy diet, although there is reason to believe the savings would be substantial. A report prepared for the American Dietetic Association estimated that if the Medicaid system in the United States provided coverage for nutritional therapy (services provided by a dietician) for patients with diabetes and cardiovascular disease, the system could save US$65 million over six years (American Dietetic Association, 1997). The North Karelia Study in Finland aims to control cardiovascular disease through diet: changing the type of fats used, lowering sodium intake and increasing vegetable and fruit consumption. The programme has witnessed a dramatic decrease in cardiovascular death between 1972 and 1997 with a saving greater than the cost of implementing the programme (Pietinen et al., 2001). The WHO *World Health Report 2002* (WHO, 2002a) reported that population-based intervention programmes to reduce the risk of non-communicable diseases through diet and changes in behaviour are largely cost-effective.

1.3.4 Underestimated cost of poor occupational safety and health

It remains difficult to estimate the impact that poor nutrition has on occupational accidents, injuries and fatalities, but this is clearly a concern for employers as well as governments. Worldwide, workers suffer approximately 270 million occupational accidents per year, of which 355,000 are fatal (ILO, 2003, p. 9). The annual global cost is upwards of US$1,250 billion in losses in global GDP (ILO, 2003, p. 15). These statistics, however, underestimate the true rate and cost of accidents. The connection between nutrition and fatigue and drowsiness is well known. Fatigue, or lack of energy, often reflects overwork or a nutritional deficiency, most commonly iron but also B vitamins. Drowsiness can accompany a lack of access to food. While it is true that we become sleepy after a big meal, smaller midday meals such as lunch keep us awake. Hypoglycaemia, or low blood sugar, which can occur when one skips a meal, can shorten attention span and slow the speed at which individuals process information (McAulay et al., 2001). Snacking on sugary foods and drinks, which the body quickly digests, causes a short surge in energy but ultimately leaves the body more tired.

Divorcing nutrition from long working hours as the cause of fatigue and a particular accident is difficult. Such analysis may not be needed. A more appropriate approach, discussed further in Chapter 3, is for governments and employers to view the meal break as an opportunity for workers' nutrition, rest and refuelling, and in relation to workers' welfare, occupational health and safety, and productivity. Indirectly, particularly in developing countries, a dedication to workers' food services ultimately benefits family health when it ensures workers' health (and continued employment) and leaves more food at home for the family.

Information for this section was provided by Alexandra Cameron.

1.4   The rationale for employers

Employers absorb the indirect costs of poor nutrition, yet it is difficult to dissociate the costs attributed to lost national productivity mentioned above. Concerning obesity, the annual economic costs – including insurance, paid sick leave and other payments – to American business in a 1998 study was US$12.7 billion, with US$10.1 billion the result of moderate to severe obesity and US$2.6 billion attributed to mild obesity (Thompson et al., 1998). Also in the United States, diabetes has cost businesses US$39.8 billion annually in lost work-days, restricted activity and permanent disability (Hogan, Dall and Nikolov, 2003). In Latin America, the cost of lost production due to diabetes exceeds direct health-care costs by 500 per cent (WHO, 2002b). In China and India, lost productivity due to diet-related non-communicable diseases amounted to 0.5 per cent and 0.7 per cent of their GDPs, respectively (Popkin et al., 2001).

The United States based Lewin Group, a health policy research firm, prepared a report for the United States Department of Defense that estimated annual net savings of US$3.1 million if nutrition therapy was a covered health-care benefit (Lewin Group, 1998). Nutrition promotion offers numerous benefits for a company, including decrease in absenteeism, decrease in staff recruitment and training costs through reduced staff turnover, reduction in the number of worker compensation claims and gains in productivity through improved health and morale (United States DHHS, 1996). In Canada, the cost-effectiveness of workplace health promotion programmes is estimated to be CAN$1.75–6.85 for every corporate dollar invested, based on reduced employee turnover, greater productivity and decreased medical claims by participating employees (Cowan, 1998). In a two-year study of 40,000 blue-collar workers, United States based Dupont found that its workplace health promotion programme, which included nutrition, led to a 14 per cent decline in disability days and a return of US$2.05 for every dollar invested (United States DHHS, 1996, p. 35). Similarly, the United States based Travelers' Insurance estimated that it saved US$3.40 for every dollar invested in its Taking Care programme, with absenteeism declining an average of 1.2 days per participant (United States DHHS, 1996, p. 35).

Many employers and employers' organizations recognize the importance of the nutrition issue and are actively engaged. For example, in the Manaus region of Brazil, the Finnish company Nokia provides full-time employees with subsidized meals, a social benefit not guaranteed in the collective agreement. Multi-country economic unions are not that far behind. The "Social Protocol and Agreement" to the Maastricht Treaty on European Union in 1992 set conditions for adopting Europe-wide legislation on labour rights. These included the right to health and safety in the workplace. In South America, the Southern Cone Central Labor Coordination, comprising unions from four countries, convinced the Common Market of the Southern Cone (MERCOSUR) to ratify 34 ILO Conventions, creating a platform to discuss basic worker nutrition issues.

1.5   The rationale for employees and unions

Food is central to our lives. The word "companion" is derived from the Latin words for "with bread". Aside from providing "fuel" for work, eating together with co-workers provides a sense of camaraderie, increases morale and reduces stress. Excuse the non-scientific television reference, but even Fred Flintstone jumped for joy at the sound of the noontime whistle.

Nutrition and food safety are as important a right as occupational health and safety. Many workers spend at least a third of their day or half of their waking hours at work. Whether workers work during "business hours", after hours, weekends or seasonally, eight hours or more (not including the commute to and from work) is a long time to go without eating, particularly when the task is arduous. The availability of healthy food choices in cafeterias or from vending machines, through the distribution of vouchers, or through the provision of mess rooms, kitchenettes or safe local food can support a healthy workplace. This is especially important when workers do not eat well outside work. Surveys have shown that over 70 per cent of employees support employer involvement in workplace health promotion programmes and 85 per cent believe that workplace programmes can increase health and lower health costs (Nutrition Resource Centre, 2002, p. 8). Also when surveyed, employees report that the workplace is an appropriate place to promote health (Nutrition Resource Centre, 2002, p. 8).

Although a proper meal is valued, it is not always expected. This is particularly true for workers in the vast informal sector of developing and emerging economies, as well as for workers in industrialized nations who face the threat of redundancy, outsourcing and other cutbacks. In the 1980s and 1990s in the United Kingdom, for example, widespread redundancies adversely affected workers' entitlements. Cost-cutting and market pressures lowered the quality of food provided in workplaces, especially in the public sector. Collective bargaining strategies at the time sought to consolidate benefits into basic wages, as this affected the calculation of other entitlements such as pay for holidays, sick days, maternity, redundancy and pensions. Meal programmes, so important in building a strong workforce during the late 1940s and 1950s, were seen more as an expendable perk than a basic right and necessity. Workers are treated as adults, and the assumption is that they will find somewhere and something to eat themselves. This devaluation of meal programmes among employers and unions is an alarming trend.

The Canadian Auto Workers (CAW) union, featured in Chapter 4, countered this trend when it secured a better meal programme for Chrysler workers in 2001 and for General Motors workers in 2004. The move paid off. The programme was a popular CAW victory, increasing the union's visibility among Canadian workers. Chrysler, in turn, won the 2004 National Quality Institute Award for Excellence, a well-respected business award that recognizes efforts to make the workplace safer and healthier. Other unions are following suit. Trade unions in Austria are pushing for better workplace food and dining areas for many reasons: for health, for solidarity with food growers, to establish food safety and food ethics standards, and to ensure at least one quality meal a day, now that evening meals often are not home-made. Although in their infancy, Cambodian labour unions have fought for basic provision for nutrition during working hours. The United Kingdom's Public and Commercial Services Union is rallying support for the enforcement of the 30-minute meal break. Companies with the economic means are revamping canteens to offer more healthy foods, at the request of their workers. Other companies that struggle to remain profitable are seeing basic meal programmes, requested by their workers, as a wise investment. We may be witnessing a meal programme revival.

Opportunities abound. Mess rooms and kitchenettes enable workers to bring their own lunch, which can be a healthy and inexpensive alternative to eating out. Canteens can provide nourishing food at a discount. This can provide workers with the opportunity to eat healthy foods, such as vegetables, which they may not buy for home or may not know how to cook properly (and therefore avoid). Vending machines these days can provide a variety of nourishing foods, even hot soups, yet occupy little space and cost far less for businesses too small to operate a canteen. Vending machines can serve shiftworkers and night workers after hours. Vouchers give employees a choice of foods and restaurants and can be an attractive perk in a benefits package. Vouchers are ideal for mobile workers as well as urban workers. Providing food options in general that are at or near the workplace facility also enables the worker to rest properly. In many situations, particularly in the developing world, a meal at work might be the most nourishing meal of the day – and make the difference between life and death.

The importance of adequate nutrition is clear. The next chapter provides an overview of the scientific consensus on what constitutes good nutrition.

2

A NUTRITION OVERVIEW

Photo: WHO/P. Virot

"Food comes first, then morals."

Bertolt Brecht, The Threepenny Opera *(1928)*

Key issues

Energy

- Nutritionists have established the energy expenditure for men and women for a variety of activities. Sedentary office work requires 1.8 kcal per minute; sitting requires 1.39 kcal per minute; farming, mining, forestry and construction can require 5 to 10 kcal per minute worked.

- Poorer nations are more likely to rely on manual labour; and workers in poorer nations are more likely to consume inadequate calories for these labour-intensive tasks.

- Consuming more calories than expended will result in weight gain. Consuming fewer calories than expended will lead to weight loss, fatigue, low productivity and accidents.

Macronutrients

- Macronutrients are broadly defined as those food components present in the diet in quantities of one gram or more. They include proteins, carbohydrates and fats.

- Recommended daily intake of protein for adults is 0.8–0.9 grams per kilogram of body weight; 8–15 per cent of the total energy consumption should come from protein. In regions where diarrhoea is prevalent, health experts recommend increasing the protein intake by 10 per cent.

- Protein deficiencies may lead to mental retardation or stunted growth among children, or a loss of muscle mass among adults. Deficiencies are rare in developed countries but still of great concern in developing countries.

- Fats contain more than twice the number of calories compared with equal measures of carbohydrates or proteins – on average, 9 kcal per gram.

- Active, non-obese adults may derive up to 35 per cent of their energy from fat and sedentary adults may consume up to 30 per cent as long as no more than 10 per cent of the energy intake is from saturated fats.

- Recommended intake of carbohydrates is 50–70 per cent of total calories.

- Healthy fats and complex carbohydrates are associated with lower rates of circulatory disease and certain cancers. Unhealthy (saturated) fats and simple carbohydrates are associated with circulatory disease and diabetes, respectively.

Micronutrients

- Micronutrients, often present in minute quantities, are vitamins and minerals that are essential for proper growth and metabolism.

- More than one billion people are ill or disabled as a result of a micronutrient deficiency and billions more are at risk.

- Illnesses and conditions brought about by a micronutrient deficiency include mental retardation, depression, dementia, low work capacity, chronic fatigue, blindness and loss of bone and muscle strength.

- Iron deficiency anaemia alone affects hundreds of millions of workers. Anaemia, and more mild levels of iron deficiency, decrease physical work capacity and work productivity in repetitive tasks, yet can be inexpensively remedied.

Humans are indeed a diverse species with vastly different body types suited to vastly different environments. We have populated nearly every region of the globe, from lush rainforests and fertile river deltas to rugged mountainous terrain and cold, treeless tundra. We have adopted the foods of these regions, be it protein from the sea or from land, carbohydrates from rice or from millet, vitamin C from berries or citrus fruits. And we have also created for ourselves a world of diverse cultures, which provide structure to what and when and even how much we should eat. Yet despite these differences we remain one species, one human race requiring a uniform set of nutrients. Thus, it is possible to characterize proper nutrition at its chemical level – proteins, lipids, vitamins, minerals – and provide universal guidelines on how best to attain good health through nutrition.

Certain vulnerabilities to diseases do exist from region to region. For example, wheat and other food products grown in selenium-poor soil in places as distinct as China, Finland and New Zealand can leave local populations susceptible to Keshan disease, a heart condition. In landlocked Afghanistan, the lack of iodine in the diet has led to an epidemic of goitre in recent years. These vulnerabilities are a result of the land, however, not the people's genetic make-up. We all require the same kind of nourishment, the same basic building blocks of nutrition. The main nutritional diseases, in terms of public health, are protein energy malnutrition, micronutrient deficiencies (especially iron, vitamin A and iodine), and obesity; and these are largely a result of inadequate food security and education.

This chapter describes in general terms the current state of scientific knowledge about diet and nutrition with the focus on adults, both female and male. This is an overview independent of the social, legal, economic and logistic issues of providing workers with access to food. Some readers may wish to skip this chapter and move on to the framework and case study chapters. We have provided a more extensive review of nutrition in appendices A and B to augment this chapter because, while the topic is important, we did not want to interrupt the flow of the publication with detailed nutrition information. The appendices expand on the notion of nutrient absorption, how certain diseases limit absorption, and how certain nutrients complement or conflict with each other. Also, subsequent chapters address food security. As defined by the WHO, food security exists when all people, at all times, have physical and economic access to sufficient, safe and nutritious food to meet their dietary needs and food preferences for an active and healthy life.

To reach as broad an audience as possible, a variety of foods are listed here and in the appendices as sources for specific nutrients. For example, beef, pork, lamb, goat, fowl and fish are all legitimate sources of high-quality protein; and vegetables, including soya beans, in the right combination can supply protein needs. These foods may seem exotic, unappetizing and taboo to some. No judgement has been cast, however, regarding the "right" food to eat. Fortunately, in most situations, we do not have to compromise. Our planet provides a sizeable menu from which we can choose; and most traditional diets – barring restrictions due to war, famine or religious obligations – satisfy and often exceed the nutritional requirements of most individuals.

2.1 Energy

The first law of thermodynamics concerns the conservation of energy. What is true for a machine is true for the human body. Humans need fuel to work. Energy that is consumed as food and not used by the body will be stored and result in weight gain. Inadequate intake of food to meet energy requirements will result in weight loss and often the breakdown of body tissue. In both scenarios – obesity or undernourishment – the result is a decreased ability to work and to resist disease.

Undernourishment, or insufficient dietary intake, plagues developing nations and stunts productivity. This is a result of either low iron (Haas and Brownlie, 2001), low amounts of other nutrients, or too few calories. Poorer nations are most likely to rely on manual labour, and workers there are mostly likely to be underfed. One study has shown that some cutters and stackers in South African sugar-cane fields lose 3 per cent of their body mass as a result of high energy expenditure and inadequate calorie intake (Lambert, Cheevers and Coopoo, 1994). Protein energy malnutrition is the main nutritional disorder associated with a diet poor in quality and quantity. Obesity is an emerging pandemic. In the United States, the total cost attributable to obesity amounted to US$99.2 billion in 1995, including approximately US$51 billion in direct medical costs (Wolf and Colditz, 1998). Ten years on, the obesity problem in the United States is worse. Obesity is a growing concern in most developed countries and in many developing countries, as energy-dense foods, coupled with automation, serve to promote weight gain. Proper utilization of energy in terms of calories consumed and spent must be the foundation of any nutrition programme.

Energy requirements and energy content in food are measured in calories or joules. One calorie equals 4.187 joules, although scientifically these units are not truly comparable. The public health community prefers using the term joule or kilojoule. However, this publication will use the term kilocalorie or kcal (referred to as a calories in the United States), which is more familiar to many readers. Energy requirements vary among individuals based on body size, age and level of physical and mental activity. On average, adult males of working age require 2,500 kcal and non-nursing or pregnant adult females require 2,000 kcal.

Nutritionists have long established the energy expenditure for men and women for a variety of activities. (See *The feeding of workers in developing countries*, Food and Nutrition Paper No. 6, FAO, 1976.) For example, among males, sedentary office work requires 1.8 kcal per minute; sitting requires 1.39 kcal per minute; and sleeping requires 1.08 kcal per minute. Over the course of a day, eight hours of each activity amounts to a 2,050-kcal expenditure. In this scenario, consuming more than 2,050 kcal will lead to weight gain. Farming, mining, forestry and construction can require 5 to 10 kcal per minute energy. Substituting this for office work in the above scenario, the energy requirement for the day rises to over 3,500 kcal. Consuming fewer calories than this will result not only in weight loss over time but also an inability to perform the work.

Merely providing enough calories to workers to perform their tasks will not guarantee good health. Some workers in poorer nations are fed meals comprising mostly carbohydrates – such as corn porridge or bread – and little protein, fat or micronutrients. Workers cannot sustain their health on this kind of diet for long. Similarly, in wealthier nations, office workers could consume most of the daily requirement of 2,050 kcal in one meal of a cheeseburger, fried potatoes and a milkshake, yet receive few micronutrients, such as vitamins A and C. Energy is generic. Food choice is clearly crucial for maintaining good health.

2.2　Macronutrients

Macronutrients are broadly defined as food components present in the diet in quantities of one gram or more. This includes proteins, carbohydrates, fats and oils and also water (WHO, 1998, p. 55). Macronutrients are sometimes referred to as energy-giving foods.

2.2.1　Proteins

Proteins are needed for the growth and maintenance of muscle, bone, skin and organs, and for the synthesis of key enzymes, hormones and antibodies. Proteins are made from combinations of 20 amino acids. Of these, eight are considered "essential" and must be present in the diet because they cannot be synthesized by the body from precursors. Proteins from animal sources are mostly "complete" or "high-quality" proteins, meaning they contain all of the essential amino acids. Vegetable proteins lack one or more essential amino acids and are referred to as "incomplete" or "low-quality" proteins. A vegetarian diet can supply all the essential amino acids provided one combines complementary vegetable proteins, such as those from rice and beans. But in general, protein quality is far better in animal protein than in cereal and legume proteins.

No upper limit of protein intake has been set, but data suggest that excessive protein consumption can adversely affect the kidneys. Health experts in many countries recommend a daily intake for adults of 0.8 grams of protein per kilogram of body weight (WHO, 1998, p. 59). Diets largely composed of cereals and legumes with some animal products (meat, eggs or milk) are sufficient to supply this amount. Diets chiefly composed of low-quality proteins, however, need to provide 0.9 grams of protein per kilogram of body weight for proper nutrition (WHO, 1998, p. 59). The risk of protein energy malnutrition is high in regions where diarrhoea is prevalent. Once diarrhoea has been treated, workers should be given extra energy, proteins and also vitamins to regain the weight and nutrients lost during the diarrhoea episode. In this case, experts recommend increasing the protein intake by 10 per cent. Protein needs during convalescence increase by 20–40 per cent (WHO, 1998, p. 59). A deficiency of just one essential amino acid will result in a decrease in protein synthesis and may lead to mental retardation or stunted growth among children or a loss of muscle mass among adults. Protein deficiencies are rare in developed countries but still of great concern in developing countries.

The World Health Organization suggests that 8–15 per cent of the total energy consumption should come from protein, with the range depending on whether one is eating high- or low-quality protein or in convalescence (WHO, 1998, p. 59). Of this, 10–25 per cent of dietary protein should be of animal origin (WHO, 1998, p. 58). Virtually all unprocessed foods contain protein, even foods thought of as carbohydrates, such as rice and wheat. Animal products are considered to provide the highest-quality protein. This includes beef, pork, lamb, game, fowl, fish, some insects, dairy products and eggs. Legumes – particularly soya and other beans, chickpeas, split peas and lentils – are considered very good sources of vegetable protein, as are nuts and some seeds. Potatoes are high in protein quality but low in quantity; cereals and leafy vegetables are low in protein quality but complement legumes. Whey protein (commercially available in powder form) is a high-quality, relatively inexpensive protein source with a long shelf life suitable for warm climates and remote work locations, where meat products may be hard to secure or store.

2.2.2 Fats

Fats, although often maligned, are vital for proper nutrition. Fats provide essential fatty acids, which are not made by the body and must be obtained from food. These fatty acids are the raw materials that help regulate blood pressure, blood clotting, inflammation and other body functions. Fats are also necessary for healthy skin and hair and for the transport of the fat-soluble vitamins A, D, E and K. Fats serve as energy reserves, stored in the adipose tissue (fat cells) that helps cushion and insulate the body. The body first burns carbohydrates during physical exertion. After about 20 minutes of intense exertion, the body depends on fat for calories.

Dietary fats consist of a chain of carbon atoms with hydrogen and oxygen attachments at various positions and degrees of saturation along the chain. The metabolic fate of a particular type of fat depends on the number and arrangement of these atoms. There are three categories of fats: saturated (solid at room temperature), unsaturated (liquid at room temperature) and hydrogenated or trans fats. A saturated fat has a maximum number of hydrogen atoms along its carbon chain. This type of fat is more readily stored in adipose tissue as a long-term fuel reserve because it provides a higher energy yield compared with an unsaturated fat. Monounsaturated fat is preferentially used for energy more quickly than saturated fat.

Whether from plant or animal sources, fats contain more than twice the number of calories compared with equal measures of carbohydrates or proteins. On average, fats contain 9 kcal per gram. Experts recommend that adults derive at least 15 per cent of their energy from fats and oils and that women of child-bearing age consume at least 20 per cent (WHO, 1998, p. 59). Certain fats are healthier than others, however, and the key to proper nutrition is the proper balance of unsaturated fatty acids. Active, non-obese adults may derive up to 35 per cent of their energy from fat and sedentary adults may consume up to 30 per cent as long as no more than 10 per cent of the energy intake is from saturated fats (WHO, 1998, p. 60). In general, the need for fat increases during times of protein malnutrition. A minimum requirement for dietary (unsaturated) fat is 10 per cent of the energy intake (WHO, 1998, p. 60).

Saturated fats are largely considered unhealthy and their consumption should be kept to a minimum. Sources of saturated fat include most animal products, particularly butter, cheese, whole milk, ice cream, organ meats, fatty cuts of beef and pork and some shellfish. Coconut, palm and palm-kernel oils are also high in saturated fats. Health experts recommend avoiding or sharply limiting food products with more than 20 per cent saturated fat (NIH NHLBI, 2001). However, saturated fats in small amounts can be healthy if the sources provide other beneficial nutrients. Red palm oil, specifically, is an excellent source of vitamins A and E and serves as a nutritious, low-priced oil for populations chronically deficient in these vitamins.

Unsaturated fats help regulate a healthy balance of "good" and "bad" cholesterol – low-density lipoprotein (LDL) and high-density lipoprotein (HDL), respectively. Polyunsaturated fats lower LDL levels while mono-unsaturated fats increase HDL levels. Polyunsaturated fats, depending on their level of saturation, contain the essential fatty acids omega-3 and omega-6. The recommended ratio of omega-6 to omega-3 acid ranges from 10:1 to 5:1, with the narrowing ratio indicative of growing knowledge about how omega-3 may improve cardiovascular health (WHO, 1998, p. 60). Western diets often have an undesirable ratio of 40:1. Sources of omega-6 include the oils of sunflower, safflower, corn and soya bean. Sources of omega-3 include flaxseed and flaxseed oil, walnuts and walnut oil, and oily fish such as salmon, mackerel, herring, sild, pilchard, sardine and anchovy, cod liver oil, and whale and seal blubber. Monounsaturated food sources include nuts and nut oils (such as

Box 2.1   Dietary sources of fats

Healthier fats

Polyunsaturated, omega-3 – flaxseed and flaxseed oil, walnuts, oily fish such as salmon, mackerel, herring, sild, pilchard, sardine and anchovy, cod liver oil and whale and seal blubber.

Polyunsaturated, omega-6 – most liquid vegetable oils such as sunflower, safflower, corn and soya bean, sesame oil and most nuts.

Monounsaturated – olives and olive oil, canola (rapeseed) oil, avocado, peanuts, almonds, cashews.

Fats to use in moderation

Saturated fats – found in most animal products, such as butter, cheese, whole milk, ice cream, organ meats and fatty cuts of beef and pork, ghee (clarified butter), lard and beef tallow; also in tropical oils such as coconut, palm and palm kernel oils.

Fats to avoid

Trans fats – found in fried foods, most margarines, processed foods and commercial baked goods such as crackers, biscuits and doughnuts.

peanut oil), olives and olive oil, avocados, canola (rapeseed) oil and, to some extent, meat and butter. Although considered healthy, unsaturated fats do have their limit. Like saturated fats, they are high-caloric, energy-dense foods. High intake of any kind of fat can contribute to an increased risk of obesity, cardiovascular disease, cancer, diabetes, arthritis and gall bladder disease (A.D.A.M., 2004).

Hydrogenated or trans fats form when vegetable oil hardens. Trans fatty acids are commonly found in fried foods, most margarines, processed foods, and commercial baked goods such as crackers, biscuits and doughnuts. Trans fats have been shown to not only raise blood levels of LDL, the bad cholesterol, but also lower levels of HDL, the good cholesterol (Mensink et al., 2003). Thus, reducing, if not eliminating, trans fatty acids from the diet lowers the risk of coronary heart disease (Expert Panel, 1995).

With regard to obesity, fats can quickly add up in the daily calorie count. Fifty-five grams of fat contribute about 500 kcal (55 grams x 9 kcal/gram), which is 20 per cent of a 2,500-kcal diet. A 125-gram hamburger patty contains about 22 grams of fat, most of which is saturated fat. Reduction of fat in the diet by 10 per cent translates to a reduction of about 3 kilogram in body weight over 2 months (Mokdad et al., 2001). The increased consumption of fast-foods, high in animal fats and simple carbohydrates, combined with a decreased level of exercise and changes in lifestyles, is the main cause of obesity.

2.2.3 Carbohydrates

Carbohydrates are the main source of energy in most diets. Their primary function is to provide energy for the body, especially the brain and the nervous system. This varied macronutrient takes the form of sugars (mono-saccharides), oligosaccharides and starches and fibre (polysaccharides), all related by their simple molecular structure consisting of carbon tied to water molecules. The body breaks down carbohydrates into glucose, which acts like a pellet of fuel that cells can use to perform their many functions.

There appears to be no absolute daily carbohydrate requirement, for the human body can derive energy from fat and protein if necessary. The WHO recommends that at least 10 per cent of the energy intake should come from carbohydrates (about 50 grams) to prevent severe ketosis, a condition in which the blood becomes abnormally acidic from ketones, the by-product of burning fat for fuel instead of glucose (WHO, 1998, p. 63). A diet consisting primarily of carbohydrates, on the other hand, may cheat the body of valuable nutrients found in proteins and fats. Health experts recommend that 50–70 per cent of an individual's energy intake should be derived from carbohydrates (WHO, 1998). As with fats, however, a proper balance of certain types of carbohydrates can prevent chronic diseases such as obesity, cancer and cardiovascular disease.

Sugars are simple carbohydrates, which are most easily digested and quickly converted to glucose for fuel. Common sugars are sucrose, also called saccharose, primarily derived from sugar cane and sugar beets; fructose, from fruits and honey; and lactose, from milk. The consumption of simple sugars throughout the day – particularly sucrose and high-fructose corn syrup, as found in soft drinks – adds calories to the diet but few nutrients, and is a major cause of dental caries. Moderate intake of sugars, however, can make food more palatable. And the slight relationship between sugar consumption and obesity is offset by an inverse relationship between sugar and fat intake (Gibney et al., 1995). It should be noted that spices could be substituted for both sugar and fat to make food tastier.

Complex carbohydrates, such as starches and fibres, are large chains of sugars often containing hundreds of monosaccharides molecules. Complex carbohydrates take longer to digest and are preferred over simple carbohydrates for weight maintenance and the control of diabetes, an emerging pandemic. Slower digestion also provides a feeling of fullness, curbing hunger in between meals. This limits the need for snacking, a major cause of weight gain. Most recommendations for adults specify an intake of at least 20 grams of fibre daily, which translates to around 10 grams per 1,000 kcal, although twice this amount can be easily tolerated (WHO, 1998, p. 64). Water-soluble fibre, found in oats, barley, legumes and the flesh of fruit, seems to reduce the risk of colon cancer (Le Marchand et al., 1997) and cardiovascular disease (Bazzano et al., 2003). One drawback is that fibre interferes with the absorption of nutrients, particularly minerals. Requirements for protein and minerals need to be adjusted accordingly in the presence of a high-fibre diet.

In summary, with regard to macronutrients and the prevention of chronic diseases, experts recommend that healthy adults choose a diet with a caloric intake of 50–70 per cent carbohydrates (predominantly complex carbohydrates), 15–30 per cent fat (predominantly unsaturated fats) and 8–15 per cent protein (with some animal protein) (WHO, 1998). Saturated fats increase the risk of some cancers, cardiovascular disease and obesity and obesity-related diseases, while a proper balance of unsaturated fats reduces these risks. Excessive amounts of simple carbohydrates increase the risk of weight gain and may be associated with diabetes, while complex carbohydrates and fibre reduce these risks and may prevent certain cancers. Exercise or physical labour is also key to preventing weight gain.

2.3   Micronutrients

Micronutrients are vitamins and minerals that are essential for proper growth and metabolism. Often only minute quantities are required. Their discovery and the subsequent in-depth study of their role and importance in the diet has led to mass food-fortification efforts – an important public health achievement of the twentieth century. Micronutrient deficiencies are cited as causing or exacerbating a host of mental and physical diseases, including infectious diseases. A diversified diet will help prevent micronutrient malnutrition. Food fortification and supplementation are also useful approaches.

Despite steady gains through the twentieth century in the field of nutrition, more than one billion people are ill or disabled as a result of a micronutrient deficiency, and over two billion more people are at risk (WHO, 1998, p. 66). These figures add up to half the world's population. As with diseases associated with macronutrients, for example, cardiovascular disease, diabetes, cancer and obesity, micronutrient-related diseases cut across class, age and gender in both developing and developed countries. Examples of illnesses and conditions brought about by a micronutrient deficiency include mental retardation, depression, dementia, low-work capacity, chronic fatigue, blindness and the loss of bone and muscle strength. These conditions, many of which are reversible, directly affect the near-term health of employees and their work performance and quality. Thus, an adequate supply of micro-nutrients for the workforce is paramount. Iron deficiency anaemia alone affects hundreds of millions of workers (Haas and Brownlie, 2001). Anaemia and milder levels of iron deficiency decrease physical work capacity and productivity in repetitive tasks, yet can be inexpensively remedied. The main micronutrient deficiencies are vitamin A (largely affecting children), iron and iodine deficiency. Other deficiencies, such as folic acid, zinc and B-complex deficiencies, are a problem in certain populations.

2.3.1 Vitamins

Vitamins are organic chemicals found in plants and animals that are essential for human growth and health maintenance. There are more than a dozen known vitamins. A varied diet can supply these vitamins naturally, but supplementation is recommended for those individuals lacking vitamins as a result of famine, war, harsh climate or poor eating habits. (See Appendix B for a description of vitamins A, B-complex, C, D, E and K.) Of particular concern for adult workers are: vitamin C, because of its role in helping iron absorption; vitamin E, because of its role in preventing heart disease and cancers; and vitamin B_{12}, important in maintaining a healthy nervous system, which is lacking in vegetarian diets.

2.3.2 Minerals

Minerals and trace elements in the diet are inorganic chemicals essential for growth and fitness. Of particular public health importance are calcium, fluoride, iodine, iron, sodium and zinc. A varied diet can supply most minerals and trace elements naturally, but supplementation may be needed for fluoride and, depending on the location, certain chemicals not abundant in the soil, such as selenium, and thus not present in the local food supply. See Appendix B for a description of key minerals. Of particular concern for adult workers are zinc, often lacking from vegetarian diets, and iron.

Indeed, iron deserves discussion here, for iron deficiency cripples workers' productivity. Iron, as a constituent of haemoglobin, is needed to carry oxygen in red blood cells. Iron is also a key element in many enzymatic reactions. Even a slight reduction of blood iron (haemoglobin concentration of below 110 grams/litre) is associated with delayed learning and behaviour changes in children (Grantham-McGregor and Ani, 2001). Anaemia, a condition marked by low concentrations of haemoglobin, often results in adults in sluggishness, low endurance and decreased physical work capacity and work productivity for repetitive tasks (Haas and Brownlie, 2001). Modest falls in iron levels also increase absorption of toxic metals, such as cadmium and lead. An estimated two billion people worldwide have clinical anaemia as a result of iron deficiency, constituting a public health emergency (WHO, 1998, p. 76). Women are at greater risk of iron deficiency due to blood loss during menstruation.

Usually, anaemia can be remedied through the provision of iron-rich or iron-fortified foods. The daily recommended iron intake varies, however, because the bioavailability of iron from foods varies from 1 to 45 per cent. Vitamin C and animal foods enhance iron absorption. Fibre, tannins (found in tea), phytates (found in grains) and polyphenols (found in coffee and red wine) reduce it. The recommended daily intake of iron depends on its bioavailability from foods, defined as very low (<5 per cent), low (5–10 per cent), intermediate (11–18 per cent) and high (>19 per cent) bioavailability. Corresponding intake levels are 20, 11, 5.5 and 3.5 milligrams of iron per 1,000 kcal (WHO, 1998, p. 77). The type of iron most easily absorbed is called haem-iron. Sources include clams, oysters, organ meats, beef, pork, poultry, fish and fortified grains. Fortification of wheat or maize flour, salt and soy sauce has been shown to be successful in regions where the natural diet is low in bioavailable iron.

2.4 Other nutrients

Simple fortification or dietary supplementation in pill form, although exceedingly beneficial in some circumstances, cannot be viewed as a panacea. Food is more than a container of macronutrients, vitamins and minerals that can be isolated in a laboratory and injected directly into the bloodstream. Attaining nutrients through food instead of supplementation is largely seen as a superior means of meeting nutritional requirements. This may be due to the fact that little is known about other components in the foods we eat, particularly carotenoids, bioflavonoids, salicytates and phytoestrogens. Also, a class of chemicals called antioxidants appears to reduce the risk of age-related diseases by helping repair cellular and DNA damage caused by free radicals. Appendix B contains a description of these other nutrients.

A well-balanced diet will supply adequate amounts of most of the nutrients discussed in this chapter. According to the WHO and the Food and Agriculture Organization (FAO), the right balance is 50–70 per cent carbo-hydrates (predominantly complex carbohydrates, with plenty of vegetables), 15–30 per cent fat (predominantly unsaturated fats) and 8–15 per cent protein

Table 2.1 Ranges of population nutrient intake goals

Dietary factor	Goal
Total fat	15–30 per cent (of total energy)
Saturated fatty acids	10 per cent
Polyunsaturated fatty acids	6–10 per cent
ω-6 Polyunsaturated fatty acids	5–8 per cent
ω-3 Polyunsaturated fatty acids	1–2 per cent
Trans fatty acids	<1 per cent
Monounsaturated fatty acids	By difference[1]
Total carbohydrate	55–75 per cent[2] (of total energy)
Free sugars[3]	<10 per cent (of total energy)
Protein	10–15 per cent[4] (of total energy)
Cholesterol	<300 mg per day
Salt (sodium)	<5 g per day (<2 g per day)
Fruits and vegetables	≥ 400 g per day
Total dietary fibre	>25 g per day
Non-starch polysaccharides	>20 g per day

Notes: [1] Calculated as: total fat (saturated fatty acids + polyunsaturated fatty acids + trans fatty acids). [2] The percentage of total energy available after taking into account that consumed as protein and fat – hence the wide range. [3] The term "free sugars" refers to all monosaccharides and disaccharides added to foods by the manufacturer, cook or consumer, plus sugars naturally present in honey, syrups and fruit juices. [4] The suggested range should be seen in the light of the Joint WHO/FAO/UN Expert Consultation on Protein and Amino Acid Requirements in Human Nutrition, held in Geneva from 9 to 16 April 2002.

Source: Adapted from: WHO/FAO, 2002.

(with some animal protein) (WHO, 1998). Table 2.1 gives ranges of population nutrient intake goals. Chapter 11 lists several key documents and programmes available to help employers and health workers choose appropriate nutrition and food safety plans for workers.

3

THE WORKPLACE AS A SETTING FOR GOOD NUTRITION

Photo: ILO/C. Loiselle

"The rich would have to eat money if the poor did not provide food."

Russian proverb

Key issues

The workplace – a setting for good nutrition

- The workplace is the ultimate community-based setting for health intervention. Many workers are present at least eight hours a day, five days a week. They are often of the same educational background and face similar health concerns.

- An opportunity exists to provide employees with what may be their only wholesome meal of the day. The comparison with school lunch programmes is apt.

- An opportunity exists to intervene, to provide the employee with access to nutritious foods – through canteens, meal vouchers, kitchenettes or pleasant places to eat, on-site farmers' markets, vending machines offering healthy options, or simply provision of bowls of fruit.

- Healthy foods at work, such as fruits, vegetables and fortified food items, might not be available in the marketplace as a result of a poor food distribution system.

Opportunities

- Ideally the meal break should be a time to rest, refuel, bond with co-workers, and release stress and to physically remove oneself from the cubical or workstation.

- The meal setting should be clean and free from the noise, vibrations, chemicals and other hazards of the work area – a place to unwind.

- The workplace meal can be fortified with iron, iodine or other key nutrients that might be lacking in the local diet.

- The workplace or its environs can be a haven for good nutrition where workers can find all those foods that their doctors recommend for losing weight or lowering cholesterol: foods such as wholegrain breads, lean meats, fruits and vegetables.

- Meals must be affordable. Eating areas must be accessible. Time is needed for the walk to and from the eating area, for purchasing food and for finding a seat.

Opportunities lost

- How many workers have no access to a canteen or proper restaurant, or no place to safely store food? How many workplaces have greasy canteens? How many are surrounded by only fast-food options or street foods of questionable safety?

- How many workers in the vast informal economies in developing nations have no allotted meal break? How many skip lunch or get by on bread and water?

- How many workers must eat at their desks or in a messy backroom, have no place to wash before eating or are subjected to food-borne contaminants?

The reality

- There are few laws that stipulate when, where and how workers gain access to food.

- In many cases, workers have low expectations about feeding programmes and unions have what they consider to be more pressing concerns.

- In developing countries, only half the populations consume enough calories for normal activity, and these countries depend more on heavy manual labour.

- Nearly a billion people are undernourished while over one billion are obese or overweight.

- A cycle emerges: poor health leads to lower learning potential, leading to a poorly qualified job pool, leading to lower productivity, leading to a loss of competitiveness, high business costs and lower economic growth, leading to lower wages and greater wealth disparity, leading to poor nutrition and poor health ...

Access to healthy food (and conversely protection from unsafe and unhealthy food and eating arrangements) is as essential as protection from workplace chemicals or noise.

Many workers around the world spend at least half of their waking hours at work; eight hours or more a day, five days or more a week. Some workers live at work for prolonged periods. At any given worksite, workers are largely of the same educational background and, in many countries and job situations, of the same sex and ethnic background. Often they face the same health concerns. They need to eat and rest in order to perform their work properly. And they are a captive audience – even temporary and migrant workers and day labourers. For health educators and nutritionists, the opportunity is profound. The workplace represents a manageable community-based setting – a logical place to ensure proper nutrition.

In school lunch programmes, health experts attempt to instil lifelong healthy eating habits and to intervene when nutritional needs are not being met. Similarly, in the workplace, an opportunity exists to teach employees about proper nutrition and to monitor outcomes. An opportunity exists to intervene, to provide employees with access to nutritious foods – through canteens, meal vouchers, kitchenettes or pleasant places to eat, on-site farmers' markets, vending machines offering healthy options, or simply provision of bowls of fruit. An opportunity exists to provide employees with what may be their only wholesome meal of the day. There are food solutions that can fit most budgets and locales. Yet too often, the opportunity is missed. Even working in the largest, most economically developed of cities in the world will not guarantee access to a nutritious meal during the working day. Far from a lingering and isolated problem in developing nations, the lack of access to the very foods needed to stay healthy, alert and to be productive has become widespread. The situation only exacerbates the rising trend (and cost) of obesity and chronic diseases.

London, Paris, Los Angeles, New York – pick any city. A taxi journey through the urban expanses between the airport and the city core reveals the extent of the missed opportunity. In the city outskirts, before the skyline begins to dominate the horizon, take notice of the junkyards, mechanics' shops, printers, small factories, retail stores, telecommunications depots, police stations, roofing companies, plumbers, health clinics, beauty salons, furniture warehouses, timber yards and car dealerships. There are workers here. What type of access to food do they have? It is unlikely they will have company canteens or meal vouchers; and if they did, where would the workers use the vouchers? At a fast-food outlet? There are few proper restaurants, if any. Perhaps these workers pack a lunch. If so, where do they eat? In a back room? How relaxing is such a setting? How clean is it? Is there a refrigerator to store the food? Are the workers at risk of food-borne illnesses? Throughout any given city, many workers eat in far from ideal conditions.

Now venture into the city centre. Has the situation really improved? Yes, the larger companies may offer a canteen. But what kind of food is served? Is the dish of the day fried meat and overcooked vegetables? Is the only economical choice a burger with chips or a fried Chinese egg roll? Are the foods heavy on salt, sugar and saturated fat and light on healthy fat, vitamins and minerals? Is the one healthy option even appealing? Are the workers bombarded by an unlimited choice of sugary drinks and snack foods? Some companies offer meal vouchers. But do workers have a proper meal during their 30- to 45-minute break, or do they grab something on the run and bring it back to their desk? The reality is often less than ideal.

Calcutta, Dhaka, Mogadishu, Managua – workers' nutrition in developing countries can be dire. Only the largest of enterprises have catering services. In many locales the greatest concerns are food and water safety, and adequate calorific intake. Street vending of food is an important means of livelihood in developing countries, particularly for women; and it often represents the only access to food for workers in the extensive informal work economy of these countries. But unregulated or under-regulated food vending is a major source of food-borne illnesses. Vendors usually have no access to washrooms or lavatories, and no means to refrigerate perishable foods, and often keep food for days until it sells. Of the 1.5 billion cases of diarrhoea annually in developing countries, around 70 per cent are associated with food contamination (Henson, 2003, p. 8). Worldwide, one in three people annually suffer from a disease caused by micro-organisms in food and 1.8 million children die from severe food and waterborne diarrhoea (WHO, 2002c, p. 7). Most food-borne illnesses are not reported; and in developing nations the economic impact in terms of health and productivity can be only grossly estimated. In the United States, where food-borne illnesses are a concern but are not epidemic, the United States Department of Agriculture estimates an annual economic loss of US$6.9 billion from five food-borne pathogens: Campylobacter, non-typhi Salmonella, E. coli O157, E. coli non-O157 STEC and Listeria mono-cytogenes (Henson, 2003, p. 16). Removing vendors, the typical government reaction in developing countries, often leaves workers with no access to food. Bringing food from home (and having no place to store it) might leave less food for the family and might not be a good food solution either. Food safety issues are well described in the FAO December 2003 working paper *The economics of food safety in developing countries* by Spencer Henson (Henson, 2003).

The FAO reported that 50 per cent of populations in developing nations do not consume enough calories for normal activity, and that these countries depend more on human power than machines for heavy work (FAO, 1966). That was in 1966. Little has changed since then for workers. A recent WHO analysis found that nearly half the world's population face starvation (WHO, 2004a). If food is not scarce, often it is unsafe or too expensive. Yet food fuels productivity. Early ILO research found that a 1 per cent kcal increase resulted in a 2.27 per cent increase in general labour productivity (Galenson and Pyatt, 1964). Similarly, another study found that increasing the average daily energy supply to 2,770 kcal per person per day with adequate nutrients in a sample of countries would have increased the average annual GDP growth rate by nearly 1 per cent each year between 1960 and 1990 (Arcand, 2001). And more recently, the WHO reported that adequate nourishment (through food fortification) could raise national productivity levels by 20 per cent (WHO, 2003a). Not providing safe and nourishing foods and adequate calories in the workplace is a missed opportunity in developing nations.

3.1 Opportunities

Ideally the meal break should be a time to rest, refuel, bond with co-workers, and to release stress and to physically remove oneself from the office, cubical or workstation. The meal setting should be clean and free from the noise, vibrations, chemicals and other hazards of the work area – a place to relax. In regions plagued by war, famine or poverty, the workplace meal can be fortified with iron, iodine or other key nutrients that might be lacking in the local diet. In industrialized countries, with an abundance of unhealthy foods, the workplace or its environs can be a haven – a place where workers can find all those foods that their doctors recommend for losing weight or lowering cholesterol. These are foods such as wholegrain breads, fresh fish, lean meats, nuts, seeds, fruits and vegetables.

In the developing world, we find that WHO and FAO recommendations for proper nutrition often go unheeded, for a variety of reasons. War and government instability can make it difficult to get to work and to secure food, water and fuel at work or at home. Refugee status takes a terrible toll on nutrition. Yet even with a stable government, workers are sometimes denied meals or discouraged from taking meal breaks; or sometimes food simply is not available, particularly in the amount and variety needed for good health. Case studies presented in subsequent chapters of this publication will demonstrate that providing proper nutrition to workers at work need not be complicated or expensive and ultimately can be profitable. Simple meal plans

Figure 3.1   The cycle of poor nutrition and low national productivity

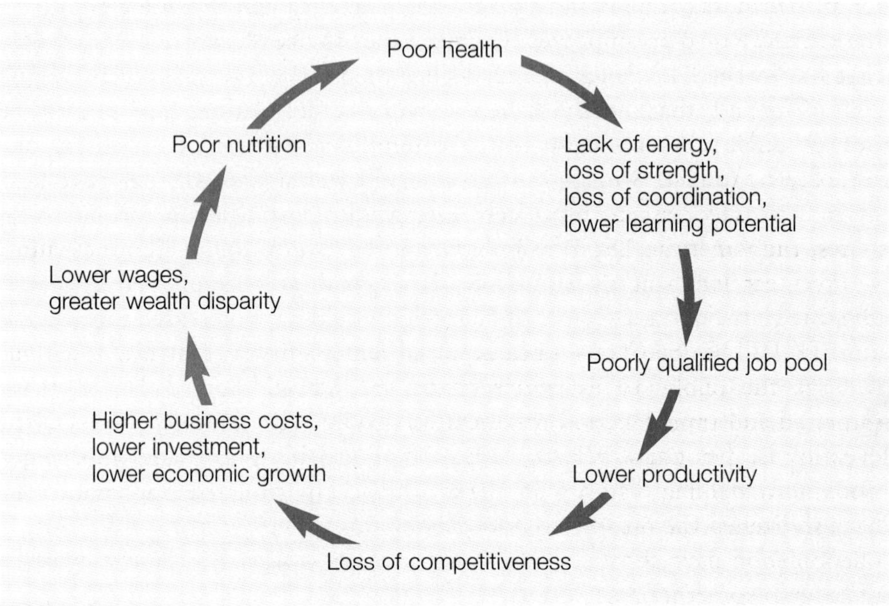

Poor health

Poor nutrition

Lack of energy,
loss of strength,
loss of coordination,
lower learning potential

Lower wages,
greater wealth disparity

Poorly qualified job pool

Higher business costs,
lower investment,
lower economic growth

Lower productivity

Loss of competitiveness

can include fortified grains and local vegetables. Improving the street food sector to minimize food-borne illnesses is another means to provide access to inexpensive and nutritious food. With proper nutrition workers will have the energy to be productive at work and, thus, earn more money, buy more food for the family and stay healthy. This is a virtuous circle allowing workers to remain productive and lift themselves out of the cycle of poor health and poverty. Yet without proper nutrition, governments, employers and workers will find themselves in the cycle captured in figure 3.1.

In the developed world, the workplace is often wrought with temptations that are sometimes worse than the ones at home. Danish pastries, muffins and cakes are standard fare at morning meetings and conference breaks. Office birthday parties bring more cake. Vending machines are usually filled with biscuits, chocolate and salty snacks. The local food van is stocked with meals for people on the go: rich sandwiches and cakes. Fast-food restaurants seem to surround the premises. Just a meal or two a week here can lead to serious weight gain (Pereira et al., 2005). Co-workers order pizza or greasy sandwiches for delivery, and the odour fills the room. The company canteen offers unlimited sugary drinks and fried potatoes every day of the week.

On top of this, many workers feel pressure to skip lunch, grab a ten-minute lunch, or stay at their desks to eat – the so-called desktop dining or SAD (stuck at desk) café phenomenon. According to a 2004 survey by the

British bank Abbey National, 70 per cent of British office workers regularly eat at their desks (Lyons and Moller, 2002). A 2004 survey commissioned by the United Kingdom Public and Commercial Service Union found that more than half of the British workforce take less than 30 minutes for lunch (Flynn, 2003). Similarly, the 2004 *Eurest lunchtime report* (Eurest, 2004) found that the British lunch hour was down to 27 minutes on average, the shortest ever recorded by Eurest. A missed or incomplete lunch will lower worker productivity, increase stress, and ultimately lead to afternoon snacking. In the United States, the American Dietetic Association found in 2003 that 67 per cent of workers eat lunch at their desks and 61 per cent snack there (American Dietetic Association, 2003).

The WHO, FAO and a multitude of national health institutes continue to urge the public to eat more fruits and vegetables, more fibre, fewer saturated and trans fats, fewer sweets and fewer high-cholesterol foods. The question is, if not at work, where and when? In this modern era, few people live within walking distance of work. Commuting times have increased and have shortened the breakfast period. Commuting and the two-worker-family phenomenon have shortened the dinner period as well. As a result, workers often grab something fast and sweet for breakfast, if anything. And there is a greater tendency to purchase prepared foods for dinner. This situation jeopardizes the success of the ubiquitous national "five-a-day" fruit and vegetable programmes. If workers have no access to fruits and vegetables at work, they will have to consume all five servings in the few hours between arriving home from work and going to sleep – an unlikely scenario. As we see, the workplace is often an obstacle to healthy eating instead of a vehicle of good nutrition.

3.2   The law

Surprisingly, there are few laws that stipulate when, where and how workers gain access to food, and none specifying what foods should be made available. The meal break is often left to cultural norms from country to country. In the United States, for example, there is no federal law mandating a meal break. The United States Code actually stipulates somewhat the opposite, that "breaks in working hours of more than one hour may not be scheduled in a basic workday" (United States Code, 2000); and the United States Fair Labor Standards Act (1938) reiterates that meal breaks are a matter of agreement between the employer and the employee. Only 19 of the 50 American states have laws concerning meal breaks. Each of these laws have many conditions and allow for only 20- to 30-minute breaks, except for New York, which requires hour-long lunch breaks for factory workers.

In the European Union, the meal break length is under debate now that France has lowered the working week to 35 hours. At issue is the definition of "working time", the time during which workers are at their employer's disposal, which some see as including the lunch break. The European Union Working Time Directive (93/104/EC) guarantees a rest break of at least 11 hours between shifts and a break during the working day when this is longer than 6 hours. Around the world rest periods and meal breaks vary: in Brazil, 1–2 hours per 6 hours; in Nigeria and the Libyan Arab Jamahiriya, 1 hour per 6 hours; in Japan, 45 minutes per 6 hours; in the United Kingdom, 20 minutes per 6 hours. South Africa and the Philippines mandate a 60-minute meal break. Other countries stipulate that the break must be at least 30 minutes during shifts longer than 5 hours. Some enterprises, such as the United States Government, section off an hour for lunch, but pay for only 30 minutes. An American civil servant's "eight-hour" working day is from 8:30 a.m. to 5 p.m. In Japan, the lunch hour can be strictly applied, with strong societal pressure not to eat early but precisely at noon with others. In many developing countries, workers feel obligated to work continuously, usually from early morning until late afternoon. In some situations, they are not allowed to take breaks. Sometimes there is no food in the vicinity, some workers feel they cannot afford to break. In these situations, workers often eat one meal a day, in the evening. The Labour Standards Act of Saskatchewan, Canada of 1978 (as amended in 1994), reflects the language of many laws regarding meal breaks:

Meal breaks – 13.3 (1994, c.39, s.8.)

(1) An employer shall grant to each employee who works six hours or more an unpaid meal break of at least 30 minutes within every five consecutive hours of work except:

(a) where an accident occurs, urgent work is necessary or other unforeseeable or unpreventable circumstances occur;

(b) where the director is satisfied that the employer and a majority of employees agree that the employees may:

(i) take their meal break at another time; or

(ii) forego their meal break;

(c) where the employer seeks and obtains the written consent of the trade union representing the employees;

(d) where it is not reasonable for an employee to take a meal break; or

(e) in any other case prescribed in regulations made pursuant to section 84.

(2) Where it is necessary for medical reasons, an individual employee is entitled to take a meal break at a time or times other than the time specified in subsection (1).

(3) Where an employee has worked five hours and the employer is not required to grant a meal break to an employee, the employer shall permit the employee to eat while working.

In India the Factories Act of 1948 makes it mandatory that companies ensure that their workforce has access to quality wholesome meals, a progressive act for any country. According to the Act, the Government "may make rules requiring that in any specified factory wherein 250 workers are ordinarily employed, a canteen or canteens shall be provided and maintained by the occupant for the use of the workers" (Viswanath, 2002). Still, the Act stops short of defining wholesome meals and the requirements of the canteen. Similarly, other countries (or, more often, regions within countries) have "labour standard" acts that define minimum length of meal breaks and exceptions to these.

The specifics about meal breaks and dining areas are often left to collective bargaining. Where there is no union, businesses are largely free to offer whatever the employee will accept. In many cases, workers have low expectations and unions have more pressing concerns. National and international trade unions and trade union federations contacted for this publication conceded that workers' nutrition and meal breaks were important issues but that these topics were not on their agenda. Notable exceptions include the Canadian Auto Workers and the Singapore National Trades Union Congress, both highlighted in Chapter 4.

The ILO has made progress in standardizing workers' access to breaks. The ILO Weekly Rest (Industry) Convention, 1921 (No. 14), and later the Weekly Rest (Commerce and Offices) Convention, 1957 (No. 106), established a minimum period of weekly rest for workers: at least 24 hours per seven-day period and preferably 36 hours. In view of the lack of broad legislation concerning meal breaks historically, and no consistency from country to country or even within countries, the ILO's Welfare Facilities Recommendation, 1956 (No. 102), includes a list of recommendations for meal provision. Adopted in 1956, it "define[s] certain principles and establish[es] certain standards concerning the following welfare facilities for workers: (a) feeding facilities in or near the undertaking; (b) rest facilities in or near the undertaking and recreation facilities excluding holiday facilities; and (c) transportation facilities to and from work where ordinary public transport is inadequate or impracticable". The text of this Recommendation is included in its entirety in Chapter 11.

3.3   Food solutions

Fifty years on, the ILO's Recommendation No. 102 remains relevant and applicable. The 1960s saw a shift in emphasis from the concept of workers' nutrition as a welfare benefit to a socio-economic benefit – that is, a necessity for increased productivity. In 1971, the ILO, along with the WHO and FAO, re-examined the state of workers' nutrition and asked a number of questions. Are workers getting enough calories and nutrients? To what extent is nutrition related to productivity, absenteeism, turnover and accidents? Who is responsible for planning and implementing meal programmes? And how can such programmes be financed? Their recommendations were published in May 1971 in the *Report of FAO/ILO/WHO Expert Consultation on workers' feeding*. In building upon the ILO's 1956 Recommendation, the authors reaffirmed that the scope of statutory obligations "should not be governed by the size of the unit, should embrace all types of industry in both urban and rural areas, and should be related to the needs of the workers and the industry" (FAO, 1971, p. 6).

The main recommendation of the report read: "that governments promulgate laws and regulations requiring the establishment of workers' feeding programmes with a view to improving the health, welfare and productivity of workers ... Such laws and regulations should have as their objective the adequate feeding of the worker and his family; should be designed to stimulate the establishment of appropriate food services ... and should recognize the economic limitation of the worker, the undertaking, the industry and the country" (FAO, 1971, p. 11).

There are a number of key points to consider in creating a meal programme.

3.3.1   Cost and place

What constitutes a successful feeding programme? First, employers must consider their space and budget. Canteens can be an ideal food solution. The company can ensure that workers have healthy foods at a reasonable price. Canteens are clearly an expensive option, though, and they require space. There is the cost of building the structure, acquiring equipment and hiring staff. (Hiring a caterer might reduce costs.) Vouchers allow the employer to avoid some of these costs. Workers use vouchers to choose from local restaurants. Yet for vouchers to be useful, there must be local restaurants. This is not always an option. Mess rooms can be less expensive than vouchers, although these too require space. In their simplest form, mess rooms are merely rooms in which food is served. An outside company could provide the daily food; the employer is merely providing accommodation. This solution can work well for small companies that aren't near restaurants. Companies can also consider offering kitchen areas with a refrigerator or box to store food and a way to heat food. This allows workers to save money by bringing their own meals, and it costs the company very little to maintain. At a minimum, workers need some place away from their workstations that is sheltered from the extremes of weather.

Cost to the employee is also important. Workers in Western Europe, Australia and North America pay about US$5–7 a meal (US$100–140 a month) yet earn around US$4,000 a month. Workers fortunate enough to have a subsidized meal programme pay about US$6 in Belgium, US$4–5.25 in France, US$4 in Germany and Spain, US$2.50–5.25 in Sweden, US$1.25–2.50 in Italy, and US$1.25 in the Czech Republic, according to internal Sodexho Alliance statistics. These workers on average spend no more than 3.5 per cent of their pay on workplace meals. In the 1971 FAO report referenced above, the authors recommend that the meal price should not exceed 5 per cent of the daily wage of the lowest-paid worker (FAO, 1971, p. 7). Russian workers featured in Chapter 8 pay only US$2 a meal, but this is about 16 per cent of their take-home pay, far too much. Most workers cannot afford this, and they skimp on lunch as a result.

Enterprises in remote locations, for example, mines and farms, must be prepared to properly house and feed workers and possibly their families. Abuses are common, as relayed in the Ugandan case study in Chapter 6. Workers are sometimes given grains as a sole source of nourishment. Two case studies in Chapter 4 about mines show how a meal programme can attract workers to remote areas.

3.3.2   Time, timeliness and rest

Time is always a pressing concern. Many workers are increasingly spending more hours at work or getting to work. The extra hours create stress and place constraints on morning and evening meals. The length of the meal break needs special consideration. Employers have to ask whether, for example, 30 minutes is enough time for employees to walk to the food service, choose a meal, pay, find a seat, eat and return to work. The type of work must be considered too. Workers performing hot, exhausting labour need more time to rest. Industrial workers need extra time to change from their protective clothing and wash.

The proposed food solution must fit the time allocation. Voucher use may require more than a 30-minute meal break, or else the company will find the employee bringing food back to the workstation to eat. Building a canteen that cannot serve workers quickly, or that does not have enough seats, is a poor investment. Crowded canteens or mess rooms can accommodate workers better if the lunch hour is staggered. If management holds firm on short breaks, then unions and workers must petition for food solutions that work within this context. In Chapter 6 we present a case study of a rose farm in Kenya that provides a two-hour midday break because it is simply too hot to work. Another manufacturer in Kenya built a mess room so that workers do not have to walk several kilometres for street food; and workers accepted a cut in the meal break (now 35 minutes) so that they could leave earlier at the end of the day.

Workers naturally must be allowed to utilize the time given to them for the meal break. Workers at hospitals or those who deal with the public, such as clerks and operators, often cannot leave for a break until another worker is available to replace them. Their break is sometimes shortened or completely eliminated. Other workers feel pressure to work through lunch, eating at their desks. Still others – as a result of understaffing, impossible targets, piece-work pay, forced overtime or harassment – cannot stop for a meal. Employers must remove such barriers to proper nutrition, and unions must remain diligent in demanding that the break times secured in collective bargaining are a reality for workers.

3.3.3 Comfort and accessibility

Canteens and mess rooms can offer workers a place to relax and bond; they should be within safe walking distance from the work area, offer affordable food, and be sheltered from the weather. In Singapore, workers revamped the Glaxo Wellcome Manufacturing cafeteria to create a more pleasant, relaxing atmosphere with a greater selection of healthy foods. Without it, workers would have at least a 20-minute round trip to a restaurant or street food vendor, which would significantly cut into their 40-minute meal break. The Musselwhite Mine in Canada has special refuge stations underground to provide a clean, quiet, safe and convenient spot for lunch and breaks. Workers have a place to change clothes and wash before eating. Without it, workers would have to return to the surface and travel across the mine to the canteen, which would take some time. These two examples, the subject of case studies in subsequent chapters, demonstrate how properly designed dining areas can help workers maximize their time to enjoy a meal.

Regardless of the time allotted for a break, the food service must be accessible. Workers with physical handicaps or other impairments should not be forced to travel far for a meal. Workers should not be expected to travel across busy areas of traffic or through dangerous parts of town. Special consideration must be given to shiftworkers and to night workers, who toil after hours when the canteen or local stores are closed. Vending machines stocked with nutritious meals are one solution here. Yet shift work and night work can have adverse effects on the heart and digestive health

(Spurgeon, 2003). Employers must be aware of the toll of prolonged shift work or night work and its interference with natural biorhythms, rest and the body's ability to absorb nutrients from food; and they must act accordingly, with regular health examinations, and provide ways for shiftworkers and night workers to eat wholesome meals. Workers on the road, such as truck drivers and sales people, are usually left on their own to find food. They often have little time or resources to eat properly each day. Meal vouchers can help ensure the worker has the funds to secure a proper meal. These vouchers are a signal from the employer that proper meals and rest are important.

Health education can help these workers understand which foods to eat and which to avoid.

3.4 Marginalized employees

3.4.1 Non-core workers

Policy-makers and union representatives cannot assume that all workers work during "business hours" at the same location each day or that all workers at a single location share the same entitlements. Aside from shiftworkers, night workers and mobile workers mentioned above, there are temporary workers, migrant workers, day labourers, part-time workers, contractors who perform non-core work such as cleaning and catering, and contractors who perform core work such as accounting and computer support; and their numbers are growing.

Consider the situation in the United Kingdom in the 1990s when large-scale and widespread redundancies led to increased outsourcing and subcontracting. This fragmented the workforce and affected workers' contractual entitlements, culminating in fewer core staff (permanently employed with entitlement to job security and benefits) and more "peripheral" workers (precariously employed with a different and usually inferior set of benefits). In the United States many government facilities are largely staffed by contracted workers hired by myriad contractors who compete for government contracts. American government workers have benefits such as public transportation vouchers that many contracted workers are denied; and it would not be surprising to find a situation in which contracted or temporary workers have inferior access to meal vouchers or other meal arrangements, such as a canteen discount.

At any given workplace, all employees must have equal access to meals and rest. Employees working outside business hours should be able to benefit from meal vouchers, access to safe food storage, or access to vending facilities. Day labourers should benefit from meal vouchers, local catering, safe food storage or access to safe street foods (see Chapter 7). Migrant farm workers should benefit from temporary shelters to eat, safe places to store food and access to clean water to drink and wash. Migrant factory workers from rural areas living in urban slums should benefit from two or three meals each day at the factory because they often have little means to store or cook food in their ramshackle dwellings. Ensuring proper nutrition for the multitude of marginalized workers is a great challenge but nevertheless paramount due to the sheer number of those who find themselves in such a category.

3.4.2 Gender

Female workers sometimes have specific nutritional needs not met at work. Women of child-bearing age are at risk of low blood iron as a result of poor nutrition coupled with menstrual bleeding. Adequate nutrition before, during and after pregnancy is crucial for healthy babies, a nation's future. Folic acid is one key nutrient required before and during pregnancy to prevent certain birth defects. Pregnancy and nursing make enormous demands on the body, and women need extra calories and additional rest during these periods. Safe food and water become all the more important during pregnancy. Access to healthy foods during pregnancy and nursing, as well as the right to nurse at work, will help ensure better health for the baby (cognitive and physical development) and mother (protection against osteoporosis and other diseases.) Women working through menopause sometimes must increase their fluid intake to combat dehydration or hot flushes brought on by hormonal changes.

In general women are more susceptible than men are to anaemia and osteoporosis; iron- and calcium-rich foods, respectively, can help ward off these diseases. Women do not necessarily require fewer calories than men. Many women must work at work and at home; and the work at home (carrying water, cleaning, gathering fuel) can consume a significant amount of calories. Employers who provide just enough calories for their employees to get through work may find their workforce chronically tired and unproductive as a result of insufficient nutrients and calories.

3.5   Occupational safety and hygiene

Malnutrition will make workers lethargic, mentally and physically, which increases the chance of workplace accidents. Contaminated food or water can sometimes sicken workers within minutes and can also lead to falls, spills or other accidents that can kill or injure a large number of workers. Employers must approach nutrition as they would other aspects of occupational safety and health. Food and water and dining areas must be free of chemicals or other hazards that could be ingested. Workers need facilities with soap and water to wash before eating. Food and water must be stored in suitable containers intended for food storage. Food handlers must understand the principles of proper hygiene. If employers do not offer a canteen, they must learn about the local food providers (street vendors, restaurant owners) and take special precautions to ensure food safety if necessary, such as providing vendors with access to clean water. A bout of food poisoning from one meal can sicken an entire workforce and could be as deadly as a toxic spill. Workers at the garment factory Kukdong in Mexico went on strike in part because of rotten food that made them sick. In Uganda, sugar-cane harvesters quarrelled with the cook over bad food. Food quality is an important concern among workers.

Workers working outdoors need protection from the elements. Some, but clearly not all, construction sites set up clean tents or trailers for the construction workers to escape the cold, heat or dirt of the construction site. As relayed in Chapter 7, construction workers often have poor access to proper meals and rest. In summary, workers have a right to protection from heat, cold, rain, workplace chemicals, noise and other workplace hazards during the meal break.

3.6   Special diets

Workers on special diets for health or religious reasons often are faced with a limited selection of food options at work. Employers need to understand the dietary needs of the employees, whether these workers refrain from meat products, pork, foods high in salt, fat or cholesterol, or foods that might cause an allergic reaction. Culture often dictates when one can eat as well as what one can eat. Muslim workers, for example, fast from dawn to dusk during the month-long period of Ramadan. Understanding these needs will help employers with food provision, labelling and timing. Workers with HIV/AIDS and other conditions that suppress the immune system are particularly vulnerable to colds, flu and more serious diseases; proper nutrition and foods free from pathogens (bacteria, parasites) are very important. HIV/AIDS affects over 25 per cent of adults in certain regions of sub-Saharan Africa; and millions more are infected in India, China and other parts of Asia, making this a pressing workplace concern.

3.7   International equality

The ILO has consistently advocated for international standards so that workers everywhere can enjoy the same rights. Multinational corporations can help in this regard too. An instructive example is the Nike code of conduct for subcontractors, featured in the Chapter 4 case study on Tae Kwang Vina in Viet Nam. Employers are more willing to invest in meal plan improvements knowing that their competitors must make similar improvements.

Progress has been made on the workers' nutrition front. A few governments, most notably Austria, Canada and Singapore, each highlighted in this publication, have established programmes to help businesses provide workers with access to nutritious foods during working hours. Some businesses on their own, too, have come to understand the value of a properly fed workforce and have made improvements. The following chapters in this publication highlight a multitude of food solutions. There is no single solution for all enterprises, no "one size fits all". As stated in the 1956 ILO Recommendation No. 102, food solutions may entail a canteen, a trolley, or a mess room. Some companies now offer meal vouchers, another food solution. In some places street vending is emerging as a solution.

This chapter began with a demonstration of how practical the workplace is for addressing the topic of nutrition. Whether this realization is a key priority difficult to tell. The WHO *Global strategy on diet, physical activity and health*, published in 2004, allocates only 60 words to the topic:

> Workplaces are important settings for health promotion and disease prevention. People need to be given the opportunity to make healthy choices in the workplace in order to reduce their exposure to risk. Further, the cost to employers of morbidity attributed to non-communicable diseases is increasing rapidly. Workplaces should make possible healthful food choices and support and encourage physical activity. (WHO, 2004b)

The WHO provides no guidance beyond this. *The Fifth Report on the World Nutrition Situation*, published in 2004 by the United Nations System Committee on Nutrition, is a 143-page document and it makes no mention of the workplace whatsoever (United Nations, 2004). Little information is available in the scientific or business literature.

Chapters 4 to 8 contain case studies of food solutions involving canteens, vouchers, mess rooms and kitchenettes, and local vendors, respectively. Chapter 9 contains solutions to an often-overlooked issue in nutrition, access to clean water. These case studies serve as a snapshot of current provision and by no means represent industries or countries in their entirety. The reader may notice a hierarchy among food solutions. This is unavoidable. Canteens and vouchers are usually a more advanced social benefit compared with mess rooms and access to safe street foods. Canteens serve large enterprises quite well; and they are difficult for smaller enterprises to maintain because of the investment and maintenance costs involved. Vouchers cut across enterprise size. Investment will improve food solutions, but much can be accomplished with small budgets.

Figures 3.2 and 3.3 provide graphical representations of the practicality of various food solutions depending on an enterprise's budget and location.

Figure 3.2   The food solution continuum. Investments in infrastructure or food subsidy will improve any food solution, leading to a range of effectiveness

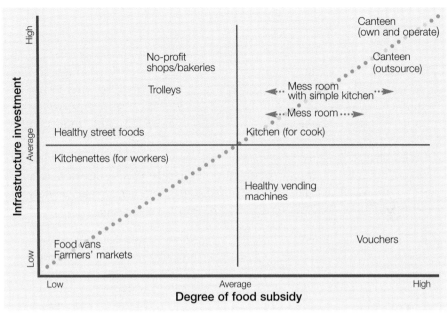

Figure 3.3   Decisions on food solutions might come down to budget and space

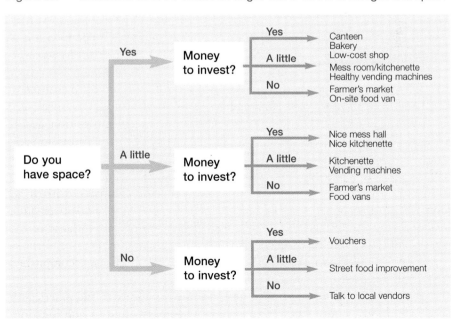

The first depicts the food solution "continuum". The second sums up an employer's choice with two questions: Is there space? What's the budget? Following this, we begin the case studies.

PART II

CASE STUDIES:
FOOD SOLUTIONS FROM THE FIELD

4

CANTEENS AND CAFETERIAS

Photo: Unilever/M. Winograd

"Laughter is brightest in the place where the food is."

Irish proverb

Key issues

The canteen

- A canteen is a facility where freshly prepared, hot food is served from behind a counter or self-served from buffets. Also called "cafeteria" and "mess".

- The 1988 ILO publication, *Canteens and food services in industry: A manual* (Brown, 1988), provides instructions on how to operate a canteen within a wide budget range.

Pros of running a canteen

- A popular canteen is a reflection of a well-run enterprise, a place where workers can eat a decent meal in pleasant surroundings with friends and colleagues.

- The canteen can offer physical and psychological benefits, enabling employees to rest, nourish themselves, relieve stress, and escape the monotony or industrial hazards of their workstations, even for only 30 minutes.

- Canteens are well suited for remote sites, such as mines and factories, where there are no local food options. Pleasant canteens help attract and keep employees.

- Most governments offer tax breaks for food and canteen equipment.

- The company can set the price and control the health quality and safety of the meal. The company can also keep employees safely on the grounds during breaks.

Cons of running a canteen

- Upfront investment and maintenance costs are often high. Ample space is needed.

- Dedication is needed. Special detail must be given to food safety, food delivery and storage, waste removal, cooking, cleaning and maintenance. One slip – one health code violation – could scare off workers and jeopardize the investment. A professional catering company can manage these day-to-day concerns.

Novel canteen examples

- Dole Food Company (United States) and Husky Injection Molding Systems (Canada) have essentially stripped their canteens of unhealthy foods. The costs of the healthiest foods are heavily subsidized.

- San Pedro Diseños (Guatemala) assessed the nutritional needs of its workforce and designed a menu to combat micronutrient deficiencies. Investment is made in food quality, safety and subsidy; the kitchen and dining area are simple.

- Glaxo Wellcome Manufacturing (Singapore) remodelled its canteen at the workers' request. Workers chose the new look, new menu and new pricing scheme. This has resulted in high morale and better health.

- Akteks Acrylic Yarn (Turkey) revamped its kitchen and dining area with a focus on hygiene. Better storage capacity allows for greater food variety. Meals are tasty, varied, healthy and free.

- Tae Kwang Vina (Viet Nam) adopted Nike's code of conduct after being cited for environmental and labour violations. Among the many improvements is a varied, well-balanced free lunch for workers.

- Voestalpine Stahl (Austria) runs a canteen based on a union initiative that calls for healthy foods either grown locally or purchased from vendors with established "fair" pro-worker values.

- Canada and Singapore have strong government and union initiatives to improve nutrition in the workplace, as well as in the community at large.

We begin Part II, the case study section, with a series of case studies about canteens, the most investment-intensive food solutions presented in this publication. This will be followed by solutions that require less investment. Many enterprises choose to provide their workers with a canteen. The decision may be one of practicality. For example, at remote sites, where workers stay for many days at a time, there may be no other option than to operate a kitchen. Other enterprises may offer a high-quality canteen to attract and maintain workers. Still others may be compelled to offer such a food service under national law. Regardless of the motive, a popular canteen is a reflection of a well-run enterprise, a place where workers can eat a decent meal in pleasant surroundings with friends and colleagues. The canteen can offer physical and psychological benefits, enabling employees to rest, nourish themselves, relieve stress, and escape the monotony or industrial hazards of their workstations, even for only 30 minutes.

Establishing a canteen as a food solution brings with it many advantages. Canteens can promote camaraderie among the workforce, bringing workers together instead of sending them out to find food. Canteens are convenient, saving employees the trouble of leaving the workplace for a meal. This is particularly beneficial for physically impaired workers. Most governments offer tax breaks for food and canteen equipment. The enterprise can control the menu, choosing to serve food it thinks best benefits the worker. The enterprise can control the price and subsidize only those foods that are healthy while still providing a "choice" of foods. The enterprise can also control the operating hours, keeping the canteen open in the early evening hours to accommodate shiftworkers and night workers, as relayed in the Peugeot-Citroën case study. Canteens should have ample seating to minimize the worker's task of obtaining food and to maximize the time for rest.

Establishing a canteen is no simple undertaking. Some enterprises choose to maintain complete control, hiring their own staff to cook, serve and clean. Others choose to outsource the task to a catering company. Both paths involve investment and commitment, as if operating a business within a business. A successful canteen requires adequate space and ventilation, a talented cooking and serving staff, a dedication to food safety, reliable equipment for cooking and storage, a reliable energy source, reliable supplies, a menu that fits the cultural and dietary needs of the staff, areas for workers to wash, staggered meal services to handle shifts and efficient rubbish collection. Just one slip – such as a careless server, or rubbish attracting flies or rodents – could lead to serious health code violations or mistrust among the customers. Space allocation is indeed a major concern and disadvantage. A company may have the financial resources to operate a canteen but no space. This can be true for companies in urban centres, where the price of space is high.

Attention to food safety cannot be overstated. Regardless of how fine a canteen might be, food-borne pathogens can sneak into the kitchen and ultimately harm hundreds of workers after only one meal. A single harmful bacterium can multiply into millions in only a couple of hours if food is not kept below 5°C or above 60°C. The risk of food contamination increases with the number of food handlers – from harvesters, to processors, to food delivery personnel, to the cooking and serving staff. Common sources of food poisoning are undercooked chicken, inadequately washed raw foods such as salads, and even improperly handled ice. Sometimes the signs of food contamination are obvious, as with the smell of spoiled milk; other times there are no sensory clues. Only vigilance and proper hygiene and food handling can prevent a disease outbreak. The WHO Food Safety Department and many national governments publish guidelines to advise food handlers on this topic, and several publications are listed in Chapter 11. Food and water safety is an occupational safety and heath issue, complete with storage, removal and supply chain concerns.

Most large enterprises have at least one company canteen. This chapter is not intended to persuade employers to establish a canteen nor to teach employers how to run one. Rather, this chapter provides a snapshot of the types of canteens around the world that are particularly healthy, inexpensive or otherwise practical (or impractical). For example, a trend in business catering today in wealthier nations is "better-for-you" menus. Enterprises that care for the long-term health of their workforce, or at least want to portray themselves as progressive, are contracting with caterers to provide foods high in nutrients and lower in calories, saturated fats, salt and sugar. Menus are also reflecting the new tastes of the post-1950 generation. In many countries throughout Australia, Europe and the Americas one will find workplace meals with an international flare. The German sausage in Germany is being complemented, if not entirely replaced, with tortilla-wrap sandwiches and six-green salads. America's macaroni and cheese is being ousted by balsamic chicken and polenta with red pepper and basil. Grilled and steamed food is replacing deep-fried. "Sauce on the side" is replacing "smothered in gravy".

Not surprisingly, earning the coveted spots in annual "top 100 businesses to work for" listings from *Forbes Magazine* and the like are those companies with progressive canteens. While such canteens don't come cheap, smaller companies or fiscally strapped enterprises can significantly improve the food quality of their canteens with little or no additional investment. What is needed, as some of the following case studies will show, is commitment and the courage to break old habits. Salad bars, for example, are cheaper than deep fryers and far easier to clean. And all the major caterers offer some type of healthy menu plan, sometimes at little extra cost.

The 1988 ILO publication, *Canteens and food services in industry: A manual* (Brown, 1988) provides instructions on how to operate a canteen, with a checklist and extensive bibliography. This chapter highlights enterprises with canteens that are successful in offering healthy food and that are accessible and pleasant, serving the two key elements of nutrition and rest. The selection represents many types of enterprises, large and small, across seven continents, providing the reader with a sample of ideas transferable to his or her own locale.

A word of clarification – in the English-speaking world, the definitions of the terms canteen, cafeteria and mess room vary from country to country. In British English, "canteen" refers to a restaurant in which customers are served at a counter, pay at a register and then carry their food to a table, usually on a tray. (A canteen, in America, is a flask to carry water; a mess room is for the military.) Many Australians, especially in an industrial setting, use the word "mess" for what Americans would call a cafeteria. This publication will use the British English term "canteen" for a food facility where freshly prepared, hot food is served from behind a counter or self-served from buffets. Local terms are used sparingly.

4.1 Dole Food Company, Inc.

Westlake Village, California, United States

Type of enterprise: the Dole Food Company is the world's largest producer and marketer of fresh fruit, vegetables, flowers and packaged foods. The company's 2002 revenues were US$4.8 billion. The following case study concerns Dole's corporate headquarters in Westlake Village, California, United States. (http://www.dole.com)

Employees: 300.

Food solution – key point: new canteen with subsidized healthy foods.

Among industrialized nations, the United States has felt the brunt of the obesity epidemic, with nearly two-thirds of its population overweight or obese. The trend cuts across class and age group, but it is particularly acute among traditionally poorer groups in the United States, such as African Americans and Latinos. Most disturbing is the rising incidence of "adult-onset" Type 2 diabetes among children, a result of diet and not genetics. Dole, being in the fresh fruit and vegetable business, naturally saw an opportunity to help reverse this trend. The company has an extensive educational outreach programme aimed at communities and schoolchildren and is active in the national "five-a-day" nutrition programme.

Food solution

In a fitting example of "practise what you preach," Dole has radically reorganized its canteen for its employees at its corporate headquarters. The main changes include: an overhaul of the menu which is now dominated by healthy food choices; discounts on healthy foods, such as the US$1.50 salad bar; a "smoothie" machine, which makes a thick drink by mixing fruits, vegetables, herbs or teas often with yoghurt; and healthy fat-free or low-fat desserts. These changes are part of the Dole Employee Wellness Program (DEW), launched in October 2003. The DEW also features free morning and afternoon fruit and vegetable breaks, vending machines with healthy options, on-site weekly access to a farmers' market, and an on-site dietician, as well as bi-weekly newsletters on fitness and health and access to physical activities. Employees earn "Dole dollars" for participating in the DEW, which can be redeemed for gift certificates and other rewards. Approximately 75 per cent of the employees use the canteen on any given day. Others eat out or bring a packed lunch. Workers have one hour for lunch. This provides ample time to eat in the canteen and rest or even visit a local restaurant for a change of pace.

The new Dole canteen menu focuses on foods low in saturated fats; and unlike most company canteens, Dole's canteen offers a variety of vegetarian and vegan meals, listed in greater detail below. No other United States based work canteen reviewed for this publication maintains such a focus – not even the National Institutes of Health (NIH), the Centers for Disease Control and Prevention and the Department of Agriculture, the three governmental organizations encouraging Americans to eat a diet low in saturated fat and high in vegetables. Other United States enterprises, some of which are featured in this book, might offer one healthy dish beside several less healthy choices, such as fried and fatty foods. No doubt this is a good start, but too often employees eat the foods they know are not good for them. Healthy alternatives are often presented as sacrifices, and in many cases, they do not actually taste that good. Some enterprises offer low-carbohydrate dishes, for employees on the popular Atkins and South Beach diets, which are high in animal protein and fat and low in carbohydrates. Dole does not kow-tow to this diet fad but instead features a diet based on WHO and NIH guidelines.

The Dole menu does indeed offer choice by offering a variety of healthy meals. They are prepared and presented with a philosophy that healthy foods can taste good – even superior to burgers and macaroni and cheese – and that they should not be viewed as a sacrifice. Jennifer Grossman, director of the Dole Nutrition Institute who spearheaded the canteen changes, has made instilling this philosophy her primary goal. Dole attempts to remove negative connotations that many Americans have for tofu, broccoli, wholegrain bread and other so-called health foods. The canteen offers breakfast, lunch and take-away dinners, which are heavily subsidized, particularly considering the quality of the meals. Breakfasts cost around US$3.00, and lunches US$4.75 on average, which is about half the cost of restaurant meals of similar quality in this part of California. The "Daily Dole" is a lunch special costing US$4.25.

There is no beef, pork, cream, whole milk or sugary drinks. Protein sources are chicken, turkey, fish, soya and other beans. Traditional beef dishes such as hamburgers are served with meat substitutes, such as soya or vegetable meal with the same consistency as beef. Chile con carne is served as "chile non carne". A typical daily lunch menu includes cilantro (coriander) black bean soup, grilled halibut with melon salsa, turkey cutlet pomodoro, vegetable curry with marinated tofu, shrimp focaccia sandwich with herb mayonnaise, tuna melt with organic potato chips and three-grain trio salad.

Possible disadvantages of food solution

Dole has taken a bold all-or-nothing approach. Change came swiftly and thoroughly. From an American perspective, the Dole menu may seem radical

Dole Garden Court Cafe

Week of Monday April 5

Monday

SunCreek Breakfast:	Buckwheat Waffles with Fresh Berries	$2.75
Copper Pot:	Gazpacho Blanco	$1.35/$1.85
Chefs Features:	Grilled Chicken Breast with Olive pesto Crust	$5.25
Daily Dole:	Poached Sole with Roasted Red Pepper Sauce	$5.25/DD$4.25
Sage Deli:	Mediterranean Pita	$4.25
Selona Grill:	Mushroom Turkey Burger with Grilled Onions	$4.25
Exhibition Salad:	Tropical Fruit Spinach Salad Tossed with Citrus Vinaigrette	$4.95

Tuesday

SunCreek Breakfast:	Smoked Salmon Omelet with Chives	$3.25
Copper Pot:	Onion Soup with "Parmesan" Croutons	$1.35/1.85
Chefs Features:	Sautéed Mexican Grouper with Avocado Salsa	$5.25
Daily Dole:	Vegetable Curry with Marinated Tofu	$5.25/$4.25
Sage Deli:	Waldorf Chicken Salad Sandwich	$4.25
Selona Grill:	Santa Fe Style Chicken Breast Sandwich w/ Black Bean Salsa	$4.25
Exhibition Salad:	Honey Glazed Chicken Over Mixed Greens with Vinaigrette	$4.95

Wednesday

SunCreek Breakfast:	Cinnamon- Raisin French Toast	$2.75
Copper Pot:	Cilantro Black Bean Soup	$1.35/$1.85
Chefs Features:	Grilled halibut with Melon Salsa	$5.25
Daily Dole:	Turkey Cutlet Pomodoro	$5.25/DD$4.25
Sage Deli:	Shrimp Focaccia Sandwich with Herbed Mayonnaise	$4.25
Selona Grill:	Tuna melt with Organic Potato Chips	$4.25
Exhibition Salad:	Three Grain Trio Plate	$4.75

Thursday

SunCreek Breakfast:	Strawberry Banana Pancakes	$2.25
Copper Pot:	Mushroom Barley Soup	$1.35/$1.85
Chefs Features:	Sautéed Blackened Tilapia	$5.25
Daily Dole:	"Beef" Lasagna with Vegetables	$5.25/DD$4.25
Sage Deli:	Turkey & Avocado Wrap	$4.25
Selona Grill:	Open Face Sandwich w/ Marinated Vegetables & Couscous	$4.25
Exhibition Salad:	Almond Turkey Salad w/ Cranberry Vinaigrette	$4.95

Friday

SunCreek Breakfast:	Spanish Scramble with Spicy Potatoes	$2.50
Copper Pot:	Potato Leek Soup	$1.35/$1.85
Chefs Features:	Chicken Fajita with Pasilla Pepper	$5.25
Daily Dole:	Wild Fresh Salmon with Mango Jicama Salsa	$5.25/DD$4.25
Sage Deli:	Chicken Caesar Wrap	$3.95
Selona Grill:	Vegetable Burger with Tomato and Avocado	$4.25
Exhibition Salad:	Strawberry Field with Chicken Tossed with Balsamic Vinaigrette	$4.95

A typical weekly menu at the Dole canteen. Main courses are low-fat. Vegetarian dishes are available daily and healthy food is subsidized.

and may even be unwelcome in certain parts of the country. America is a meat-and-potato culture, and many Americans would view the Dole menu as fancy or exotic. Californians may be more familiar with diverse cuisines compared with other parts of the United States, particularly the central part of the country. Nevertheless, Dole faced a challenge in getting its employees to accept the menu changes. The pricing, presentation and, of course, taste have slowly won over most of the employees. Despite the obvious advantages of removing unhealthy foods from the workplace, it is not clear whether the Dole approach would work in a largely blue-collar, industrial setting with burly men resentful that they are forced to eat tofu. In Dole's defence, there is nothing stopping employees from packing a lunch or visiting a nearby restaurant.

Costs and benefits to enterprise

The expense to the company has not been trivial. The added cost of the canteen has been approximately US$100,000 for the first year, and another US$100,000 has been spent on other aspects of the DEW, such as the free yoga classes.

Dole views the DEW as both an investment and an experiment, and the company is not expecting an immediate pay-off. With approximately 59,000 employees worldwide, Dole will make changes to some extent at its other facilities if it deems the headquarters' DEW to be successful. Dole has. Success is loosely defined. Dole's goal is not necessarily to make the canteen profitable. Dole hopes to reduce health-care costs but also attract and retain employees with the attractive benefit of an inexpensive and pleasant canteen. The DEW is less than a year old, at the time of writing. Dole is working with an independent clinic to evaluate the programme's health impact on a group of 50 volunteers. For now, anecdotally, Ms. Grossman reports that employees are losing weight – sometimes without trying – and have come to view the canteen as a perk. Dole also sees itself as an industry leader and hopes to raise the standard of American workplace nutrition. From a public relations perspective, the move has paid off. The DEW was announced with fanfare in October 2003, and Dole has since received positive press in newspapers and industry journals. The United States Under Secretary of Agriculture, Eric Bost, spoke highly of the DEW during a non-related interview, and he could think of no other programme that comes close to Dole's.

Government incentives

None, other than standard tax exemption.

Practical advice for implementation

As the reader will see in other case studies, the CEO's personal involvement led to a fully realized workplace health initiative. Dole Chairman, President and CEO, David Murdock, in his 80s, is a fish-eating vegetarian and fitness enthusiast. Ms. Grossman, also a vegetarian, said she could count on him to support the ambitious health programme that she and her staff created. A sparkling new facility is nothing if the employees don't use it. This is why the incentives – low prices, Dole dollars, and presentation – may be the most important aspect of the DEW. Incentives complement choices. In other companies, the healthy choice might not be chosen because it is either tasteless or expensive. While most unhealthy food has been stripped from the canteen, workers do have temptations: they can eat out or bring food from home, and these choices are unlikely to be as healthy as food at the Dole canteen. Essentially, Dole uses incentives to make it impractical to maintain an unhealthy lifestyle. One worry was that the employees would reject the changes, resenting that they were being forced to eat healthy foods. Indeed, many employees grumbled at first that their favourite, unhealthy foods were gone. Slowly, however, most have come to see the value in Dole's DEW. Ms. Grossman said she must remain careful not to come across as a food dictator. Incentives and choices, not mandates, are key.

In March 2003, Dole became a private company. Mr. Murdock said that Dole's investment in the DEW wouldn't be possible if it were a publicly traded company because of its effect on quarterly profits and shareholder pressure. Although the US$200,000 investment may seem high compared with other enterprises, one can argue that the cost is not a burden for a multibillion-dollar company, particularly in light of the excesses reported among executives at other United States companies in recent years. Mr. Murdock's statement may have more relevance if the DEW is extended to Dole's 59,000 other employees.

Union/employee perspective

The Dole headquarters has no union to offer its perspective. Employees grumbled at first about being forced to eat "health food", but most have come to appreciate the canteen. Many are losing weight, some without trying, and this has boosted the canteen's popularity. Some employee comments reflect the changing of attitudes. "My tastes are changing ... I really look forward to my salad at lunch with the same kind of gusto that in the past I would have reserved for less healthy, higher calorie meals," said one male employee. Other comments reflect the reality of staying on a diet alone, such as this from a female employee, "I wasn't doing it myself. I am eating better only because [CEO] Murdock revamped the kitchen." Other employees hoped the same changes would reach other Dole facilities.

4.2   San Pedro Diseños, S. A.

Guatemala City, Guatemala

Type of enterprise: San Pedro Diseños is a textile company founded in the early 1990s. It moved to its current location in Guatemala City in 1998. The company produces approximately 200,000 items per month – largely T-shirts, blouses, skirts, jackets, jeans, trousers and casual shorts – for Timberland, Costco and GAP, among other companies.

Employees: 250.

Food solution – key point: revamped meal programme to address workers' lack of calories and nutrients.

San Pedro Diseños workers are mostly low wage earners – operators and manual workers. The operators work on sewing machines; manual workers move supplies about. The average age is 25; the age range from 20 to 30. Approximately 60 per cent of employees are female. Most (75 per cent) come from distant parts of the country and 90 per cent have less than six years of education. The monthly salary starts at Q1,328 (quetzals) (US$170), which is the state minimum wage. Operators' wages vary based on productivity, and are usually higher than the salary for manual workers. Workers live on the margins of poverty in rented houses in the city, often with extended family members.

Several years ago the company established an occupational health and safety programme, for which it was recognized nationally. Through an initial health surveillance managers discovered the extent of poor nutrition and poor knowledge of nutrition among the workers. Workers perceived themselves as healthy in a survey, but this wasn't the case. In essence, the workers' health status reflected that of the nation, where 36 per cent of women of child-bearing years are anaemic and the average deficiency of calories is 200 kcal per day, according to the Instituto de Nutrición para Centroamérica y Panamá. The workers at San Pedro Diseños had a typically meagre and unvaried diet of rice, beans and corn tortilla, which afforded them some calories but not the recommended intake of micronutrients.

Guatemala experienced fluctuations in its food supply during the 1980s, and food availability has fallen sharply since 1995 to a current, critical level, ten years later. Approximately 60 per cent of homes do not have enough income to provide the calories and nutrients required. Since 1997, two minimum wages are needed to cover the basic food cost for a family. Child malnutrition

Workers prepare tortilla in one of three kitchens, adhering to safe food-handling principles (E. Pop Juárez).

is now a major concern, with 49.3 per cent of children aged less than 5 chronically malnourished, 26 per cent anaemic and 18.5 per cent deficient in vitamin A. Around 75 per cent of homes consume only five food products: tortilla, beans, eggs, tomato and sweet bread (PAHO 2003, p. iii).

Food solution

The San Pedro Diseños management came to realize that the majority of workers started their day without breakfast and many didn't have a nutritious lunch. The result was sluggishness later in the day and frequent illnesses. Workers said they chose their food based on price: eating rice, beans and tortilla was the cheapest way to feel full. Most complained of a lack of money to buy food or a lack of time to prepare meals. What little they understood about nutrition, which was often incorrect, came from television, magazines, and friends and family. Management started a nutritional plan as part of an enterprise policy and outlined three main strategies: food security, social services (making sure workers can afford the food) and health (general check-ups).

The basics of the new meal programme include: cooking facilities; a dining area; subsidized meals; an hour-long meal break; free sweet bread (*pan dulce* or

The dining area is simple but pleasant, with room for all 250 workers (E. Pop Juárez).

pan de manteca) and coffee during the breaks; and a healthy, varied menu. The company's dining room is about 120 square metres and accommodates 150 workers comfortably. The area is pleasant and clean. There are two facilities to cook food and another one to make corn tortillas. The food is prepared and served daily. Fresh products are used each day, such as vegetables, meats and fruits. The managers and owners share the same facilities and eat the same food.

Typically workers can now enjoy breakfast and lunch. Complimentary sweet bread and coffee is offered before work and also at 10 a.m. during the 15-minute break. A serving of sweet bread contains about 150 kcal. Workers have the option to buy breakfast, too, at a low cost. During the 60-minute lunch break, workers make the short walk to one of two serving areas to purchase a meal. There is a place to wash before eating. Then they walk to a common, indoor dining area. Some workers play sports before lunch, so the 150-seat dining area is large enough to facilitate 250 workers eating lunch at different times during the long break. Workers who bring a packed lunch also eat here.

Lunch contains 1,000–1,100 kcal, about half the daily requirement to perform the type of work at San Pedro Diseños. There are three or four main items on the menu each day, and this includes meat, soup, rice, fresh vegetables, salad, tortilla, pasta and a beverage. Lunch is priced at Q6 (US$0.75), which is about a third of the actual value. The full cost is Q18–Q20, and the company pays the remaining share. Workers don't have to pay immediately; credit is extended to the end of the week. So, the total weekly cost to the workers for a decent daily meal is Q30, which is about 9 per cent of the lowest factory wage. On Saturday, an optional working day, the company provides a free meal voucher. Also, throughout the company, there are dispensers with clean water.

Before 1998 the company maintained three factories in different locations, each with a small, overcrowded canteen. These were ordinary canteens for Guatemala and not particularly well liked. The new facility has space for three kitchens: two to cook meals and one to make tortillas. A caterer prepares the food. The kitchens each have three or four cooks who have licenses issued by the Ministry of Public Health. The kitchens are inspected by a government agency. The two main kitchens employ workers from the older canteens. They maintain separate menus, and they each cook about 125 meals each day.

Possible disadvantages of food solution

There are few disadvantages of the new meal programme. The FAO recommends that a meal should cost no more than 5 per cent of the daily wage of the lowest-paid worker. The San Pedro Diseños meal costs 9 per cent, but it is not clear how many workers earn only the minimum wage. The company has now recognized the need to educate the workers about nutrition and will implement a programme in the future.

Costs and benefits to enterprise

The lunch subsidy costs the company roughly Q5,000 (US$640) a day, which is Q20 for each of the 250 workers. The cost of sweet bread and coffee was not mentioned but assumed to be marginal. The cost of hiring cooks was not disclosed, but this was more expensive than hiring unlicensed, untrained cooks, a temptation in poorer nations. (The company saves on food safety issues in the long run.)

According to the managers, since the creation of the new meal programme there have been many rewards. Workers are more productive and more satisfied; morale is higher; absenteeism and the need for rotation due to illness have fallen; and medical costs are down. Since 2001, production has increased by around 70 per cent and annual earnings have increased approximately 20 per cent.

Government incentives

None.

Practical advice for implementation

San Pedro Diseños does many things right. With a modest budget the company offers a canteen as impressive as the Dole canteen presented in the preceding case study. The San Pedro Diseños dining area is not fancy, but it is pleasant nonetheless. The company saves money by offering simple chairs and tables, which can be moved easily. The long break eases crowding in the dining area. This also gives workers sufficient time to rest, which is particularly important in the hot climate. (Convenient access to clean water helps here too.) The kitchens are small and simple, but clean and efficient. The company does not skimp on food safety and nutrition. Fresh foods are brought in daily, and few perishables need to be stored. San Pedro Diseños uses licensed cooks trained in safe food-handling practices. The menu reflects a deliberate effort by the company to supply workers with adequate amounts of macro- and micronutrients. Fresh vegetables and meats are foods most workers would not eat outside the workplace. This is a company that investigated the nutritional needs of its employees and decided upon an economic means to facilitate those needs.

The managers share the same food as the employees, a wise move to spread goodwill among the workers. Free coffee and sweet bread are an inexpensive perk that also significantly boosts the workers' positive attitude towards the company. San Pedro Diseños could consider offering juice at least once a week along with coffee (which has few nutrients) or a culturally appropriate substitute for sweet bread (which is a simple carbohydrate). Depending on its budget and the need, San Pedro Diseños and similar companies could consider distributing food for workers' families to help combat malnutrition at home. Childhood malnutrition is an acute problem in Guatemala, and it is compromising the prosperity of the country for years to come. Bulk distribution of fortified grains or milk can combat iron, vitamin A and other micronutrient deficiencies.

Union/employee perspective

There is no union. Through focus group discussions and key informant interviews, workers were asked to describe the nutritional programme implemented by the company: that is, name the issues affecting their food choices, their eating habits and working conditions. Workers stated that food assistance – such as complimentary sweet bread, coffee and Saturday meal vouchers, and low-cost, nutritious lunches every day – is greatly appreciated and that it has improved their health. Yet one worker said, "We buy and eat cheap foods because we have no choice. Beans, rice and tortillas are great because you can eat enough food for a day in one meal." This seems to imply that workers can get one square meal a day at the workplace, which no doubt eases the family burden of food provision. But low salaries and the lack of affordable nutritious foods in the city (and not nutritional information) make it difficult to feed their families.

Workers indeed commented that the lack of money due to low incomes is the most common barrier to achieving good nutrition. Many workers agreed that San Pedro Diseños is different from other companies because of the social benefits, health services, meals and decent treatment. The company pays on time, too. All of these factors, said the workers, made them feel motivated. Managers mentioned that they needed to improve food safety knowledge and skills among workers.

This case study was prepared by Dr. Edín Rolando Pop Juárez.

4.3 Spotlight on Canada: Government and unions help improve workers' nutrition

With its long, harsh winters and a traditional cuisine famous for bacon and creamy dairy products, Canada has grown alarmed in recent years over an increasingly sedentary population with expanding waistlines. In Ontario, one of the ten Canadian provinces and home to the nation's capital, Ottawa, more than 50 per cent of men and 34 per cent of women are overweight; 80 per cent of women do not get enough fibre; 75 per cent of adults do not consume enough wholegrain products; and more than 50 per cent eat too much fat (Nutrition Resource Centre, 2002). Nationwide, the rising rate of chronic diseases – cancer, heart disease and diabetes – mimics that found in some other Western industrial nations.

The Canadian Auto Workers initiated wellness programme

The Canadian Auto Workers (CAW) union has taken an active lead in making a change. In 1996, the CAW began to negotiate a comprehensive wellness programme at the Chrysler and General Motors (GM) plants in Canada. Workers wanted better access to exercise facilities, health education, health check-ups and healthy food. The union-initiated million-dollar programmes were finally in place at Chrysler by 2001 and at General Motors by early 2004. Regarding nutrition, both of these companies now serve a greater variety of healthy foods in the canteens. Often such wellness initiatives come from management. However, at GM and Chrysler (now called DaimlerChrysler Canada), the programmes would not have come to fruition without unwavering union and worker commitment. According to the CAW Director of the Health and Safety Training Fund, Lyle Hargrove, the fact that the union initiated the change has enabled the CAW to retain greater control of the programme. Over half of the members of the wellness committees belong to the union.

Hargrove describes the eating facilities at GM and Chrysler as good canteens that got better. Most of the changes have concentrated on menus. The CAW would like to see additional improvements. The lunch break is 30 minutes. Although the canteens are located close to the factory floor, this still leaves barely enough time to eat. The CAW would like to see a better food subsidy arrangement too. Subsidizing healthier foods, such as vegetable-based dishes, would encourage more workers to try them. Currently such meals are more expensive than, for example, less healthy, fried options. (The Dole Food Company canteen featured in this publication has demonstrated success in subsidizing healthy food options.)

The wellness programme has paid off for the union and, it seems, for Chrysler. The wellness programme has been a popular CAW victory, greatly increasing the union's visibility among Canadian workers. The CAW hopes to extend similar programmes to its other sites. Chrysler, in turn, has won the 2004 National Quality Institute Award for Excellence. This well-respected business award, developed in association with Health Canada, recognizes efforts to make the workplace safer and healthier.

Eat Smart! Workplace Cafeteria Program

Canadian health officials also recognize that the workplace is a natural place to address the issue of poor nutrition because workers spend a significant amount of their time there and eat at least one meal during working hours. There are many workplace nutrition efforts across the country. In Ontario alone, the 37 local public health units promote workplace health using a variety of resources and programmes. One innovative effort in Ontario is the Eat Smart! Workplace Cafeteria Program, which is a programme of health standards introduced in 2001. This builds upon Ontario's successful Eat Smart! Healthy Restaurant Program, which started in 1999.

The restaurant programme started as a partnership among the Ontario Ministry of Health and Long-Term Care; the Canadian Cancer Society (Ontario Division); the Heart and Stroke Foundation of Ontario; the Ontario Ministry of Agriculture, Food and Rural Affairs; Toronto Public Health; local health units; heart health programmes; the food service industry; and consumers. Essentially, Canadians were growing concerned that restaurant food, albeit tasty, was becoming increasingly unhealthy and was partly responsible for the burgeoning epidemic of obesity. This was similar to the situation in the neighbouring United States. Restaurant portions were often large and high in saturated fats and salt, with few vegetable options. Many Canadians on restrictive diets for health reasons – trying to reduce their cholesterol, for example – had few healthy menu options to choose from. Health experts were also concerned about cigarette smoke and unsafe food-handling practices.

Eat Smart! addresses some of these concerns through a voluntary programme that brings together the food service sector and a multitude of health organizations. The Nutrition Resource Centre, part of the Ontario Public Health Association, manages Eat Smart! through funding from the Ontario Government. Restaurants apply and pledge to serve food in a smoke-free environment with healthier choices available on the menu and by request. Eat Smart! restaurants offer more options of wholegrain products, vegetables, fruit, and main courses and desserts with less fat. Customers can also ask for healthy substitutions at no extra charge (for example, salad instead of fries). Restaurants that meet these requirements can display the Eat Smart! logo in their window. To ensure quality, restaurants are assessed annually.

The Eat Smart! Workplace Cafeteria Program places this scheme into the company canteen. (There is also a school cafeteria version.) Companies are not left to implement the programme on their own, however. Documents from the Nutrition Resource Centre are quite specific about how to set up and launch Eat Smart! For example, manuals include information on how to negotiate contracts with caterers, how to educate employees, how to display point-of-purchase (POP) messaging, how to add variety to the menu from season to season and how to self-monitor the programme. One other important aspect of Eat Smart! is its recognition of healthy meals for shiftworkers and night workers, an often neglected group who must fend for themselves after the canteen has closed.

Eat Smart! is run by the local public health units. Of the 37 units in Ontario, 32 implement the restaurant programme and 18 currently implement the workplace programme. So far, 45 workplace canteens participate; and there is high expectation that many more will enrol in the coming years, as more local health units get involved. While Eat Smart! is one of many Canadian health programmes, its most striking characteristic is the degree to which it has been thought out and implemented. Many of the workplace health programmes around the world researched for this book seem to be nothing more than recommendations. These recommendations – as generic as "eat right and exercise" – are either rarely or half-heartedly implemented. With Eat Smart!, Canadian health experts took an established idea and extended it to the workplace; thus the new programme benefits from name recognition. Inclusive from the start, they gathered opinions from all groups, taxing as it was to work with scores of organizations and offices, and incorporated their inputs. Several workplaces have since been evaluated, revealing successful aspects of the programme as well as points that need to be addressed.

Healthy Eating at Work and Food Steps

Two other workplace health programmes in Canada are Healthy Eating at Work and Food Steps. These programmes are tailored towards individuals. Food Steps is a research-based programme centred on the "stages of change" theory to reduce fat from one's diet week by week, or step by step. Food Steps is sometimes offered to workplaces by public health units implementing workplace health programmes. It is a self-help, correspondence programme, which makes it a good fit for workplaces, although it is also used in the general community as a complement to individual nutrition counselling and group programmes. Healthy Eating at Work is based on the "vitality" concept developed by Health Canada to promote healthy food, active lifestyles and a social acceptance of a wider range of body types.

Research has shown that better nutrition at work boosts productivity and morale. Businesses, however, receive no direct financial incentive to join Eat Smart! The Nutrition Resource Centre and its two key partners in the Eat Smart! programme, the Heart and Stroke Foundation of Ontario and the Canadian Cancer Society (Ontario Division) offer the "Cafeteria Award of Excellence", which is a modest incentive. By comparison, Singapore, in addition to awards, offers small financial incentives to encourage businesses to adopt healthy workplace canteen practices (see Spotlight on Singapore, p. 94). California is experimenting with tax incentives (see Spotlight on California, p.219). Similar incentives in Canada might encourage more businesses to join Eat Smart! However, this is merely an outside opinion and does not reflect the programme's agenda.

Information about the Eat Smart! programme is available in French or English at: http://www.nutritionrc.ca and http://www.eatsmart.web.net. The CAW web site is http://www.caw.ca, although there is no substantive information about the wellness programme online.

4.4　Husky Injection Molding Systems Ltd

Bolton, Ontario, Canada

Type of enterprise: Husky is a leading supplier of injection molding equipment and services to the plastics industry, with US$816 million in sales in 2003 and approximately 2,800 people employed worldwide. Husky employees make machines and machine parts used to create plastic products. Husky regularly ranks among the 50 best employers in Canada and is recognized as having the "best physical work environment" in Canada according to the 2004 ranking. (http://www.husky.ca)

Employees: 1,380 at Bolton campus.

Food solution – key point: canteen with subsidized, healthy foods.

Like many companies, Husky has a holistic approach to health care with a focus on education and prevention. The company excels in encouraging its staff to be physically active. Its four largest sites – in Canada, the United States, Luxembourg and Shanghai – have on-site fitness centres. If space does not allow for an on-site facility, then the company provides workers and their families with a fitness subsidy to join a local gym. Husky's nutrition programme is just one aspect of the wellness initiative, yet it too is above average. The focus of this case study is the canteen system at the Bolton campus, approximately 20 kilometres north of Toronto. However, each Husky site is similar in the canteen and health benefits offered.

Food solution

The Husky canteens offer employees healthy food choices that promote wellbeing and energy. Four out of the five Bolton buildings have a canteen and around 80–90 per cent of the employees use them. The nutrition agenda features fresh fruits and vegetables (local and organic when available), high-fibre wholegrain breads, wild rice, meat alternatives such as polenta (not exactly mainstream in Canada), cholesterol-smart meals (no red meat), environmentally responsible food selection and preparation practices, and consideration of employees' food sensitivities and allergies. Unlike other enterprises featured in this publication, Husky did not design its canteen menu in reaction to health problems such as diabetes or obesity. Husky's workforce is fairly engaged in health and is healthy. That said, Canadians are not immune to chronic diseases. Husky sees its nutrition programme as a preventive measure.

For example, red meat is not served because of its levels of saturated fat and hormones, and also because of the negative impact of ranching on the

The Husky canteen is noted for its healthy, subsidized menu and pleasant atmosphere.

environment. Deep-frying is non-existent. This reduces the employees' exposure to saturated and trans fats. Every meal comes with three servings of vegetables or a side salad. Vegetarian meals are more highly subsidized than poultry and fish dishes. Coffee is sold at fair market prices, but herbal teas are free. The main theme – reduction in saturated and trans fats (see Chapter 2) and an increase in vegetable consumption – is in line with recommendations from Canadian health authorities as well as the WHO as a way to reduce the risk of cancer, cardio-vascular disease and obesity. While scientists are not in agreement over the health risks of hormones and caffeine, Husky takes the approach that these are not needed in the diet.

The lunch break varies from 30 minutes to an hour, depending on the operation and type of job performed. Husky addresses the issue of timeliness by locating canteens across the facility. Still, 30 minutes can be tight to grab a meal, pay, sit, eat and return to work. All canteens serve breakfast and lunch and none serve dinner; however, prepared meals are available for reheating. The average cost for a full meal including vegetables or salad is CAN$4–7 (US$3.35–5.90). The sub-sidy depends on the food cost and varies between CAN$1–2 (US$0.85–1.70) per meal. The final price is less than most local restaurants serving a comparable meal.

Husky's Bolton campus does not have vending machines. Snacks, available through the canteen, are generally as healthy as possible. The only potato chips sold are all-natural and contain no trans fat. Other common snacks include energy bars, granola, nuts and fresh fruit. There are no chocolate bars.

Education is a large component of the Husky wellness programme. The company offers monthly educational sessions on a wide variety of health topics. Husky employs multidisciplinary clinicians who use education as one of the primary components of their treatment plan. The Wellness Center team includes two medical doctors, two occupational health nurses, a chiropractor, a naturopath (alternative medicine practitioner), a physiotherapist, two massage therapists and an administrative assistant. One doctor, nurse and assistant are kept full time. Dr. David Doull, a chiropractor at Bolton interviewed for this case study, is responsible for its global health plan; a second chiropractor works part time. As mentioned briefly above, Bolton has an on-site fitness facility that is free to all employees, their spouses and children over 18 years of age. It features cardiovascular and strength equipment and lunchtime fitness classes for aerobics, yoga and karate.

Possible disadvantages of food solution

Similar to Dole's canteen, Husky offers no unhealthy options. This works at Husky because of the company's culture. Some workers in other settings might resent a lack of choice, a concept discussed further in the "advice" section below.

Costs and benefits to enterprise

Husky's annual operating budget for its environmental, employee services and wellness activities is approximately US$2.5 million. This covers the wellness programmes (on-site health care, prevention programmes and education); fitness programmes; a child development centre; food service; and environment, health and safety. The canteen budget is approximately US$480,000.

Husky estimated the savings to the company as a result of the health and safety initiatives to be approximately US$6.8 million for 2003. Husky's saving are a result of: a low rate of absenteeism (half the industry average); lower drug costs (a quarter of the industry average); low injury rates (70 per cent below industry average); energy audits and recycling programmes; and the convenience of on-site services (increasing time spent at work). The calculations do not include a productivity benefit. Husky does not isolate the impact of its nutrition programme. It sees synergy in its holistic approach.

Government incentives

None, other than standard tax exemption.

Practical advice for implementation

As with the Dole Food Company, Husky CEO Robert Schad has made health a top priority at his company. Mr. Schad, at 75, is himself a health enthusiast and looks at least a dozen years younger. He is a vegetarian and financial supporter of naturopathic research. At the Bolton campus, he has managed to instil a culture of healthy thinking and environmental responsibility. For example, the extensive landscaping is maintained without pesticides. Approximately 85 per cent of the company's waste is recycled. Bicycles are provided for transport between buildings.

The Husky staff is largely health conscious as a result of health education and the progressive corporate culture. Subsequently, health initiatives succeed because there is a demand. After all, a healthy canteen is useless if employees don't use it. The Husky employees seem to willingly purchase healthy food at work and take advantage of other health benefits. In many companies, the majority of employees appear not to want healthy foods. Food vendors are therefore against providing healthy food because it won't sell. At best, only one healthy dish is offered at the company canteen. Husky seems to have broken out of this rut. Dr. Doull said the Bolton food service is more expensive than traditional canteen fair, but the company chooses to serve it because it is healthier for the employee. There does not appear to have been a "revolt", as seen in other companies presented in this publication, where healthy foods were removed from the menu for lack of sales. Husky employees do have options. Fast-food restaurants surround the facility. The employees choose to at the workplace.

There's an important distinction between Dole and Husky; both with their healthy canteens. The Dole canteen is at corporate headquarters. The Husky canteen is essentially the same at all of its facilities. Husky is a manufacturer, and the workforce is far more diverse than the Dole headquarters workforce. Here we have an example of blue-collar workers enthusiastic about healthy food options. This implies that healthy food need not be only for the "elite", higher-educated corporate worker. All types of workers may come to enjoy and benefit from the types of food recommended by the WHO and national governments. Husky provides the same benefits at all its locations, even those overseas, which is admirable.

Union/employee perspective

Husky is a non-union site. The employees interviewed for this case study were very pleased with the canteen. All were impressed by the variety of healthy options, with a salad bar "second to none", according to one worker. The menu allows them to easily meet the "five-a-day" fruit and vegetable goal and other healthy eating recommendations promoted by the Canadian Government. The canteen has also changed the way these employees shop for food and cook at home. Some regularly ask for recipes from the cooks. One female employee spoke about her child, who is a vegetarian. She can now cook for her child and ensure the child has a nutritionally balanced diet, which some vegetarians (especially young ones) lack. Another employee has changed eating habits at home to help lower her husband's cholesterol level. Morale seems to be high at Husky, and one employee said this is because they view the canteen as a sign that management cares about their health.

4.5   Placer Dome, Inc., Musselwhite Mine

Northwestern Ontario, Canada

Type of enterprise: Musselwhite is an underground gold mine located in northwestern Ontario, a fly-in operation nearly 500 kilometres north of Thunder Bay. Commercial production began in April 1997. Reserves are expected to last until 2012. The mine is a joint venture owned by Placer Dome (68 per cent) and Kinross Gold Corporation (32 per cent). Placer Dome, which operates it, is one of the world's largest gold mining companies, producing over 3 million ounces of gold per year and with reserves of approximately 60 million ounces. The Vancouver-based Placer Dome operates 18 mines on five continents. (http://www.placerdome.com/operations/musselwhite/musselwhite.html)

Employees: 400.

Food solution – key point: canteen with highly trained chefs and selection of healthy foods; indigenous workforce.

The Musselwhite Mine is a sprawling site with a canteen for morning and evening meals.

Musselwhite is a remote site with unique challenges in providing workers with access to food. The weather can be daunting, with blinding snowstorms that can last for days, occasional high humidity, and temperatures ranging from −45°C to +35°C between the seasons. Trucks deliver food once a week, an 8- to 10-hour ride from Thunder Bay depending on the weather. Employees are flown in. They bunk at the mine for two-week rotations and need to be fed three meals a day. The food must be both filling and nutritious to keep the miners happy, healthy and alert during 10- to 12-hour shifts. Many employees have special health concerns. Placer Dome has a good reputation in Canada due to its environmental sustainability policy, adopted in 1998, and commitment to indigenous peoples and their lands. Through a special agreement with the First Nations communities (indigenous groups in northwestern Ontario), Placer Dome maintains food and transportation contracts and directly employs people of indigenous descent. Over 90 per cent of the camp staff (cooks, housekeepers) and, in total, approximately 30 per cent of all employees fall into this category. This population is at an extreme high risk of developing diabetes. Foods are made available to reduce this risk and also to control blood sugar levels.

Food solution

The Musselwhite Mine's canteen supports the 250 workers at the facility. Workers essentially have unlimited access to food during canteen operating hours at no charge, a common practice at remote sites. They are treated as adults in as far as not being instructed about how much they need to eat. One advantage of "free" food is that employees might sample a vegetable or healthy dish risk free out of curiosity – something they always wanted to try but not buy. The workers' caloric requirements vary greatly. Workers in the underground mines have the most physically demanding tasks. Mining is largely mechanized, but occasionally miners will need to perform physically demanding tasks, placing their caloric demands over 5 kcal per minute, or about 3,000 kcal per 10-hour work shift.

Musselwhite maintains two basic work shifts, day and night. Employees make long journeys from across Canada to work at the mine. Thus, they choose either 10- or 12-hour work-days to bundle into their two weeks and then spend two weeks away with their families. Workers eat breakfast and dinner at the canteen, and they pack a lunch. Night workers awake to a "breakfast" of dinner fare but seem to adapt well. In the mines, workers are allowed several breaks, including a 30-minute lunch break. The mine property covers approximately 150 square kilometres, but current mining and associated plant processing equipment buildings occupy about 15 hectares.

Nevertheless, it is not practical to return to the canteen during working hours. Lunch is taken at refuge stations, where there is ample room to clean up and sit down at tables.

Colin Seeley, Manager of Aboriginal Affairs and Corporate Relations, said there is a tendency at the mine to overeat. Placer Dome has several safeguards, however, to help workers control their weight. The executive chef is hotel-trained with four apprentices, each of whom are trained in nutrition. The food served is healthy and diverse, particularly for this region of Canada during the winter months. The selection is low-salt, low-starch and low-fat with little saturated and trans fats. Only olive and canola oils are used. The menu features fresh vegetables, fruits and salads, wholegrain breads, low-fat (1 per cent) milk, and hot dishes that meet the standards of Ontario's Eat Smart! programme (refer to "Spotlight on Canada"). As a seasonal treat, the chef sometimes prepares a fresh, local fish called pickerel. As detailed below, some employees are at risk of diabetes or are diabetic. The canteen offers diabetic desserts. Many employees might very well eat more healthily at the mine than at home.

Workers also have year-round access to exercise. Musselwhite has a recreation centre with a gymnasium and an exercise room. During the summer, workers take advantage of nearby Opapimiskan Lake for catch-and-release fishing, swimming, kayaking and hiking. There is always an occupational nurse

Workers eat in clean, convenient underground refuge stations during working hours.

at the mine for emergencies and general health questions. The nurses (and others at the camp) subscribe to the Wellness Letter, an award-winning advertisement-free newsletter from the University of California, Berkeley; and this too factors into decisions at the mine about health and nutrition.

About 30 per cent of employees are of indigenous decent and live relatively nearby. (The closest town is over 100 kilometres away.) Diabetes is a top health concern. The Ojibway and Cree peoples of Sandy Lake, a few hundred kilometres north of Musselwhite, have some of the highest rates of diabetes in Canada – estimated to affect over 26 per cent of the population, including 2 per cent of children, three times the national average (Ontario Ministry of Health and Long-Term Care, 2004). This disease was virtually unheard of 50 years ago. The epidemic is thought to be fuelled by a change in traditional lifestyles and access to processed and sugary foods. Processed foods tend to be digested quickly and elevate glucose levels, placing strain on the pancreas. Several Musselwhite workers are diabetic or have elevated blood-sugar levels, and they are under the supervision of the company nurses.

Managing diabetes is difficult in the remote, northern regions of Canada. Fresh vegetables and non-processed foods are expensive and difficult to obtain in the winter. Fresh food must be flown in – the region's small markets sell produce at nearly twice the price of food in Toronto. Indigenous workers have little access to healthy foods outside the mine other than the lean game meat that they hunt. There is no guarantee that these workers will eat the most appropriate foods to control diabetes while at work. However, given the extended period "confined" to canteen food, one- or two-week shifts far away from the temptations and limited selections of their local stores, there is a great opportunity for the local population to significantly improve their long-term health.

Possible disadvantages of food solution

When food is unlimited, workers may eat too much or waste food. One solution is to offer smaller portions, assuming the workers can return to the food counter for seconds.

Costs and benefits to enterprise

Placer Dome budgets approximately CAN$1 million (US$840,000) for the canteen food, not including transportation and labour. This comes to CAN$11.30 (US$9.50) per day per worker, slightly above the industry average. Placer Dome estimates that an extra dollar per worker per day is spent to provide the quality and diversity of food required by the Eat Smart! programme.

Musselwhite is a fairly new operation, and no studies have been conducted on improved body mass index (BMI) ratios, cholesterol levels and other health indicators. Placer Dome made the decision early on that the menu would by diverse and appealing – that is, none of that stereotypical gruel served to miners in remote areas in centuries past. The menu was originally designed to meet the workers' caloric and nutritional needs and also to attract and keep workers, and not to address any specific health concerns. Tweaks to the menu have brought more healthy food options. Placer Dome measures the pay-off in high morale, few sick days and good safety record.

Government incentives

None, other than standard tax exemption.

Practical advice for implementation

Camp Manager, Larry Shaw, noted that meat and fatty foods can cost as much as fruits and vegetables, so a healthier menu – if designed properly by a knowledgeable chef – need not cost more money. Similarly, maintaining hotel-trained chefs costs more in salaries; but these chefs are experts in finding and preparing high-quality, lower-cost foods. So while companies can cut costs by sacrificing food quality and variety, they can find savings in other ways. Regardless, Placer Dome maintains the belief that providing cheap food will ultimately lead to poor health, lower morale, accidents and lower productivity. Nutrition is seen as an investment in productivity. Engaging the local population has been a win-win situation, far beyond the scope of this nutrition case study. Briefly, it is worth noting that Placer Dome's agreements with the First Nations Council has positively affected the company's reputation in Canada. Placer Dome also benefits from the local workforce, who are eager to work at the mine, particularly because of the company's good standing with the First Nations. And the indigenous workers benefit from nutritious foods they might not otherwise have access to.

Union/employee perspective

The Musselwhite Mine is a non-union site. However, provincial labour laws require an employee health and safety committee chaired by a non-management employee. All sectors of the mine are represented on this committee, which meets at least once a month to discuss issues concerning health and safety. Keith Horner, a workers' representative committee member interviewed for this case study, praised the nutrition programme at

Musselwhite. Employees have a choice of food, and some choose "french fries and gravy" each night, he said. But healthy options are plentiful, clearly labelled and, most important, tasty. He himself asks the cooks for recipes to prepare at home. Musselwhite has one of the best canteens he has encountered in his 20-plus years of mining. An apprentice chef interviewed for the case study detailed the diligence taken in preparing "heart healthy" meals with little saturated fat and baked rather than fried dishes.

4.6   Akteks Akrilik Iplik A. S. (Akteks Acrylic Yarn Industry and Trade Company)

Gaziantep, Turkey

Type of enterprise: Akteks Akrilik Iplik S. A., founded in 1984, produces acrylic and other types of yarn at a rate of 3,000 tons per month. It is one of the top 200 largest companies in Turkey with a US$70 million turnover and around 2,000 employees. Akteks yarn is sold domestically as well as internationally in Europe, Africa and the Middle East. The following case study concerns the Akteks 2 factory, which produces acrylic yarn in Gaziantep, southeastern Turkey. (http://www.akteks.com)

Employees: 1,025 men, 20 women.

Food solution – key point: vast improvements in food safety, along with menu changes; meals are complimentary.

Most of the workers come from the local region and are in good health. The average age is about 29. The improvements that have taken place at the Akteks 2 factory were to prevent food-borne illnesses and improve nutrition. Akteks 2 has since become a model for other factories.

Food solution

The workers' union recommended that the company take part in a worker-management education project organized by the ILO to address a variety of issues. One of the issues was the canteen. The factory kitchen was an unhygienic wooden shanty open to the environment and insects. Workers were not chronically sick from the food served at the factory, but they didn't like the eating conditions and food. Improving the eating conditions became one of the action plans agreed as a result of participation in the ILO project. The ILO provided health and safety training. Akteks management used its newly learned skills to design and implement a food safety programme, and had strong support from the workers and their union.

With an investment of US$72,000, Akteks revamped the canteen at the Akteks 2 factory in Gaziantep. The floors and walls of the kitchen and dining areas were converted to glazed tiles. The kitchen was designed to be washed down easily each day. The tables and the chairs, once plastic, are now Verzalit, which is more hygienic than plastic or wood. Kitchen equipment and related tools were updated. There is now a cool store and separate storage places for dry and wet food, unlike before. This has enabled the storage of a greater variety of foods.

The meals are often regional. The cook generally uses lamb meat, sunflower oil, tomato, rice, all sorts of vegetable, yoghurt and various spices. Before the canteen improvement, meals were basic and less nutritious. Meals were once as simple as chickpeas and boiled wheat porridge. The new menu, which changes from day to day, is free to employees and costs the company about US$0.90 per meal. To accommodate the four working shifts, meals are served around the clock – breakfast, lunch, dinner and evening. The meal break is 30–60 minutes. The dining area is close to the factory, and there appears to be enough time to eat and rest. The dining area is well ventilated, protected from the elements and seats about 250. This is adequate space, reflecting the average number of workers per shift. There is a washroom stocked with soap nearby. Most workers use the canteen. There are no vending machines. There are nearby restaurants, but the price can be high for daily use. Workers eat the canteen food for the taste, not because it is free. Before the improvements, workers typically did not finish their meals and food was wasted. Workers eat reasonably well outside work, but at work the food is as healthy, if not more healthy, than food at home.

Possible disadvantages of food solution

There can be few disadvantages expected when employers listen to employees and earnestly strive to make improvements.

Costs and benefits to enterprise

The canteen renovation in 2004 cost US$72,000.

Anecdotally, the factory managers can report higher productivity and more. They emphasized that the employees are very happy with the changes. The improvements are recent and, as yet, no detailed assessment has been made.

Government incentives

None.

Practical advice for implementation

The food is tasty, nutritious and free of charge – three ideal conditions not always met at other companies. Employers must bear in mind that street food can be tasty but unhealthy and insanitary; and meals can be free but unappetizing and not nutritious. In fact, meals at Akteks before the changes were sometimes wasted because they weren't tasty. A free meal not eaten is a poor investment. Changes were initiated upon completion of ILO worker-management training.

Union/employee perspective

The union, Turkiye Tekstil Iscileri Sendikasi, recognized a need for change and a means to accommodate that change. Both the workers and their unions are pleased with the improvements and remain active in maintaining the new higher standards of hygiene and nutrition.

Information for this case study was provided by H. Müge Çamligüney.

4.7   Tae Kwang Vina

Dong Nai, Viet Nam

Type of enterprise: Tae Kwang Vina is a Korean-owned garment company established in 1995 that provides sports shoes and high-tech running shoes to Nike. The company produces about 900,000 pairs of shoes per month.

Employees: 14,500 workers (85 per cent female).

Food solution – key point: vast improvements in canteen and other working conditions after adopting Nike's code of conduct.

Tae Kwang Vina is located in an industrial area in the Dong Nai province, close to Ho Chi Minh City. The company was one of five enterprises established by Korean and Taiwanese subcontractors to support Nike's venture in Viet Nam during the mid-1990s. Tae Kwang Vina quickly developed a bad reputation among local workers and labour watch groups over its many labour violations. Major complaints included industrial solvents that made workers sick, and other environmental violations, illegal overtime and hiring practices, low salaries, and verbal and physical abuse. Most workers were migrants from the north and central parts of the country because few local people wanted to work at the factory. Non-governmental organizations (NGOs), such as Vietnam Labour Watch and Global Exchange, as well as American-based activists raised awareness of the abuses taking place at Tae Kwang Vina with the hope of holding Nike responsible. By 1999 Nike began to take proactive measures, starting with an audit of its Viet Nam subcontractors and then the implementation of its code of conduct, modelled after several ILO Conventions. The improvements that followed have been lauded by various labour groups, who continue to monitor the Vietnamese factories. Today about 70 per cent of Tae Kwang Vina's workers are from the region.

Food solution

Nike has eliminated the use of toxic solvent-based cleaners and glues in most of its subcontractors' factories. This and other improvements are reported in the 2003 World Bank document, *Nike in Vietnam: The Tae Kwang Vina Factory* (World Bank, 2003), part of the World Bank's "Empowerment Case Studies" series.

The remainder of this ILO case study concerns the meal programme. Workers at Tae Kwang Vina now receive a free lunch or dinner of rice, soup, meat and vegetables. The rice is unlimited. The meal is cooked on-site by a dedicated kitchen staff. The company serves a different meal each day of the week in order to offer variety in tastes and nutrients. The menu is usually determined a week in advance. Lunch or dinner is offered depending on the workers' shifts. The company also serves breakfast at a 50 per cent discount to encourage workers to eat at the factory and not from street vendors, a common source of food-borne illnesses in this region.

Tae Kwang Vina has two canteens, each with room for around 1,100 workers and located within 50 metres of the work areas. Workers can wash with soap and water before eating. Space in the canteens can be tight. The company provides a 30-minute lunch break and rotates workers through the canteen by staggering the meal break. The canteens are ventilated with ceiling and wall fans. An outdoor area with additional seating is shaded with umbrellas, and an accompanying library provides more space to relax after the meal. Each canteen also has four televisions. Essentially all the workers take advantage of the free meal. Their other food options are street vendors and a local shop with snacks. There are no vending machines.

Tae Kwang Vina takes several steps to ensure food safety and quality. Foods are fresh and delivered daily, and no meals are prepared more than 24 hours in advance. Dishes and trays are washed by machine. Nike helped Tae Kwang Vina establish a nutrition programme and continues to provide technical support. The emphasis of the programme is to ensure workers have sufficient calories and micro- and macronutrients to perform their tasks and remain healthy. Annual surveys reveal that workers are satisfied with the meal selection. Internal studies reveal that workers are not deficient in iron or other micronutrients, and new workers often gain weight. For these workers, meals at work are generally as nutritious and often more nutritious than meals outside work.

Employees in each workshop have unlimited access to clean drinking water tested quarterly by a local health centre. The results of the testing are posted at the water dispensers.

Possible disadvantages of food solution

Tae Kwang Vina seems committed to good nutrition and hygiene. The company offers a meal programme that is well above average. It is not clear whether 30 minutes is enough time for adequate rest in this warm climate. While the canteen is close to the work area, extra time is needed to grab a meal and sit down, particularly in light of the sheer number of employees and the limited seating.

Costs and benefits to enterprise

Each lunch or dinner costs around VND 5,000 (US$0.32), which includes food, water, electricity and labour. All changes associated with the meal programme amounted to a 5 per cent increase in operational costs.

Productivity has improved noticeably. Workers are now trained to perform multiple tasks, instead of just one, and this has led to fewer defects. The number of B-grade shoes has decreased from 120,000 pairs in 2001 to 90,000 pairs in 2004. The company said that the combination of better nutrition and improved management were responsible for increased productivity. Morale is considerably higher at the factory. The rate of sick days and employee turnover is at its lowest.

Government incentives

None. Improvements are considered a company investment.

Practical advice for implementation

Nike initiated the changes at Tae Kwang Vina. Without activism on the part of NGOs and other concerned parties, it is not clear when or if improvements in working conditions would have been made. Nonetheless, Tae Kwang Vina did not go about implementing changes half-heartedly. The company could have skimped on various aspects of the meal programme. Meals could have been partially subsidized, for example, or the meals could have been less diverse. Instead of skimping, Tae Kwang Vina decided to offer well-balanced meals with consideration given to proper hygiene as well as workers' opinions. The company also maximizes the number of workers the canteens can handle by rotating meal breaks and providing extra space for rest outdoors and in a library.

Union/employee perspective

The union was ineffective at remedying the workers' problems when the factory first opened. Tae Kwang Vina controlled the union through representatives chosen by the management. Workers were largely migrant and stayed less than two years, which made organizing difficult. The union has been more representative of the workers' concerns since the adoption of Nike's code of conduct. Aside from overseeing meal programme changes, the union took the lead on food hygiene, such as the half-priced breakfasts and the general cleanliness of the canteens. No union representative could be reached for comment. A representative from Global Alliance (an NGO) based in Viet Nam, however, was pleased with the factory improvements and recommended that Tae Kwang Vina be included in this publication.

4.8　Spotlight on Singapore: The Workplace Health Promotion Programme

For a country comprising only 692 square kilometres, the island city-state of Singapore looms large as a leader in the area of workplace health initiatives. Singapore is one of the few governments to have established a programme to address nutritional health issues specifically at the worksite, as well as community-based programmes.

Through its Health Promotion Board, a statutory board of the Ministry of Health, Singapore established the Workplace Health Promotion Programme in 1984. The programme's current objective is to cover 70 per cent of the private sector workforce with an effective workplace health promotion programme by the year 2005, and it is close to that goal. Almost all public sector organizations have an ongoing relationship with the programme. The programme's activities, explained in greater detail below, include administering a health promotion grant and providing free consultancy services.

Singapore can boast of one of the highest life expectancies in the world, but it is not unique among industrialized nations in terms of its health concerns over diet-related chronic diseases. The two leading causes of death, by far, are cancer and cardiovascular disease (Singapore Ministry of Health, 1999). The average obesity rate, 6 per cent, belies the Indian and Malay ethnic groups' rates of over 12 per cent and 16 per cent respectively (Singapore Ministry of Health, 1999, p. 25). Also, the definition of obesity among Asians has recently been called into question, for the relationship between body fat percentage and BMI is different between Asians and Caucasians (Deurenberg-Yap et al., 2000). Singapore subscribes to WHO Expert Consultation recommendations that public health action levels along a continuum of BMI measurements be introduced to enable countries to better manage health risks linked to obesity. For certain Asian countries, such as Singapore, action levels corresponding to increased and high risks for cardiovascular diseases are 23 kg/m^2 and 27.5 kg/m^2 respectively, which are lower than those for Caucasian populations (WHO Expert Consultation, 2004). Thus, Singapore is particularly diligent about lowering BMI.

Over 1.1 million males and nearly 1 million females in Singapore (half of the total population) work in the formal sector, in businesses as diverse as manufacturing, commerce, transport, communications, and financial and business services (Singapore Ministry of Manpower, 2003). Although Singapore experienced an economic downtown at the end of the 1990s, with the collapse of Asian stock markets, and, more recently, the 2003 Severe Acute Respiratory Syndrome (SARS) epidemic, its economy remains relatively stable

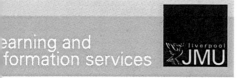

No....... 73 111 6 ....

Self collection of holds

(last 6 digits of barcode no. located on bottom of your University card)

Please issue the item at the self service machine before you leave this area.

www.ljmu.ac.uk/lea

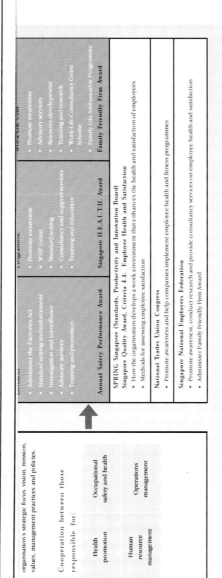

A flowchart of the Workplace Health Promotion Programme.

and lay-offs are uncommon. Singapore's GDP for 2003 was S$159 billion (US$97 billion) with per capita GDP of S$38,000 (US$23,300) (Singapore Ministry of Trade and Industry, 2004). In stable financial environments, enterprises can have a positive influence on workers' health by creating healthy work settings, ensuring that organizational policies are conducive to good health, and by providing health promotion programmes and services at work. This is the philosophy of the Workplace Health Promotion Programme.

In September 2000, the Tripartite Committee on Workplace Health Promotion (TriCom) – representing employers' federations, the employees' unions and the Government – articulated a strategy framework to guide the further development of workplace health promotion in Singapore. Those strategies included: establishing standards and indicators linked to business outcomes; recognizing achievement with a Singapore Helping Employees Achieve Lifetime Health (HEALTH) award; promoting workplace health by industry; collaborating with the occupational health and safety movement; creating a comprehensive support infrastructure; integrating with the productivity movement; and equipping company personnel with the skills to manage workplace health programmes.

The Workplace Health Promotion Programme is currently implementing the range of recommendations identified in the TriCom report and is guided by the Intersectoral Management Committee on Workplace Health Promotion, which comprises representatives from unions, employers and Government. The recommendations fall neatly within the programme's main activities: organizing workplace health promotion campaigns; administering the Workplace Health Promotion Grant; conducting industry-based promotional campaigns; providing free consultancy services; providing a range of training courses and educational seminars; and developing a workplace health promotion toolkit of handy references and resources, including "Best Practices in Workplace Health" and the "Directory of Health Promotion Services".

The Workplace Health Promotion Grant helps organizations develop and sustain a health promotion programme. The modest grant (a maximum of S$5,000) can be used for facilities and equipment, screening programmes and other health interventions. The organization must co-fund the project by contributing an equal or higher amount. The Singapore HEALTH award gives national recognition to organizations with commendable workplace health promotion programmes. More than a plaque, the award is desirable because it reflects proficiency in employee health and satisfaction, one criterion of the Singapore Quality Award, a highly valued national award.

This publication contains case studies of two HEALTH award winners, Boncafé and GlaxoSmithKline. Several of Singapore's unions share the Government's vision on health promotion and disease prevention. "As a labour movement, the Singapore National Trades Union Congress (SNTUC) has been encouraging workers to adopt a healthy lifestyle and helping workers improve their health," said Mr. Yeo Guat Kwang, a Member of Parliament and the Director of the SNTUC. "We see it as part of our efforts to improve the lives of workers."

In 2003, the SNTUC initiated a Workplace Canteen Programme with support from the Health Promotion Board. The two organizations work with management to promote healthy eating habits and make healthier food choices available in workplace canteens. Under this scheme, canteen committee members and stall holders/chefs were trained to prepare healthier food choices for workers. In total, 60 companies have participated in the pilot programme.

4.9   Glaxo Wellcome Manufacturing Pte Ltd

Singapore

Type of enterprise: GlaxoSmithKline (GSK), headquartered in the United Kingdom, is the world's second largest research-based pharmaceutical and health-care company, with a £6.7 billion (US$11.9 billion) pretax profit in 2003. Glaxo Wellcome Manufacturing Pte Ltd (GWM), located in Singapore, produces GSK products. This facility is a segment of GSK operations in Singapore and does not represent GSK in Singapore nor GSK as a whole. (http://www.gsk.com)

Employees: 500.

Food solution – key point: canteen revamping, initiated and supervised by employees.

Glaxo Wellcome Manufacturing is a winner of the Singapore HEALTH award for its commitment to employee health and wellness. The company offers free comprehensive health screenings and a redesigned canteen featuring a variety of healthier food options compared with what was served in the past. Employees are also able to participate in workplace health activities during working hours, including physical activities.

Food solution

The revamped canteen is called D'Café. The "D" stands for "delight". The company always had a canteen; the facility is located in an industrial area with no nearby restaurants, so a canteen was a necessity. D'Café is a marked improvement over the older canteen. A volunteer committee of GWM employees initiated and supervised all changes to the canteen, starting in 2000, based on inputs from fellow employees. By 2002, D'Café was ready. Structural improvements include new floor tiles, larger windows to allow for more natural lighting, a new stereo system, and additional seating. The structural changes provide a bright, clean, relaxing atmosphere. The canteen seats about 250. This is larger than before, and the new layout allows workers to purchase their lunch more quickly, leaving more time to eat. Employees have 40 minutes for lunch. The canteen is only a five-minute walk away for most employees. Thus, the concern for timeliness is addressed with an on-site canteen with fast service.

Employees seem to largely understand what constitutes good nutrition. Through worksite health screening and health education, they understand the

Employees designed the GSK canteen with bright light and space.

kinds of food they should eat for better health, but they had expressed concern that they had little opportunity to eat healthily. The D'Café committee strove to improve the canteen's look and provide a wider range of healthy foods to encourage workers to use the facilities. Many employees eat two meals daily at D'Café, breakfast and lunch. Food choices at D'Café can contribute significantly to good nutritional health.

Menu changes include a salad bar, fruits, more grilled and steamed dishes, and fewer fried and oily dishes – all of which were employee requests. Singapore cuisine is heavily Chinese in style, representing the majority ethnic group on the island. Although Chinese dishes often include large servings of vegetables, they can also be oily and salty. Glaxo Wellcome Manufacturing hired a dietician to teach the D'Café cooking staff how to cook with less oil and salt, as well as other healthy tips, such as removing chicken skin from chicken dishes to reduce cholesterol. Each day the D'Café offers at least one "heart healthy" dish that is low in saturated fat and cholesterol, labelled as such. The D'Café also prepares take-away dinners, a feature that is popular with working mothers. The same opportunity to eat healthy meals (prepared under the guidance of a dietician) is extended to workers' family members. Over 90 per cent of the employees at GWM use the canteen; others bring a packed lunch. Canteen food during lunchtime and overtime is discounted by around US$1. The salad bar is 80 cents, so with the lunchtime discount it is technically free.

Workers have access to water at newly installed water coolers around the GWM complex. The company's intent is to have the staff drink more water and fewer sugary drinks, and signs are posted around the building reminding employees that water has no calories, whereas coffee has 130 and soda pop has more. Four times a year, GWM sponsors "Fruit and Vegetable Day" when employees get free fruit or vegetables and learn about their importance for lowering the risk of heart attacks and cancer. During bread fairs, a dietician teaches GWM employees how to make healthy sandwiches using wholegrain breads. (Bread is not a traditional Asian food.) At health fairs, vendors are allowed on site to sell health products and vitamin supplements. The nutrition initiative at GWM is complemented by an emphasis on physical activity and stress reduction.

Possible disadvantages of food solution

There are no apparent disadvantages.

Costs and benefits to enterprise

The water coolers cost around S$10,000 (US$6,100), annually, to maintain. Revamping the canteen cost approximately S$300,000 (US$184,000).

In the past few years, GWM has recorded significant changes in employee health and productivity. Since 2000, medical expenses have dropped by 13 per cent. Since 2001, the percentage of employees with high levels of triglycerides (fats in the blood) has dropped from 31 per cent to 24 per cent; with high blood pressure, from 16 per cent to 13 per cent; with BMI greater than 30, from 7 per cent to 6 per cent; and with high cholesterol, from 61 per cent to 51 per cent. Since 2002, the average annual absenteeism rate has dropped from 3.7 to 1.9 days. Water consumption has increased by 50 per cent, and consumption of sugary drinks has dropped by 15 per cent.

Government incentives

The Singapore Health Promotion Board offers up to S$5,000 in grants to encourage health programmes at work. Glaxo Wellcome Manufacturing used a grant to conduct health screening but not canteen changes.

Practical advice for implementation

Workplace health seems to be enforced not through policies but rather encouraged through personal involvement from the general manager and the staff, who were wholly responsible for the changes at the canteen. Ms. Adeline

Chew, the Employee Wellness Officer, describes a slow process of changing many of the employees' eating habits. "It was not easy," she said. "When we were trying to encourage healthier dishes, we did get some push-back. Now things are changed. Sometimes I even hear feedback from my colleagues at the D'Café asking, 'Why is everything fried today?' or 'Why are the desserts so sweet today?' This shows that awareness levels of some staff have increased." Health screening and education played a role here. Many employees were told that they needed to reduce their cholesterol or blood pressure level. The choices at D'Café made this a little easier.

Union/employee perspective

The D'Café was initiated by the employees. The Singapore unions have been very supportive of workplace health initiatives and hold a yearly national campaign on the topic. (See "Spotlight on Singapore".) Glaxo Wellcome Manufacturing union representative, Tan Chee Tiong, said that the workers are particularly pleased with their canteen's environment and the salad bar but continue to advocate for more nutritious foods on the menu. The unions are not part of the D'Café committee.

4.10 Spotlight on Austria: Light, healthy and fair eating in the workplace

Set in the heart of Europe, Austria maintains a well-diversified and developed economy and a high standard of living. Its labour force comprises just over half of its 8.1 million total population, with around 4–5 per cent unemployment for the past several years. Its GDP was approximately 15 billion (US$18.9 billion) in 2003 (Statistik Austria, 2004), divided by sector as 65 per cent services, 33 per cent industry and 2 per cent agriculture. Buoyed by a strong economy and social awareness among the Austrian people, six Austrian trade unions have established a catering concept called "*Gesund – Leicht und Fair Essen im Betrieb*" or "Light, Healthy and Fair Eating in the Workplace". The six unions are Gewerkschaft Agrar Nahung Genuss (ANG), Gewerkschaft der Privatangestellten (GPA), Hotel, Gastgewerbe Persönlicher Dienst (HGPD), Gewerkschaft Metall Textil (GMT), Gewerkschaft der Chemiearbeiter (GdC) and Gewerkschaft Druck Journalismus Papier (DJP).

The "light and healthy" part of the slogan signifies a deliberate effort to address the trend of unhealthy eating and rising obesity and chronic disease rates in Austria. In the early 1990s the proportion of total energy derived from fats was 42 per cent, one of the highest figures in Europe, a considerable increase from the 1970s (WHO ROE 1998, p. 25). Consequently, 8.5 per cent of the population was obese and 14.5 per cent were overweight (Kiefer et al., 1998). The prevalence of overweight increases with age; over age 45, nearly one in three people were overweight or obese in the early 1990s (WHO ROE 1998, p. 24). Today, nearly 12 per cent of the population is obese (Ulmer et al. 2001). Overweight is two to three times more frequent among less wealthy and less educated Austrians; and it is also more prevalent in the east, with about twice as many obese men and women in Burgenland, Kärnten and Lower Austria than in Tiroland Vorarlberg (WHO ROE, 1998, p. 24). Cardiovascular disease, diabetes and cancer risk factors have mirrored the rise in BMI, with rates among the highest in Western Europe (WHO ROE, 1998, p. 9).

The "fair" part of the union slogan refers to whether the food served in canteens was produced and acquired in an environmentally and socially friendly manner. According to this concept, deciding what kind of food is put on the menu (or dinner table at home) also means deciding whether to accept or refuse food produced by monoculture or unfair competition, which can cause social and environmental harm and entail speculative gains at the expense of the poor countries of the South, and toxic residues on the food. The trade unions naturally felt that workers – particularly workers within their unions – should have access to foods produced and acquired in a fair manner, for this ultimately corresponded to fair treatment of fellow workers in the food and agriculture sectors. The "fair weekly menu" concept was first offered at a symposium held in June 1999. A team at a Vienna hospital developed the menu for the 450 symposium participants. Foods on the menu were, as far as possible, organically produced, predominantly of local or regional origin, matching the season, purchased from farmers practising species-appropriate animal husbandry or from fair-trade outlets, and contained sound raw materials.

The impact of such a programme can be broad, for about 1.5 million workers in Austria use workplace canteens every day, consuming hundreds of thousands of tons of food in the process. Eating out during the day is increasingly more common, too, as long commuting times prevent workers from going home for lunch. Life's hectic pace can limit the time workers have in the morning to pack a lunch, particularly those from single-parent and two-worker households, also increasing the demand for workplace food options. The food industry comprises about 530,000 workers, and they too are affected by the "fair" movement.

A brochure entitled "Fair Eating for a Better World" was specially produced for the June 1999 symposium to provide information on the topic for shop stewards, kitchen managers and environmental managers. Since then, union-led visits to company canteens and food production establishments have been a regular feature of this programme (reversing the slogan "from farm to fork"). The idea is to promote fair and healthy meals in the workplace by enabling an exchange of first-hand experience and information among colleagues.

A second symposium was held in November 2002. This focused on how to successfully improve dietary habits and menus in company and factory canteens. A brochure devoted to these topics presented ideas and reports from the field and offered advice on how to implement them. Because healthy and high-quality food in the workplace depends not least on what is purchased to produce it, the trade unions decided to participate in an additional project intended to collect, discuss and publish proven purchasing criteria and supplier requirements. This project is called "Developing a List of Quality Assurance Criteria for Company and Factory Canteen Procurement as a Means to Promote Healthy and High-Quality Food Offerings in the Workplace". The idea behind this step was that the quality of the menus offered in company and factory canteens can be influenced on various levels: for instance, when purchasing ingredients or ready-made meals or when outsourcing the whole catering process. In this context, quality criteria that meet customer requirements for fresh, high-quality, tasty and healthy food, even if it costs a bit more, are becoming increasingly important.

Decision-makers in company and public sector catering facilities are called upon to discuss these criteria with their suppliers and to specify them in formal and informal invitations to tender. One important goal of the project is to promote the exchange of ideas and experiences between all relevant parties and to reach a common understanding on such issues as food quality, healthy eating and appropriate quality criteria. A final event, where the project results were presented, was scheduled for December 2004. Participation in this project is intended to provide further support for activities aimed at promoting healthy and fair eating in the workplace.

In summary, the initiative hopes to be a boost to local agriculture, to global development and social responsibility, and to human rights and workers' rights. For more information, contact Gerhard Riess of ANG (ang@ang.at) or visit http://www.ang.at.

4.11 Voestalpine Stahl GmbH

Linz, Austria

Type of enterprise: Voestalpine Stahl GmbH is the largest company within the Voestalpine Group. The Stahl division produces hot- and cold-rolled and surface-coated flat steel products in its production site in Linz. Total sales for financial year 2002–2003 were 1.54 billion (US$2 billion). Catering at the Linz facility is handled by Caseli, an umbrella brand name for the gastronomic services of Voestalpine Stahl GmbH and the Cateringer und Betriebsservice, GmbH.

Employees: over 6,000.

Food solution – key point: subsidized canteen with a healthy new menu that reflects the union-based programme *"Gesund – Leicht und Fair Essen im Betrieb"* or "Light, Healthy and Fair Eating in the Workplace".

Voestalpine provides its workers with a large and pleasant canteen system managed by its local catering company Caseli. The canteen has two unique albeit slightly overlapping features. First, the canteen follows the principles of the Fair Essen movement. In short, this movement advocates health and social and environmental responsibility. (Fair Essen is explained in greater detail in the preceding "Spotlight on Austria" section.) Second, Caseli offers Voestalpine workers its own healthy catering programme, called *"Fit und Vital"*. Although Voestalpine is its largest client, Caseli caters in another 60 companies and schools. Caseli also operates small shops throughout Linz and handles events catering, and is positioned to provide a variety of services to Voestalpine.

Food solution

Fifteen cooks and 75 kitchen helpers prepare and serve over 5,000 meals a day. Food is prepared in a central kitchen and served in 13 dining areas. These dining areas serve only a midday meal. (Workers can take advantage of 15 vending machines with meals anytime and 18 Caseli shops.) Voestalpine subsidizes the canteen meals, which are under 5 (US$6.50). There are a variety of healthy options, such as a low-fat meal alternative labelled "GERNE". This is the German word for "gladly", and the letters stand for *"gemeinsam ernährung neu erleben"* or "experiencing new nutrition together". A massive salad bar makes available 12 different kinds of salads, in addition to a vegetable buffet. Caseli serves at least three hot meals each day, usually one that is vegetarian and one without pork. Workers on special diets for health or religious reasons can usually find something to eat each day. As part of the Fair Essen requirement, when possible, food comes from local sources, is organic or seasonal, and reflects a respect for the rights of the workers who grew or distributed the food.

Voestalpine workers are allowed only 30 minutes for lunch. The facility is about 5 square kilometres and getting to a central canteen after taking the time to wash would be overly time-consuming. Voestalpine resolved this problem by distributing dining areas across the facility. Some workers bring a packed lunch. They can eat this in the dining areas, at their desk, at outdoor areas around the facility when the weather is fine or in lounge areas indoors. Other workers buy a snack or sandwich from one of the 18 Caseli shops or 15 vending machines. The shops and vending machines offer the type of "*Fit und Vital*" food found in the dining areas. These too are conveniently located and save workers time, leaving more time to eat and rest. Shiftworkers and night workers frequent the vending machines, which like old-fashioned "automats" serve whole meals and not just snacks. Some workers purchase food from the vending machines to take home at the end of the working day.

Possible disadvantages of food solution

None. Food is healthy, convenient and inexpensive, a perfect trio.

Costs and benefits to enterprise

The cost of the special health menu comes at a slight additional cost over ordinary catering, mostly for the organic food, which Voestalpine subsidizes.

Voestalpine has not conducted studies on weight loss, health improvement and morale, etc. The company employs a dietician and offers seminars on exercise as well as nutrition. Anecdotally, Caseli reports that the number of sick days has decreased in recent years.

Government incentives

None.

Practical advice for implementation

All the key factors come together at Voestalpine: healthy, convenient, inexpensive – and a new concept for workplace meals, socially conscious.

Clearly not all companies can offer such a complete programme. A strong union is needed, and the company must be a strong economic performer. Individual aspects of the meal programme are easily transferable to other enterprises, though. Serving wholesome food in vending machines is a convenience to workers. Vended meals are less expensive to serve than canteen meals because staff members need not be present. Meals can remain hot for hours for the employee to purchase anytime. This is particularly a great benefit for shiftworkers and night workers who work after hours when the canteen is closed. Enterprises which cannot afford a full canteen can indeed opt for a vending machine only as the main mechanism for workers' meal provision. Meals can be produced locally or contracted to a local caterer.

Low-cost shops can also stand on their own as food solutions, as they require few resources. A converted broom closet is large enough to house a shop worker and prepared lunch foods and drinks. The Caseli shops are far more extensive, but even the simplest of shops stocked with healthy foods can save a worker time in preparing a lunch or buying from outside the company. The social aspect of the Voestalpine meal is important. The concept seems logical for unions looking out for the welfare of fellow workers around the world. The emphasis on organic food may seem excessive to many people. The provision of local foods is healthy, because this food is inherently fresher and picked riper. There are no convincing scientific data to support the notion that organic foods are healthier than conventional foods, nor is there evidence that organic production can feed large populations. Nevertheless, if employees value organic foods, then this is a fine addition to the meal programme, assuming the company can cover the extra costs.

Union/employee perspective

Six unions were instrumental in creating the Fair Essen concept: Gewerkschaft Agrar Nahung Genuss (ANG), Gewerkschaft der Privatangestellten (GPA), Hotel, Gastgewerbe Persönlicher Dienst (HGPD), Gewerkschaft Metall Textil (GMT), Gewerkschaft der Chemiearbeiter (GdC) and Gewerkschaft Druck Journalismus Papier (DJP). The food programme at Voestalpine is a gem of the Fair Essen initiative, and employees are very happy with it. Refer to the preceding section ("Spotlight on Austria') for more details.

4.12 PSA Peugeot Citroën

Rennes, France

Type of enterprise: PSA Peugeot Citroën is the second-largest car manufacturer in Europe. Sales in 2003 exceeded 50 billion (US$66 billion) and the net income was 1.5 billion (US$2 billion). As of January 2004, PSA Peugeot Citroën employed over 200,000 workers worldwide. The PSA group maintains several plants around the world, including one in Rennes, France, the subject of this case study. The Rennes plant was opened in 1961 and has since produced over 10 million vehicles. The workforce is largely blue-collar.

Employees: 8,000.

Food solution – key point: changes made in canteens and shops with renewed emphasis on healthy foods tailored to individual employees; strong educational-outreach component; partly subsidized by Government to follow a national health programme.

Starting in 2002, PSA Peugeot Citroën (PSA-PC) began to layer a nutrition-based health programme on top of its existing Cap Santé health programme, which emphasizes education and disease prevention. The new nutrition programme, called Santal, represents a partnership with Sodexho (the contracted caterer) and Préviade-Mutouest (the mutual fund provider). Santal is the only privately run nutrition programme in France that receives a subsidy through the National Nutrition-for-Health Programme, known by the French initials PNNS (Programme National Nutrition Santé). As such, Santal follows PNNS recommendations and is closely monitored by both PNNS administrators and PSA-PC.

Food solution

The Rennes facility has two canteens serving over 2,400 meals a day, plus smaller outlets (vending machines, trolleys and stands called Relais Gourmand) serving 3,500 items, excluding drinks. One canteen has capacity for 1,600 workers; the other seats 800 workers. Canteens and food outlets are situated so that no worker has a long walk for food or refreshments. The meal break is 45 minutes for those workers who have lunch or dinner in the middle of their working day. (Shiftworkers, who eat before or after work, have a 21-minute break over 6 or 7 hours.) Before Santal, the daily menu provided healthy and balanced options. Sodexho improved the menu by adding healthy options aligned with PNNS recommendations and the broader educational outreach effort. This was aimed at enabling workers to better recognize the healthy options they had read about or had been recommended. Two key features of the programme are educational outreach and individual contact with a dietician.

The goal of Santal is to convince employees that they can improve their health through better nutrition. Although this is a straightforward concept, change can be difficult because eating habits in France are deeply embedded in the culture. The French diet can be high in fat, particularly animal fats such as butter and cream. Changing lifestyles in France – namely, less need for physical activity – coupled with the traditional French diet of high-fat and high-cholesterol foods, as well as an influx of processed foods, have led to an alarming rise in obesity and associated chronic diseases. A 2003 national study found that over 41 per cent of French men and women were overweight or obese, a figure that has been rising steadily year by year for the last decade, according to PSA-PC press materials (Peugeot, 2004). The company's study at Rennes found that 36.6 per cent of women and 49.8 per cent of men in the body shops and on the assembly were overweight or obese (Peugeot, 2004).

The rise in overweight employees is what first prompted PSA-PC, in 2002, to make changes in its health education programme. Employees received brochures about nutrition while the Santal programme was being developed. In November 2002 the company hired a dietician to work two to three days a week. A goal is for all 8,000 employees to meet with the dietician; to date 700 have done so. This is voluntary. Some employees met with the dietician because of a change in their life, such as pregnancy or the desire to participate in a new sport. Others were strongly recommended by the company medical officer to see the dietician.

The PNNS/Santal educational outreach component is organized into two- to three-month campaigns focused on a particular food group: dairy, vegetable, fish, or fruit so far. Employees encounter the campaign in many ways. Posters are hung in workshops, canteens and around other eating areas. Each employee receives a "hungry to know" pocket-size pamphlet about the campaign. These explain how the particular campaign food – for example, vegetables – contributes to good health. There are recipes to take home. During the first week of the campaign, a special stand is set up just to serve a first course, main dish and dessert associated with the campaign. Following weeks bring dozens of variations on the campaign theme with the goal of demonstrating how tasty and non-repetitive healthy eating can be. The average cost of a meal is 3.20 (US$4.20). In general, campaign meals in the canteen are priced the same as alternative meal options.

Trolleys, Relais Gourmand stands and vending machines also offer campaign foods, when available. Santal sandwiches are always available, and they are low in fat, served on enriched bread, and priced the same as traditional sandwiches. Vending machines have stickers and nearby posters encouraging workers to drink more water. The canteens are open for lunch and dinner. The smaller outlets remain open for workers on the night shift. As this is a large factory in an industrial area, employees have few meal options outside work. There are only a few shops nearby, and they sell snacks. One would need to drive into town for a restaurant, and meals there are more expensive.

After meeting with the medical officer and dietician, employees learn what is the most appropriate diet for them based on their weight, cholesterol levels, family history and other key health indicators. These workers then use software called NutriGuide, provided by Sodexho, that recommends a custom-made diet for each day, right down to the salt, fat and calorie content. This software is available to all employees to plan out a weekly meal regimen. The software is built into an entertaining, easy-to-use, interactive web site. Employees can play with different nutrition scenarios. Like many clever web sites, though, this service could be largely unused. As yet, no data are available on employee usage.

Possible disadvantages of food solution

There are few disadvantages. In addition to offering nutrition education, the company can subsidize the healthiest options so that it makes economic sense for workers to participate in the nutrition campaigns. The 21-minute break for nightshift workers is long enough to grab a snack, but it might not provide adequate rest during 6 or 7 hours of work.

Costs and benefits to enterprise

For the three years 2002/2003/2004, Santal cost 345,000 (US$455,000), which includes extra materials, training and staff time. About 37 per cent, or 127,000 (US$167,000), was recouped: 37,000 (US$9,200) from PNNS and 90,000 (US$119,000) from Préviade-Mutouest.

Santal is a long-term programme. Health or productivity gains are hard to assess in the short time since the programme has been active. Nevertheless, PSA-PC has documented positive changes. In general, employees with serious diet concerns have met with a dietician. Also, all employees and, in all likelihood, most of their families have been exposed to PNNS campaigns. The study carried out by the medical service in July 2003 on 139 employees who undertook a nutrition assessment found that 75 per cent of the employees in the study had

A PSA Peugeot Citroën nutrition poster.

"changed their eating habits", 51 per cent remembered the recommendations made during the assessment, and 54 per cent felt that the recommendations were easy to apply. Also, 24 per cent of employees who followed the recommendations lost weight. These results encouraged management to enable employees to have regular meetings with the dietician in 2004. Among employees regularly coached by a dietician, 72 of 88 (82 per cent) lost weight.

A Sodexho survey found that 83 per cent of patrons in one canteen and 79 per cent in the other are satisfied with the food; these figures are 11 and 13 percentage points higher, respectively, compared with surveys a few years ago. Changes implemented by management are, at a minimum, recognized and positively received by employees; and ultimately these changes might lead to concrete health and productivity gains. During the respective campaigns, there was a 9 per cent increase in vegetable consumption and an 11 per cent increase in fish consumption. About 12 per cent of sandwiches sold were Santal sandwiches. Management said that one long-term goal of the Santal programme is to lower the morbidity index (the number of illnesses that require more than 21 days off the job) to a level below the national level in five to ten years.

Government incentives

PNNS grant for 37,000 (US$48,000).

Practical advice for implementation

The nutrition-based Santal was built upon a successful health education programme called Cap Santé. This programme (promoting flu injections and alcohol moderation, among other health concerns) helped establish Santal because a distribution system was in place and employees were used to receiving health education. Santal is a logical extension of Cap Santé. Having a health education component in place before starting a nutrition programme is not a necessity, but it certainly helps. The company was clever to save resources by teaming up with interested parties. The French Government wanted to promote and test its nutrition programme, so it offered PSA-PC a subsidy in 2002 and 2003. Sodexho was interested in promoting its healthy menu and NutriGuide software system, which it hopes to bring to other clients. Préviade-Mutouest offered money and its graphics facility to produce the professional-quality educational outreach materials, which can be very costly. PSA Peugeot Citroën and Sodexho were also wise to train the entire food-service staff in the Santal/PNNS health programme. This made the staff knowledgeable and eager to promote Santal.

PSA Peugeot Citroën reached out to night-shift workers, a group often neglected. Most night-shift workers cannot make use of the canteen unless they come in early for dinner. They can, however, grab healthy snacks and light food from the stands and vending machines. They also have access to nutritional information and recipes. Unlike Dole and Husky, PSA-PC did not simply remove less healthy foods from the canteen. Were there fears of employee revolt if all the food became healthy? The answer is, probably, yes. French workers are more opinionated about their food and probably would not stand for the removal of butter or other animal fats. This is a feature in the following case study from Iowa, where beef and pork are important to the local economy. Employers must consider the local food culture before making radical changes to the menu. Otherwise they might find no one using the canteen.

Union/employee perspective

Although management initiated Santal, the unions approve of the programme and provide regular oversight and input. The unions participate in a canteen and food services committee and a hygiene and working conditions committee. No union representative could be reached directly. Employees generally like the improvements made to the canteens and other eating areas. Most are familiar with the campaigns and many participate by trying the recommended foods.

4.13 Wellmark Blue Cross Blue Shield

Des Moines, Iowa, United States

Type of enterprise: Wellmark Blue Cross Blue Shield of Iowa provides health-care coverage for more than 1.5 million Iowans. Total assets for 2002 were US$1.1 billion, with a total surplus of US$5.1 million. Wellmark is part of the Blue Cross Blue Shield Association, a network of 41 health plans insuring 88.3 million people, or 30 per cent of Americans. Wellmark's main office is in Des Moines, the state capital. (http://www.wellmark.com)

Employees: 1,505 (Des Moines).

Food solution – key point: canteen with healthy and flexible menu.

Wellmark is in the health business, and disease prevention has long been part of its agenda. Through newsletters, mass mailings, and its web site, Wellmark tells its members about the importance of proper nutrition and exercise to maintain good health. Wellmark's employees get that same message. In 2001, Wellmark revamped its ageing canteen. The new canteen was to have two special features: a pleasant ambience and a healthy menu. That healthy menu has matured to its current incarnation, a canteen plan offered by Sodexho USA called "Your Health Your Way" (YHYW), which includes breakfast and lunch.

Wellmark employees have a paid 45-minute lunch break. Some employees, depending on their job position, can extend this to 60 minutes by juggling other breaks. About 40 per cent of the employees use the Wellmark canteen on any given day. Others either eat a packed lunch or take advantage of the restaurants in downtown Des Moines. One can walk for miles downtown without stepping outside via the city's extensive system of skywalks. This is quite useful during Des Moines' cold, snowy winters and hot summers. For many Wellmark workers, time is a concern. The on-site canteen is only a five-minute walk for most employees, leaving them over 30 minutes to dine, a comfortable break. Walking to and from downtown restaurants can easily consume at least 20 minutes of the meal break. The advantage of leaving the workplace is that it offers a bit of exercise. A disadvantage, aside timeliness, is that the quality of the food might not be as good as that served in the canteen. Price is also an employee concern. Canteen meals are subsidized by around 26 per cent. A typical lunch costs US$4–6, as opposed to US$6–9 at local restaurants.

Food solution

Sodexho has managed the Wellmark canteen for several years. In late 2003, Wellmark adopted Sodexho's new YHYW. The key features are the focus on health, taste and flexibility. Obesity is a well-known health concern in the United States, and the Iowa obesity rate mirrors the national rate at over 20 per cent. Unsurprisingly, many Americans are on diets to reduce weight. The problem is, these diets vary wildly. They can be broadly classified as low-carbohydrate (high-fat/protein), low-fat or low-calorie. Passing no judgement on the legitimacy of these diet plans, YHYW accommodates most dieters. The menu is not fixed, and substitution is easy. For example, someone on a low-carb diet can request sandwich meat in a low-carb wrap instead of on bread. The menu also features vegetarian foods, low-fat dishes and a large salad bar. Most foods have cards displaying the food's nutritional information. Other features of YHYW are food variety and presentation. The menu changes regularly, and the platters have a restaurant-like presentation. These are YHYW criteria. Some of the food may even be pleasantly exotic to some customers, because there is far more than simply the "meat and potatoes" that many Iowans are used to. Many meals reflect an ethnic or regional theme: Mexican, Asian, Italian, and Southwest American, for example.

In general, most meals contain no more than 3 grams of saturated fat and have less than 30 per cent of their calories from fat, less than 100 milligrams of cholesterol, less than 1,000 milligrams of sodium, less than 600 calories and at least 3 grams of fibre. Models of the featured food items are displayed at the canteen entrance with their price and nutritional information. The YHYW programme also provides catering for meetings and home, so there is an opportunity to bring healthy foods into the home. Wellmark will soon offer cooking lessons, which will extend the possibility of providing healthy food for the family.

Possible disadvantages of food solution

There are no obvious disadvantages, although the concept of offering choice (between healthy and less healthy) is discussed below.

Costs and benefits to enterprise

Wellmark did not disclose the costs of the canteen renovation, canteen upkeep or the YHYW programme during its interview. However, renovations needed to be done; the costs were thus unavoidable. The renovation was more of an opportunity to promote wellness by providing a modern look with food selections more reflective of America's diversity – that is, with Latin, Asian and other ethnic-inspired dishes. The YHYW programme comes at a nominal expense to the company above a traditional menu.

The canteen plan is part of a wellness programme, so it is difficult to isolate the contribution it has had on employee health and morale. The YHYW menu has only been in place since late 2003. The company does, however, view the canteen improvements as a health investment and a means to attract and keep employees.

Government incentives

None, other than standard tax exemption.

Practical advice for implementation

Wellmark does well in terms of time and timeliness. Workers have at least 45 minutes for lunch; and the canteen is in the same building that houses most of the workers, only a five-minute walk. This saves the worker the time it would take to walk to a local restaurant or to pack a lunch, the latter being difficult in many hectic households with children. Wellmark's headquarters is located in one building, so providing a canteen there was a natural solution to the timeliness concern. Wellmark's YHYW menu offers choice – that is, a choice between healthy and less healthy options. The unhealthier foods are not removed from the menu, as is the case at Dole headquarters in California. The choice comes at the risk of employees consistently choosing foods that may contribute to obesity or chronic diseases. Wellmark minimizes this risk through aggressive nutrition and health education. Wellmark employees understand which foods are healthier for them, and the canteen provides these foods. This is a vast improvement over other companies that merely offer education but no access to healthy foods. The decision to offer choice is sometimes cultural: Americans tend to value choice, rather than being told what they cannot eat. Also, Iowa is largely an agricultural state with large-scale cattle and pig farming. Not serving beef or pork at the Wellmark canteen could cause an uproar. Understanding the local culture is important in choosing a canteen programme.

Union/employee perspective

Wellmark employees are not unionized. The decision to offer a new canteen plan came from management, although many employee groups continue to provide input.

4.14 WMC Resources – Phosphate Hill

Queensland, Australia

Type of enterprise: WMC Resources (formerly Western Mining Corporation) produces nickel, copper, uranium oxide, phosphate fertilizers and a range of intermediate products at mining, concentrating, smelting and refining facilities across Australia. Phosphate Hill is the site of the Duchess phosphate mine and plant for phosphate ore processing, ammonia production and granulation to manufacture ammonium phosphate fertilizer for use in agricultural cropping. WMC's net assets at the close of 2003 were approximately AUS$4 billion (US$3 billion), with an after-tax 2003 profit of AUS$246 million (US$185 million). (http://www.wmc.com)

Employees: 380–600, on rotation.

Food solution – key point: canteen changes, in response to study by a local university.

Phosphate Hill has the distinction of being the most remote chemical plant in the world. The nearest landmark is Mount Isa, 140 kilometres to the north-west; the nearest large city is Townsville, over 700 kilometres to the northeast. The location's remoteness, hot and arid climate (routinely over 40°C in the summer), and diverse workforce present a variety of challenges in providing workers with access to nutritious food. Employees bunk at the mine for up to ten days at time and must be fed three meals a day. Many employees are of Aboriginal descent, a group that is more susceptible to diabetes and kidney disease compared with the rest of the Australian population.

Food solution

Phosphate Hill contracts with Compass-Eurest to provide food, and it works with the James Cook University School of Public Health and Tropical Medicine (JCU) to assess the health and nutritional wellbeing of its workers. Workers arrive by plane and are transported from site to site by bus or light vehicle. Fresh vegetables and other foods are brought in by truck. Meals are free at the canteen (which the company calls the "mess") on an all-you-can-eat basis, typical of remote site facilities. Workers eat breakfast and dinner at the canteen and bring a packed lunch, usually salads and cold meat sandwiches. Work shifts are 12 hours, day and night, starting at 6 a.m. and 6 p.m. All the worksites are above ground; this is an opencast mine. Workers are given a 30-minute break for lunch as well

Phosphate Hill workers eat in the "crib" during working hours and partake in more substantial evening meals in the "mess" or canteen.

as other breaks during the shift. Most eat lunch or other meal breaks in small, clean rooms called crib rooms. These rooms are cleaned and checked regularly for mine contamination. Much of the mining, processing and production at Phosphate Hill is mechanized, and a worker's caloric requirement is not particularly high, unlike in traditional mining or heavy labour.

A JCU study in 2001 identified that high BMI was a health issue requiring intervention. Rising BMI is a concern across Australia. The prevalence of obesity and overweight in Australia based on BMI in 2000 was nearly 60 per cent, a rate that has more than doubled in the past 20 years (Cameron et al., 2003). WMC responded by offering its employees more options for healthier foods and exercise. The company has hired two lifestyle coordinators, working opposing shifts, and this has significantly increased participation at the gym and in organized sporting events, such as indoor cricket, football and netball. The coordinators perform personal assessments and develop individual programmes for the workers for improving health. Eurest provides clearly labelled healthy meal options. These include daily low-fat and vegetarian dishes and a greater variety of fresh vegetables. Eurest employs a full-time nutritionist who regularly visits the site and contributes to the monthly newsletter. The canteen changes have the potential to markedly improve health, for the canteen is the sole source of all food for Phosphate Hill workers for four to ten days at a time, depending on their work cycle.

Twenty-five employees are of Aboriginal decent, a group facing a diabetes epidemic. Type 2 diabetes and its related symptoms, cardiovascular and renal diseases, are the major causes of premature death in Australian Aboriginal populations. The Type 2 diabetes rates are estimated to be between 10–30 per cent among indigenous groups, up to four times the rate in the non-Aboriginal population in Australia (Australian NHMRC, 2000, p. 158). A major risk factor is weight gain. The epidemic is thought to be the result of a rapid change from a traditional diet (uncultivated plants and wild animals) to one heavy with processed and sugary foods. The food at Phosphate Hill is clearly not traditional, but it is healthier than the food that dominates the modern diet of Aboriginals: processed salty and fatty meats, white flour, sugary carbonated drinks – all consumed in quantities above the national average – and few fruits and vegetables (Better Health Channel, 2004). Phosphate Hill's canteen offers foods to control or lower the risk of diabetes, which are clearly labelled.

Possible disadvantages of food solution

As posited in the Placer Dome case study, unlimited access to complimentary food may encourage overeating and obesity. Companies need to take precautions by offering, for example, exercise facilities, a health counsellor or smaller first servings.

Costs and benefits to enterprise

The annual budget to maintain the entire camp is AUS$8.5 million (US$6.6 million). WMC was not able to provide financial information concerning the added costs of its health improvements: university studies, nutritionist, coordinators and food variety. However, Support Services Manager, Tom Magee, said that offering healthier food options comes at no significant added cost.

A recent JCU study found modest improvements in BMI from 2001 to 2003, which was attributed to diet and exercise. Safety and morale have improved in combination with a number of factors, but healthy lifestyle has played a significant part. The JCU study has not yet uncovered significant improvements in other health measures, such as cholesterol and blood pressure.

Government incentives

No financial incentives in terms of tax breaks or subsidies are available for these programmes.

Practical advice for implementation

The JCU study on BMI raised awareness among the staff of a serious health issue. This was a valuable input, one that has helped foster change, because the advice came from health professionals and not the human resources manager. Employees seem to have taken the word of the academics to heart. The health coordinators have made a serious impact as well. Employees see themselves losing weight and, interestingly, some see work (where they live for four to ten days at a time) as a place where they can lose weight. Phosphate Hill walks a thin line, however, in offering healthy foods while keeping less healthy foods on the menu. The management doesn't want to limit choice. Fly-in operations, such as Phosphate Hill, which are so remote that the most convenient access to them is by small plane, can be stressful and can place strains on family life. Phosphate Hill attempts to minimize that stress by creating a pleasant atmosphere. Unlimited, tasty food is one tool to keep employees happy; and switching to a 100 per cent health menu might adversely affect morale. However, WMC, unlike many Western companies, does not go as far as paying to import luxury foodstuffs – primarily for its non-Aboriginal staff.

Union/employee perspective

Phosphate Hill is a non-union site. However, the mine maintains an Environment, Health and Safety Committee made up of employees, who provided feedback for this case study. The committee said the company does an excellent job providing a variety of healthy and tasty food while keeping freedom of choice. Some joked about eating more healthily at work than at home. On some nights certain dishes are not well received. Echoing the worker-representative from the Musselwhite case study, one committee member noted that there will always be some workers who load up on the fatty foods. He finds that most of the younger generation choose to eat well, adding, "I don't think you could do much to improve on what is already a top-class facility." This could mark a positive trend if young mineworkers elsewhere also choose to eat healthy foods and companies provide those foods as a job incentive. The health coordinator added that he is limited in recommending the types of foods to be served, so he instead focuses on guiding employees to the right choices for their needs from among the foods on offer.

Another committee member, also satisfied with the taste and variety of food, voiced minor concerns about lunch, which is brought from the canteen to the worksites. One option is hot food, which can cool during the 30- to 45-minute trip from canteen to crib room, raising a small risk of food-borne disease. A second option is cold cuts of meat, which tend to be fatty. A third option is meat pies and quiches, which are also fattening. One solution would be to provide catered food and a server in the crib rooms. Lunch does need to be substantial to help the workers through their 12-hour shift.

4.15   Spotlight on Argentina: Hard economy, hard habits

Argentina at the beginning of the twenty-first century is in some ways a country of contrasts. The poorer northern regions suffer disproportionately from infectious diseases, while the wealthier southern regions have higher rates of chronic diseases. Within a period of only a few years, Argentinians have seen a near total collapse of their economy, falling from the position of being a top economic force in South America in the 1980s and 1990s to suffering high unemployment and malnutrition. In 2002 approximately 20 per cent of the population was unemployed, 50 per cent lived at or below the poverty line and over 25 per cent were living in destitution and facing malnutrition, according to the World Bank. The situation is improving albeit marginally. This situation is not unlike the Great Depression which hit the United States in the 1930s.

Argentina has one of the highest meat consumption rates per capita, and this too stands in contrast to most countries: red meat is more readily consumed by lower-income classes; and fruits, vegetables and grains are largely eaten by wealthier individuals. Meats provided approximately 50 per cent of total energy intake and nearly 70 per cent of total protein (Navarro et al., 2003). Changing this dietary habit is difficult, for the meat-dominated food culture stretches back several centuries. Meat has a high social value, and the meat barbecue (*asado*) is a cherished tradition.

It is not surprising to health experts that, by far, the leading cause of death in Argentina is cardiovascular disease, contributing to about 37 per cent of all deaths, followed by cancer (17 per cent) and infectious diseases (7 per cent) (Verdejo and Bortman, 2000). Also, an increased risk of colon cancer was found among those consuming relatively large amounts of cold cuts, sausages and bovine viscera (but not lean meats) (Navarro et al., 2003). Fortunately, despite a diet high in fats and meat, Argentina has not experienced rising obesity to the same extent as other nations. However, obesity is not uncommon among the lower-income population, with its diet high in saturated fat, trans fatty acids, salt, sugar and very few fresh products such as fruit, vegetables, fish and whole grains. Many in this group have micronutrient deficiencies caused by the poor intake of iron, calcium, vitamin C and zinc, among others.

Access to food at work, especially vegetables and fruits, can contribute greatly to the health of Argentinians, particularly as the country starts to emerge from the period of economic downturn. The peso devaluation that occurred in 2002 caused steep increases in basic food items, coupled with unemployment. The average monthly income fell to 534 pesos (US$180), below the poverty line of 817 pesos. This has meant that families without two incomes have great difficulty purchasing even their basic necessities.

4.16 Unilever

Buenos Aires, Argentina

Type of enterprise: Unilever is an international company based in London and Rotterdam, employing 247,000 people worldwide. The company maintains two core divisions: foods, and household and personal care products. Its 2003 operating profit was 2.7 billion euros (US$3.6 billion). Unilever maintains ten manufacturing plants and two distribution centres in Argentina, employing approximately 4,000 workers. This case study concerns Unilever's Fraga facility in Buenos Aires. (http://www.unilever.com.ar)

Employees: 600 at Fraga office.

Food solution – key point: healthy, subsidized canteen food despite poor economy, meat-eating culture.

Food solution

The Fraga facility comprises white-collar workers. The Unilever canteen is very pleasant, with large windows, natural lighting and an outdoor section. The canteen was built in the 1970s but renovated in 1998. Workers come to unwind and socialize. The canteen food is heavily subsidized; workers only pay around US$2 a meal, approximately three times lower than the real cost or the cost of an outside meal. As a result of the low cost, most employees use the canteen even though there is enough time to visit the many nearby restaurants. The canteen is in-house; and workers can reach the canteen and purchase food all within a few minutes, allowing themselves more time to enjoy lunch. The meal break is 45 minutes.

According to Dr. Miguel Stariha, the medical department manager, the main health concerns facing all Unilever employees are overweight, obesity, high cholesterol and high blood pressure. He attributes this to a poor, meat-based diet, very long commutes and a sedentary lifestyle. The canteen menu has foods that can improve these health conditions. Unilever contracts Sodexho to provide a special healthy menu, and this is clearly labelled. The menu includes traditional fare (red meat and pork) but also alternatives: chicken, fish (once a week), vegetarian dishes, an extensive salad bar and fresh fruits as dessert. Most employees still do not meet the national health goal of consuming five servings of fruits or vegetables a day, but the Unilever canteen provides the foods that would aid in achieving this goal. The canteen has message boards filled with information about nutrition and exercise, including organized exercise events.

A combination of food choice and pleasant surroundings at the right price (M. Winograd).

Possible disadvantages of food solution

The canteen is pleasant and convenient, and the food is inexpensive. The only possible disadvantage would be the temptation of the unhealthy food items on the menu.

Costs and benefits to enterprise

The company spent approximately US$50,000 to renovate the canteen, making it more pleasant (large windows, natural lighting) and health-accommodating (salad bar, tea station). The special healthy menu provided by Sodexho is of no additional cost to Unilever, a valued (i.e. large) customer.

Unilever has not conducted a formal health study to measure the positive benefits of the canteen, but Dr. Stariha offered several anecdotes. Only two employees have had coronary events since 1998, and both had a prior history of heart disease. Vital statistics such as weight, blood pressure and cholesterol have improved for many employees. Absenteeism is very low, a statistic Dr. Stariha attributes to the food programme and also other perks at the company. Knowledge about nutrition has increased greatly.

Government incentives

Aside from basic tax incentives for operating canteen and meal voucher programmes, the Government offers no specific incentive to serve healthy food designed to reduce the risk of chronic diseases. Low-income workers' children may receive a free school meal, which must meet nutritional criteria (unlike workplace canteen food).

Practical advice for implementation

Unilever's size provided leverage to reduce Sodexho's price for its healthy menu. Facilities of similar size can do the same. Unilever also proves that even in an economic crisis, high-quality subsidized food does not need to be cut. Unilever faces a tough fight in encouraging its workers to eat healthier foods, though. Healthy snacks don't sell. Workers prefer coffee with cream, croissants with butter, and fatty foods instead of fruits, vegetables and juices. This is part of their cultural heritage. Unilever said it has greater success in neighbouring Brazil in helping its workers reach the "five-a-day" goal. Dr. Stariha said that change is coming slowly through health education and availability of healthy foods.

Union/employee perspective

The canteen and medical service regularly rank at the top of worker opinion surveys. The Fraga facility will move to another building in late 2004; 120 workers were in the new building by May 2004. These workers are asking management for a canteen similar to what they had – that is, pleasant, healthy and inexpensive – because they are currently eating vendor foods and at local restaurants and not enjoying the experience. Some employees said that they feel changes in their bodies and that they are becoming unhealthy.

A few years ago, the push for healthier food had come from management. In fact, this is still the case at many of Unilever's facilities. While Fraga isn't unionized, most other facilities are. However, because Unilever's factory workers have not voiced concern for healthy foods, it is not a union concern. A healthy canteen or issues over meal break length have not been part of collective bargaining agreements. Quite the opposite, for blue-collar workers in Argentina, healthier foods – vegetables, fish and chicken – are not considered satisfying or rewarding for hard work. We see a paradox: management wanting to improve canteen food (as a health and productivity investment) and workers resisting changes. The Fraga office is the one facility where the Unilever management has succeeded in changing the food service

The fresh fruit section and a salad bar are becoming popular (M. Winograd).

because the white-collar staff has been largely accepting of the changes. Now employees seem to cherish it even more. Will this change of attitude influence other facilities? Unilever has recently purchased Refinerías de Maíz, and workers there are more resistant to changes in food services. Currently they bring packed lunches; there is no canteen. This will be an interesting case to follow. Will there be union demands for a canteen? The union did not respond to requests for an opinion or review of this case study. One last important point is that all Unilever workers value the subsidized meal, healthy or not.

This case study was prepared by Mariano Gabriel Winograd with Rodrigo Clacheo.

4.17 Total Austral

Patagonia, Argentina

Type of enterprise: Total is a French-owned multinational energy company with 110,783 employees and operations in more than 130 countries. Total is the world's fourth largest publicly traded oil and gas company, with 2003 sales exceeding 104,000 billion (US$131,000 billion). Businesses are divided into three segments: upstream (oil and natural gas exploration and production), downstream (trading, shipping, refining, marketing) and chemicals. This case study concerns Total Austral and its upstream activities in Neuquén and Tierra del Fuego; 2003 sales were 601 million pesos (170 million/US$214 million) (http://www.total.com)

Employees: 509.

Food solution – key point: clean and quiet canteen, no cost to employees.

Total Austral and its affiliates operate several facilities in Neuquén and Tierra del Fuego. There are two sites in Neuquén, located inland in south-central Argentina close to the Chilean border. There are four sites (and two more offshore sites coming soon) in the Tierra del Fuego region. Some sites are hundreds of kilometres from cities. Because of the remote locations, most employees work on 21-day rotations. Over 70 per cent of the workers live in cities somewhat near the site, but most choose to bunk at the sites. Total Oil must provide three meals a day for these workers. At the land site, workers eat their three meals at a canteen, described below. Workers at the two offshore sites in Tierra del Fuego "commute" by helicopter and do not sleep on the offshore rig. They pick up a catered lunch, which they heat and eat on the rig. For breakfast and dinner, these workers visit a canteen on the shore near their bunking facility.

Food solution

As at most remote sites worldwide, employee meals are included at no charge. This can translate into a "family" food solution, particularly in Argentina, which has been hit by an economic downturn which it is only now slowly recovering from. As explained in the "Spotlight on Argentina" section, a sizeable percentage of the population can barely afford food. Providing food for workers on site for 21 days at a stretch means more food for the family at home. Eurest does the catering for Total Austral, with a kitchen at each site.

Eurest obtains fresh food from local vendors when possible, although some food products must be flown in from Buenos Aires, some 3,000 kilometres north of Tierra del Fuego. The food can be dry, fresh or frozen. Delivery schedules vary by site.

Total sites have similar menus worldwide. There are healthy appetizers, including a large and diversified salad bar. The daily main course is not repeated for an entire month. There are vegetarian and meat dishes. Desserts include a variety of fruits. There is a "snack island" of tasty albeit high-calorie and somewhat unhealthy food. Creating an island away from the healthy alternatives helps workers understand that the snack food is fine on occasion but unhealthy when consumed in large amounts. However, there is no nutritional information delineating the health content of any given menu item. A non-Eurest nutritionist reviews the quality and nutritional value of the foods served at the canteens, and the company occasionally organizes lectures on the topic of nutrition.

Despite the rugged and remote environment of the sites, the lunch rooms are quite civilized and cosy. They are colourfully designed with excellent ventilation and ample natural light. The clean and pleasant canteens provide a nice contrast to what is often grimy work in oil exploration. Employees are

Total's canteens are a refuge from the grimy work at the petroleum facility. Meals are heavy on meats, but Total hopes to introduce fruits and vegetables into the workers' diets (M. Winograd).

able to wash before meals. It is forbidden to enter the lunch room in work clothes. Because it takes time to change and return to the canteen, workers are given 90-minute breaks for meals. Outside, the weather can be extreme, particularly at the Tierra del Fuego sites, where temperatures dip as low as –30°C. On offshore platforms workers' meals are normally served in a special marmite dish heated in a microwave.

Possible disadvantages of food solution

With no-cost food comes the increased risk of weight gain, as noted elsewhere previously. Also, Argentina has developed a "5-a-day" fruit and vegetable programme, called "*5 al día*" (www.5aldia.com.ar), but Total Austral has not yet subscribed to it.

Costs and benefits to enterprise

Information on costs was not made available.

Total Austral benefits from high worker satisfaction, above-average employee health and a low number of accidents. The accident rate is so low that the company is exempt from certain reviews by its labour insurance company. There is no information available about increased productivity as a result of food quality.

Government incentives

In Tierra del Fuego, food and service fees are free from VAT, which is normally around 21 per cent. In Neuquén the law (No. 24.700) exempts companies from paying social security charges on the cost of meals provided to workers. Such laws offer a strong incentive to provide food.

Practical advice for implementation

Total has addressed the timeliness concern by extending the length of the meal break. This reflects two important features of the meal programme, keeping the canteen clean and ensuring that workers have time to eat and relax. Removing gear and cleaning up can take some time. Without an extended meal break, workers would be forced to eat with grimy hands in grimy clothes, degrading the quality of the meal and the appearance of the canteen. Total also offers a simple solution to meals on offshore rigs. These meals are provided to workers, who bring them from the mainland to the platform and heat them at noon. This saves time and money (the expense of an offshore cooking facility or flying back to shore), while allowing workers to maximize their break and relax. The length of meal breaks varies depending on the type of job, corresponding to the time needed to clean and travel to the canteen.

Companies need to understand the culture of their host countries when considering a food programme. In Argentina, high value is placed on red meat dishes and high-calorie foods heavy with salt, fat and sugars. Thus, given these options in an all-you-can-eat, no-cost environment, some employees may indulge. The food programme must be balanced with a culturally relevant nutrition education programme.

Union/employee perspective

Eurest is improving its study of workers' needs and desires. Food provision is not a particularly important topic for the unions these days, and they offered no opinion about Total Austral's food programme, nor did they have any input into it. The workers and their unions have made no complaints about the food programme for the past 16 years, since it began. The switch from Sodexho to Eurest for catering was purely a management decision.

This case study was prepared by Mariano Gabriel Winograd with Rodrigo Clacheo.

4.18 Moha Soft Drinks Industry S. C.

Addis Ababa, Ethiopia

Type of enterprise: Moha Soft Drinks coordinates the production, marketing and quality control of Pepsi-Cola products with bottling plants in Addis Ababa, Dessie and Gondar. This case study concerns the Saris-Gotera branch in Addis Ababa, located in the southeastern industrial district of the city. This branch, along with the Tekle-Haimanot branch in Addis Ababa, is owned by the billionaire Sheik Mohamed Al-Amoudi, the largest foreign investor in Ethiopia. The Saris-Gotera branch produces Pepsi-Cola, Mirinda, 7-UP and tonic water. Moha has thousands of market outlets throughout Ethiopia.

Employees: 897 (616 male, 281 female).

Food solution – key point: a discounted canteen, managed by a committee delegated by union workers and factory management.

Lunch is not on the menu for many Ethiopian workers across the country. At Moha, about 200 workers, or about 22 per cent of the staff, purchase lunch at the canteen. Another 30 per cent eat packed lunches from home. The rest usually do not have lunch, relying instead on a heavy breakfast and early dinner at 5:30 p.m. or so. Lunch is typically eaten between noon and 1 p.m. Workers are allowed around an hour for their meals. The canteen is approximately 50–100 metres from most workstations – a two- to three-minute walk. Workers store their packed lunches in cupboards at their working places, not in a refrigerator, while they are working.

Food solution

The canteen serves breakfast, lunch and dinner, the latter being for nightshift workers. The types of food items served in the canteen are traditional Ethiopian: largely cereals: *teffe*, wheat, barley, maize ; and legumes: beans, peas, lentils, chickpeas (*shero*, *kik*, *miser*). Occasionally beef or lamb stews are served with or without peppers. Fruits and leafy vegetables are rarely served. Vegetables are limited mostly to potatoes, tomatoes and kale. Milk is served in the morning and afternoon. Other dairy products, such as yoghurt or cheese, are rarely available. Servings are small with relatively few calories. Most factory workers are slim or underweight and weak.

Meals are inexpensive, up to about 50 per cent cheaper than meals offered by nearby vendors. A canteen meal costs about 3 birr (approximately US$0.35). Lunch outside of the factory costs 4–6 birr. The company does not subsidize canteen food. The price is low partly because the canteen operates at a low-profit margin, just enough to pay the 19 canteen workers. The food taste, quantity and quality, being so cheap, are not as good as that in the local market. The canteen is clean and pleasant. Workers who pack lunches eat in the canteen, in offices, or in the open air in the shade. Workers who skip lunch get free time to walk around; or they play indoor games such as chess, *dama* (draughts) and cards, enjoy hot and soft drinks at the canteen, or go out of the factory to nearby snack bars.

Possible disadvantages of food solution

The traditional Ethiopian food served in the canteen is largely cereal with some legumes, occasionally with meat but rarely with other vegetables and fruits. The servings contain fewer calories than needed for factory work. Clearly the quantity and quality of food would not lead to obesity, yet it does contribute to vitamin and iron deficiencies and low blood pressure. Also, packed lunches in cupboards offer some protection from food pathogens, but refrigeration would be better. Company finances would be better spent on a food subsidy than refrigeration, though.

Costs and benefits to enterprise

The cost to the company is rather low. Moha pays only for the physical structure and maintenance of the canteen plus water, electricity and telephone.

Moha can boast of very little direct pay-off for its minimal food programme investment. The food programme is not a morale booster. Workers are generally weak, and some are sluggish and anaemic (especially the female workers) according to the factory clinic's register book. However, one male worker spoke of how pleased he was with being able to save on the cost of lunch. "I usually save nearly 45 to 65 birr per month [US$5–7.50] by having my lunch at the canteen, and this is exactly what I need to pay for my daughter's monthly expense for transport to and from her school and her daily allowance."

Government incentives

No government incentives in terms of tax break or subsidies are available for the food solution in the canteen. In fact, owner Mohamed Al-Amoudi regularly complains of high taxes minimizing the profit margin.

Practical advice for implementation

Providing a low-cost canteen with just enough profit to pay canteen employees might be a practical way for small companies to afford a canteen. That is, the company need not allocate funds for a food subsidy if it establishes a "non-profit" canteen. Moha succeeds by offering adequate time to rest in a pleasant setting. However, the canteen still needs to serve meals with the proper quantity and quality need to ensure adequate nutrition. Moha's canteen falls short of this standard. Given Ethiopia's long struggle with malnutrition and low productivity, implementing a nationwide, subsidized workers' meal programme could benefit both the people and the economy. Such has been the case in Brazil. (See Brazil case study in Chapter 5.) Meals can be served for a pittance a day in Ethiopia. Meals at a cost of US$0.50 per day for 900 workers five days a week for a year would cost about US$112,000. This is a small investment for Pepsi-Cola, if not for the Moha owner.

Union/employee perspective

The union's collective agreement with factory management provides for free health services (medical examination and treatment) and monetary compensation for accidents and injuries, as well as protective gear. This was no easy victory for the union. Food is not part of the collective agreement. A committee delegated by union and management oversees the canteen to ensure that meals are provided to workers at an affordable price. Many workers seem to be unhappy with the salary and food situation. The average salary is 648 birr (US$75.20) per month; the lowest salary is 230 birr per month. Said one female worker earning the average salary, "I spend 35 per cent of my salary to purchase food, which is about the same amount for most of my fellow factory workers. With this salary scale, my and other workers' daily food intake is too low to fulfil the daily caloric output. That is why you see me thin and weak." (It should be noted that workers can receive a bonus, based on factory earnings. In 2003, all employees received a one-month salary bonus, which they used to supplement their meagre living status.)

This case study was prepared by Dr. Kassahun A. Belay and Dr. Abera Kume.

4.19 Kotebe Metal Tools Works Factory

Addis Ababa, Ethiopia

Type of enterprise: Kotebe Metal is a publicly owned factory that produces metal tools, such as sickles, axes, utensils and various farming and gardening tools. Kotebe Metal is a very popular factory among the rural farmers in the country, because it produces important farming and gardening tools.

Employees: 180 (149 male, 31 female).

Food solution – key point: a discounted canteen, managed by a committee of union workers accountable to the union.

In recent years Ethiopia has privatized many of its factories. Moha Soft Drinks in the preceding case study is one such example. Kotebe Tools remains a government-controlled factory. Its food solution for workers, however, is similar to that of Moha: a meagre offering of canteen food at a discounted price compared with locally available meals. The workers' union oversees the canteen through a delegated committee. The committee's responsibility is to ensure that meals are provided to workers at affordable prices. This committee has greater authority than the committee at Moha.

Food solution

The Kotebe canteen serves breakfast, lunch and dinner for the night shift. There are eight canteen workers. About half of the factory workers use the canteen. About 40 per cent bring a packed lunch from home. They store their packed lunch privately in offices, in cupboards at the canteen and even in their clothing lockers. There is no refrigerator to keep the food cool nor microwave oven or small stove to heat food. The remaining 10 per cent of workers skip lunch, opting instead for a heavy breakfast and early dinner. Lunch is typically eaten at noon. Workers are allowed about an hour for meals. The canteen is approximately 20–150 metres from most workstations – a two- to three-minute walk. This leaves plenty of time to eat or rest.

The canteen food is nearly identical to that found at Moha Soft Drinks, traditional Ethiopian: largely cereals: *teffe*, wheat, barley, maize; and legumes: beans, peas, lentils, chickpeas (*shero*, *kik*, *miser*). Occasionally beef or lamb stews are served with or without peppers. Fruits and leafy vegetables are rarely served. Vegetables are limited mostly to potatoes, tomatoes, kale, onions and garlic. Workers receive a half litre of milk or they have the option of receiving cash instead, which is discussed below. Other dairy products, such as yoghurt or cheese, are rarely available. Servings are small with relatively few calories. Most factory workers are slim or underweight and weak. This finding is very similar to the general population at large.

Meals at Kotebe (located in the outskirts of Addis Ababa) are less expensive than meals at Moha Soft Drinks (located in the city proper) and cost about 50 per cent less than meals in the local markets. Meals cost about 2 birr (US$0.23). Lunch outside the factory costs 4–6 birr. The price is low partly because the canteen operates at a low-profit margin, just enough to pay the eight canteen workers. The food taste, quantity and quality, being so cheap, are not as good as that in the local market. The canteen is clean and pleasant to the eye. It is well ventilated with enough light. Workers who bring packed lunches eat in the canteen, in offices or in the open air in the shade. Workers who skip lunch get free time to walk around, or they go to the canteen to play indoor games, chat among themselves, listen to the local radio station or watch television.

Possible disadvantages of food solution

We see disadvantages similar to those found with the Moha Soft Drink meal plan. The traditional Ethiopian food served in the canteen is largely cereal with some legumes, occasionally with meat but rarely with other vegetables or fruits. The servings contain fewer calories than needed for factory work. Clearly the quantity and quality of food would not lead to obesity, yet it does contribute to vitamin and iron deficiencies, and low blood pressure. This affects health and productivity; and based on the clinic manager's report for this case study interview, sick leave is very common.

The opportunity to receive cash instead of milk seems shortsighted. One worker said that he prefers cash because he can then purchase other food, usually at the canteen. Clearly for workers receiving low salaries, the extra cash can be used to purchase many useful non-food items. Some workers, however, use the cash for tobacco or alcohol. Providing cash instead of food to poor (and undernourished) workers is rarely beneficial because of the large possibility that the cash will be misused: gambled, stolen or lost. This is why so many factories and countries, as a whole, issue vouchers or some other coupon that can be used to buy specific items. One Kotebe worker said, "Although it is not in our collective agreement provisions, we use the cash given for milk to fulfil other interests, including to buy cigarettes. We feel ashamed when we see some workers use the money for alcohol consumption."

Costs and benefits to enterprise

The cost to the company is rather low. Kotebe pays only for the subsidized milk and canteen maintenance, water, electricity and telephone. (The Government considers maintenance and utilities as a food subsidy, otherwise the meal price would be higher.)

Workers having their meals in the canteen minimize out-of-pocket expenses. The saving can be applied to other living expenses. Said one worker, "I save quite a good amount of money per month by having my lunch at the canteen, and I use the money to cover my bills for electricity and water." It is not clear, however, whether most workers appreciate the meal plan and whether the factory management benefits from increased morale.

Government incentives

No government incentives in terms of tax break or subsidies are available for the food solution in the canteen.

Practical advice for implementation

Kotebe's canteen meals are cheaper than Moha's because Kotebe is located in the outskirts of Addis, where the cost of meals at nearby restaurants is even less in comparison with the restaurants where Moha is located at Saris/Gotera. The meals are not very good, however. At best, they provide some workers with a little mid-day food. For countries that have long struggled with malnutrition, such a system offers one advantage: workers who may have had no meal get a small meal. Self-sustaining, profitless canteens serving inexpensive food can be a basic food solution in similarly poor countries. They cost the company virtually nothing to run, and they offer the workers a little extra that they might not ordinarily get. Given the initial investment in the physical structure of the canteen, it seems logical that companies and governments – with just slightly more investment – can vastly improve the nutritional status and productivity level of their country.

Union/employee perspective

The collective bargaining agreement at Kotebe is similar to that at Moha Soft Drinks: free health services (medical examination and treatment) and monetary compensation for accidents and injuries. In addition, as part of a collective agreement, Kotebe workers receive half a litre of milk each day or its equivalent in cash. The union is working for more benefits in terms of improvements in the quantity and quality of food offered in the canteen. It is asking for more fresh vegetables and milk products to be made available by a substantial subsidy from the factory.

One worker from Kotebe's union said, "Every factory has a workers' union in Ethiopia, where workers come together to fight for their benefit packages. But the strength of the union differs from factory to factory. The unions in public factories seem stronger than those in the private ones. This is because hiring and firing are simple in private factories [that is, there is less job security]. In public factories, the procedure to fire and hire workers is more complicated. This [protection] offers a better chance for workers in public factories to negotiate with the management, whereas the private factories ... can fire a worker if he fights for his benefits package, and no one can save him from being fired. If he takes the case to court, it will definitely take him not less than ten years to get a final court decision. I know friends who suffered for the last seven to eight years before they got decisions for their cases from the court, because the judiciary system in our country is not yet well organized to cope with the demands of innocent workers."

This case study was prepared by Dr. Kassahun A. Belay and Dr. Abera Kume.

4.20 McMurdo Station

Ross Island, Antarctica

Type of enterprise: McMurdo Station is an international science facility operated by the United States National Science Foundation (NSF). McMurdo is Antarctica's largest community, one of 16 science stations on the continent and one of three operated by the United States. McMurdo is located 3,500 kilometres south of New Zealand on the Hut Point Peninsula on Ross Island, the farthest southern solid ground accessible by ship. (http://www.nsf.gov/od/opp/support/mcmurdo.htm)

Employees: as high as 1,200 in summer; 250 in winter.

Food solution – key point: a diverse menu despite remote location and harsh weather conditions.

McMurdo Station covers approximately 400 hectares with over 100 buildings and other structures. The dining facility is located in building 155, close to the dormitories and at the centre of activities. Building 155 also has offices, a retail store and dormitories for year-round residents. The dining facility serves breakfast, lunch, dinner and, in the summer, a midnight meal. The length of meal break varies by department, but most have an hour for lunch during the nine-hour day. (Kitchen employees have two 30-minute meal breaks because their shifts are not standard.) Employees working outdoors must often travel several minutes to the dining area and then remove their thermal gear. However, the full hour break provides enough time to go to the dining facility, get a lunch, and sit down and enjoy a meal with some rest before returning to work. Workers are given some leeway.

Food is free (that is, included in a scientist's research grant or employee's salary), and portions are unlimited, except for occasional speciality foods, such as lobster. What is striking about the menu is its diversity and similarity to canteens "back home". Breakfast, served between 5:30 and 7:30 a.m. in buffet style, includes two types of hot cereal, scrambled eggs, fresh eggs to order (in the summer), hash browns (fried potato cake), sausages or bacon, yoghurt, fruit (canned, but fresh in summer), baked items, juice (from concentrate) and milk (from powder). Lunch, from 11:00 a.m. to 1:00 p.m., is typically deli style with cold cuts. Dinner, from 5:00 to 7:30 p.m., includes meat, fish and vegetarian dishes with a salad bar.

McMurdo can offer such "ordinary" food at the very edge of the world through careful, clever and efficient planning, employing techniques easily

McMurdo Station's canteen in Antarctica is bright, warm and pleasant.

transferable to enterprises in similarly remote locations, such as those in arctic regions. Non-perishable food items are shipped only once a year, from California, and arrive in February, which is the end of the peak summer period. Shipping is expensive, and a single yearly order saves money. The food is stored at McMurdo in special freezers and cold rooms designed to reduce freezer burn. Unlike at the South Pole station, McMurdo's temperature does pop over the freezing point in the summer, sometimes as high as 8°C, so food needs to be kept at a constant, frozen temperature. Included under the definition of non-perishable, here, are meats, egg liquids and vegetables that are frozen. There are limitations on what can be ordered. International law prohibits the importation of live materials, plants and soil. Fresh foods and vegetables are allowed, but they first undergo careful inspection in New Zealand. The menu is planned around these restrictions.

McMurdo generates its own fresh water from seawater through reverse osmosis, approximately 150,000 litres a day in the summer. Most of Antarctica is a desert, and McMurdo has virtually no precipitation in the summer and only snowdrift precipitation during the other months. Ample drinking water is needed because of the dry conditions. The water system is another money saver. Reverse osmosis is not inexpensive, but it is cheaper than shipping and

A greenhouse grows enough vegetables to feed the winter crew, providing a fresh "crunch" and a psychological lift during the dark months.

storing water. This water is used for the entire station: cleaning, drinking, cooking and in the hydroponics greenhouse.

Dining facility workers grow vegetables year-round in the greenhouse under artificial light. The greenhouse can provide nearly the entire winter community with a salad once every four days, along with herbs and vegetables for the chefs to incorporate into their menus. During the summer the greenhouse is a supplement to fresh food flown in from New Zealand. Sally Ayotte, a dietician and executive chef for the United States Antarctic Program, explained that the fresh lettuce and other "greens" provide the "crunch" that is missing from prepared frozen vegetables. Crunch equals freshness and provides a psychological lift for the workers, particularly during the nine months of winter and isolation. The dining facility also offers freshness through its homemade yoghurt and breads.

The difference between winter and summer at McMurdo is like night and day. From late April to late August, there is no sunlight. The bay is frozen by March. There are no scheduled flights between late February and late August. Emergency lifts and drop-offs are possible, weather permitting. Winter residents essentially hunker down for eight months of cold, dark isolation. Daily flights resume in late October with the return of 24-hour sunlight and last until the end of January. So for about nine months a year, McMurdo's dining facility can offer no fresh foods other than greenhouse and bakery goods (made with frozen ingredients). The quality of frozen food has improved markedly in recent years, and the food is nutritious, but Ms. Ayotte recommends that workers take a daily multivitamin to ensure proper intake of key nutrients, such as vitamin C. McMurdo gets busy in the summer months of October to February. Fresh food is ordered from New Zealand once a week. Windstorms can ground flights, however, so shipments are sometimes late or missed.

Workers must be healthy to live at McMurdo and they must stay healthy while they are there, because emergency medical evacuations can be difficult. One health criterion for the NSF Office of Polar Programs is that workers and visitors maintain a healthy cholesterol level. The inclusion of hot cereal such as oatmeal and wholegrain breads on the menu addresses this health criterion. Weight is another concern. Workers engaged in outdoor activities tend to maintain a healthy weight from burning calories through labour-intensive work in a cold environment. Office workers tend to gain weight, tempted by the full-scale bakery. To help control weight, manage cholesterol and limit fat intake, the dining facility staff predominantly cooks with canola (rapeseed) oil, serves steamed and baked dishes, with heavy gravies and sauces offered separately.

Workers and scientific visitors can ship and store their own food or purchase items from a McMurdo store. In-home cooking is prohibited, however, because of the extreme fire hazard. McMurdo personnel can use dining-facility microwave ovens. Alcohol can be purchased at McMurdo, but it is rationed to one bottle of liquor, two bottles of wine, or one case of beer (24 cans) per week.

Possible disadvantages of food solution

Unlimited access to free food may encourage overeating and obesity. Companies need to take precautions by offering, for example, exercise facilities, health counsellors, or smaller first servings. McMurdo does have several exercise facilities. There is no on-site nutritionist, however, and no information readily available about nutrition. Healthy (or unhealthy) foods should be labelled as such and health information should be posted on a dining facility bulletin board or in a newsletter.

Costs and benefits to enterprise

Information on costs was not provided.

No obvious pay-off stands out, such as lower blood pressure and weight or improved safety, absenteeism and morale. Most of the workers are visitors, and many spend only a few weeks in Antarctica. Long-term health studies of wintering employees would be interesting.

Government incentives

None.

Practical advice for implementation

The greenhouse has been a unique and resourceful addition to McMurdo Station. Such greenhouses can benefit any remote worksite and are recommended. Aside from providing fresh vegetables and "crunch" during a nine-month winter, the McMurdo greenhouse also serves as a lush, warm oasis with colourful flowers for workers to visit.

As we saw with the Musselwhite and Phosphate Hill case studies, the McMurdo management must offer high-quality food at no extra cost to workers, but at the risk of encouraging unhealthy weight gain or raising blood pressure, blood sugar or cholesterol levels., Caught up in the excitement of visiting Antarctica, scientists visiting McMurdo for a month might be willing to "rough it" with camp rations. Year-round workers will not. They want the comforts of home, and this includes foods that can be unhealthy if not eaten in moderation. McMurdo offers delicious desserts to compensate for the inconvenience of working so far from home. (Home visits are not possible.) Wintering personnel usually stay for eight to ten months, beginning around January. Twelve-month contracts begin in October. Raytheon Polar Services, which supports the United States Antarctic Program, knows it cannot attract workers if the dining facility serves flavourless gruel from the days of early polar explorers. Prospective employees are assured that they will not have to make major food sacrifices. In these situations, when food is a selling point, companies need to offer nutritional guidance to ensure the health of their workers.

Union/employee perspective

This is a non-union site, and no union regulations influenced the food programme. The dining facility is popular with the workers. It is a centre of activity, a place to meet and socialize. Long-term workers often form clubs and socialize in various buildings, but everyone comes together at the dining facility sooner or later. Workers provide valuable feedback about the dining facility; and, in fact, employees came up with the idea to build a greenhouse, which was approved by the NSF prior to construction and staffing. Major programme changes come from management.

4.21 Ministry of Defence and Armed Forces

United Kingdom

Type of enterprise: the Ministry of Defence and Armed Forces (MoD) is responsible for defending the United Kingdom and promoting international peace and security. The modern MoD was created in 1971 as a fusion of old ministries, the oldest of which dated back to the sixteenth century and King Henry VII. Meals are provided through the Defence Catering Group, formed in 2000. (http://www.mod.uk)

Employees: over 200,000 regular forces and 100,000 civil servants.

Food solution – key point: new nutrition programme for military bases and field operations; innovative ration packs for active duty.

The reader should not be surprised to see a case study of the military amongst the factories, mines and offices featured in this book. Soldiers are workers; and the similarities between military operations and business operations are many. For the military, proper meals are needed for performance and morale. The food also must be plentiful and diverse to accommodate taste preferences and, often, the religious obligations of troops. The military is in fact a hyper-business: distribution and logistics can be daunting; catering conditions are extreme, in hot, cold, rainy and dry environments; and good food can mean the difference between life and death. All the case studies presented thus far share some common ground with the military.

The British military has a long history of improving its meal programme. On a 1747 voyage to the Plymouth Colony (New England) aboard the HMS Salisbury, Dr. James Lind found that citrus fruits cured scurvy. By 1795, the British Royal Navy was providing a daily ration of lime or lemon juice (both called limes at the time) to all its men, earning English sailors the nickname "limey". During the Crimean War from 1854 to 1856, more soldiers died from poor nutrition and poor sanitation than from bullets. Through the efforts of Florence Nightingale, kitchen departments in army hospitals and barracks were systematically remodelled. By the First World War, daily rations for soldiers in the trenches reflected the early twentieth century understanding of proper nutrition, yet they also catered to the tastes of foot soldiers: fresh, preserved or salted meat, bread or biscuit, bacon, cheese, fresh or dried vegetables, tea, jam, sugar, mustard, lime juice and sometimes rum and tobacco. Ration packs have come a long way since then. So too has the barracks canteen, which will be the first focus of this case study.

Food solution

Today the scourge of the British military is obesity, not scurvy. Despite being fit and physically active, British soldiers are not immune to weight gain and the chronic diseases associated with it. Military canteens have long aimed to please, and soldiers can eat their fill of steak and chips. The MoD is in the process of overhauling its canteens (called messes) to provide a better balance of fats, proteins, carbohydrates, vitamin and sugars, all without sacrificing taste. The new menu will reflect a better understanding of nutrition garnered over the last several decades. The change will be far-reaching, even affecting field kitchens and ration packs. The MoD is teaming up with QinetiQ and Campden and Chorleywood Food Research Association (CCFRA), two European research organizations, to implement the change, which will take over a year to complete.

It is not possible to report on what kind of food will be served, other than to say there will be a greater focus placed on serving fresh vegetables, wholegrain products and leaner meats, all of which will be labelled clearly to reflect their healthy attributes. The most significant change in British military catering in decades is the "pay as you dine" (PAYD) programme, now being tested at several barracks in the United Kingdom and Germany and, soon, in Cyprus and Gibraltar. The earliest trials began in the autumn of 2002. The PAYD system replaces the "single living-in service personnel" food charge, which is around £100 (US$190) per month. Service personnel, particularly the junior ranks, have long complained about this fee. In a 1999 survey of 20,000 service personnel, the junior ranks expressed an "overwhelming desire for change" and requested a better choice of what and when they eat. With PAYD, personnel will pay only for the meals and services they choose while on base. Those who eat less or take their meals elsewhere will no longer be disadvantaged.

Meals at the barracks are generally available three times a day, in the morning, midday and evening. Soldiers with families generally eat off base. The core menu will be subsidized and less expensive than local restaurants. The MoD hopes that the consumer-based PAYD will offer the diversity and profitability found in commercial establishments. The radical change has not been free of hitches. Contracted caterers had reported financial losses until recently. The Defence Catering Group reports, however, that caterers are now turning the corner into profit due to improved local management and better menu planning.

Another change in military catering is the design of the messes, which increasingly resemble canteens in large companies. Long benches and tables and long serving queues have given way to smaller self-service stations and comfortable chairs. This applies to the three types of messes: officers, senior non-commissioned officers and junior ranks. With PAYD, MoD civilians are able to

The UK MoD has revamped most of its canteens on military bases, with a modern, casual atmosphere to complement the new menu and payment system (UK MoD).

use the messes, for they now have a means to pay for the food. (The decision will be up to the commanding officer at each barracks.) Civil servants already use messes where they are entitled to; the key to extending the catering market into the wider defence arena will include contractor staff working on bases, as well as making it possible for families and relatives to eat in the appropriate messes, according to Brigadier Jeff Little, Director of the Defence Catering Group.

There are no specific time allowances for meals. One advantage of PAYD will be longer operating hours, allowing servicemen and women to fit meals around their duties without detriment to their output. Messes are typically spread around the barracks, and reaching them can often significantly diminish the time available to eat. The future formation of "super garrisons" and centralized garrison messes will improve this situation.

Payment only applies to food on base. Soldiers assigned to operations or training receive food free of charge. These soldiers gain access to meals at temporary base messes or field kitchens, or they receive a daily ration pack, properly known as an Operational Ration Pack (ORP). Ration packs are wonderfully designed. A daily pack weighs about 1.8 kg and contains a morning, midday and evening meal plus a hot drink and snack. They measure about 45 by 45 cm; and they are made to break apart, meal by meal, so that soldiers can place them in their pockets or gear in ways that best suit them. A combination of high-quality vacuum packing and dehydration ensures that the rations have a three-year shelf life. This enables the packs to be stockpiled

A soldier prepares to boil part of his 24-hour Operational Ration Pack. The pack breaks apart into morning, midday and evening meals with a snack and a drink (UK MoD).

for availability at short notice. The packs are durable, too, and stand up to mass shipping by plane, ship or truck over difficult terrain.

The ORPs are the backbone of operations. Approximately 3 million packs have been shipped for Operation Telic in Kuwait and Iraq (approximately 2.5 million are produced each year.) The food can be eaten hot or cold. This is essentially a boil-in-the-bag design that includes fuel tablets called hexamine blocks. There are over 20 different ORPs, including vegetarian, halal, kosher and Sikh/Hindu. There are also a number of variants: hot-climate rations (extra drinks); patrol rations (lightweight, dehydrated food); four-person rations and more. The rations contain around 4,000 kcal, which are on average 60 per cent carbohydrate, 25 per cent protein and 15 per cent fat by calorie, comparable with WHO guidelines. Soldiers on rations are usually in heavy training or real combat. The packs are designed so that soldiers can eat at their discretion. Convenience is a key feature. The MoD actively seeks feedback from soldiers. Two recent additions to the ration packs, as a result of feedback from missions in Afghanistan, are hot pepper sauce packs and anti-bacterial wipes.

Although the ration packs are healthy, soldiers are not expected to need them for more than 15 consecutive days, unless in prolonged battles, not seen in

Soldiers out of immediate harm's way eat at field kitchens, which offer a greater variety of foods than their combat rations (UK MoD).

decades. The packs may lack key nutrients to sustain soldiers for more than 30 days. The initial phase of operations pushes the ORP to the limit. Wherever and whenever possible during operations, the MoD provides soldiers with fresh meals at field kitchens. Field kitchens are set up quickly in battle zones once a relative level of safety has been established. Military chefs are trained to cook in adverse conditions. Mobile field kitchens may utilize ten-person food packs, which can stay fresh for 18 months. These feed ten people for one day and require little skill to prepare. Supplies can often be delivered to a combat troop every few days.

Depending on the climate, soldiers might pack several litres of water a day and drink up to 6 litres per day. This too marks a departure from past operations, when soldiers were given sterilizing tablets. The change is the result of soldier preference. Water is sometimes shipped in greater quantity than food (28,000 soldiers consuming 6 litres per day totals 784,000 bottles per week or 234 one-ton pallet loads). The MoD also distributes fruit drinks and fruit concentrate for variety.

Possible disadvantages of food solution

None apparent.

Costs and benefits to enterprise

The MoD's food budget is £120 million (US$230 million). Ration packs are expensive, about £7 each. The Defence Catering Group doesn't expect the healthy new menu to cost much more than the old menu.

For the MoD, food is more than fuel. Food is a source of morale, a critical factor in combat. Soldiers might grumble, but their grumbling appears to translate into changes. Surveys reveal that soldiers are increasingly pleased with the food provision. No studies have been conducted, nor are any planned, to assess the impact of the new food programme on key health measurements: weight, blood sugar and cholesterol.

Government incentives

None.

Practical advice for implementation

Ministry of Defence catering success owes much to careful planning by the Defence Catering Group, comprising only 60 people, and its primary supplier, 3663. (The name 3663 refers to the letters for "food" on a telephone keypad.) Key lessons from the MoD experience are: willingness to modernize and reorganize; willingness to weather out change; willingness to seek and accept employee feedback; and precision distribution, constant research and development, and thoughtful preparation. The MoD also benefited from a nationwide effort to improve canteen food quality, called the Public Sector Food Procurement Initiative (PSFPI) (see Chapter 11). The initiative aims to improve the food supply chain, support small and local food producers, and increase the consumption of healthy foods. The initiative offers guidance on these topics, and the MoD food supply chain was the subject of a PSFPI case study.

Union/employee perspective

The MoD is not bound by a collective bargaining agreement. However, employees – that is, the soldiers – do have considerable say in the development of the meal programme. No troop leaders want their men and women grumbling about lousy food. An army moves on its stomach, as the saying goes. And high morale is crucial for successful operations. The modern incarnation of ration packs and barracks food owes much to employee input, both formal and informal. No companies interviewed for this book seem to have the same dedication to employee opinion. This reflects the importance of morale for the MoD.

4.22 Canteens and cafeterias summary

The preceding case studies provide only a sample of workplace canteens around the world. The most successful canteens presented here owe their success to one or more of the following components: government participation; union participation; employer or employee enthusiasm; convenience; affordability; and healthiness. Thus, one take-home lesson is that while canteens might be commonplace, the canteens most valued by employees come through investment of will.

We also find that in most nations with well-developed economies, the emphasis is shifting toward healthy canteen food – that is, not only providing enough food but offering the right foods to eat. This is logical, now that concerns about feeding the workforce have given way to concerns over obesity and chronic diseases in developed countries. In troubled economies, such as Argentina, we see how employers value canteens and would offer them if the budget allowed. In developing nations, with their vast informal work sector, canteens are a rarity. Here, getting enough calories and nutrients is the biggest concern, and this need often goes unfulfilled. Multinational corporations operating in developing nations should provide local populations with the same high-quality meal plans that they offer in wealthier nations. Because of weak unions and workers' lower expectations, this is not always the case. The author had difficulty obtaining information from such enterprises.

Canteens are useful, particularly in keeping employees safe at work. Workers do not need to cross roads or venture into what might be unsafe parts of town. Employers can take personal care in providing safe and healthy food. A nearby canteen also enables workers to spend less time searching for food and more time resting. Workers with disabilities greatly benefit from accessible canteens. A summary of key elements in case studies from this chapter follows.

Dole Food Company, Inc.

Dole headquarters takes an extreme approach and offers only healthy foods in the canteen. Foods are subsidized; fruit is free. This makes eating healthy foods the practical choice. The plan was initiated by a health-conscious management and CEO. The positive: a generous plan. The negative: costly to operate.

San Pedro Diseños, S. A.

This garment factory did much with a modest budget. The company first identified the nutritional needs of its workforce (micronutrient deficiency, inadequate calories) and specifically addressed them with a new, subsidized meal programme that did not skimp on food safety or quality. The positive: nutritious, low-cost meals, perhaps the only full meal of the day. The negative: none.

Husky Injection Molding Systems Ltd

Husky, like Dole, has particularly healthy canteens initiated by a health-conscious CEO. The company complements nutrition with health education. The company spaces several canteens throughout the facility for worker convenience. The positive: a generous plan; convenient access. The negative: none.

Placer Dome, Inc., Musselwhite Mine

The Musselwhite Mine uses food as a means to attract workers. Musselwhite employs a local indigenous workforce. Canteen food is free. Highly trained chefs subscribe to health newsletters, cook healthy foods and find bargains. The positive: good morale. The negative: none.

Akteks Akrilik Iplik A. S.

Akteks revamped its kitchen and dining area with a focus on hygiene. Better storage facilities allow for a greater variety of food, which is free to workers. The positive: food is safe, tasty, nutritious and free, an ideal combination. The negative: none.

Tae Kwang Vina

This subcontractor for Nike in Viet Nam made extensive improvements in working conditions after being cited by NGOs and activists for environmental and labour violations. The company adopted Nike's code of conduct, which included a proper meal programme. The positive: free, nutritionally balanced meals for workers. The negative: none.

Glaxo Wellcome Manufacturing Pte Ltd

GWM's canteen remodelling was spearheaded by employees. Food is subsidized and healthier than before; salads are free. The canteen atmosphere is pleasant with more space now, to avoid queues and delays. The positive: good morale. The negative: none.

Voestalpine Stahl GmbH

Voestalpine excels in convenience, with a large and pleasant canteen and a network of shops. This is a union-based canteen programme incorporating "fair trade" concepts. The positive: good food; modest subsidy. The negative: costly to maintain.

PSA Peugeot Citroën

PSA Peugeot Citroën combined educational outreach with a new, subsidized healthier menu. The positive: workers participate in nutrition campaigns; shiftworkers and night workers benefit from healthy vending machines when the canteen is closed. The negative: none.

Wellmark Blue Cross Blue Shield

Wellmark needed to remodel an ageing canteen, so it decided to offer an entirely new menu and a pleasant atmosphere, with health as its impetus. The company takes advantage of a professional caterer healthy food option, a growing trend. The menu is sensitive to local culture. The positive: the flexible menu fits many special diets. The negative: none.

WMC Resources – Phosphate Hill

Like Musselwhite, Phosphate Hill uses good food to attract workers to its remote location. Food is tasty and now healthier. University researchers evaluated worker health and recommended changes. The positive: good food. The negative: none.

Unilever and Total Austral

These Argentine locations have kept a meal programme despite the economic downturn. The management stresses healthier diets, but workers choose fatty meats and no vegetables and resist change. Total takes special care in providing enough time for workers to wash and eat. Canteens are otherwise average. The positive: encouraging sign from management that the company cares about nutrition in the midst of an economic downturn. The negative: not much healthy variety.

Moha Soft Drinks Industry and Kotebe Metal Tools Works

These Ethiopian factories offer a canteen with a relatively affordable meal, although the food is meagre, largely cereal (carbohydrate) with little fat, protein and micronutrients. The positive: long break; food cheaper than local vendors. The negative: low on nutrients and calories; low on morale-building.

McMurdo Station

Based in Antarctica, McMurdo employs many clever strategies to reduce costs and provide the comforts of home in an isolated and hostile environment. The positive: nourishing food similar to that from home boosts morale. The negative: none.

United Kingdom. Ministry of Defence

The British military has taken a business approach to non-combat catering. Catering during combat involves impressive coordination and creativity. The military remains particularly responsive to soldiers' opinions, for food is a major morale builder during operations. The positive: commitment to healthy eating. The negative: none, if civilians are included in the meal programme.

Canada, Austria and Singapore

These countries have some of the best union- and government-initiated workers' nutrition programmes.

5

MEAL VOUCHERS

"One cannot think well, love well, sleep well, if one has not dined well."

Virginia Woolf

Key issues

The food and meal voucher system

- Vouchers are food and meal tickets provided by the employer to employees, or sometimes their families, for food and meals at select shops and restaurants.

- Vouchers are a social benefit regulated by national law, first adopted formally in the 1950s in the United Kingdom with the stated goal of feeding workers. Employers usually contribute 50–100 per cent of the face value of the voucher.

- Laws specify maximum tax exemption and employee contribution, as well as the types of shops and restaurants that can participate, the types of items that can be purchased (no alcohol or tobacco, for example) and the daily use (number of vouchers accepted, no change given, etc.). Laws vary from country to country.

- A successful system requires tax exemptions and a harmonious relationship between employers, employees, restaurants/shops, governments and voucher issuers.

- Vouchers are usually in paper form with rigorous anti-counterfeit elements; electronic "smart cards" are gaining popularity.

Pros of vouchers

- Meal vouchers are ideal for urban companies, where rental space is expensive and eateries are plentiful, and for companies with mobile or telecommuting workers.

- A meal voucher scheme can be a great equalizer, allowing small companies that cannot afford a canteen the ability to grant meal benefits to their employees.

- Savings include the cost of canteen construction, equipment, cooking staff and insurance for legal responsibility in case of accident or food poisoning.

- Vouchers help in tax collection by forcing food establishments to keep all transactions on the books. Tax revenue generated from increased activity in the food sector can exceed taxes lost from voucher tax exemptions.

- Unlike cash hand-outs, vouchers can only be used for certain items, such as meals.

- Vouchers can rejuvenate urban centres with the creation of new restaurants and the additional jobs and pedestrian traffic this generates.

- Food vouchers for use in shops can extend the social benefit to families.

Cons of vouchers

- A variety of restaurants must be near the company for meal voucher use.

- Employers cannot control the quality of food, as they can with a canteen.

- Employers must grant employees enough time to leave the workplace for a meal. A 30-minute break is not usually enough time.

Novel voucher examples

- Brazil's voucher programme reaches nearly 9 million workers, about 30 per cent of Brazil's 30 million workers in the formal sector. The programme has fuelled the economy, sharply reducing malnutrition while increasing productivity.

- Hungary has the greatest percentage of workers enrolled in a voucher plan compared with other countries; over 80 per cent of its approximately 2.75 million workers. Hungary initiated a voucher system to better regulate tax collection, to improve the health of its workforce and to "catch up" with Western Europe.

To label meal vouchers as simply tickets for a free meal downplays the relationship among the players in a successful voucher scheme: employers, workers, restaurants, governments and voucher issuers. On one level, the concept is straightforward. A company unable to offer its employees a canteen instead provides coupons covering most or all of the cost of a meal at a nearby restaurant. For such a scheme to remain economically viable, however, governments must provide tax incentives; restaurants must provide meals that match a worker's budget, schedule and tastes, and that are free from food-borne pathogens; voucher issuers must collect and reimburse counterfeit-proof vouchers on a timely basis; and workers, of course, must use the vouchers.

5.1 Meeting a social need

The formal meal voucher system had its origins in the early 1950s in the United Kingdom, ironically now a country with one of the weakest meal voucher systems because of recent changes in tax laws. (See the United Kingdom case study.) Business lore has it that a fellow named John Hack was lunching with some friends when he noticed people paying for their meals with slips of paper. Hack asked a waiter about this. He was told that nearby companies had made an arrangement with the restaurant to reimburse it for meals eaten by company workers. Post-war Britain had only just seen the end of food rationing, and the national priority to rebuild the economy involved ensuring that workers (many of whom were returning soldiers) had a proper meal each day. Companies without a canteen were in a difficult position regarding provision of food for their employees.

Hack thought the process through. Companies had to print vouchers, establish relationships with restaurants, count the returned vouchers and issue payment to the restaurants – a hassle for companies with no experience in this sort of work. Hack started his own company to oversee the voucher scheme for a service charge. The popularity of luncheon vouchers, or LVs as they soon were called, grew. By 1954, the British Government granted LVs full exemption from the National Insurance Contribution, which meant that £1 was worth £1.33. In addition, up to 15 pence per voucher was tax free. Typically, LVs in the early days were for either 15 pence or 3 shillings (30 pence). Other European countries followed suit through the 1960s.

Meal vouchers were introduced in order to meet a social need. This is the reason why voucher systems are always established by a State and implemented by law. By law, vouchers are issued over and above salary provision. The meal voucher system is no blanket solution to feeding employees in all countries in all regions, but it does offer several advantages for companies under certain situations. A voucher scheme can be a great equalizer, allowing small companies which cannot afford a canteen the ability to give meal benefits to their employees. The savings include the cost of constructing a canteen, purchasing equipment, hiring staff or catering service, and purchasing insurance for legal responsibility in case of accident or food poisoning (all of which are tax deductible). The cost that would have been spent on canteen or mess room food subsidies can be applied to vouchers. Vouchers are also ideal for companies in urban settings, where rental space for an internal canteen is expensive and eateries are plentiful, and for companies with mobile or telecommuting workers. For the employee, vouchers can offer more choices for lunch and an opportunity to escape the work environment and dine with co-workers or even friends from different companies in a relaxing setting. The walk to lunch serves to burn off excess calories.

5.2   Tax revenue and boost to local economies

Governments benefit from meal vouchers in several unique ways. Vouchers help in tax collection. Strictly regulated and essentially counterfeit-proof, vouchers force restaurants and other food establishments to keep all transactions on the books. Vouchers cannot be used in the black economy, and this fact has spurred voucher acceptance in Eastern Europe particularly. Vouchers generally cannot be used with street vendors, who are a primary source of contaminated food in many countries. Restaurants participating in the voucher system, in fact, are usually inspected by government health workers, and this helps to improve food safety standards nationally. As we will see in the Brazil case study, vouchers have led to the creation of over 400,000 food outlets. Increased revenue from restaurants and related supply-chain services – local food production and food delivery – ultimately leads to additional tax collection, enabling governments to recoup taxes "lost" from tax-exemption policies.

A study by the consulting firm Arthur Andersen commissioned by the French National Meal Voucher Commission found that the French Treasury will initially lose approximately 1.75 euros (US$2.35) per voucher, or a total of 850 million euros (US$1140 million) per year, as a result of tax exemptions on meal vouchers (ICOSI, 2004, p. 61). (Yet keep in mind that canteens are 100 per cent deductible.) The meal vouchers issued in one year have a face value of around 3 billion euros (US$4 billion). This is subject to value-added tax (VAT) at restaurants and take-away food services, representing 82 per cent and 18 per cent of voucher use respectively. With a VAT rate of 19.6 per cent for sit-down food and 5.5 per cent for take-away food, the tax generated per year on vouchers is around 510 million euros (US$680 million). Of this, 33 per cent is tax deductible for the concerned food sectors, lowering the recouped tax to 340 million euros (US$340 million). Additional taxes are collected, however, on profits generated by vouchers, which Arthur Andersen estimated to be 80 million euros (US$110 million) (corporation tax), plus 55 million euros (US$75 million) (*taxe professionnelle*), plus 93.5 million euros

(US$125 million) (income tax on food sector employees). Rounding up slightly, the total is currently around 570 million euros (US$765 million). A 2003 report by the Institut de Coopération Sociale Internationale (ICOSI) for voucher issuers interpreted this figure as reflecting a profit to the Treasury of approximately 500 million euros (US$670 million) when considering the 1 billion euros tax exemption for canteens (ICOSI, 2004, p. 62).

Vouchers can rejuvenate urban centres with the creation of new restaurants and the additional jobs and pedestrian traffic this creates. Vouchers have also been shown to stabilize food prices – a result of increased restaurant competition and an attempt to offer meals at the face value of vouchers. The specifics of voucher schemes, as the following set of case studies demonstrates, vary from country to country. Companies usually pay between 50 and 100 per cent of the voucher face value, although this isn't a general rule; employees make up the difference from pre-taxed salary. Sometimes vouchers bear the name or an identification number of an employee or employer. National laws determine voucher use. Meal vouchers sometimes may only be used for hot meals, sit-down meals, or must be of a specific caloric content. Sometimes rules regulate the number of vouchers that can be used per day, per week or per month, with an expiration date on the voucher. Vouchers are sometimes only valid within a particular neighbourhood or city. In all countries, vouchers cannot be used to purchase tobacco and cannot be used in exchange for cash; and restaurants cannot offer change. Vouchers have a key advantage over cash in that employers can be sure that the allowance is used for its intended purpose: that is, vouchers are used for food, whereas a cash hand-out or bonuses can be used to purchase anything.

5.3   Types of vouchers

Vouchers are usually paper but a few countries, such as China, have switched to electronic cards. This is somewhat surprising because electronic cards are convenient but have upfront costs that discourage their use in emerging economies, namely equipment and wiring costs. Nevertheless, electronic cards are the way ahead for voucher schemes. Once the infrastructure is in place, electronic cards (also called magnetic or smart cards) can reduce costs by eliminating paper purchase and collection. Electronic cards also have the advantage of removing the stigma sometimes associated with purchasing meals or food with vouchers, which are often given to the lower-income segment of the population and not just workers.

Food vouchers extend the social benefit to families. Of the 34 countries with government-sanctioned voucher systems, 18 allow food vouchers as a substitute or addition to meal vouchers. Food vouchers are used at

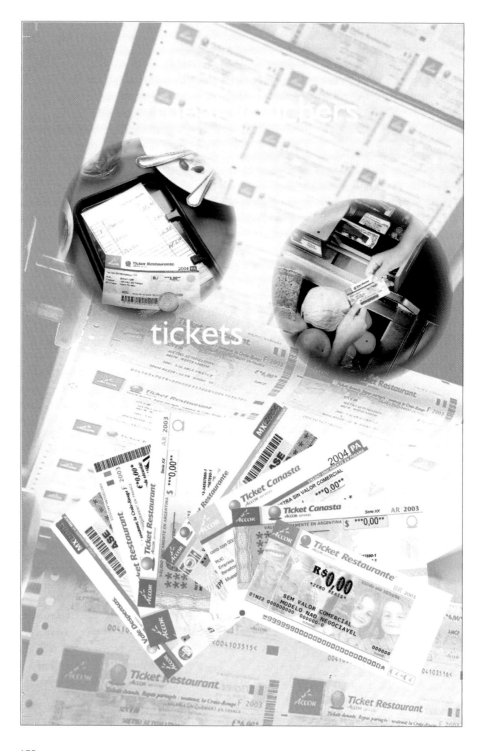

participating food stores for basic food necessities. Often only an employee or an employee's spouse is allowed to use the voucher. Some so-called food vouchers can be used broadly. The *Ticket Canasta* in Argentina, for example, is used to purchase food, medical and hygiene products and school equipment. In Mexico, the *Vales Despensa* can be used by anyone in the employee's family. Food vouchers work well in countries such as Romania where big or long lunches are not the cultural norm, or where restaurants are expensive or uncommon. A variety of vouchers exists, which an employer can use as a performance bonus: there are entertainment vouchers, cultural vouchers, dinner vouchers, hotel vouchers, etc., all contributing to the rest and well-being of the employee. These kinds of vouchers are a motivation tool and thus inherently different from meal vouchers.

5.4   Voucher pros and cons

Most unions see vouchers as a useful social benefit but understand the current system's limitations and opportunities for abuse. As defined by national law, meal vouchers are supposed to be given on top of salary. Yet this sometimes can be difficult to regulate. After all, what is a base salary? An employer could lower salaries slightly yet entice potential employees with "free" meals. In such a scenario, the employer saves on social security and retirement payments. This is an abuse of the system, however, and the unions as well as the other players in the system serve as watchdogs. Vouchers currently are of little benefit to workers in the informal sector, which constitutes much of the employment in many parts of Africa and Asia. This disadvantage is not inherent in the system, though. Brazil might extend its voucher scheme to the informal sector; this is a case to watch. The bottom line is that strong union involvement in the voucher scheme appears to strengthen the system and guarantee equity, as is readily apparent in France with the involvement of over a dozen major unions. It can be demonstrated that, in practice, there is little abuse and that figures in many countries illustrate that users are very happy with the meal vouchers system.

Meal vouchers are not ideal for all situations. Clearly, a variety of restaurants must be near the company, preferably within walking distance. For companies in remote locations and, often, in suburbs, the meal voucher scheme is not possible. (However, food vouchers can work wherever there are shops selling food, and there is no time constraint – food vouchers can be used outside working hours.) In dense, urban environments, meal vouchers are still not a guaranteed solution. Employers must consider the quality of restaurants available to accommodate workers. Employers who operate a canteen have direct control over food safety, food quality and serving time. Employers who offer vouchers transfer that control to local shops and restaurants. For the most part, local food providers have shown themselves to be up to the task, offering dishes that match the needs of workers as well as the face value of the vouchers. Indeed, studies show that meal vouchers raise the food quality in participating restaurants and stores. To gain permission to accept vouchers, restaurants commonly must open their doors to regular inspections; and street vendors, who often have poor food handling skills, generally cannot accept vouchers. Yet one cannot deny the proliferation of fast-food restaurants and the negative impact on health that such establishments can cause. A meal voucher offered in the absence of decent eateries could become a government- and employer-subsidized ticket to obesity, hypertension and diabetes. Meal vouchers offer choice, but choice is not necessarily a good thing. Workers will not necessarily choose what is best for them. Temptations abound. If there are no suitable restaurants near the workplace, employers could consider food vouchers, which allow workers to purchase foods to make their own lunch.

5.5   Successes and new possibilities

The aim of a voucher is to guarantee purchasing power dedicated to food, which is especially important in poorer countries such as India and Venezuela. Vouchers have been widely successful in meeting this goal. Unlike cash hand-outs, vouchers can only be used for food. Using vouchers for unhealthy food can be an unintended consequence. Such has been the case in Brazil for low-income workers (Veloso and Santana, 2002). This need not be the case. The voucher system has so far succeeded in meeting the social need to combat hunger, its primary intent. The voucher system has also been a boost to local economies, particularly in the food sector. A third benefit has been its effect on reducing the black economy. Yet another benefit could be reducing the risk of obesity and chronic diseases with "health vouchers" in countries most vulnerable.

The United States, which does not have a formal meal voucher system, offers an instructive example. Its culture is so fundamentally different from Europe and South America that the creation of a voucher system could be disastrous if not properly regulated. Most workers in most cities would need to drive to a restaurant, increasing pollution and road wear. And in most cities, fast-food establishments far outnumber healthier alternatives. Health experts in the United States are in near total agreement that dining out regularly leads to weight gain and contributes to poor health. Meal vouchers in the United States would need to be health vouchers, an exciting concept for many nations. Such a system can ensure a proper meal by restricting the types of foods that can be purchased. This, in turn, would encourage restaurants to offer healthier alternatives in order to attract voucher business. This scenario is quite plausible.

The successful American WIC (Women, Infants, Children) programme, with its high standard of nutrition, has led to the creation of low-sugar and fortified foods created by food manufactures to tap the lucrative WIC market. For example, the manufacturer of the popular cereal Cheerios lowered its sugar content so that it could be purchased with WIC coupons. Canada has a system of healthy restaurants called Eat Smart! (see "Spotlight on Canada" in Chapter 4). While Canada does not have a formal meal voucher system, the country is well positioned to establish health vouchers that could be used in qualifying "Eat Smart!" restaurants.

The food politics battlefield is littered with landmines, with the dairy, sugar, beef, pork, poultry, fish, agriculture, snack food and fast-food industries pushing their own agenda. None of these foods is inherently unhealthy. In excess, however, they can be unhealthy. In the United States in 2004, one fast-food company promoted deep-fried chicken as a diet food because of its high-protein, low-carbohydrate content. Other restaurants offer so-called healthy salads with dressing containing more saturated fat than a cheese-burger. Consumers get mixed messages. Europe also has a growing number of less-than-healthy eating establishments in urban centres. Coupled with a worker's desire (or pressure) to eat quickly and return to work, the combin-ation can lead to poor health. Policy-makers and employers must be committed to maintaining the integrity of a healthy meal voucher system. Meal vouchers were never designed to combat obesity. Obesity is a modern problem. The original goal of meal vouchers, circa 1950, was to ensure workers had a proper meal. Malnutrition remains an issue in parts of Eastern Europe (Romania, Slovakia), South America (Brazil) and Asia (China, India), where vouchers exist. Elsewhere, with the rising prevalence of obesity and chronic diseases, the focus can switch to healthy meal vouchers for the meal voucher system to take on a new, added benefit.

One final point must be made concerning time and timeliness. This refers to the length of time available to workers to eat, the times of the day when they can eat, and the amount of time it takes them to reach the food service, be served and then return to work. Vouchers clearly offer the opportunity for a bit of exercise and fresh air – that is, the walk to the restaurant. It is reasonable to assume that in most circumstances, walking to and from a local restaurant will take at least 15 minutes, with additional time needed for service and payment. A half-hour meal break may not provide enough time for workers to have a proper and relaxing meal. Enterprises offering meal vouchers for their employees need to take into consideration the proximity of eateries and length of the meal break. The meal break may need to be at least 45 minutes. Otherwise, employers might find their employees returning to work harried or with a sandwich or fast-food to be eaten at the desk or workstation, an undesirable outcome either way. If meal break times cannot be increased, and if the costs of establishing an on-site cafeteria are prohibitive, then enterprises might consider building a kitchenette or dining hall or allowing a caterer with a meal trolley to enter the facility. Vouchers still could be used instead of cash to purchase catered food.

The following pages contain case studies from several of these countries. Figure 5.1 gives a schematic representation of the voucher scheme, and table 5.1 summarizes key features of meal vouchers in the countries that use them. This information comes from Accor Services, a major provider of food vouchers. Various other sources, such as *Key Indicators of the Labour Market* (ILO), Eurostat and the United Nations Development Programme (UNDP), confirm wage information. Table 5.1 shows that tax exemptions in general promote voucher use. Without exemptions, voucher use is minimal, as seen in Ireland, the Netherlands and the United Kingdom. Yet even with exemptions, voucher use varies widely from country to country, regardless of minimum and average income versus maximum or average voucher exemption. This implies that other factors must also drive voucher use. Note that figures are expressed in euros in this table instead of American dollars, because much of the information comes from European sources.

Figure 5.1   The voucher scheme

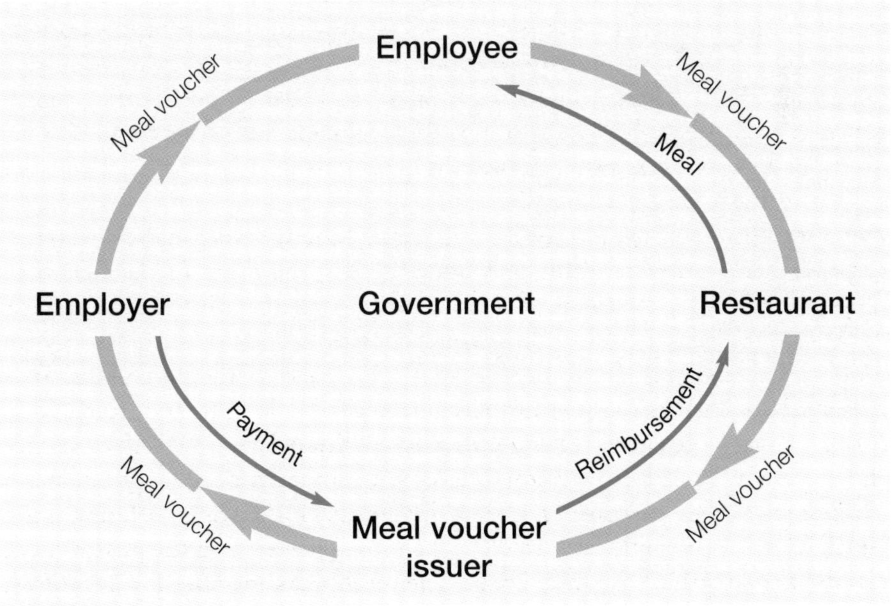

Source: Adapted from Accor Services.

Table 5.1 Meal vouchers of the world

	Last update to law	Workforce enrolled (%)	Maximum daily employer exemption (in €)[1]	Average voucher value (in €)[1]	Average monthly wage (in €)[1]	Minimum monthly wage (in €)[1]	Exemption /minimum wage (%)
Europe							
Austria	1994	10.0	4.40	1.96	1,811	1,200	7.9
Belgium	2003	25.0	4.91	5.00	2,032	1,290	7.5
Czech Republic	2002	28.3	1.52	1.57	430	150	21.9
Finland	2003	2.9	3.20	7.00	1,900	No law	n/a
France	2001	10.5	4.60	6.50	1,850	1,090.50[2]	8.8
Germany	2002	1.8	3.10	4.04	2,270	1,155	5.8
Greece	1995	0.6	2.70[3]	2.50	1,000	528	11.0
Hungary	2004	80	1.22	1.10	433	204	12.3
Ireland	1965	0.7	0.19	1.53	1,800	1,072	0.42
Italy	1998	10.1	5.29	4.94	1,735	1,077	10.6
Luxembourg	2001	16.7	5.60	8.25	2,032	1,290	9.4
Netherlands	2001	0.2	0	5.68	1,808	1,050	n/a
Poland	1998	0.4	2.30	1.60	530	210	23.7
Portugal	2003	2.2	6.09	3.41	645	356	38.8
Romania	2002	17.3	1.60	1.60	125	70	43.4
Slovakia	2002	5.2	1.74	1.43	316	144	26.2
Spain	1999	1.4	7.81	4.34	1,813	450	37.5
Sweden	1991	4.1	0	6.60	2,000	No law	n/a
Switzerland	2000	0.9	4.74	5.73	3,185	1,910	7.6
Turkey	2002	2.9	3.86	1.70	800	377	25.4
United Kingdom	1999	0.3	0.217	4.18	2,950	1,022	0.5
Americas							
Argentina	2003	7.6	3.01	6.60	500	200	20
Brazil	2002	10.6	3.60	1.43	247	72	108
Chile	1997	1.6	5.28	2.40	305	137	81
Colombia	1998	0.4	10	3.90	517	155	139.4
Mexico	2002	9.6	3.64	2.87	442.59	110.58	100
Uruguay	1996	4.0	1.60[3]	1.60	160	40	20.0
Venezuela	1998	7.1	3.41-6.82	6	586	200	55.2
Asia and Near East							
China	n.a.	n.a.	n.a.	n.a.	n.a.	n.a.	n.a.
India	2001	0.2	1.15	0.6	230	75	33.1
Lebanon	1999	1.1	3.82	4.00	400	220	37.5

Notes: [1] As of 5 December 2004, €1 was equal to US$1.34. [2] = reflects 35-hour work week. [3] = average exemption. n.a. = data not available

Source: Accor Services; exchange rates in this and other tables in this chapter calculated in euros in early 2005 (€1 equalled approximately US$1.28).

5.6 Brazil

Table 5.2 Meal voucher system in Brazil

Last update to law	Workforce enrolled (%)	Maximum daily employer exemption (in €)	Average voucher value (in €)	Average monthly wage (in €)	Minimum monthly wage (in €)	Exemption minimum wage (%)
2002	10.6	3.60	1.43	247	72	108

Contribution – key points

Both employer and employee participate in this programme. The employee's contribution cannot exceed 20 per cent of the face value of the voucher. For companies and organizations with limited budgets, meal vouchers are distributed to lower-wage employees first. Meal vouchers are fully tax exempt for both employer and employee under most circumstances. Both large and small companies offer vouchers.

Usage – key points

The voucher programme in Brazil reaches nearly 9 million workers, around 30 per cent of Brazil's 30 million workers in the formal sector. (The 10.6 per cent in table 5.2 reflects the missing informal sector.) Brazil's programme is unique in its specification of calories and content. Each voucher-paid meal must be at least 1,400 kcal for most occupations (1,200 kcal for non-strenuous labour; 300 kcal for breakfast). The net dietary protein calories (NDpCal), a measure of protein quantity and quality, must be at least 6 per cent, comparable with a plate of rice and beans. Employers cannot reduce or suspend voucher allowance for disciplinary reasons. Employees can receive vouchers six months beyond the end of a labour contract. The meal vouchers, called *voucher refeição*, are used to purchase prepared meals in restaurants and other eating establishments during the working day, which includes commuting time. Brazil also has food vouchers, called *voucher alimentação*, to pay for foodstuffs from supermarkets and similar stores. In either case, the store or restaurant owner cannot give change back on voucher use. Each day, approximately 5 million food vouchers and 4 million meal vouchers are used. Multiple vouchers can be used at one time.

Voucher physical characteristics

The majority of vouchers in Brazil, particularly those issued by small companies and in remote regions, are in paper form. However, nearly 2 million magnetic card vouchers are now in use. Paper vouchers contain a serial number, company name and sometimes the employee's name. The vouchers state whether they are for meals or for food, because the two types of vouchers cannot be used interchangeably. A common denomination for a meal voucher is 8.50 reais (US$3). Yet some vouchers are as low as 4.00 reais, which cannot buy much.

Voucher programme

Brazil's voucher programme is part of the larger Worker Food Programme, known as the *Programa de Alimentação do Trabalhador* (PAT). Nearly 90 per cent of the PAT relates to vouchers; the remaining 10 per cent involves canteens. The PAT was established in 1976 with the primary goal of providing food to low-wage workers – those making up to five times the minimum wage. This population has been the most vulnerable to chronic nutritional deficiencies. Over 46 million people were living below the poverty line in 2001, according to the Instituto Brasileiro de Geografia e Estatística (IBGE) national survey of data from households. The IBGE is a governmental organization. The PAT represents a concerted, nationwide effort to improve nutrition, increase productivity and remain competitive in the world economy. The Brazilian Government committed itself to providing tax incentives; businesses committed themselves to absorbing most of the cost of food; and workers committed themselves to allocating a percentage of their salary, an upfront sacrifice by all parties. Although there are still some rough edges, the PAT is largely considered a success in feeding many workers and spurring economic growth.

In 1977, the PAT reached 760,000 workers through 1,300 companies. Today, over 115,000 companies in all sectors of the economy provide vouchers to their workers. This represents an average increase of 3,600 companies per year. An increasing number of small- and medium-sized enterprises (SMEs) are joining the PAT. Over 60 per cent of the workers who participate in the PAT earn less than five times the minimum wage, the Government's targeted income bracket (up from 50 per cent in the mid-1990s). However, broken down, this number reveals that the poorest workers, making less than twice the minimum wage, comprise only 16 per cent of PAT beneficiaries. A quarter of PAT beneficiaries earn more than seven times the minimum wage.

Over 200,000 restaurants and food outlets accept vouchers. According to the Brazilian Association of Food Industries (ABIA), the number of restaurants in Brazil has grown from 320,000 in the 1980s to 756,000 by 1997 – roughly the number of restaurants in the United States – and the ABIA attributes the growth partially to vouchers. For a food outlet to qualify to participate in the meal voucher programme, the establishment must offer ready-made meals and respect a standard of hygiene set by the Brazilian health department. Most street vendors cannot legally accept vouchers. Qualifying outlets include restaurants, snack bars and bakeries. Many agricultural workers use vouchers to purchase "food baskets" containing a variety of foods that can be shared. The ABIA said the food sector registered US$58.8 billion in invoices in 2003, up from US$49.7 billion in 1994. The PAT generates hundreds of thousands of jobs annually in the food sector, and PAT trade constitutes nearly 1 per cent of the GDP.

Prior to 1976, Brazil exhibited features typical of developing nations: poor worker nutrition and subsequent sluggishness, and poor mental and physical dexterity, leading to low productivity and high rates of accidents, absenteeism and worker turnover. This is well documented in a 2001 White Paper from the University of São Paulo entitled *Programa de alimentação do trabalhador: 25 anos de contribuições ao desenvolvimento do Brasil*, by Professor José Afonso Mazzon, who has written extensively on this topic. Professor Mazzon found that the number of work-related accidents rose from 1.3 million in 1971 to 1.9 million in 1977, a 46 per cent increase. By 1996 the number had fallen to 395,000 while the active working population had doubled since 1975. Each major city saw improvements. For example, in Pernambuco, accidents with time off work per worker per year fell from 1.8 in 1975 to 0.7 in 1980. The average number of days off with a medical certificate per worker per year in Pernambuco fell from 4.6 to 2.9 days. Also, from 1991 to 1998, national productivity increased by 2.5 per cent per year, comparable with the United States. The industrial sectors (oil and steel) and service sector (telecommunications) had the highest productivity increases, most of which participated in the PAT (Mazzon, 2001).

During his inaugural address in October 2002, President Luiz Inácio Lula da Silva announced that eradicating hunger in Brazil would be his administration's highest priority. He subsequently created the Special Ministry of Food Security and Combating Hunger (MESA), which initiated the Zero Hunger (*Fome Zero*) programme. With the focus on this programme, delegates from labour and government met in April 2004 to discuss increasing the scope of the PAT to include an additional 15 million workers, including domestic servants and people who work in the informal economy. Meeting participants included representatives from MESA, the National Food and Nutritional Security Council (CONSEA), the Ministry for Labour and Employment, the Inter-Union Department for Statistics and Socio-Economic Studies (DIEESE), trade unions and federations, and companies that provide meals and meal vouchers. MESA plans to issue a report in 2005. However, MESA reportedly is having difficulty moving forward with this plan and progress is slow.

Possible disadvantages of voucher programme

The extensive meal and food voucher programme in Brazil seems to miss a key population of workers who could most benefit, that is, the poorest workers. Many work in the informal sector or for small companies excluded from the PAT for a variety of bureaucratic reasons. This situation only further skews the distribution of income. The very poor are less well organized and have a weak political voice compared with the Brazilian middle class. Some poor individuals are receiving 50 reais (US$18) per month via electron cards, part of the *Fome Zero* programme.

Some meal vouchers have a face value of 4 reais (approximately US$1.40), which cannot buy much. Counterfeiting is not known, but vouchers can be easily traded or exchanged for many types of non-food products, for the final recipient (the restaurant or food provider) often is not concerned with where the voucher comes from. Laws are needed to prevent abuse of the voucher system. Health researchers found that being covered by the food programme was positively associated with unhealthy weight gain (Veloso and Santana, 2002). The authors of this report suggest that the programme's approach, which is limited to dietary recommendations concerning the caloric content of meals, should be revised to better promote the health of the workers participating in the programme.

Cost to government

The cost of the PAT tax benefit has fluctuated recently: 96 million reais (US$34 million) in 1998, 90 million reais (US$32 million) in 1999, 155 million reais (US$55 million) in 2000, 103 million reais (US$36 million) in 2001. Regardless, the amount is consistently less the 1 per cent of the total tax deductions for the country, even in 2000, according to the Federal Department of Taxation. The fiscal cost is about 10 reais (US$3.60) per worker per year. The PAT-generated fiscal collection is 16 times greater than the programme's fiscal waiver, according to the University of São Paulo's Fundação Instituto de Pesquisas Econômicas (FIPE).

Practical advice for implementation

The PAT was mandated by law in 1976, Bill 6321. One striking feature of the PAT is that it was started from scratch in a massive country with widespread poverty and modest infrastructure. The Labour Ministry and Labour Secretariats remained committed to the programme, even during economic downturns. Although PAT is government regulated, it is totally run by the private sector, making it nearly free of any operational cost from public coffers. The system would fall apart without the commitment of the three main players: the government tax incentive, albeit small, remains enough of an incentive to encourage the private sector. Companies, operating in a moderately poor nation, resist the temptation so common in developing (and, now, developed) countries to minimize the bottom line. Workers, many of

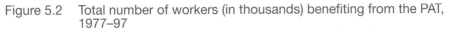

Figure 5.2 Total number of workers (in thousands) benefiting from the PAT, 1977–97

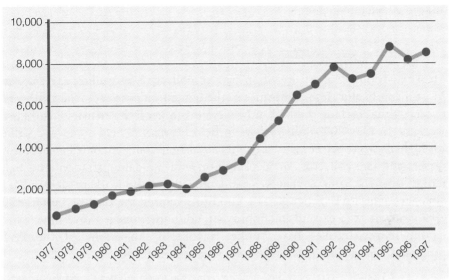

Source: University of São Paulo, Fundação Instituto de Administração, José Afonso Mazzon.

Figure 5.3 Total number of participating companies, 1977–97

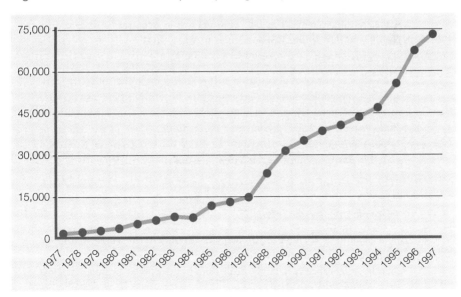

Source: University of São Paulo, Fundação Instituto de Administração, José Afonso Mazzon.

whom earn low wages, allocate part of their salary for a meal. The voucher amount is free from the high Brazilian social taxes, and this is a great additional encouragement.

Union/employee perspective

Meal and food vouchers are often part of collective bargaining agreements. Most medium and large companies in the biggest cities in fact maintain work contracts that include the PAT, now viewed as a necessity to attract and keep workers. In May 2002, rail workers in Belo Horizonte held a one-day strike for higher wages, better health benefits and larger voucher contributions. Bus drivers and fare collectors in São Paulo organized a demonstration later that month over the same demands. This demonstrates the workers' demand for vouchers. The PAT is viewed as a good programme that can be better; and efforts are afoot to expand and improve it, not undermine it. Government and labour representatives have spoken favourably in public of the PAT programme in recent years as the following quotes illustrate:

- "The PAT is a way to invest in bettering the work and health conditions of the Brazilian workers." *Rinaldo Marinho, general coordinator of the Safety and Workers Alimentation Actions of the Labour Ministry, December 2003.*

- "The PAT works with very little state interference ... The State simply gives the incentives to the enterprises. The companies and their workers make the adjustments. The PAT continues to look better." *Antonio Neto, president of the Central Workers Union (CUT), 2003.*

- "The PAT is vital to the lowest workers' categories, those less organized and with less power of negotiation ... It is important in the collective work contract negotiation not only because of the benefit itself but also because of its educational effect, providing workers the necessary alimentation." *Paulo Pereira da Silva, president of Força Sindical, one of the two main labour federations in Brazil, and of the Metal Workers Union of São Paulo and Moji das Cruzes, the largest union in Latin America, 1996.*

- "The defence of the PAT is a worker duty." *Jose Zunga Alves de Lima, president of the Federacao Interestadual dos Trabalhadores em Telecomunicacao, Fittel, 1996.*

- "The benefits of the PAT are immediate, not only to the worker but to his family too. Alimentation is fundamental to the workers' development, their learning capacity in study, health and to their life as a whole." *Senator Paulo Paim, 1995.*

These quotes were translated from their original Portuguese.

5.7 Hungary

Table 5.3 Meal voucher system in Hungary

Last update to law	Workforce enrolled (%)	Maximum daily employer exemption (in)	Average voucher value (in)	Average monthly wage (in)	Minimum monthly wage (in)	Exemption minimum wage (%)
2004	80	1.22	1.10	433	204	12.3

Contribution – key points

Both large and small companies offer vouchers. The employer's contribution is deductible up to the tax limit. The employee's contribution is not compulsory. Like Brazil, Hungary has a system of meal and food vouchers. From January 2004, the monthly tax-free limit for both types of vouchers increased: meal vouchers increased from 4,000 HUF (US$21.25) to 6,000 HUF (US$31.90); food vouchers from 2,000 HUF (US$10.60) to 3,500 HUF (US$18.60). The tax-exemption increases have led to greater employer participation and contribution. The tax-free value of the voucher can cover 50 per cent of lunch during the working week. It is legal for an employer to give an employee up to a year's allowance of vouchers retrospectively.

Usage – key points

Hungary has, by far, the greatest percentage of workers enrolled in a voucher plan compared with other countries, over 80 per cent of its approximately 2.75 million workers. Vouchers are used by civil servants and those in private industry. Meal vouchers can be used only at affiliated eating places serving ready-to-eat meals. These include thousands of affiliates comprising restaurants, fast-food outlets, some company canteens and, increasingly, food-delivery companies. Meal voucher use has increased by 393 per cent since 2001 for Accor Services and significantly for Sodexho Pass, two voucher providers. Food vouchers can be used at over 10,000 shops selling food, as well as for hot meals. There are no rules regulating voucher use for purchase of alcohol. There are three professional voucher issuers with a total of 1.2 million users and a system of supermarkets and hypermarkets with another 1 million users.

Voucher physical characteristics

Vouchers in Hungary are printed on paper. Meal vouchers are typically issued in 100-, 200-, 500-, and 1,000-HUF notes. Vouchers do not need to contain information about the employer and employee, but some companies request this as an added security feature, a free service depending on the issuer. Vouchers contain a 20-digit bar code or optical character recognition (OCR).

Voucher programme

Hungary emerged from communism earlier than other Eastern-bloc countries. Hungary began liberalizing its economy in the late 1960s, introducing so-called "goulash communism". The country held its first multiparty elections in 1990 and initiated a free-market economy. Hungary joined the North Atlantic Treaty Organization (NATO) in 1999 and the European Union in May 2004. The population in 2003 was 10 million. Hungary is a poor nation compared with Western Europe (with about half the per capita income) but has demonstrated strong economic growth in recent years. Its inflation rate dropped from 14 per cent in 1998 to 4.7 per cent in 2003, for example. Only 8.6 per cent of the population now live below the poverty line (as opposed to 12.7 per cent in the United States). In 2002, its real growth rate was 3.3 per cent and its GDP was US$134 billion. Major industries include agriculture, mining, metallurgy, construction materials, processed foods, textiles, chemicals (especially pharmaceuticals) and motor vehicles.

Among Hungary's big health concerns are cardiovascular disease, obesity and cancer, which are largely diet related. These health concerns and many others (smoking, alcoholism) are addressed at the national level through the 2003 Johan Béla National Programme for the Decade of Health. The rate of premature deaths from cardiovascular disease is three times that of Western Europe and higher than the average in Central and Eastern Europe (Hungary MoH, 2003, p. 15). Half of all deaths are from cardiovascular disease, and a quarter are from cancer (Hungary MoH, 2003, pp. 15, 89). Two-thirds of males and one-half of females are overweight or obese (Hungary MoH, 2003, p. 50). The culprit appears to be a diet high in calories, animal fat, cholesterol and salt, and very little fibre, fruit, vegetables and whole grains. The proportion of animal fat to total fat in the diet (a measure of saturated fat intake) is one of the highest in the world, over 75 per cent (WHO, 2003a).

As part of the Johan Béla national programme, Hungary has started the National Food Safety Programme, which includes workplace initiatives on food safety and nutrition. Goals of the national programme include reducing the energy-from-fat ratio to 33 per cent from 38 per cent; reducing saturated fat to 12 per cent from 16 per cent; increasing vegetable intake from 300 to 450 grams per day; and doubling the number of people who eat three servings of vegetables a day. Efforts have concentrated largely on education – mass media campaigns on proper nutrition. The consensus among Hungarian health experts is that better nutrition needs to be integrated into mass catering, coupled with improved food labelling. As of 2005, this has not yet happened.

One positive legacy of communism is a concern for workers' well-being. So it is not surprising that over 90 per cent of companies offer some type of subsidized meal, through either a canteen or the voucher system. During the earlier communist regime, however, much of the food policy was aimed at self-sufficiency and cheap food supplies. Food subsidies constituted a large percentage of Hungary's national budget, and this led to a greater presence of fatty and sugary processed foods, including sausages and few vegetables (FAO, 1998). Less was known then about the relationship between diet and chronic diseases, so there was no concern to change this system.

The free-market economy of the 1990s brought a rise in private industry, including foreign investment. Gone were the large, government-owned factories with canteens. Hungary's tax-free food voucher system started in 1993. The first issuers were supermarkets and other food stores, which today constitute about 40 per cent of the voucher market share. Accor Services and Sodexho Pass were operating in Hungary by the mid-1990s, followed very recently by Chèque Déjeuner. Meal vouchers were introduced in 1996 and have been growing in popularity, particularly with the rise in tax exemptions. The ratio between food and meal vouchers in 2002, 2003 and the beginning of 2004 was 90:10, 80:20 and 75:25 respectively. The limiting factor appears to be a lack of good-quality, reasonably priced lunch providers, yet this is slowly improving.

Possible disadvantages of voucher programme

The current voucher scheme might exacerbate Hungary's major health problems of obesity and cardiovascular disease. Vouchers can be used to purchase any type of food, and they are accepted at fast-food restaurants. Because a fast-food meal is cheaper than a sit-down restaurant meal, and because the price is closer to the face value of the meal voucher, there is a strong temptation to use the voucher for these less-healthy foods. The concept of a worker's meal was born in a time of food shortages. However, hunger is no longer a large concern in Hungary, now that the population living below the poverty line has fallen to only 8.6 per cent.

Cost to government

The tax-free limit of vouchers was unchanged for many years. Then, in January 2003, the monthly tax exemption increased from 1,400 (US$7.40) to 2,000 HUF (US$10.60) for food vouchers and from 2,200 (US$11.70) to 4,000 HUF (US$21.25) for meal vouchers. In January 2004 the exemptions shot up again: up to 3,500 HUF (US$18.60) for food vouchers and 6,000 HUF (US$31.90) for meal vouchers. This amount is exempted from tax for both the employer and the employee. The tax exemptions nearly quadrupled the number of enterprises participating in the meal voucher programme. No figures could be found giving estimates of the net cost to public coffers. However, if the situation is similar to that of Brazil and France, then substantial tax exemptions on vouchers may be a boost to the economy, leading to greater tax revenue, an increase in the number in restaurants and a stronger food sector. Only recently have more restaurants been established to accommodate voucher users.

Practical advice for implementation

The Hungarian Government has stressed its commitment to "catching up" with other European Union members in terms of market reforms and health. Regarding health, the Johan Béla national programme is a strong start. The Government is aware of how diet is related to chronic diseases and how healthy workers are vital to the economy. Hungary imported the meal and food voucher system to ease the rapid transition from a centralized economy with government- or quasi-government-owned factories (with workers' canteens) to a free-market economy with smaller, private companies and fewer canteens. The tax laws reflect how the Government views vouchers as a logical substitute for canteens: the tax exemption for vouchers and canteens are nearly identical. The former communist countries of Central and Eastern Europe, with a shared history of food subsidies and workers' rights, can benefit from the voucher system in similar ways. As mentioned earlier, however, safeguards must be in place to ensure that workers have access to healthy food, not simply fast and fatty foods that ultimately could cripple the workforce and the economy.

Union/employee perspective

The Hungarian Association of Food Voucher Issuers (EUFE) comprises members from Sodexho Pass, Chèque Déjeuner and Accor Services, who work closely with trade unions, professional associations and employers' organizations. The unions have been supportive of vouchers since their introduction in Hungary. Recently Hungarian trade unions have pressed for a reduction of working hours in their bargaining demands. Working time is regulated by the Labour Code and is usually not an issue for sectoral or company-level collective agreements. The trade unions propose two one-hour weekly reductions that would ultimately bring the working week to 38 hours. Related to this effort, the National Association of Hungarian Trade Unions (Magyar Szakszervezetek Országos Szövetsége – MSZOSZ) is proposing a change to the Labour Code to increase the 20-minute meal break now defined.

5.8 Romania

Table 5.4 Meal voucher system in Romania

Last update to law	Workforce enrolled (%)	Maximum daily employer exemption (in)	Average voucher value (in)	Average monthly wage (in)	Minimum monthly wage (in)	Exemption minimum wage (%)
2002	17.3	1.60	1.60	125	70	43.4

Contribution – key points

Romania is unique among voucher systems in that employee contribution is not possible. The contribution burden falls entirely on the employer. The maximum tax exemption on a voucher is 61,000 lei (US$2). Any amount above this is treated as employee income and is taxable. Every six months the maximum face value (i.e. exemption) is recalculated based on an official food price index. The Romanian voucher market has a quota, a maximum number of 1.6 million users a day. Civil servants and workers at companies who have debts with the State are not entitled to vouchers, although there is a movement afoot among trade unions to change this. Both large and small companies offer vouchers.

Usage – key points

Romania provides workers with food vouchers only, not meal vouchers as in other countries. Nevertheless, the food voucher can be used in any affiliated eating place or food shop. There are about 24,000 participating shops, over 90 per cent of food retailers. Employees can receive one voucher per day worked, but they can use two food vouchers per day. There are 1.5 million users, close to the quota. Eating places and shops are not allowed to return change. Vouchers cannot be used for tobacco or alcohol.

Voucher physical characteristics

Food vouchers, called "table tickets", are paper and must bear the name and address of the issuer; the period of validity (until the end of the current year); a sequential serial number; a warning that vouchers cannot be used for alcohol or tobacco; and a blank area where employees write their names and the name and address of the eating place or shop once the voucher is used, and the date.

Voucher programme

Romania emerged from its centrally planned economy to a free market only recently, after the 1989 overthrow of Nicolae Ceausescu. Poverty doubled through the 1990s, and today Romania is among the poorest of Eastern European countries, with over 25 per cent of its 22 million people living below the poverty line (United Nations, 2003, p. 11). Over 15 per cent live in acute poverty with an income of less than US$1 per day (WHO ROE, 1999, p. 6). Widespread poverty, corruption and red tape are said to hinder foreign investment. A 2001 International Monetary Fund (IMF) Standby Agreement has led to small gains in privatization, deficit reduction and inflation curbing. Major industries include agriculture (40 per cent of active population), textiles and footwear, light machinery and auto assembly, mining, timber, construction materials, metallurgy, chemicals, food processing and petroleum refining. Romania's GDP was €48 billion in 2002 and €50 billion in 2003, and its growth rate was 4.9 per cent (based on Eurostat data; €50 approximately US$66). Romania could enter the European Union by 2007. Regarding health, Romania had the lowest rate of deaths due to cardiovascular disease in Europe in 1970, but now has one of the highest: 35 per cent of deaths under age 65 and 77 per cent of deaths over age 65. Life expectancy in Romania is 70 years (WHO ROE, 1999, p. 11).

Romania has a workforce of nearly 11 million, with 8.63 million currently employed and 4.6 million receiving monthly wages, according to the Central Bank of Romania. The quota of 1.6 million vouchers – a number greatly increased recently and now reviewed quarterly – is strictly regulated. In one financial quarter in 2003, for example, 200,000 new daily vouchers were allowed (and 100,000 more in early 2004), which were distributed among the eight voucher issuers in the country. In the past, demand has often exceeded supply but still, currently, this strictly controlled distribution system may favour long-established players. The average voucher face value is 60,500 lei (US$2), reflecting the 61,000 lei maximum tax exemption. Companies can deduct the cost of vouchers as an expenditure, compared with canteen costs, which are considered benefits-in-kind and must be included in the company's accounts and are taxed as salary.

Romania doesn't have a lunchtime break culture, so it is natural that the voucher system favours prepared food over the hot lunch. The tradition is to eat a large breakfast, a quick and small lunch, a large dinner, and a light meal later in the evening. Most workers pack a lunch prepared at home with materials purchased with food vouchers at stores. Restaurants are too expensive compared with the average salary, and employees tend not to use them for lunch breaks. A relatively small number of them, mainly local and international fast-food restaurants, accept vouchers.

In its report on European meal vouchers prepared for voucher issuers, ICOSI (Institut de Coopération Sociale Internationale) concluded that the social advantage of food vouchers in Romania far exceeded those of the other countries under study. ICOSI went as far as stating that vouchers contribute to the solvency of the economy. Up to 30 per cent of the food sector's turnover stems from voucher use. (This figure reflects the estimated 12 per cent of transactions at general stores and 30 per cent of business at retailers selling only food.) Vouchers represent around 20 per cent of the average monthly wage and 40 per cent of the minimum wage. With nearly 45 per cent of the population living below the poverty line, and with food comprising 50–80 per cent of the average household budget, vouchers help ensure that workers and their families have enough to eat. While the employer receives and signs the voucher, any family member can use it. The fact that vouchers cannot be used for alcohol or tobacco further guarantees that this social benefit is used for food and not to support addictive habits. In the same report, ICOSI wrote that Romanian companies view vouchers as a social policy tool, an inexpensive means to recruit workers and reduce absenteeism, which is high in Romania (ICOSI, 2004, p. 34).

It seems that the quota system played a role in the success of the vouchers in Romania. The quota was very small at the beginning and the vouchers quickly became a scarce good that companies fought to obtain.

Possible disadvantages of voucher programme

According to ICOSI, the voucher system is far too regulated. The quota policy restricts supply, while the tax solvency and public sector limitations restrict demand. (Public servants cannot join the scheme unless there is employment turnover, so only some public hospitals can distribute vouchers.) There is a lack of permanency, too, as companies regularly join the scheme but are kicked out depending on the amount of tax they owe. The Government explains its approach as a requirement of the International Monetary Fund (IMF). The face value of the voucher is usually not enough to cover a meal at a restaurant. A slightly higher allowance might be a spur to the restaurant economy, as seen in other countries. Those vouchers used for restaurants, albeit a small number, tend to be for fast-food businesses. It is not clear whether eating each day at such establishments in Romania will someday contribute to a rise in chronic diseases. So far, the price of meals in internationally-owned fast-food restaurants has been much higher than the value of a voucher. So going to such restaurants is still not very common and considered as a special occasion by many Romanians.

Cost to government

No data could be found on the cost of this voucher programme to the Government. Thus, it is unclear whether and to what extent the Government benefits from the additional revenue generated in the food sector from vouchers. It does appear to benefit from a reduction of the black economy, which ICOSI estimated to be 20–30 per cent of the GDP. Vouchers enable some companies to transform wages paid illegally in cash into a perfectly legally declared amount for approximately the same cost.

Practical advice for implementation

Romania maintains a popular voucher programme that continues to grow with each new tax-exemption increase. Demand among employers, employees and unions is strong. Romania demonstrates that a voucher system can thrive in a poor country amidst heavy regulation, and that it might perform very well if regulations were lifted. Similar nations, once tied to the former Soviet Union, such as Croatia and Latvia, can benefit from a voucher system if Romania can.

Union/employee perspective

Vouchers have become an important negotiation element for the unions. Potentially, over 4.5 million Romanians can receive vouchers. Trade unions are petitioning the Government to liberalize the system, lift the quota and expand privileges to public servants, such as railway workers – a hot topic in 2004. The unions also hope to bring small- and medium-sized companies inside the scheme. From an employer's perspective, vouchers help in hiring and retention and are often requested.

5.9 France

Table 5.5 Meal voucher system in France

Last update to law	Workforce enrolled (%)	Maximum daily employer exemption (in €)	Average voucher value (in €)	Average monthly wage (in €)	Minimum monthly wage (in €)	Exemption minimum wage (%)
2001	10.5	4.60	6.50	1,850	1,090.50	8.8

Contribution – key points

Both large and small companies offer vouchers. Employers and employees contribute nearly equally to the voucher value, with the employer contributing by law a minimum of 50 per cent and a maximum of 60 per cent, and the employee making up the difference. Under these conditions, the employer's contribution is exempt from social security and other taxes up to €4.60 (US$6). Any sum above this limit is considered employee income and is subject to tax for both employer and employee. The exemption is periodically updated; the €4.60 exemption came in 2001.

Usage – key points

French law permits tax-exempt meal vouchers, which can be used to purchase ready-to-eat meals in affiliated eating places. A special commission within the French Ministry of Finance oversees the programme. Only one meal voucher can be used per working day. (Two vouchers are sometimes tolerated.) Vouchers usually cannot be used on Sundays and holidays. The law stipulates that vouchers must only be used for food. Eating places cannot give back change. Unused vouchers can be reimbursed in many situations.

Voucher physical characteristics

Meal vouchers are only in paper form. Vouchers by law have the issuer's name and address, the period of validity, a sequential number for tracking, and the name and address of the eating place once the voucher is used.

Voucher programme

France, with over 60 million inhabitants and a GDP of US$1600 billion, is a leading economic force in the European Union. France also has one of the oldest and most mature meal voucher systems, which was modelled on the British system but has since far exceeded it in scope and volume. The French luncheon voucher was born in 1962 and became official (by law) in 1967. It should be no surprise, then, that France is home to the three largest international voucher companies – Chèque Déjeuner, Accor Services and Sodexho Pass – and also a smaller company called Natexis Intertitres. France has a labour force of 27 million workers; 2.8 million receive meal vouchers. This number increased in 1992 when the Ministry of Finance extended voucher privileges to its own civil servants. Today, more and more civil servants receive vouchers. A survey conducted by the EDHEC Business School in Lille revealed that 83 per cent of French workers consider meal vouchers as a social benefit. The benefit is not insubstantial. Employees essentially pay for only about 50 per cent of their lunch. For the employer, a voucher costs about €715 (US$940) per year per employee: an average of €6.50 x 50 per cent x 220 vouchers a year.

Vouchers fit a variety of eating habits and demands. The lunch break is usually 45 to 60 minutes. Traditionally the French have taken long, sit-down lunches. Only 7 per cent of French employees take a packed lunch, in stark contrast to Romanians in the previous case study. About 28 per cent eat in company canteens, 30 per cent eat at home, and over 35 per cent leave their place of work, according to a Coach Omnium study (Eurostaf, 2001). Of those who leave work, 82 per cent eat at sit-down restaurants and 18 per cent buy prepared food from a bakery or fast-food shop. Meal vouchers, with an average face value of €6.50 (US$8.50), encourage workers to seek a proper meal when they venture out as opposed to fast food. As a result, the amount spent on lunch by workers has increased by 28 per cent (ICOSI, 2002, p. 72). Many French restaurants serve healthy meals, and 92 per cent of France's general medical practitioners surveyed said that meals taken outside the workplace make a positive contribution to employee well-being (ICOSI, 2004, p. 30). So there is some agreement that voucher use can lead to better health because of a healthy food infrastructure. But not all French food is particularly healthy, as mentioned in the PSA Peugeot Citroën case study in Chapter 4.

Meal vouchers were introduced in France in order to meet social needs. Employers wanted to contribute to their employees' lunches, and in the 1960s there were only two ways: the canteen, which was only possible for major companies (because of the cost and infrastructure) and which was reserved for people at head office, a socially unfair solution; or cash, which left it uncertain that employees were using the money for lunch. Once the French Government adopted the voucher system, studies showed that dedicating funds by way of vouchers had social as well as economic impacts.

Possible disadvantages of voucher programme

No disadvantages are apparent.

Cost to government

As referenced earlier, a study by the consulting firm Arthur Andersen found that the French Treasury, will initially lose around 1.75 euros (US$2.35) per voucher, or a total of 850 million euros (US$1,140 million) per year, as a result of tax exemptions on meal vouchers. The tax collection on food and food services, however, is around 570 million euros (US$765 million). It is much more difficult to take into account the induced effects, especially the impact on health and productivity.

Practical advice for implementation

France represents a mature voucher system, with strong commitment from the Government, employers and employees, coupled with an extensive restaurant and food sector. All the pieces (cultural, social, economic) are in place.

Union/employee perspective

Over 80 per cent of French workers strongly value meal vouchers. France has established the National Meal Voucher Commission (Commission Nationale des Titres Restaurant). The Commission has 22 members, all unpaid, who represent employer and union organizations. The Commission is particularly representative of restaurant unions and voucher issuers. The following unions support the voucher system by their action as members of the Commission Nationale des Titres Restaurant. Positions are taken in that commission only when a consensus among the different parties emerges. The commission's objective is to defend the development of the meal vouchers system. Union members include: Confédération Française Démocratique du Travail (CFDT) – FORCE OUVRIERE, Confédération Française de L'Encadrement, Confédération Française des Travailleurs Chrétiens (CFTC), Confédération Générale des Cadres (CFE-CGC), Confédération Générale du Travail (CGT), Confédération des Professionnels Indépendants de l'Hôtellerie (CPIH), Groupement National de la Restauration (GNR), Mouvement des Entreprises de France (MEDEF), Président Adjoint Confédération Nationale de la Boulangerie Française (CNBF), Président Confédération Française de la Boucherie, Charcuterie, Traiteurs (CFBCT), Président Confédération Nationale des Charcutiers-Traiteurs et Traiteurs (CNCT), Président Union des Métiers de l'Industrie Hôtelière de France et d'Outre-Mer (UMIH), Secrétaire Général Confédération Générale de l'Alimentation de Détail (CGAD), Syndicat National des Hôteliers Restaurateurs Cafés et Traiteurs (SYNHORCAT), and Union des Métiers et des Industries Hôtelières (UMIH).

5.10 United Kingdom

Table 5.6 Meal voucher system in the United Kingdom

Last update to law	Workforce enrolled (%)	Maximum daily employer exemption (in)	Average voucher value (in)	Average monthly wage (in)	Minimum monthly wage (in)	Exemption minimum wage (%)
1999	0.3	0.22	4.18	2,950	1,022	0.5

Contribution – key points

Contributions are exempt from taxes only up to 15 pence (US$0.25). Above this, contributions are considered employment income subject to tax for both employee and employer. Both large and small companies offer vouchers.

Usage – key points

Vouchers are non-transferable and can only be used for meals. Lower-paid staff are given preference over higher-paid staff in voucher distribution, if availability is limited. As usual, no change is given back on a meal.

Voucher physical characteristics

Vouchers in the United Kingdom are paper, although recently some companies have requested smart cards. The voucher displays a face value, typically £1 (US$1.90–3.80), an expiry date and two sets of serial numbers. Accor Services is the only voucher issuer operating in the United Kingdom.

Voucher programme

Government-regulated meal vouchers – called luncheon vouchers (LVs) in the United Kingdom – were invented in England in the early 1950s as a substitute to providing a canteen. The tax exemption set in 1958, 15 pence, which was once enough to buy a proper meal, has never been increased; and as a result, there are few participants in the British voucher scheme. (Adjusted for inflation, 15 pence in 1958 would equate to around £3 (US$5.70) today.) Most of the 2,300 participating companies are small and do not have the resources for a staff restaurant. Several larger companies that participate have a cafeteria at the corporate headquarters but not at smaller branch locations. Approximately 72,000 workers receive luncheon vouchers daily, at an annual cost of £17 million (US$33 million). The United Kingdom has a workforce of 29.6 million, similar to France and Italy, where over 2 million workers receive vouchers.

The British tax system seems to benefit company canteens. The average tax subsidy is at least £1.14 (US$2.20) per person per day for private company canteens, and £1.37 (US$2.65) per person per year for public sector canteens (Deloitte and Touche, 1997), compared with the £0.15 (US$0.25) for voucher users. This raises concerns of business equity, where larger firms with canteens receive preferential tax treatment. The most recent blow for the voucher scheme came in 1999, when the British Government lowered the exemption of the National Insurance Contributions (NIC), once at 100 per cent of the face value, down to 15 pence. This means that the tax and NIC break is only £36 (US$69.50) per year. This change is thought by many to be the result of the Great Yarmouth, or "Asda", scandal in 1997, when it came to the attention of the Government that an elder care home in Great Yarmouth was paying employees £60 (US$116) a week plus £70 (US$135) more in Asda super-market vouchers to avoid NIC. The Government hoped to nip in the bud such abuse of the tax system. Today, the British voucher scheme hobbles along, driven not by pure economics but intangible benefits, such as improved morale and hiring enticements. The biggest drop in participation came in 1999. At its peak, the voucher scheme reached over 3 per cent of the workforce. With a lack of a realistic tax exemption in line with inflation, this rate slowly dropped to around 1 per cent by the early 1990s, when there were a quarter of a million users. By 2001, after the NIC slash, participation was down to around a third of this figure.

Of great concern in the United Kingdom is the rise in "desktop dining". A 2004 survey by Abbey National, a British bank, found that 70 per cent of British officer workers regularly eat at their desks (Lyons and Moller, 2002). Time spent on lunch has shortened. The 2004 *Eurest lunchtime report* found that the British lunch hour is now down to 27 minutes on average (Eurest, 2004). The United Kingdom's Public and Commercial Service Union found that more than half of British workers take 30 minutes or less for lunch (Flynn, 2003). The union is petitioning the Government for longer and guaranteed meal breaks. Some in this union see vouchers as a means to facilitate this, for vouchers represent a clear signal from the employer or manager to the employees that they can and should take a meal break.

Vouchers encourage workers to take longer lunches outside the work-place, which can relieve stress and promote exercise. A ten-minute walk to a sandwich shop consumes 50 calories, while eating at the desk consumes 10 calories. But food quality is important. In France, we find that most general medical practitioners recommend eating out for lunch, because healthy food options are available. In the United States, most doctors recommend not eating out because of the high-fat, high-salt, high-sugar and high-calorie content of food. The United Kingdom is in transition. Its rates of overweight and obesity are the highest in Western Europe. If the food options for voucher recipients comprise nothing more than a multitude of unhealthy food outlets, then voucher use might not lead to better health and the related economic benefits: that is, fewer sick days, greater productivity, fewer accidents, etc. One option to avoid this scenario – should the United Kingdom radically adjust voucher exemption status and demand resume – is to create a system of health vouchers, in which only healthy meals could be purchased with a voucher. This concept is now under discussion. The health voucher is no simple solution. Dedication is needed to determine and regulate what is labelled "healthy".

Possible disadvantages of voucher programme

The tax exemption for United Kingdom luncheon vouchers provides no incentive for companies to offer them to employees.

Cost to government

The current cost to the Government is insignificant because voucher use is not common. Accor Services estimates the tax cost to be £30 million (US$58 million), a figure that wouldn't necessarily increase with greater voucher use due to positive effects on the food service sector. Currently, no real impact on the economy can be measured.

Practical advice for implementation

A lack of tax incentives has led to poor voucher participation. Year by year, as food prices rose and tax exemption values stayed the same (at the 1958 level), more and more companies dropped vouchers from their list of employee benefits. Then in 1999, when the NIC exemption was stripped, another two-thirds of the participating companies left the system. The numbers are irrefutable. If a country is serious about a voucher system, then suitable tax incentives must be in place – usually at a level comparable with the tax breaks offered to cafeterias – or else businesses simply won't participate in the scheme.

Union/employee perspective

There is little union and employee activity because voucher use seems to be a forgotten concept in the United Kingdom. Some may see a social stigma attached to vouchers, because a similar concept, the milk token, is distributed by the Government to the poor to buy food staples. Others may see luncheon vouchers as antiquated, something that their parents used in the post-war era. The Public and Commercial Service Union is one union that could include vouchers in collective bargaining agreements to help ensure longer and regular meal breaks. One representative from this union, at a small meeting arranged by Accor Services, said his group was thinking about this. No examples of vouchers playing a part in collective bargaining agreements could be found. The issue may soon come to the front as many cafeterias (particularly in the public sector) have been closed for financial reasons, and workers are left with no substitute.

5.11 Sweden

Table 5.7 Meal voucher system in Sweden

Last update to law	Workforce enrolled (%)	Maximum daily employer exemption (in)	Average voucher value (in)	Average monthly wage (in)	Minimum monthly wage (in)	Exemption minimum wage (%)
1991	4.1	0.00	6.60	2,000	No law	n/a

Contribution – key points

Tax exemption for meal vouchers in Sweden was eliminated in 1991. Meal vouchers are taxed fully as employment income. Employers customarily pay half the face value. Both large and small companies offer vouchers.

Usage – key points

An unlimited amount of vouchers can be used per day at any affiliated eating place, day or night. About 95 per cent of restaurants accept meal vouchers, called *rikskuponger* in Swedish. To join the voucher network, restaurants must serve hot food and have a sit-down area, although vouchers can be used to purchase take-away food as along as these two requirements are met. Vouchers cannot be used to purchase tobacco or alcohol. Change can be given on meal vouchers up to 10 Swedish krona (US$1.50).

Voucher physical characteristics

Vouchers are printed on paper with a face value in Swedish krona in the following denominations: 2, 5, 10, 20, 40, 50 and 60. No physical characteristics are required by law.

Voucher programme

Sweden presents an interesting case of a voucher system surviving, albeit barely, despite the incentive of tax exemptions. The reason it stays alive might be due to Sweden's long history of social benefits for workers and a relatively robust economy. Sweden's 2002 GDP was US$230.7 billion, substantial for a country of only 8.8 million. The Swedish workforce numbers 4.4 million with approximately 4 per cent unemployment.

In 1991, Sweden removed the tax advantages of meal vouchers. Previously voucher use was growing, with turnover rising from 1 billion krona

(US$147 million) in 1984 to 6 billion krona (US$884 million) in 1990. With the removal of the tax incentive, the turnover dropped virtually overnight to 2 billion krona (US$294 million) and has remained stable since. There are approximately 175,000 users. In France, in contrast, voucher use has grown by 87 per cent since 1991. Interestingly there appears to be a threshold of companies that will offer employees vouchers as a social benefit no matter the financial incentive.

The Swedish lunch break is 30 to 45 minutes, longer than other Scandinavian countries. Dinner is the most important meal of the day. Swedes will sacrifice lunchtime if it means they can leave work earlier, although they do value free, quality meal breaks for school children. According to the French Centre for Foreign Trade, 65 per cent of Swedes regularly eat outside the home, which represents 6 per cent of the total household budget and 23 per cent of the total food budget. This is the third highest rate of dining out in Europe. Thus, Swedish workers value lunch outside the workplace. Most restaurants prepare a daily special (*dagens rätt*) with salad and coffee for around US$7.50–9, the average face value of a meal voucher. All the elements of a successful voucher programme seem to be in place except for a tax incentive.

Possible disadvantages of voucher programme

Without a tax incentive, the voucher system is not popular and thus provides no stimulus to the economy.

Cost to government

None.

Practical advice for implementation

As we saw in the United Kingdom case study, a lack of tax exemptions starves the voucher system. A robust system requires government incentives. Sweden, one of the most socially minded countries in the world, can only muster 4 per cent voucher use without tax incentives, and other countries won't do much better.

Union/employee perspective

Sweden has a high rate of trade union membership: about 85 per cent of blue-collar workers and 75 per cent of white-collar workers. Although vouchers are not a major concern for Swedish trade unions, the topic of workplace stress is.

Studies have shown a connection between stress and the rising trend of absenteeism in Sweden, now the highest in Europe. Studies have also shown that work-day breaks reduce employee stress. Meal vouchers, and the promise of an extended lunch break beyond the company walls, may soon reach the bargaining table.

5.12 India

Table 5.8 Meal voucher system in India

Last update to law	Workforce enrolled (%)	Maximum daily employer exemption (in €)	Average voucher value (in €)	Average monthly wage (in €)	Minimum monthly wage (in €)	Exemption minimum wage (%)
2001	0.2	1.15	0.6	230	75	33.1

Contribution – key points

The employee's contribution is allowed but not mandatory. It is fully deductible and exempt from tax and social security contributions up to 50 rupees (US$1.10). This translates into the following savings: 4,680 rupees (US$103) at the 30 per cent tax bracket per annum; 3,120 (US$67) rupees at the 20 per cent tax bracket per annum; and 1,560 (US$34) rupees at the 10 per cent tax bracket per annum. Vouchers are used largely among middle-class workers.

Usage – key points

Meal vouchers are used at affiliated eating places, up to 50 rupees (US$1.10) per day. Meal vouchers are non-transferable and cannot be turned into cash. Vouchers are used at thousands of affiliated eateries in more than 150 cities. Vouchers issued between January and September expire at the end of December; vouchers issued after September expire at the end of the next calendar year.

Voucher physical characteristics

Vouchers are printed on paper and contain the basics: face value, validity period, name of issuer and sequential number. The meal vouchers come in a booklet, with different denominations of meal vouchers ranging from 5 to 50 rupees, according to the employer's discretion.

Voucher programme

The voucher system in India began informally in the late 1980s organically, similar to the British system in the 1950s. The management at the TELCO factory in Mumbai, which is owned by the TATA group, decided to provided tickets to employees to purchase lunch in the dozen or so eating places situated very close to the factory. Some of these eating places on the roadsides and sidewalks were not very clean, and the food was not very nutritious. So TELCO created coupons of a set value that could be used at better restaurants. The concept spread. In 1995, the Indian Government granted a 35-rupee (US$0.75) tax exemption on coupons for meals during working hours. In 2001, the Government passed a law to regulate voucher use and increased the exemption to its current level, 50 rupees (US$1.10). Today, around 180,000 workers receive vouchers. The system largely serves the country's growing middle class, with participating eateries mostly mid-price establishments.

Providing a canteen is a statutory requirement for employers with more that 250 employees at a facility. This is part of India's Factories Act of 1948. Companies can bypass this rule by offering vouchers.

Possible disadvantages of voucher programme

This is a new system that works well for the middle class but has not quite reached the poorer classes. The potential to do so is apparent.

Cost to government

So far, minimal.

Practical advice for implementation

Vouchers offer emerging economies such as India many advantages. New businesses can capitalize on the voucher system to save money on canteen or mess hall construction, while still offering employees subsidized meals. (The Indian growth rate is 8 per cent, an indication that new, small businesses are flourishing.) Affiliated restaurants must maintain a proper level of hygiene to participate in the voucher scheme, and this reduces the risk of food-borne diseases, which can be a problem in India's warm climate. Vouchers have the potential to benefit the poorer classes because the payment – in voucher form and not cash – cannot be used for alcohol, tobacco, gambling or other potentially harmful activities. Vouchers can help secure a proper meal for these workers and leave more money in their pockets for the needs of their families. Even an allotment of 5 rupees (around US$0.11) is enough to purchase a simple yet nourishing meal in many parts of India. Unlike in Brazil, however, vouchers do not reach the poorest segment of the population.

India has a massive, diverse, informal street food economy, as is discussed in the case study on Calcutta street foods in Chapter 7. In recent years, in fact, street food vendors have put some restaurants out of business because they are able to offer foods more cheaply to the large number of migrant workers pouring into the cities in search for jobs. Street foods can be nutritious, but the risk of food-borne illness is high. Vouchers can help remedy this situation. The Government can regulate street foods and permit street vendors to accept vouchers on the condition that they undergo training in food handling and hygiene. Employers with a modest budget can offer 5- to 10-rupee vouchers, which can cover the cost of a meal on the street. Government benefits from reeling in the unregulated street food sector, and the food safety and tax revenue improvements this brings; vendors benefit from legal status to sell food and a steady flow of customers; employers benefit from a nourished workforce; and employees benefit from a meal they might not have had otherwise.

Union/employee perspective

No specific union perspective could be obtained. Trade unions in India see vouchers as a positive social benefit, but other priorities (such as pay and safety) occupy their time.

5.13 Lebanon

Table 5.9 Meal voucher system in Lebanon

Last update to law	Workforce enrolled (%)	Maximum daily employer exemption (in €)	Average voucher value (in €)	Average monthly wage (in €)	Minimum monthly wage (in €)	Exemption minimum wage (%)
1999	1.1	3.82	4.00	400	220	37.5

Contribution – key points

The employee's contribution is allowed but not mandatory. It is fully deductible and exempt from tax and social security contributions up to LBP 5,000 (US$3.30). This translates into a tax savings of up to LBP 335,000 (US$220) per year per employee. Recently small companies have joined larger ones in offering vouchers.

Usage – key points

Meal vouchers are used at affiliated eating places, one voucher per day. This includes approximately 1,000 restaurants, coffee shops, sandwich bars, mini-markets, bakeries and major supermarkets.

Voucher physical characteristics

Vouchers are printed on paper and contain: face value, name of employee, name of employer and validity period details.

Voucher programme

Lebanon has made considerable progress toward rebuilding its political and economic institutions since 1991. The 1975–91 civil war seriously damaged the country's infrastructure, reducing national output to half and ending its position as a banking hub in the Middle East. A financially sound banking system and a multitude of resilient small- and medium-scale manufacturers have aided economic recovery. The economy rebounded in the early 1990s, slowed at the close of the decade, and has since rebounded again. In 1999, the Lebanese Government introduced a law to encourage companies to provide additional benefits to their employees. One of these benefits is the meal voucher for employees enrolled in the social security fund. Contributions up to LBP 5,000 (US$3.30) per worker per working day are not considered additional salary in submissions to the social security programme (21.5 per cent rate) and are exempt from income taxes.

Large institutions – mainly banks and insurance companies – offer their employees meal vouchers, but smaller companies have also joined the system recently. Interestingly, Lebanon businesses demonstrate canteen and voucher compatibility. The bank Société Générale has had a canteen for years but is now one of the biggest voucher users. The voucher system otherwise is standard. Lebanon is mentioned here mainly for two reasons: it demonstrates voucher use in helping an economy ravaged by civil war; and it is one of two examples (along with Turkey) of a voucher system in a predominantly Muslim culture.

Possible disadvantages of voucher programme

As in India, this is a new system that works well for the middle class but has not quite reached the poorer classes.

Cost to government

So far, minimal.

Practical advice for implementation

Countries rebounding from war can learn from Lebanon's example. As a result of "Horizon 2000", the Government's US$20 billion reconstruction programme, real GDP grew 8 per cent in 1994, 7 per cent in 1995, and 4 per cent in 1996 and in 1997; it slowed to 1.2 per cent in 1998, -1.6 per cent in 1999, -0.6 per cent in 2000; and it has rebounded slightly, 0.8 per cent in 2001 and 2.0 per cent in 2002 (World Fact Book, 2004b). During the 1990s, annual inflation fell to almost 0 per cent from more than 100 per cent. The 1999 law that enabled voucher use represents the latest effort to raise the quality of life in Lebanon. Furthermore, Muslim culture has a long tradition of the wealthy helping the less fortunate. Social benefits such as meal vouchers fit soundly within this tradition and can resonate in other Muslim countries. In fact it is surprising that Turkey is the only other predominantly Muslim country with a formal voucher system.

Union/employee perspective

Lebanon is one of the few countries in the Middle East with a comparatively well-developed labour movement. Trade unions have secured some tangible gains, such as fringe benefits, collective bargaining contracts and better working conditions. During the civil war, divisions in many of the trade unions weakened their normal functions, and many of their members joined the warring factions. Many others emigrated. Economic factors, such as the current recession and a very high unemployment rate of 30 per cent, have escalated a further decrease in the union's power. The minimum wage, for instance, has not increased since 1996. The union will not start bargaining for the food vouchers for another year or two, as other requests are of higher priority.

5.14 China

Contribution – key points

No national laws regulate food and meal cards. The Chinese tax administration treats contributions as a part of taxable income like any allowances in cash or lunch boxes. Employers receive a 30 per cent tax exemption.

Usage key points

The electronic meal cards can be used in affiliated restaurants, fast-food outlets, cafés and bakeries. Meal cards are recharged each month with the amount the employer decides to distribute.

Voucher physical characteristics

It is a paperless system. Rechargeable electronic cards bear the name of the employee; disposable cards do not.

Voucher programme

Accor Services established electronic meal cards in China in 2000, along with a fitness card. This represents a brand new system for a massive country undergoing tremendous economic and social change. Thus, it will be interesting to see how this system evolves. Accor and other players are advocating for a clear income tax and social charges exemption for both employers and employees. The voucher system is relatively too small and new to report in practical detail here, although two issues stand out: China's willingness to entertain a meal card system demonstrates the feasibility of voucher use spreading to other Asian cultures. (Vouchers are predominantly a concept common in Europe and in South America and Mexico, which have been culturally influenced by Europe.) The adoption of meal cards in China also illustrates the shift in workers' benefits in recent years. Under the older communist Government, workers had greater access to free or subsidized meals during working hours. With the rise of capitalism in this communist country, however, many workers have seen some of their benefits taken away. The need to eat has not changed, of course; and some businesses are finding it a good practice to provide workers with meals.

Possible disadvantages of voucher programme

The system is not yet mature. Currently the system suffers from a lack of government incentive and, thus, business incentive.

Cost to government

None.

Practical advice for implementation

A mature meal card system in China can help the country control food-borne diseases and the black economy.

Union/employee perspective

As seen in Europe and the Americas in years past, unchecked capitalism can lead to worker exploitation. If the Government supports the meal card programme through tax incentives, then businesses can more easily afford to provide workers with a meal benefit. Workers and unions, then, would have one more tool in their collective bargaining agreements. Big companies in China have a large budget for social benefits, and trade unions are now considering bargaining for vouchers – a new concept in China.

5.15 Meal vouchers summary

The voucher system has few disadvantages. Enterprises that cannot, for a variety of reasons (finances, space, number of remote workers, etc.), operate a canteen can offer their employees meal or food vouchers. Vouchers are ideal for small, medium-size and large enterprises. Economy of scale doesn't apply. Only two basic requirements need to be met: that there are nearby restaurants, and that there is enough time to eat lunch. As we saw in the preceding case studies, the countries with the fullest participation among the voucher "players" have the strongest voucher systems. The players are the government (establishing the rules, providing tax incentives), restaurants (providing reasonably priced food), employers (willing to offer a meal subsidy) and voucher providers (providing efficient service). A summary of key elements in the case studies from this chapter follows.

Brazil

Strong government support has led to widespread use and has boosted the economy as well. The programme reaches nearly 9 million workers. The voucher plan has a unique calorie and protein requirement for each meal. The positive: reduces hunger among lower-income workers. The negative: not yet effective in Brazil's large informal economy.

Hungary

Trade union commitment has helped make the voucher plan successful. Over 80 per cent of the workforce use them, including civil servants, the largest percentage by far among any country. The positive: used by the government to "catch up" with Western Europe in terms of efficient tax collection, health and productivity. The negative: often used to purchase less-healthy, convenient foods.

Romania

Romania also has strong union participation. The country is unique in its requirement that contributions must be 100 per cent from the employer. Romania doesn't have a lunchtime break culture, and restaurants are expensive, so vouchers are for food from shops, not meals. The positive: adapts to the culture by becoming a food voucher instead of a meal voucher. The negative: heavily regulated with quotas.

France

France is home to the most established meal voucher system, with broad use and union support. Rules established in France are copied by many countries: work-day use only, no change given, one voucher per day per worker and a minimum of 50 per cent employer contribution. The positive: good relationship among players. The negative: none apparent.

United Kingdom

Vouchers had their origin in England, but the voucher system is barely surviving there for lack of tax incentives. Less than 0.5 per cent of workers use them, the lowest rate among countries with voucher laws. There is some discussion of creating "health vouchers", which would be used only for healthy foods. The positive: the system is still hanging on. The negative: lack of tax incentive cripples the system.

Sweden

Tax incentives were eliminated in Sweden, but the system continues on with a respectable 4.1 per cent use among workers. Around 95 per cent of restaurants accept vouchers, one of the highest rates. The positive: the Swedish sense of social welfare has kept the system alive. The negative: lack of tax incentive keeps the take-up low.

India, Lebanon, China

The voucher concept, born in Europe and adopted across South America, is taking root in Eastern countries. Usage is low but growing. In Lebanon and India, the system largely serves the emerging middle class, but there is no reason why companies employing lower-wage workers cannot use vouchers. Vouchers are very new to China and are in a somewhat experimental phase, carefully watched by both government and voucher providers.

6

MESS ROOMS

Photo: Boncafé

"Hunger: one of the few cravings that cannot be appeased with another solution."

Irwin Van Grove

Key issues

The mess room and kitchenette

- A mess room is a place where employees eat food prepared elsewhere. There is minimal food storage. Local vendors or caterers bring food for daily consumption. Employees can reheat their own food. Vending machines might be available.

- A kitchenette is a small kitchen, often with an adjoining dining area where employees can store, cook or reheat food brought from home. Typical appliances include a small refrigerator, a microwave, a hotplate or a small stove.

Pros of running a mess room or kitchenette

- Mess rooms and kitchenettes can be considerably cheaper than canteens or vouchers, yet they still provide employees with a meal option.

- Mess rooms and kitchenettes require less space than a canteen and are easy to clean and maintain.

- Mess rooms and kitchenettes can be as grand as the employer desires. A mess room might be merely a semi-enclosed structure with benches. Add decor. Add heat or air conditioning. Add food subsidy. Add options for nutritious meals.

- Similarly, kitchenettes and dining areas can be greatly improved with small investments in appliances and recreational elements, such as television, radio or games.

- Mess rooms and kitchenettes can send a message to employees that the employer cares enough to offer at least something in the way of a food solution.

- Mess rooms and kitchenettes can minimize traffic at a co-existing canteen.

- This solution can work well in the informal sector.

Cons of running a mess room or kitchenette

- The variety of food available is usually less diverse than that available through a canteen or voucher system.

- Poorly maintained mess rooms and kitchenettes attract insects, rodents and bacteria.

- Employers with a large workforce who offer drab mess rooms or kitchenettes instead of a canteen or voucher system might be perceived as mean.

Novel mess room/kitchenette examples

- Workers at MexMode in Mexico went on strike in part because of bad food in the mess room. The company improved service by offering a greater variety of food with a full subsidy. Morale and productivity are up; sick days and accidents are down.

- K. Mohan and Co. in India worked with the NGO Global Alliance to improve food safety and nutrition for what amounted to a few cents per worker per day.

- American Apparel in California improves its mess room year by year with new additions. The company works with a local university to offer subsidized, nutritious and ethically appropriate meals.

- Simbi Roses in Kenya began serving free meals when the managers realized workers were skipping lunch. The company hired a local cook to prepare a simple but relatively nutritious meal to be served every day, cooked in a semi-enclosed shed and eaten usually outdoors. The company saw a rise in productivity and is now constructing a permanent, enclosed structure for cooking and dining.

In this publication we are defining mess rooms as rooms in which employees eat meals cooked elsewhere. Canteens are facilities with kitchens that store, cook and serve a variety of food. Mess rooms can be a simple, empty shell to which food is brought. Food is delivered to the mess room already cooked by a local caterer. This chapter also features enterprises with kitchenettes, which are small kitchens with an adjoining dining area where workers can cook or reheat food brought from home.

One advantage of a mess room or kitchenette over a canteen is that they are inexpensive to maintain. The kitchenettes require no staff. In many cases, workers are responsible for keeping the area clean. Companies can supply ovens or heating trays, refrigerators, tables, chairs and a sink to wash dishes and pots. The mess room requires no extensive investment in kitchen staff or equipment. Mess rooms might consist of only tables and chairs, and a place to wash up. For enterprises that cannot afford a canteen but have some space in their grounds, mess rooms might be the appropriate food solution. Indeed, the companies featured in this chapter are small or without the financial resources for a canteen.

One can argue that mess rooms are a step below canteens and vouchers in the food solution hierarchy. This is true at some level. For example, one business in the Netherlands downgraded its canteen to a mess hall in the face of financial hardship, offering less food variety and meal subsidy. From an employee point of view, a canteen or meal voucher will probably seem grander than a mess hall. Yet mess rooms and kitchenettes can send a message to the employee that the employer cares enough to offer something in the way of a food solution.

This solution can work well in the informal sector, which is common in many parts of Africa and Asia. The mess room in such cases would provide shelter from the elements and a clean place to eat and rest. Mess rooms can double as meeting rooms. Special features can be added one by one. For example, companies can invite a local food vendor at no cost into the facility to sell food in the mess room. This local vendor benefits from a reliable customer base, as well as a place to wash up, unlike on the streets. Employees benefit from the convenience of having food brought to them. The employer can make the arrangement sweeter by offering a food subsidy, a simple arrangement between the employer and the vendor. Kitchenettes also improve with layering in which more additions – such as 'a refrigerator, an oven, comfortable chairs, fans or a window – contribute to a pleasant dining experience. The kitchenette can cost the employer nothing (except water and electricity) if workers bring in their own used appliances. The employer can buy new appliances or the occasional bowl of fruit. The eating area, a necessary accompaniment to the kitchenette, improves with proper ventilation, clean water, air conditioning, television, games and even artwork.

Food safety is an important concern for the mess room and kitchenette. Because such as area may be deemed as a more casual dining solution compared with a canteen, employers might become lax about cleaning. Employees are often responsible for keeping the kitchenette cleaned. As with the "law of the commons", kitchenettes get dirty quickly because no one person owns or is responsible for equipment. Spoiled food, even in refrigerators, can promote mould growth and contaminate the entire kitchenette. Mess rooms, viewed by some employers as simplified canteens, often have no dedicated cleaner. Harmful bacteria or mould can quickly spread on eating surfaces if they are not cleaned regularly with hot, soapy water. Employers who provide a dirty place to eat may soon realize they are not doing the employees any favours.

Building a small mess room with a space to heat up or cook simple food can be done with scrap materials for a low price. Consider the following snapshot of a garment factory in Haiti. Each day when their work stopped at 11 a.m. for a 30-minute lunch break, all 300 workers of Confections et Emballage used to leave the factory, buy their food from small businesses in the neighbourhood, and consume it where they could. Conditions were far from ideal because the hot and dusty environment around the factory offers little opportunity for eating and relaxing in a proper way. The hot climate makes rest and recovery particularly important after hours spent in a working environment where, despite ventilation, temperatures can be quite uncomfortable. This recovery is essential both for the workers' health and safety and to maintain their level of performance at the required level.

Confections et Emballage built a mess room within the factory in two weeks, using primarily scrap materials. The iron bars used as a framework for the construction were found abandoned; the material for the roof was left over from a separate roof construction project. Only bricks, cement and labour had to be purchased. The total cost of the construction amounted to approximately US$1,000, an investment of US$10 for each of the 100 workers it could accommodate. The new construction, inaugurated on 20 May 2003, offered a clean, healthy environment where workers could eat in the shade and have a proper seat and the opportunity for social interaction. (We are sad to report that Confections et Emballage burned down in the Haitian riots of 2004. Lessons learned from its efforts remain viable.)

6.1   MexMode

Atlixco, Mexico

Type of enterprise: MexMode is a Korean-owned garment factory located in northern Mexico, one of over 3,500 *maquiladoras* (garment assemblers) in Latin America. Major clients include Nike and Reebok. MexMode changed its name from Kukdong in September 2001. No financial information about the company was made available.

Employees: approximately 700, 75 per cent male.

Food solution – key point: a new mess room with subsidized food as the result of the formation of a union and subsequent collective bargaining.

MexMode's new mess room was the result of a yearlong struggle of work stoppages, letter-writing campaigns, union formation and collective bargaining, all beginning late in 2000. The Kukdong garment factory, as MexMode was known at the time, had a poor reputation among workers' rights groups. Complaints against the company included verbal and physical abuse, low pay, firings and generally dismal working conditions. In January 2001, 800 employees staged a work stoppage. Among the complaints was the rotten food served in the factory mess room. The mess room was particularly appalling: plates and utensils were routinely dirty; the food contained worms and human hair; and diarrhoea and other food-related illnesses were commonplace. (Most workers travel great distances to reach the factory, so the mess room is one of the few meal options.)

A quick summary of the labour struggle follows. In July 2001, Nike did not place any more orders after an order for its hooded fleece product was filled, citing a lack of "shared values regarding Code of Conduct related issues with Kukdong factory management", according to an e-mail message from Dusty Kidd, Vice President of Compliance at Nike. With work orders drastically reduced, Kukdong was forced to temporarily lay off workers and its finances were in jeopardy. By September 2001, workers succeeded in forming an independent union called SITEMEX (Sindicato Independiente de Trabajadores de la Empresa MexMode – Independent Union of Workers at the MexMode Factory) with about 95 per cent worker participation. A new and better mess room was part of the collective bargaining agreement. By 2002 Nike re-established its working relationship with the company.

Food solution

The old mess room could only accommodate 500 workers. There was one food supplier, a caterer, with whom Kukdong contracted. The new mess room has room for 2,000. Over 90 per cent of the employees use it. The new mess room is cleaner and far more pleasant – spacious and bright, with 40 windows. Several workers were hired to keep the mess room clean. There are now five vendors who serve food. These vendors bring food every day and use the facilities at MexMode to cook or reheat meals. MexMode offers workers 14 pesos (US$1.26) a day, six days a week, to buy lunch at the mess room or to use at local stores to purchase materials for a packed lunch. Mexico has a long, rich tradition of street food vendors; and those workers who don't use the MexMode mess room usually purchase a "take-away" meal from a local vendor.

Meals at the mess room cost about 14 pesos, which is less expensive than a meal on the street. The lunch break is 60 minutes. The mess room is close to the factory, so this provides ample time for the workers to eat and rest. Mexican culture once called for a two- to three-hour lunch accompanied by a nap, called a siesta. Modern demands are slowly eroding this tradition across Mexico. The mess room vendors offer breakfast and dinner too. The company pays for dinner for workers on overtime and allots 30 minutes for the break.

Possible disadvantages of food solution

It is hard to complain about the radical changes in mess room food, price and cleanliness at MexMode. This has been a windfall victory for workers' health. MexMode has been generous to offer not only a variety of vendors but to cover most of the cost of the meal, a 100 per cent turnaround. We must, however, question the cash allowance for food. MexMode could issue vouchers or tokens for use at mess room vendors or local stores instead of cash to ensure the payment is being used for food and not for less healthy options: tobacco, alcohol or gambling. While the vended food isn't always healthy (fatty, salty), there have been no complaints of food-borne illnesses.

Costs and benefits to enterprise

The meal programme costs MexMode 84 pesos (US$7.56) per person per week (14 pesos x 6 days), or about 57,000 pesos (US$5100) for the 683 workers employed, at the time of the case study, for the weekly food budget.

Morale has never been higher at the factory, and accidents and sick days have never been lower. Productivity is up, although there are no official statistics on this. This is anecdotal information supplied by SITEMEX.

Government incentives

None.

Practical advice for implementation

The MexMode workers' tale is an old-fashioned union success story, in which a handful of workers took great risks to organize and make substantial changes. Best of all, MexMode appears to be doing well financially as a result, as measured by the increased demand for overtime to meet work orders. Nike, for one, re-established business ties with MexMode as a direct result of improved working conditions. SITEMEX was not alone in its struggle, however. The union's success would not have been possible without the coordinated support provided by the Workers Support Centre (CAT) in Mexico, Students Against Sweatshops groups at universities across the United States and Canada (major purchasers of MexMode products), labour organizations including the American Federation of Labor-Congress of Industrial Organizations (AFL-CIO), and solidarity groups including the United States Labor Education in the Americas Project (US/LEAP), Campaign for Labour Rights, Global Exchange, Sweatshop Watch, the European Clean Clothes Campaign, the Korean House for International Solidarity, and the Maquila Solidarity Network.

Establishing a new mess room was not difficult for MexMode. Aside from the generous 14-peso subsidy, MexMode merely allowed five food vendors to come to its facility. Food is brought to MexMode each day. This arrangement saves MexMode the cost of establishing its own canteen with its own staff. Even without the subsidy, this would be a simple and useful food solution to bring safe food to workers during working hours.

Union/employee perspective

The Government does not specify the quality of worker mess room or length of meal break. Nor does the Government monitor food safety and quality in the *maquiladoras* sector. SITEMEX realized that food quality and safety for the workers would need to be the company's responsibility and added this to the collective agreement. SITEMEX has heard that other *maquiladoras* factories also have dismal mess rooms. The new mess room has been such a morale booster that change in the area of workers' nutrition may sweep the *maquiladoras*.

6.2   Boncafé International Pte Ltd

Singapore

> **Type of enterprise**: Boncafé, a purveyor of gourmet coffees, coffee drinks, teas and hot chocolate, operates a multi-million dollar, state-of-the-art factory in the heart of Singapore's food manufacturing belt. (http://www.Boncafé.com)
>
> **Employees**: 60.
>
> **Food solution – key point**: employee-operated kitchen areas.

Boncafé is a winner of the Singapore HEALTH award for its commitment to employee health and wellness. The company does not have a canteen or space for a large dining area. Street vendors are relatively close, but employees do not care to eat this type of food on a daily basis.

Food solution

In 2000, Boncafé began a concerted effort to improve the health of its employees. One key change has been the enhancement of kitchen areas (which the company calls "cooking points" or "pantry rooms") to encourage home cooking, which is usually healthier than nearby street food in terms of nutritional content and food safety. Cooking facilities, located in several areas within the multi-level factory, may include a steam cooker, an oven, a food warmer, a refrigerator, a sink, pots and, of course at Boncafé (as if the pervasive factory aroma of coffee wasn't enough to perk you up), a coffee maker.

Male employees often bring warm, home-cooked meals to work, which they place in a food warmer to keep warm. Ideally, foods should be kept cold or hot, below 5°C or above 60°C, to stop or slow the growth of food-borne pathogens. It is not clear whether the food warmer routinely achieves this; but, in tropical Singapore, placing food in a food warmer is a better choice than leaving it at room temperature. Female employees usually reheat food or cook at work. Typical healthy dishes include fish porridge, *bee hoon* soup, tuna fish sandwiches on wholegrain bread and rice with green leafy vegetables, broccoli, beans or peas. Occasionally the women prepare *popiah*, a type of spring roll with vegetables, which needs to be prepared and eaten fresh because the texture and taste quickly degrades. There seems to be ample room for employees to cook and eat together, and many look forward to preparing food at work.

Workers often prefer to eat together.

Factory manager Eric Huber, who has initiated many of the changes at the cooking points, occasionally purchases apples and oranges for staff consumption. Water coolers have also been placed throughout the factory. Mr. Huber said one of his objectives is to inculcate healthy habits – namely a proper and healthy diet and regular exercise. As such, he takes a personal approach to his staff's health by regularly dining with them. The company doesn't believe in mandates (other than the no-smoking policy on factory grounds), but rather tries to encourage healthy habits through the posting of nutrition information in the eating areas and through occasional invited talks by medical experts. Mr. Huber has noticed a significant change in employees' diets in the past three years, with far less "junk food" and far more vegetables and fruits now that the workplace has become conducive to change. The company takes a three-pronged approach to wellness: education, facility (the kitchenettes) and physical activity. Physical activity includes organized walking, jogging and stretching led by Mr. Huber, who is a former military officer and exercise instructor.

Boncafé evaluates its wellness efforts every quarter. A recent evaluation revealed that although 30 per cent of the staff had some form of improvement in their health screening results, 23 per cent showed no improvement at all. The number of employees with blood pressure at the "normal-high" level rose

Workers at Boncafé can cook soups and other healthy meals in the "cooking points".

by 13 per cent; "bad" cholesterol levels rose by 8.34 per cent; and the BMI of those employees overweight increased by 5 per cent. So the wellness programme has shifted to target those employees with poorer health.

Possible disadvantages of food solution

None apparent.

Costs and benefits to enterprise

Boncafé did not need to purchase any of the cookware or food storage and cooking appliances, because these have been donated by the employees themselves. Water (for water coolers and distilled water) costs the company S$144 (US$88) per month.

Medical costs have dropped since 2002 by 37 per cent and medical leave has dropped by 25 per cent. Absenteeism is nil, and staff morale remains high despite a small lay-off and economic downturn due to the SARS outbreak. There has also been a noticeable improvement in the incidence of stroke and diabetes, although of course the sample size (60 employees) is small. The health of one employee diagnosed as having a mild stroke due to hypertension and high cholesterol has improved significantly; within a year, through diet and medication, his blood pressure and cholesterol levels have dropped to normal. As a result of worksite health screening, three cases of diabetes were detected at an early stage. These workers now can control their blood sugar levels through diet and exercise. The true pay-off of intervention cannot be measured, because the many conditions associated with diabetes – such as nerve damage, weakness, poor eyesight, heart disease, stroke and kidney disorders – can, if left unchecked, lead to untold expenses as a result of medical leave and accidents.

Government incentives

The Singapore Government, through its Health Promotion Board, offers the Workplace Health Promotion Grant to encourage the establishment of health programmes at work. The maximum grant is S$5,000, which must be at least matched by the company. Boncafé has not applied for a grant but does make use of the boards' posters and lectures.

Practical advice for implementation

Mr Huber said that employees certainly don't "jump into the bandwagon and go with the flow" when it comes to changing diet and exercise patterns. Changes at Boncafé were no overnight success but rather the result of three years of persistent persuasion. (Changing dietary and exercise habits, however, has been easier than persuading employees to quit smoking. Only 3 of 14 smokers have quit in the past couple of years despite numerous talks, posters and brochures.) Setting a personal example seems to have had a strong effect on changing employees' habits. For example, Mr. Huber and now many other employees walk the approximately 1.2 km each way to the MRT (public transit) station, which has had a snowball effect on getting other employees to exercise and think about health in general.

Union/employee perspective

The Food, Drinks and Allied Workers' Union (FDAWU) Assistant Executive Secretary, Samuel Tan, notes that, in general, the FDAWU supports employers providing cooking points to workers in factories. Management at several factories with FDAWU members are already providing cooking facilities and a pantry with, for example, microwave ovens and toasters. These electrical appliances are especially useful for workers performing nightshift duties. The union has supported various programmes organized by the National

Trades Union Congress (NTUC) Quality Lifestyle Department to improve workers' health and safety. From time to time, the unions organize talks on healthy food choices to educate workers on the need for proper diet and nutrition. These are public talks, such as an event staged in August 2004 at a busy MRT station. The August event was called the Healthier Food Trail; and union members picked up useful tips about nutrition, including healthy street food, healthy supermarket shopping, and cooking demonstrations.

Many employees have worked at Boncafé for more than ten years, and several have been with the company for over 25 years. There appears to be a casual, family-like atmosphere, which led to changes at the cooking points – that is, the use of shared appliances. Bonding among staff is quite common, and employees sometimes cook together. Employees seem to appreciate the cooking points as a means to have more control over what they eat and to also save money. "We used to eat at the hawker stalls during lunch," said one female employee. "Now that we have our own cooking points, we are better able to manage healthy eating, being in control." A male employee, in an interview with a television news reporter, said he ignored the health talks and posters offered at work through Singapore's Workplace Health Promotion Programme, and he continued to smoke and eat oily, salty foods. Then a heart attack came. He has since been able to eat healthier foods at work as a result of the cooking points, he said.

6.3   K. Mohan and Co.

Bangalore, India

Type of enterprise: K. Mohan is a garment manufacturer and exporter for the United States and European markets, which comprise about 70 per cent and 30 per cent of its business respectively. Clients include Nike, Banana Republic and Gap. (The complete list is at the end of this case study.) K. Mohan operates six factories all within a ten-kilometre radius near Bangalore city centre. Its average sales volume is US$40 million a year. In 2002, the company produced 3.5 million units, nearly equally divided between shirts/blouses and pants/shorts. The company has been operating since 1973, although a parent company dates back to 1954. (http://www.kmohan.com/)

Employees: 5,600 at six factories.

Food solution – key point: subsidized mess room with unlimited servings, soon with iron-supplementation programme.

K. Mohan and Co. has received high grades over the years for its treatment of workers. The factories are generally clean, comfortable and well lit, and the company offers many social benefits, such as childcare for its largely female workforce and access to medical care. To ensure decent factory conditions, the company works with the Global Alliance for Workers and Communities (GA), a partnership of private, public and non-governmental organizations. The GA regularly visits the K. Mohan factories and offers training and recommendations for improvement. Various aspects of K. Mohan's operations are described in the GA document *Developing health care programmes in associated factories* (Global Alliance, 2003b) The focus of this case study is K. Mohan's mess rooms.

Food solution

The K. Mohan mess rooms, for the most part, are large, clean and well ventilated. Full-time maids are responsible for their upkeep. Water quality is checked every six months. There are a few health concerns from facility to facility. Employees and food servers sometimes do not have adequate resources to clean up before eating or serving (no soap or towels, etc.), for example. Food is catered by outside companies and brought into the mess rooms, a common practice in India. The catering facilities are usually close by, within a couple of kilometres. These facilities are usually family-owned and handle one or a few clients a day, a total of a few thousand meals. Each catering facility has its own food safety concerns: no refrigeration, dirt floors and old cooking utensils, for example.

Most employees, depending on the factory, are treated to a free mid-morning coffee or tea break, at 10:30 a.m. Lunch is served at different times. Some factories break at 12:15. The Singasandra factory, the largest of the six with over 1,800 workers, has two lunch breaks, from 12:30 to 1 p.m. and 1 to 1:30 p.m. The mess room is located at the factory within an easy walk, a few minutes away, so workers have time during the break to actually eat and not spend their break obtaining food. Lunch is mandatory and subsidized, in clear contrast to most other (garment) factories in Bangalore. Workers elsewhere often bring a small packed lunch, if anything. The lunch at the K. Mohan factories costs Rs 7.50–8.00 (US$0.17–0.18) per worker per shift. The company pays Rs 5.50–6.00 (US$0.11–0.12), and the worker pays Rs 2.00–2.50 US$0.04–0.05). In Bangalore, Rs 2 (US$0.04) will buy a cup of tea on the street, so this is a good price for a full lunch. The average monthly salary is about Rs 2,800 (US$64) for an eight-hour day six days per week, comprising accrual of statutory benefits such as bonuses, gratuity, etc.

Lunch varies from day to day, factory to factory, but typical foods are rice, *rasam* (a spicy lentil soup), *sambar* (a rice lentil soup), beans, vegetables, pickles and buttermilk. After GA intervention, *pappad* (lentil cracker) was replaced by salads and sprouted grains (such as sprouted sunflower seeds) to offer a more balanced diet. Also, fried items were removed from the menu, ordinary salt was replaced by high-quality ionized salt and leafy green vegetables are now served twice a week. Workers are allowed unlimited amounts of staples such as rice and *rasam*. Other foods are restricted to one serving. Corporate managers in some factories have their own, separate lunch at a price of Rs 10 (US$0.20). This is essentially fancier food with better service. The average caloric content from lunch is about 750 kcal but could be higher considering that unlimited servings are available for some foods. Workers eat hardily. The average amount of protein per meal is 20 grams; the average iron amount is 18 mg; and the average beta-carotene amount is 400 mg. On first look, this may seem like enough iron, but supplementation is needed because iron-uptake is lower in a predominantly vegetable-cereal diet.

Anaemia is widespread in Bangalore. In some factories, up to 75 per cent of the female workers have anaemia. As detailed in Chapter 2, anaemia in adults, a condition marked by low concentrations of haemoglobin or "blood iron", often results in sluggishness, low endurance, and decreases in physical work capacity and work productivity for repetitive tasks. Global Alliance has proposed to treat anaemia with iron and folic acid supplements along with vitamin C. This is part of a planned worker awareness programme on nutrition

Workers at K. Mohan enjoy a new meal plan that includes unlimited rice and rasam *at a very affordable price.*

and sanitation. (Workers will be de-wormed too.) The intervention started in June 2004, and it is too early to report results.

Possible disadvantages of food solution

K. Mohan is generous with its meal subsidy compared with other garment factories in the region. And in that regard, considering this population is at risk of malnutrition as a result of poverty, the company should be commended. Time and timeliness concerns are well addressed, for workers have adequate time to eat and relax at an on-site eating facility. However, K. Mohan appears to have little control over food safety. The risk of mass food contamination is high. Global Alliance cited many food safety hazards at the off-site caterers and has made recommendations accordingly. Hazards include a lack of basins or restrooms for cooks and food handlers to wash their hands; poor staff knowledge of proper hygiene; poor storage facilities for perishable and non-perishable food, which invites insects and rodents; in some situations, a 45- to 60-minute travel time in warm weather between caterer and K. Mohan facility; old or faulty cooking equipment; questionable quality of iodized salt; and questionable freshness of food, possibly purchased in bulk at a discount. These concerns have been or are being addressed. K. Mohan workers receive medical examinations once a year. Previously, workers at the caterers did not receive such check-ups and were not tested for worms or communicable diseases. This changed after a recent GA visit and subsequent recommendations; these workers are now examined every six months. So, the "disadvantages" are rapidly disappearing.

Costs and benefits to enterprise

K. Mohan's cost of maintaining mess rooms is minimal, just soap and basic cleaning. The food subsidy costs about Rs 6.6 million (US$145,000) (4,000 workers, 300 meals, Rs 5.50 contribution). The de-worming tablets (albendazole) cost Rs 2.50 (US$0.05) and are taken once every six months. Iron and folic acid tablets are supplied by government hospitals free of cost. (The tablets are available commercially for about Rs 49 (US$0.98) for 30 tablets.)

Before the mandatory, subsidized lunch and tea break, in April 2001, the attrition rate was 7.39 per cent. This dropped to 5.3 per cent by April 2004. Similarly, absenteeism was 9.46 per cent in 2001 and 4 per cent in April 2004. There is no clear evidence, however, that changes in the catering service were responsible for this. Global Alliance will now monitor the effectiveness of the anaemia intervention. The factory managers report anecdotally of better morale and better health.

Government incentives

There is no government incentive to serve healthy food. Providing a canteen or mess room is a statutory requirement for employers with more than 250 employees at a facility. This is part of India's Factories Act of 1948.

Practical advice for implementation

K. Mohan is but one of many garment factories operating within developing countries or emerging economies with a focus on wealthy United States and European markets. Similar factories with similar economic resources in India and Southeast Asia pale in comparison with K. Mohan with regard to workers' nutrition. However, we see that little financial investment is needed to provide for basic nutrition. The K. Mohan approach could represent a lower-level, bare-minimum standard for the garment industry. With slightly more investment, big-name, image-conscious Western companies who purchase goods from factories in poorer nations could repair or upgrade the existing food-service infrastructure to ensure high-quality, safe and nutritious foods. A few tens of thousands of dollars per factory (and its caterer) per year can go a long way in helping hundreds of garment factory workers and their families.

Union/employee perspective

This is a non-union site. K. Mohan has a "workers' committee", as required under law, to address the workers' grievances. There is also a canteen managing committee, which deals with all problems related to the canteen. K. Mohan works with these committees and Global Alliance to improve the meal programme. Employees are generally happy. The canteen committee meets once a month or if there are any issues warranting a meeting. All of the proceedings are minuted and displayed in the local language on a notice board. The GA Bangalore team orchestrated several changes. After performing an appraisal (and in consultation with the management), GA helped change the menu to reflect a balanced diet. GA also helped train the cooking staff in proper hygiene; provided the cooking staff with a checklist for self-monitoring; instructed the garment workers on proper nutrition through plays and newsletters; and instructed pregnant and lactating mothers on the topic of good nutrition for pregnancy and nursing. The aforementioned Factory Act concerns the quality and quantity of food, the level of hygiene, the times of meals and the running of canteens. The Factory Act isn't always followed to the letter across India. Global Alliance and its recommendations, which seem to work as a de facto collective bargaining agreement, greatly improved workers' access to nutritious food. Global Alliance's approach seems widely applicable.

Information for this case study was extracted from several reports from Global Alliance including *An appraisal report on the improvement of nutritional aspects (canteen food, hygiene, water) and reduction of iron deficiency anaemia (IDA) in workers at their workplace*, prepared by Tara Gopaldas (Global Alliance, 2003a). The K. Mohan staff and the GA team (Beatrice Spadacini and Mary Sandhya Christopher) provided additional information. Note that other K. Mohan clients are Ralph Lauren, Polo Jeans, Jones Apparel Group, Decathlon, Lane Bryant, Kohls, Vetir, Shopko, J.C. Penney and Sears.

6.4 Spotlight on an NGO: The Global Alliance for Workers and Communities

The Global Alliance for Workers and Communities (GA), a partnership of private, public and non-governmental organizations, was established in 1999 to improve the workplace experience and future prospects of workers involved in global production and service supply chains in developing countries. The majority of these workers are young adults. Global Alliance was active from 1999 to 2004 in five countries (China, India, Indonesia, Thailand and Viet Nam) and reached over 330,000 workers in 54 factories.

The NGO worked with managers and workers in recommending and implementing change within the workplace. The organization's scope encompassed far more than the topic of workers' nutrition, which is subject of the preceding case study of the K. Mohan and Co. garment factories in India. Its focus was on worker development. This goes beyond code compliance to enhance workers' knowledge and skills in critical areas relating to health, workplace issues, personal finance and personal skills while also improving the workplace environment. It accomplished this through workers' surveys, factory visits and employee and management training. Global Alliance has indeed trained over 10,000 managers and supervisors, more than 100,000 factory workers and thousands of peer educators on a wide range of health and personal empowerment topics.

Its approach seemed to work well at K. Mohan, a non-unionized garment manufacturer for Western companies where workers have no formal representation. Employing a scrupulous methodology, similar to that of academics, GA staff and local consultants visited K. Mohan's six factories, examined the facilities, interviewed workers, organized health screenings and made a series of recommendations concerning nutrition. Essentially, GA recommended relatively simple and inexpensive yet crucial improvements to the canteens, along with a vitamin and mineral supplementation programme. K. Mohan already had a decent meal programme established, so improvements could be quickly implemented. Similar changes are being implemented in other garment factories in other countries where GA is active.

In many garment factories worldwide today, workers are now allowed breaks, including meal breaks, yet they have poor access to nutritious food. They are often left with the option of either street-vendor food, which they cannot afford in any significant quantity (assuming it is safe and nutritious), or packing a meagre lunch box (with no place at work to store it safely). As a result, workers are often sluggish or ill due to a lack of calories or nutrients. Earning the right to breaks is a significant victory. A subsidized, nutritious meal is the natural counterpart to a break. If one gets both, all the better. K. Mohan workers got both. In Bangalore, such a meal costs far less than a dollar or euro per day per worker.

Global Alliance's main corporate sponsors were the United States-based Nike and Gap companies. These companies appeared to rely on GA programmes to improve the workplace environment and to offer learning opportunities to the employees of their contract factories. For example, when this author approached Nike and Gap about the topic of workers' nutrition in the garment sector, both companies recommended speaking with GA. Representatives at Nike and Gap said that keeping track of working conditions at supply facilities worldwide, which they do not own, is an arduous task. (Representatives at the United States-based Starbucks company voiced a similar concern about coffee suppliers, as did Dole Food Company and Tropicana Products Inc.) Whether multinational companies are merely passing the buck should not be an issue here. K. Mohan is a Gap and Nike supplier, and through GA improvements were made. With little investment, large companies – as a sign of goodwill or to protect their corporate reputation – can greatly improve working conditions within today's vast supply chain by "outsourcing" responsibilities to organizations such as GA. To maximize its effectiveness, GA employed local experts who understand the culture in which the suppliers operate. Better understanding of social boundaries (such as "rankism" and gender roles) enables an organization to successfully implement improvements.

Global Alliance was an initiative of the International Youth Foundation. It also received technical and/or financial support from the Spanish apparel company Inditext, the World Bank, St John's University (in New York) and Pennsylvania State University. The web site is www.theglobalalliance.org.

6.5 Spotlight on California: 5-a-Day Worksite Program and Task Force on Youth and Workplace Wellness

Mention the word California and many images may come to mind. One often thinks of svelte Hollywood starlets, "hippie" vegetarians in San Francisco and endless beaches with endless sun cast upon fit, tanned bodies. Everybody, it seems, is in shape, partaking in the latest sport or diet fad. The reality of America's Golden State, however, is sobering.

Nearly 60 per cent of Californians are overweight or obese (California DOH, 2003a). Inactivity, overweight, and obesity cost the state an estimated US$24.6 billion a year in direct medical, lost productivity and workers' compensation costs, the highest in the United States (California DOH, 2003b). And although California produces more fruits and vegetables than any other state in America, Californians consume on average only 3.9 servings a day, far below the recommended five to nine servings to maintain an ideal weight and lower the risk of chronic diseases (California DOH, 2001). One of the most common reasons that Californians gave for not eating fruits and vegetables was that they were "hard to get at work", cited by 61 per cent of survey respondents (California DOH, 2001).

But change is afoot. In late 2002, the California 5-a-Day Worksite Program interviewed 40 business leaders chosen randomly, a list that included CEOs, human resource managers and benefits directors. The goals were to identify the type of unhealthy behaviours that affect employees and determine what was being done at worksites to improve employee health. The programme also conducted a series of focus groups throughout the state with low- and middle-income working women. The goal here was to identify barriers to healthy eating and physical activity at the workplace, and to describe factors that would encourage workers to eat more fruits and vegetables and perform more physical activity at work. In the end, a set of recommendations was extensive, with several categories organized by expense and ease of implementation (Backman and Carman, 2004). Recommendations targeted mess rooms and local vendors in particular. Among the programme results were the following:

- Assure that foods served at meetings are nutritious. Replace doughnuts, coffee and sodas with 100 per cent fruit or vegetable juice, fruits, vegetables and wholegrain bagels as standard fare for meetings.

- Provide large baskets of fresh fruits or vegetables for employees to eat throughout the day.

- Work with catering trucks to encourage them to offer low-cost healthy choices, with an emphasis on fruits and vegetables.

- Establish an on-site or neighbourhood farmers' market at a workplace or among several workplaces in collaboration with a group of employers.

- Provide appealing menu options at all workplace food services and mess rooms that meet healthy nutrition standards at reasonable prices.

- Provide food choices in vending machines that meet healthy nutrition standards. These can include fresh, canned and dried fruits, 100 per cent fruit or vegetable juice, plain or mixed nuts, low-fat bagged snacks, non-fat yoghurt and milk, salads, etc.

California has no laws in place that provide financial incentives to businesses to adopt these recommendations, such as tax breaks or subsidies. Pending approval as of early 2005 is California Senate Bill 74, which would require vending machines on state property to include at least 50 per cent healthy items. State property includes government buildings, state parks and roadside rest stops. The California Health Insurance Act of 2003 requires employers to help pay for employees' medical insurance. There is a provision that meals provided at the convenience of the employer are tax deductible, and this could include catered healthy food, yet few businesses seem to be aware or take advantage of this new tax deduction.

Incentives to provide healthy food at work largely come through business awards (and resulting publicity) and educational outreach tools from the California Department of Health Services and the California Task Force on Youth and Workplace Wellness. The Department of Health (DOH), a state-funded agency, oversees the California "5-a-Day" campaign", which encourages Californian adults to consume five or more servings of fruits and vegetables every day and be physically active at least 30 minutes a day. Specifically, the 5-a-Day Worksite Program – still in a developmental phase as of January 2005 and independently funded by a grant from the Centers of Disease Control and Prevention and the Department of Agriculture – is designed to increase fruit and vegetable consumption and physical activity among low- and middle-income employees. The programme views the workplace as a viable arena in which to promote health because over 70 per cent of working-age Californians are currently employed. Aside from undocumented migrant workers, most Californians are employed in the formal sector, and they spend nearly half of their waking hours at work (Trinkl, 1999). For the past decade nationally and in California, however, the five-a-day campaign has focused almost entirely on schools and communities.

The California Task Force, created by an act of state congress in 2002, also addresses the critical issues of fitness and nutritional health in California's schools and workplaces. In 2003, the task force presented its first California Fit Business awards to seven businesses of various sizes. In essence, these companies were recognized for meeting the aforementioned recommendations for changes in the mess rooms and in their approach to office foods, local vendors and health education. The strategy to include small companies, whose efforts were small but noteworthy, was intended to send a message that all businesses can apply similar improvements in the area of workers' nutrition, usually at a minimal or no cost.

The 2003 winners include American Apparel and San Mateo County, and their food solutions are described in the following two case studies. Another winner was L-3 Communications, a small United States Defense Department contractor who declined to be featured in a case study. L-3 has a variety of health and nutrition education programmes, along with kitchen and dining areas attached to recreational facilities (such as billiards and table tennis). The arrangement encourages workers, who have only 30 minutes for lunch, to get away from their desks and to cook and eat together instead of driving for take-away food. University Health Services (UHS) of the University of California, Berkeley, won the California Fit Business award for encouraging local shops to serve healthier foods. (UHS doesn't have a canteen or mess room.) The Contra Costa County Schools Insurance Group, with fewer than 50 employees, won the award for healthy changes to vending machines; monthly brown bag "lunch 'n' learn" presentations on topics such nutrition and physical activity; and its switch from pastries to fresh fruit and bagels at on-site meetings – an example of how little things can make a difference.

In California and across the United States, providing fruit and vegetables at the workplace appears to be a missed opportunity. California sees itself as a leader among states regarding health initiatives and environmental activism. California is well known in the United States, for example, for its voter referendums, which mandate government actions concerning food and product safety. The five-a-day campaign was born in California in 1988 through a grant from the United States National Cancer Institute, and today California has the largest budget among the 50 American states to promote the campaign, US$4 million in 2004. Thus far, the campaign's primary success has been increasing awareness of the importance of fruits and vegetables for maintaining a healthy weight and reducing the risk of chronic diseases. That is, more people are aware of what they are supposed to eat. Success in increasing fruit and vegetable consumption has been minimal: only 40 per cent of women and 29 per cent of men eat at least five-a-day, and only 13 per cent of women and 4 per cent of men eat the upper-tier recommendation of nine-a-day

(DiSogra and Taccone, 2003). The lack of success may be the result of focusing efforts on the community as a whole, which often leads to awareness but not change.

Pilot studies finally undertaken in schools in 2002–03 that provided healthy food alternatives in vending machines, cafeterias and schools stores have shown greater success in changing poor dietary habits (Baer and Hausman, 2003). This may imply that the American workplace could also benefit from a targeted five-a-day programme that provides healthy food alternatives. Denmark is one country that has succeeded in increasing fruit and vegetable consumption among adults with its Free Fruit at Work campaign (see Chapter 7). California's 5-a-Day Worksite Program is just beginning, and it is not yet clear whether this will be largely education based or will involve increasing the availability of healthy foods at work. Produce companies such as Dole Food Company, Inc., who have worked closely with schools in recent years, may find new business opportunities working with manufactures and other enterprises.

Further information about California's 5-a-Day Worksite Program and the California Task Force on Youth and Workplace Wellness is available at: http://www.ca5aday.com and http://wellnesstaskforce.org, respectively. The 5-a-Day Worksite Program press kits are available at: http://ca5aday. netcomsus.com/index.php/press_kit.html.

6.6 American Apparel

Los Angeles, California, United States

Type of enterprise: American Apparel is the largest garment factory in the United States, with the capacity to produce over 200,000 pieces per day. Nearly every aspect of production is performed at the company's downtown Los Angeles facility, and this includes knitting, cutting, sewing, photography, design, marketing and distribution. (http://www.americanapparel.net/)

Employees: 2,100.

Food solution – key point: dining area with subsidized, catered, healthy foods for the predominantly minority workforce.

American Apparel was a winner of the 2003 California Fit Business awards for its commitment to employee health and wellness. The majority of the employees are women, mostly Latin American, although there are also a substantial number of Asian employees. Many employees are also recent immigrants from Mexico, Central America, China or Southeast Asia who came to the United States to escape war or poverty in their homelands. Traditionally, such immigrants in the United States have had limited access to health care, and they experience higher levels of stress and violence, higher rates of death from chronic diseases and greater risk of excessive weight gain, particularly the Latin American groups. Thus, receiving a proper meal at work in a relaxing setting significantly adds to their quality of life.

Food solution

American Apparel provides subsidized healthy breakfasts and lunches to employees, including daily salads and fruit offerings. The meals are freshly cooked and brought in every day by a company called the Market Place. The company sells US$15 lunch cards, good for five meals (hence US$3 per meal, which is nearly half the price of a similar quality meal outside the factory). The breakfast menu includes omelettes, pancakes, french toast, ham and eggs and breakfast sandwiches. The lunch menu reflects the ethnic makeup of the staff: *quesadillas, enchiladas, posole* (a stew with potatoes and maize), *cocido* (a stew with chick peas), chicken *mole*, rice and beans, teriyaki chicken and chow mein noodles. The menu also includes fruit salads, vegetable salads and soups. In

223

addition, there are two lunch trucks just outside the factory and vending machines in the dining area. The vending machines offer coffee, soft drinks, juices, milk, snacks and healthy options such as chicken, tuna or egg sandwiches and bean burritos. A local restaurant is allowed into the factory to sell fruit to employees at between US$1.25–2.75 per bowl.

Workers are allowed 30 minutes for meals, along with two 15-minute breaks during the day. The dining area is the centre of the workers' community, a place to socialize. Several hundred meals are sold each day. Many employees bring a packed lunch or purchase food at the lunch trucks or vending machines. The catered lunches were introduced partly to reduce congestion in the dining area. Too many employees needed to heat their lunches in microwave ovens, leaving only around ten minutes to eat. (The constant microwave usage was a drain on power too, setting off circuit breakers.) Congestion is now greatly reduced, and employees can spend most of their break eating, socializing and relaxing. Having easy food options at work can mean less time preparing food in the morning. This is particularly important for female workers with children, because culture and gender roles tend to dictate that they are the ones who must prepare meals for their children. Some employees form informal "teams" and bring potluck-style lunches. Each member of the team is responsible for bringing one item. This adds variety to lunch and saves money.

American Apparel is working with California State University, Northridge, specifically with its departments of Kinesiology, Health Sciences, and Family Consumer Sciences. One goal is to provide healthier prepared food. The company is bringing together nutritionists from the university and the Market Place to meet this goal. The Health Sciences Department is also developing an education outreach and activity plan. Nutrition information in Spanish and Asian languages is available on site through a collaborative effort with the non-profit Garment Worker Center.

Together with the Kinesiology Department, American Apparel is devising better ergonomic conditions at work. The company already offers free massage therapists to reduce repetitive motion injuries, and it is currently building an on-site health and wellness facility, which will provide drop-in health counselling, as well as exercise classes to be held before and after business hours and during lunch breaks.

Possible disadvantages of food solution

Although the menu is ethnically appropriate, some of the items offered – namely, fatty pork and beef dishes – might contribute to obesity. The new menu designed by nutritionists will address this issue, though. It is not clear why more workers don't take advantage of the US$3-lunch. This might be still too expensive for some workers, such as those with large families. Or maybe packing a lunch or eating only a snack for a midday meal is part of their culture. Beverages are not included with the meal, and this has led to an unexpected advantage where employees sometimes choose free water over sugary drinks. While the vending machines have healthy options, it is unclear whether the lunch trucks (serving tacos, for example) are a source of unhealthy food. The enduring presence of the trucks and the number of repeat customers would indicate that food safety is not a concern.

Costs and benefits to enterprise

American Apparel buys meals in bulk for around US$4 and sells them for US$3. Northridge provides its consultation for free. This is "real life" training for graduate and undergraduate students. Translation costs are minimal.

American Apparel has a remarkably stable and loyal workforce, and benefits in general have led to reduced absenteeism and substantially less turnover in comparison with the industry as a whole.

Government incentives

The California Health Insurance Act of 2003 requires employers to help pay for employees' medical insurance. There is a provision that meals provided at the convenience of the employer are tax deductible, and this could include the catered food that American Apparel brings in daily. The company doesn't seem to be aware or take advantage of this new tax deduction.

Practical advice for implementation

American Apparel has employed many practical, cost-saving ideas to provide employees with better access to healthy food, and other small companies can do the same. The nutritional and ergonomic advice is free, from a local university. This is an interesting contrast to the paid consultation at the Phosphate Hill mine in Australia, a company with far deeper financial resources. Professor Steven Loy of Northridge, who helps oversee the programme, says there are students yearning for the opportunity to put the theory they have learned in the classroom to work in the real world. He has created a model that can be duplicated at other universities; and he is hoping to persuade administrators and politicians to expand this model across California to help other workers (and students).

The dining area itself is low budget: basically a room that needs to be kept clean. Food is brought in, so no additional funds are needed for a mess room staff. Vending machines complement the catering, and they too require little funding. Inviting a vendor inside the plant to sell fruit is an excellent and essentially free way to help workers reach the national five-a-day fruit and vegetable goal. The potluck teams add to diversity and morale with no extra cost to the employer.

Union/employee perspective

American Apparel is a non-union site. Many of the company's improvements are a result of direct feedback from the employees. For example, at first employees did not like the food programme because there were few options. They voiced that complaint, and now they can have a different dish every day. Yet the basis for most of the company's benefits – the free massages, the food programme, the exercise programme which includes free bicycles for commuting, non-monitored bathroom breaks, natural lighting, paid vacation, relatively high wages (nearly three times the minimum wage, on average), family health care and employee training – stems from a core company value of being a "sweatshop-free" enterprise. As in the Husky case study, once again we see a charismatic company founder, Dov Charney, being the impetus for change.

6.7   San Mateo County Municipality

Redwood City, California, United States

Type of enterprise: this is a county government. San Mateo County is located immediately south of the city and county of San Francisco, a relatively wealthy urban and suburban county with a population of approximately 730,000 and a geographic area covering 1,163 square km. (http://www.co.sanmateo.ca.us)

Employees: approximately 700, 75 per cent male..

Food solution – key point: a new mess room with subsidized food as the result of the formation of a union and subsequent collective bargaining.

San Mateo County was a winner of the 2003 California Fit Business awards for its commitment to employee health and wellness. The county maintains a diverse workforce with widely varying services typical of a county government. The largest departments are the San Mateo Medical Center and Clinics, the Health Services Agency, the Sheriff's Office and the Human Services Agency. There are over 70 offices situated throughout the county, including facilities that operate continuously (correctional facilities, a juvenile hall and the hospital). Some employees are peripatetic, in remote locations or on 10- or 12-hour shifts. Due to the nature of their work, many workers cannot leave their workstations without someone taking their place. The meal break varies from 30 minutes to one hour, depending upon operational needs and work schedule.

San Mateo County workers have no central canteen, and the canteens vary in quality. The Medical Center has a canteen offering healthy food choices (low-fat dishes, fruits and vegetables), as well as accompanying nutritional information and occasional nutrition education campaigns. This is typical of American hospitals and health clinics in recent years. Another canteen, operated by a contractor of the State Department of Rehabilitation, offers a soup and salad bar in addition to made-to-order grill selections and packaged snack food. There is no central vending machine policy regarding food selections.

Food solution

In face of this diversity of working conditions, the county has developed an education-based nutritional programme along with a few incentives so that workers can make healthy choices wherever they are. The county's Employee

Health and Fitness Program has had nutritionists on contract since 1994. Educational outreach includes: "lunch 'n' learn" seminars that include healthy cooking demonstrations; regular courses on blood pressure, cholesterol and diabetes; and nutrition e-mail campaigns that highlight healthy foods in an A-to-Z format or featured colours. To reach employees in a cost-effective and timely manner, the county makes use of e-mail and the Internet to post course offerings.

Financial incentives include a modest (US$5) reward for following the national five-a-day fruit and vegetable regime by maintaining health logs, and larger cash rewards (US$75–200) for enrolling in the Blue Shield Healthy Lifestyle Rewards Program and adopting a healthier lifestyle. (Blue Shield is a United States-based health insurance company.) For the past 20 years, San Mateo County government has provided access to the Weight Watchers at Work programme and for the past ten years it has offered a financial incentive to participate: eligible employees receive a 50–100 per cent reimbursement for attending class and losing weight. Complementing the county's efforts on nutrition is an emphasis on physical activity. Programmes include a self-directed fitness incentive programme, on-site exercise classes and fitness education workshops. On-site exercise classes require a fee and are performed during non-working hours.

Possible disadvantages of food solution

Employees are largely left on their own. Employees might be too busy or otherwise uninterested in reading e-mails. Such a system might not go far enough in helping employees overcome the temptation of skipping lunch or grabbing a quick lunch of unhealthy food as a result of having no nearby healthy option or having the pressure of relieving co-workers at a service desk.

Costs and benefits to enterprise

The total cost for nutrition education, incentives and other services in 2003 was under US$12,000. This included the training costs and programme development costs.

From 2001 to 2003, the Weight Watchers at Work programme saw 1,066 participants (some of whom were repeats) attending 10- or 12-week programmes offered in six county locations. Among these participants, 151 received tuition reimbursement. Total weight lost among these 151 employees was 1,870.8 pounds (848.6 kg) or an average weight loss of 12.4 pounds (5.6 kg) per claim. Of those claims, 62 per cent were from employees with a BMI measurement of greater than 30. Also from 2001 to 2003, various nutritional training sessions and noontime seminars attracted 198 participants

Welcome to the fifth COLORFUL week of the 5-A-Day Nutrition Challenge!

This week we will be focusing on the colors
Orange & yellow

The Orange & YELLOW group includes oranges, tangerines, peaches, nectarines, and papayas. These fruits provide beta-cryptothanxin, a minor carotenoid that provides a very small but important fraction of the daily amount of carotenoids we all consume, and has been associated with decreased risk of cervical cancer.

Did you know that peaches are now in season, along with nectarines? The Farmer's Markets sport a wide variety of each fruit, ranging from deep yellow-orange to white; all full of juicy, luscious flavor. California produces more peaches than any other state, even Georgia, who claims it for their state fruit! Peaches contribute $943 million dollars to California's total economy.

To learn more about peaches and to taste some of their delights, go to the CALIFORNIA PEACH FESTIVAL held in Downtown Marysville, California, July 19, 2003, noon to midnight. Check it out at www.capeachfestival.com or call (530) 671-9600.

Fresh Nectarine (or Peach) Frosty

2 lg Nectarinesor peaches; pitted and sliced
1 Banana; peeled and sliced
10 Ice Cubes
2 tb Frozen Lemonade Concentrate

Combine all ingredients in a blender and, on high speed, blend until smooth. Pour into 2 8-oz glasses and serve at once.

Just Fruit Recipes - www.justfruitrecipes.com

Papayas

• Choose richly colored papayas that give slightly to palm pressure. If all you can find are slightly green fruit, don't worry — they'll ripen quickly at home.

The first page of a weekly two-page flyer about nutrition. San Mateo has alternative themes throughout the year; this theme focuses on fruit and vegetable colour.

(again, some were repeats). In addition, 165 employees participated in the five-a-day nutrition campaign and 45 per cent of the participants self-reported meeting their nutrition goal of eating five or more servings of fruit or vegetables for five or more days a week. No assessment has been made yet on whether these health improvements have contributed to a reduction in health costs for San Mateo County.

Government incentives

No financial incentives in terms of tax breaks or subsidies are available for the aforementioned programmes.

Practical advice for implementation

E-mail seems to be a successful and low-cost method to reach employees, but whether they read the information is uncertain. Ms. Pamela Gibson, the Health Program Coordinator, said that it is important not to bombard the employee with health information, yet health messages do need to arrive regularly. "Over the years we've learned not to send e-mails daily (we send one weekly message with five attachments), to keep the text at a readable length, and to offer practical tips or easy recipes to make it easy for someone to try something new," Ms. Gibson said. "We also intersperse basic nutrition information with more complex topics to meet almost everybody's interests." She added that "one sure-fire way to increase participation levels" for the nutritional programmes on hypertension, cholesterol and diabetes is to include lunch as both a teaching tool and a source of nourishment.

Union/employee perspective

The local union commented positively about San Mateo's efforts in the area of workers' nutrition. "The programs have been great. The e-mail information on nutrition has been the 'daily word' full of new and useful information," said Marlene Smith, former president of Service Employees International Local 715 and currently a steward. "San Mateo", she said, "helps us solve the 'what shall I prepare for dinner' question." San Mateo county employees generally have reacted positively to the health promotion programmes. Anonymous surveys consistently rank the hypertension, cholesterol and diabetes management courses as "good" or "excellent". Nearly all participants self-report achieving at least one of the goals set at the beginning of these courses. Criticism seems to focus on course limitations – such as availability, scheduling conflicts and crowded classes – which may improve as demand grows.

6.8　Russian-British Consulting Centre

Rostov-on-Don, Russian Federation

Type of enterprise: the Russian-British Consulting Centre (RBCC) was established in January 1997 as a result of a joint initiative of the Rostov Oblast Administration and the British Government. The centre serves as a technical aid programme of the Know-How Fund that provides independent consulting support to the business community, local authorities, companies of various ownership forms and private entrepreneurs. Its main services are business planning, investment design, development strategies, financial management, marketing research and business training. In 2003, RBCC's turnover was US$96,000. (http://www.rbcc.ru)

Employees: 12.

Food solution – key point: a kitchenette plus a shared municipal canteen with other companies in an office complex.

Most of the employees in this small company prefer to take lunch in the office. Employees at RBCC work from 9 a.m. to 6 p.m. Monday to Friday, with an hour for lunch taken by choice between noon and 2 p.m. Lunch is often taken in groups. This suits the company well because "team building" and sharing thoughts over lunch is important in the consulting business. Employees bring a packed lunch, buy lunch at a nearby shop or visit a shared canteen near the office complex and then return to the office to eat.

Food solution

The RBCC has a small kitchen with a refrigerator, microwave oven, hot water, dishes, a table and chairs. This makes storing and reheating food convenient. Employees are responsible for keeping the kitchen clean; and because the company is small, this is never a problem. The company provides many free beverages, which are kept in the kitchen. There is coffee, and black and green tea, with milk. The organization was buying bottled water, which cost around US$20 a month. In 2004 the company installed a filter on the spigot, which provides water of equally high quality at a fraction of the cost of bottled water. (See a second RBCC case study in Chapter 9.)

On any given day, three or four workers bring a packed lunch. This is the most inexpensive and potentially healthiest food option. The food is always homemade and usually contains salad and hearty bread. Another two or three workers visit a local shop. This is a short walk, and workers have plenty of time to grab something and return to eat. Shops offer cooked salads, sandwiches, sausages and canned goods at a cost of approximately US$1.70 for a decent lunch. Half the staff use a municipal canteen situated near the office complex. Here they can buy a salad, hot soup (four or five types daily), a main course (four or five types daily), baked roll or bun and fruit compote. This costs 65 rubles (US$2.00).

The canteen, called Municipal Canteen 1, is open from 9 a.m. to 5 p.m. Monday to Friday, and it can accommodate up to 100 people at a time. It is open to the 20 offices in the four-storey office complex where RBCC is situated. Such an arrangement is not uncommon in the Russian Federation. The canteen once belonged solely to the municipality but now operates as a commercial venture. Aside from local office workers, customers include city workers and others in the area who receive food tickets or similar subsidies for lunch. Municipal Canteen 1 also provides food for schools and special events. The meal is slightly more expensive than food bought at a shop; but it offers a more well-rounded and filling meal, and it is up to five times less expensive than a restaurant. A restaurant lunch would cost about 300 rubles (US$10). In typical canteen fashion, customers help themselves and bring their food to a table (or take it away). The food is simpler than restaurant fare and the interior is plain. There are no waiting staff, although a canteen worker clears dirty dishes. Canteen work is a low-paying job, too. All these factors, good or bad, contribute to the lower price.

With a full hour for lunch at RBCC and with the canteen and shops so close, employees have plenty of time to rest or to take a walk. One other feature of the RBCC meal programme worth noting is that the company gives its employees three litres of honey once a year, in July. Honey is thought to stimulate the body's immune system, and workers share the honey with their families.

Possible disadvantages of food solution

None apparent. Desktop dining is generally frowned upon in most companies because it increases stress, raises the risk of food-borne diseases and can damage computers and other equipment. The kitchenette lures workers away from their desks, and the extended lunch hour provides time to stretch and rest.

Costs and benefits to enterprise

US$30 a month for coffee, tea and milk; US$15 per employee per year for honey.

The RBCC is a small company with flexible benefits. Morale is high, and the atmosphere is friendly. The pleasant and convenient eating area at work encourages team building, a boon to the company.

Government incentives

No government incentives are received for RBCC's meal programme. Municipal Canteen 1 has small tax advantages over restaurants. One tax break is municipality electricity tax, which is 30 per cent lower than a restaurant's tax rate.

Practical advice for implementation

The centre makes the most of its small office. The water filter is a clever solution to provide clean water to employees at a low cost. Most companies, large and small, can install these commercially available filters and save up to 90 per cent on their bottled water bill. Setting aside an area in the office to store, heat and eat food is an ideal means for a small company to offer some meal benefit in lieu of a canteen. Kitchenettes are inexpensive to create and maintain. Employees who know there is a special, clean place to prepare and eat food at work are more likely to bring a healthy, packed lunch from home. This saves the worker money. Special diligence is needed, however, in keeping it clean, or it will attract insects and become an eyesore. This would certainly discourage use.

Union/employee perspective

Many of RBCC's employees have worked extensively in the United Kingdom and British colleagues visit occasionally. All are impressed that one can buy a filling meal for less than a British pound. This is a non-union site. The company is small enough to hold meetings to discuss benefits or other concerns. The workers are generally pleased with the eating arrangements.

6.9 Spotlight on Bangladesh: Turning the page on poor workers' nutrition

Despite major gains in food production and burgeoning industries, such as the garment export industry, Bangladesh remains a country with persistent poverty and malnutrition. Bangladesh has been the site of much international focus, and it is well understood that simply supplying food to this country of 135 million people is no "silver bullet" to bring about long-lasting, positive development.

The cause and persistence of Bangladesh's malnutrition epidemic is multifaceted. Historically, Bangladesh has had difficulty recovering from years of colonization. Nature itself serves crushing blows year after year with soil erosion, monsoons and flooding, some of which are thought to be exacerbated by global warming. Bangladesh is now deep in a downward spiral of malnutrition, in which adult populations themselves have suffered through malnutrition and paid the price with stunted growth (physically and mentally) and poor health – which affects their ability to work and therefore their ability to feed themselves and their families. The political environment over the years has not always fostered development, and pockets of corruption exist today, which hinder development. The Bangladeshi culture is diverse and complex, with a largely rural base rooted in subsistence farming. Knowledge of proper nutrition and hygiene varies with income, with the wealthiest being the most informed. Deep traditions of female and male expectations also can interfere with development efforts. Nationally, the literacy rate is below 50 per cent, and is lower among women, who are in charge with food preparation. This makes health education all the more difficult.

This section is not intended to describe the cultural, historical and economic factors behind the widespread poverty in Bangladesh. For a more complete treatment, refer to *Report on workers' nutrition in Bangladesh* by Professor Golam Mowlah, Director of the Institute of Nutrition and Food Sciences at the University of Dhaka (Mowlah, 2004). The 48-page report was prepared especially for this ILO publication and is available upon request from the ILO Dhaka office. This section, in contrast, is intended to serve as a snapshot of the Bangladesh workforce and as an introduction to a case study on the garment industry.

The vast majority of the Bangladesh workforce can be divided into three broad categories: physical labour, industrial labour and farming. Physical labour includes rickshaw pullers, baby-taxi and taxi operators, bricklayers and construction workers, miners and those employed digging or filling earth. Most of these activities are outdoors. Industrial labour refers to heavy and light industry, from large to small, as well as cottage and handicraft industries.

This includes garments and textiles, food processing and distribution, electronics and engineering, pottery, blacksmithing and tool making. Farming includes ploughing, tilling, planting, irrigating, fertilizing and harvesting, often performed by "landless" workers, both male and female. Over 90 per cent of the workforce are engaged in the informal sector. Access to food varies across geographical region, occupation, landholding, income and education, which themselves are clearly interrelated.

Around 84 per cent of the rural population work in agriculture. Nationally, agriculture constitutes approximately 63 per cent of the workforce (formal and informal) and contributes 32 per cent of GDP. Despite living so close to food sources, these workers are among the most vulnerable to malnutrition. This is because crop production is not necessarily diverse, and their diets tend to be largely grain based. Without land of their own, these workers have difficulty planting their own crops (such as leafy vegetables and beans) or raising chickens. Furthermore, during periods of famine, this population is hardest to reach with food relief.

Urban workers are either non-migrant or migrant, broadly defined as poor or very poor. Non-migrant workers work near their homes and, in general, have better access to food and thus a slightly better health outlook. These workers are employed in industry, particularly the established and better-paying industries such as engineering or tool making. Migrant workers are the most poverty-stricken people in Bangladesh. They take the lowest-paying jobs, such as those in the garment industry (a new industry, dominated by female workers) and involving physical labour, often paid by the day. They reside mostly in slums or shanty towns. Migration has been the result of population growth, a decrease in agricultural lands as a result of urbanization, an increase of landless people, rural unemployment, land erosion and natural calamities.

Workers in the informal sector have little guarantee of a meal or a comfortable meal break during the working day. Some workers pack a small lunch and eat this whenever and wherever they can. Informal sector employers rarely provide food but do often provide some type of break. In the formal sector, meals (snacks or lunch, free or subsidized) and breaks are far more common. These meals are often not substantial but rather just enough to help the worker continue through the day. The most pressing nutritional concerns facing workers are a lack of calories and nutrients. Up to 75 per cent of the population does not consume enough calories to perform work, that is, less than 2,100 kcal. Nearly 75 per cent of adult women are anaemic. Over 55 per cent of women aged 15 to 44 have iodine deficiency disorders.

The estimated annual cost of malnutrition in Bangladesh is US$1 billion (World Bank, 2000). This is approximately 14 per cent of Bangladesh's US$7 billion budget expenditure. The country spends about US$246 million

Table 6.1 Food intake by income in rural Bangladesh

Type of food	Minimum requirement (grams/day)	Consumption (grams/day)			Consumption as percentage of requirement		
		Poor	Middle	Rich	Poor	Middle	Rich
Grains	437	439	542	569	100	124	130
Pulses	40	14	21	25	35	53	63
Fish	48	24	41	61	50	83	127
Meat, eggs	12	4	8	20	33	67	167
Vegetables	177	151	210	257	85	119	145
Milk	58	12	29	49	21	50	85

Sources: Bangladesh Bureau of Statistics; and Mahbub Hossains: "Food security, agriculture and the economy: The next 25 years", in *Food strategies in Bangladesh: Medium and long-term perspectives* (Dhaka, Bangladesh Planning Commission, University Press Ltd., 1989).

Table 6.2 Caloric intake of selected workers in Bangladesh

Occupation	Average caloric intake in sample households					
	Rural		Urban		National	
	No. households surveyed	of kcal	No. households surveyed	of kcal	No. households surveyed	of kcal
Cultivator >100 decimal[1] of operated land	217	2 094	17	1 919	234	2 081
Cultivator <100 decimal[1] of operated land	68	1 952	5	1 893	73	1 948
Day labourer	212	1 834	19	1 744	231	1 827
Rickshaw/van puller	30	1 827	7	1 673	37	1 799
Skilled labour	76	1 762	35	1 796	111	1 773
Beggar	5	1 812		1 473	5	1 727

Note: [1] A decimal is a unit of land in Bangladesh equal to around 25 square metres.

Source: National Nutrition Survey of Bangladesh 1995/96, Institute of Nutrition and Food Science, Dhaka University, 1997.

fighting malnutrition and could lose US$22 billion in productivity costs over the next ten years without adequate health investment (World Bank, 2000). The United Nations System Standing Committee on Nutrition's *Fifth Report on the World Nutrition Situation*, published in March 2004, states that the annual "discounted present value of economic productivity losses" attributed

Table 6.3 Nutrient intake of landless workers in Bangladesh – all below WHO recommendations except for carbohydrates

Nutrients	Intake		
	Rural	Urban	National
Calorie (kcal)	1 716	1 752	1 734
Macronutrients:			
Protein (grams)	42	49	45.5
Fat (grams)	13.68	23.84	18.76
Carbohydrates (grams)	355	335	345
Micronutrients and vitamins:			
Calcium (mg)	318	359	338.5
Iron (mg)	10.27	12.53	11.46
Vitamin A (IU)	1 400	1 780	1 590
Thiamine (mg)	1.08	1.09	1.085
Riboflavin (mg)	0.43	0.49	0.46
Niacin (mg)	16.81	16.87	16.84
Vitamin C (mg)	29.99	58.83	44.41

Source: National Nutrition Survey of Bangladesh, Institute of Nutrition and Food Science, Dhaka University, 1995/96

to iron deficiency anaemia alone is estimated to be 7.9 per cent of GDP, the highest among any nation (United Nations, 2004, p. 14).

The tables opposite and above provide an overview of the nutritional status of workers in Bangladesh. Table 6.1 describes food consumption by food type and shows that Bangladesh's population consumes enough grains per day but that only the wealthiest have a full, well-balanced diet. Table 6.2 shows that, regardless of occupation, most workers do not consume enough calories. Table 6.3 shows that only the carbohydrate recommendation is met and that all other macro- and micronutrients are lacking from most diets.

Nearly 30 million workers suffer from hunger and malnutrition. The situation will remain unchanged if the benefits of growth at the national level, now finally realized, are not equally distributed among the people. Vulnerable group feeding (VGF) cards and the food-for-work (FFW) programme are not enough to alleviate poverty. Better long-term programmes are necessary, particularly those reflecting a concerted effort among the Bangladesh Government, international governmental bodies, health organizations and NGOs.

New intervention programmes such as school health education and school feeding programmes in selected regions, beginning in 2002, have proved to be cost-effective measures to improve health. These programmes are managed together by national and international groups. Similarly, studies are under way to assess the effectiveness of vitamin and mineral supplements for children and mothers. No similar projects are planned for the workplace, which is in so many ways like a school: where a known population (the workers) returns to a known location (the workplace) for a known period (the eight-hour working day), day after day and year after year. Intervention and follow-up would be easy to accomplish.

The National Nutrition Survey, to be undertaken in 2005, could provide new insights into the nutritional status of Bangladesh's workers and how to improve the situation. The following case study concerns workers' nutrition in the garment industry. This highlights a basic worker food programme, which can be viewed as a good start.

This information was compiled by Professor Golam Mowlah.

6.10 Bangladesh garment sector: I Garments, Bantai Industries and MVM Garments

Dhaka, Bangladesh

Type of enterprise: the following case study concerns the meal arrangements at three garment factories in Dhaka, Bangladesh. Each factory prepares garments on order for export, mostly to American and European companies. Garment production is a major source of foreign capital in Bangladesh. The garment sector comprises 4,000 units, directly or indirectly employing 20 million workers and grossing over US$5 billion annually. Workers are mostly drawn from migrant populations, 85 per cent female.

Employees: I Garments has 575 workers; Bantai has 480; MVM Garments has 1,200.

Food solution – key point: subsidized or free meals, clean drinking water.

Food solution

The Bangladesh Factory Act of 1965 mandates factories with more than 250 employees to provide workers with convenient access to food and an hour for lunch. Canteens and mess rooms are to be managed by a committee with worker representation. The Act also specifies what basic foodstuffs need to be served. However, only 5 per cent of garment factories maintain a canteen; the factories are either too small, or they are skirting the law. Workers are also protected under the Bangladesh Export Processing Zone (EPZ) Authority Act of 1980. This covers various aspects of health, safety and welfare, including toilet and canteen facilities. However, the Act covers export processing zones (EPZ) in Bangladesh; and these zones, created in 1980, are off-limits to trade unions until 2006. (See the "Union/employee perspective" section, below.)

Many regard the vast garment-export industry in Bangladesh as a success story in terms of craft standards and meeting the high demands of international buyers. Workers' welfare and social development also rank high, by the overall standards of industry in Bangladesh. For example, most factories strictly enforce child labour and are increasingly respecting overtime rules. The nutritional status of garment workers, however, is often at risk because these workers are mostly a migrant population from very low-income classes, often with poor health and malnutrition problems before they even set foot in a garment factory. The garment workers are particularly vulnerable to anaemia and other micronutrient deficiencies. (Chronic diseases such as heart disease and diabetes are not a great concern because, tragically, life expectancy is only around 55 years.) A study of female garment workers in Dhaka revealed that the daily caloric intake ranged between 1,567 and 1,714 kcal. The prevalence of anaemia (Hb<12g/dl) was between 37 and 52 per cent. Half of the study population was underweight, with BMI measurements below 16. In terms of recommended daily intake, calories fell short at 81 per cent, vitamin A was only 61 per cent, iron was 67 per cent, riboflavin was 37 per cent and vitamin C was only 89 per cent (Institute of Nutrition and Food Science, 1998). And these are labourers who have to work hard to make a living.

To cope with the poor nutrition of its workers, I Garments and MVM Garments provide a relatively inexpensive food service programme. Bantai Industries had a progressive programme but can no longer maintain it during the recent downturn in garment orders.

I Garments

With just over 500 employees (mostly female), I Garments is a mid-size factory. The production line comprises mostly knitted items: woven shirts, pants, jackets, skirts and evening wear. The factory also has a crew for cutting, sewing, finishing and quality-control inspection. I Garments won the 2004 Wal-Mart award for its product quality, performance and treatment of workers. No worker is younger than 18. Salary and benefits are relatively good and include a bonus for regular attendance and double pay for overtime. The working day is eight hours. Workers are entitled to 14 paid "ceremonial day" holidays, 10 casual days, 14 medical days and up to 22 earned vacation days. The salary for non-management varies between 1,000 and 2,500 taka (US$17–42) per month, which is slightly above the industry average. Social programmes include childcare, health education and health care (including family planning services), annual picnics and cultural events and entertainment. The factory itself is clean, well-ventilated and well-equipped for fire and other emergencies. Full-time cleaners keep the facility clean. Its profitability in the presence of above-average working conditions can serve as an example for other garment factories. It should be noted, however, that many workers are paid by the piece and that work can be demanding.

The dining area (about 200 square metres) is wide, well-ventilated and clean, with an attached bathroom where workers can wash. The dining area is maintained by workers and a full-time cleaner. Bathrooms are generally clean and supplied with towels and soap. Workers break for an hour, generally beginning at 1 p.m. During this time, workers take a lunch box into the dining area. I Garments, like many garment factories, offers a free tiffin, or snack, which costs the company about 5.50 taka (less than US$ 1 cent) per person. The tiffin, distributed at noon, contains bread, a sweet and either a banana or egg. I Garments had planned to offer a subsidized lunch, but workers chose the free tiffin option instead. (I Garments is still considering offering a free lunch, though.) Workers bring the tiffin, a packed lunch or both into the dining area. A caterer provides all the food, and no cooking is done in the dining area. The dining area is close to the factory floor, and workers have ample time for eating and resting. Some workers live closer than a ten-minute walk to the factory and eat lunch at home with their family.

Food safety is a matter of great concern for the whole population of Bangladesh. In the warm and wet climate with little refrigeration, foods can easily become contaminated along the entire food distribution system, from farm to fork. Foods from restaurants, shops and particularly the open market offer no reprieve. Sometimes foods are adulterated: packages do not contain what they say they contain, or the food is a cheaper grade than what is posted. I Garments tries to minimize food safety risks. The company instructs its staff on the topic of hygiene. The caterer is instructed to keep perishable food cool and cooking utensils clean. I Garments also disposes of food waste properly so as not to attract insects and rodents. Food handlers are checked regularly for worms and communicable diseases.

Bantai Industries

Bantai opened in 1991 with an initial investment of US$500,000. Within a year the company grew from 300 to 540 workers making several million baseball caps per year, largely for export to the United States. Typical of the Bangladesh garment industry, most workers are young women from rural areas in desperate need of safe and affordable shelter and access to nutritious food. Bantai found favour with NGOs and humanitarian groups with its progressive benefits: bank accounts for women (essentially unheard of in Bangladesh), relatively decent housing, access to discounted food clubs, childcare, health care and free meals. Work itself is nevertheless tiring, for most workers are paid by the piece and the work environment lacks ergonomic inputs.

Some of Bantai's social benefits are available today. But unfortunately there have been major changes, which are discussed in detail below. Bantai was once a joint-venture project with foreign collaboration, which contributed to its great success in business, social and welfare activities. The foreign partners have now left, however. Orders are down; only 480 employees remain; and benefits are being cut. Remaining benefits include health and family planning, education, entertainment and safety programmes. There is no longer a free or even subsidized meal, but there is a clean and pleasant dining area, and workers can bring a packed lunch or tiffin to it. Bantai Managing Director, Muhammad Saidur Rahman, once proud of his company's benefits, hopes to remedy the situation.

MVM Garments

MVM Garments is one of the largest garment factories in Bangladesh. Some of its benefits are comparable with those offered at I Garments. MVM Garments offers a free lunch. Lunch is typical Bangladesh fare: cereals, dhal and some vegetables. The problem with this programme, as well as lunches served in other factories across industry in Bangladesh, is that they provide minimal calories and nutrition. The meals are essentially carbohydrates intended to keep bellies filled for a few hours in order to finish the working day. The meals are alarmingly deficient in protein, vitamins and minerals and do little to combat the epidemic of anaemia and iodine deficiency. This stands in stark contrast to the Brazilian meal voucher system, in which subsidized worker meals must contain a high amount of protein and other nutrients. As such, despite some employers' efforts to provide a midday meal, garment workers remain one of the most vulnerable groups in Bangladesh for nutrition-related diseases.

All three garment factories featured here have a simple water purification system, comprising mechanisms to boil, filter or treat water with a tablet. The drinking water at work is safer than the water most workers have access to elsewhere.

Special issues

As noted, both food safety and nutrition are of great concern in Bangladesh. The Bangladesh Government, in conjunction with humanitarian groups, offers training to companies and their canteen staff on proper food handling and preparation. Training is offered in cleaning, cooking and food selection. Cleaning includes basic hygiene: washing hands before touching food; washing hands after using the toilet; washing and sanitizing all surfaces, floors, utensils and equipment used for food preparation and eating; protecting the kitchen and dining area from insects, rodents and other animals; separating raw animal foods from other foods; and using separate equipment to prepare raw animal foods. Cooking training includes how to cook meats thoroughly; bring soups and stews to the boil when reheating; reheating, chilling and freezing; and not keeping foods at room temperature for more than two hours. Food selection includes the use of safe water, pasteurized milk, fresh vegetables and awareness of expiry dates.

Anaemia is widely prevalent in Bangladesh and chronic among the garment workers due to their low intake of animal foods and general lack of understanding about nutrition. Many garment factory workers earn enough to buy nutritious food yet still remain undernourished, either because they send money home or purchase basic staples lacking nutritional variety. Many factories offer nutrition education. There are also food donation and food fortification programmes, largely aimed at children and at the community as a whole, not the workplace. For example, there are fortified school lunch programmes and programmes to supply pregnant and lactating women with iron, folic acid and vitamin C. Workplace nutrition programmes, such as iron tablets and vitamin supplementation, exist but are sporadic. None of the garment factories presented in this case study have a consistent programme, despite the fact that many workers are anaemic.

The lack of adequate housing for garment workers significantly harms worker nutrition efforts. Most garment workers are young women and most, about 90 per cent, in Dhaka live in slums and shantytowns with little or no electricity and clean water. There is no official dormitory system, as there is in other countries with garment factories. Women garment workers have little means to store or cook food, and prepare a lunch for work.

Possible disadvantages of food solution

Meals are free, but they aren't plentiful. They lack the basic calories and nutrients needed to work efficiently and stay healthy. Many workers are chronically tired and unhappy.

Costs and benefits to enterprise

From a Western perspective, the cost of the meal programme seems low – less than a dollar or euro per week per worker. Yet if Bantai Industries can serve as an example, meal programmes are apparently relatively costly to maintain and are seen as a benefit that needs to be cut during economic downturns.

The garment workers at the companies mentioned here understand that their benefits are better than those found in some other garment factories. And for this reason, they are grateful. The companies can only boast of modest gains in productivity, if any, compared with other factories with no food programmes.

Government incentives

The Government does not offer tax breaks or other incentives to establish a cafeteria or meal programme with subsidized food. Despite the Factory Act of 1965 (and revisions in 1968, 1972 and 1979) and the Bangladesh Export Processing Zone Authority Act of 1980, working in Bangladesh provides no guarantee that one will not go hungry.

Practical advice for implementation

Establishing eating facilities such as the ones mentioned here is a straight-forward affair. By law, many companies need to offer some arrangement. The most inexpensive route seems to be to provide a room reserved for eating and socializing, where food is brought in. To make this a suitable food solution, companies must consider proper food safety and nutrition. Both require some degree of investment and dedication. Training on food safety is available for free, yet maintaining a clean cooking and eating area requires staffing and supplies. Keeping a mess room clean is not difficult. The area merely needs to be wiped down and food waste needs to be removed. Companies relying on a caterer to supply a snack or lunch must demand that the caterer maintains a proper level of hygiene and, at a minimum, undertakes hygiene training.

Nutritious meals might cost more, but not too much more. Companies must understand that proper nutrition is an investment in productivity. A permanent budget must be made available for a subsidized or free meal. As we saw with Bantai Industries, a small fluctuation in the market (precipitated by a faltering United States economy) led to the cancellation of key social and health benefits, much to the chagrin of the management. The health of garment workers is too precious to be so dependent on the whims of the market from week to week, month to month and year to year. Multinational apparel companies, in an effort to reassure consumers that their clothes are not made in sweatshop conditions, can donate the few tens of thousands of dollars needed to provide nutritious meals for an entire factory for an entire year. This would guarantee a consistent workplace food programme regardless of market fluctuation. This or a similar arrangement will be increasingly important, for the garment industry is expecting a major shake-up. After January 2005, Bangladesh will no longer benefit from a quota system imposed by the WTO and must compete in the free market.

Union/employee perspective

Trade unions are currently relatively weak in Bangladesh, but change is occurring. On 13 July 2004, the Bangladesh Parliament passed the EPZ Trade Union and Industrial Relations Bill 2004, which will allow the formation of trade union bodies in export processing zones. Fully fledged trade unions will not be able to operate, however, until 1 November 2006. Until then, workers have to rely for improvements in their conditions on the Bangladesh Garment Manufacturer and Exporter Association (BGMEA), together with various NGOs. However, the BGMEA is an employers' organization and may not necessarily represent the views of the workers. It is formulating a comprehensive labour code for ready-made garments in compliance with the requirements of international buyers, and various labour and non-tariff barrier issues. Until November 2006, workers in EPZs can form committees. Committees require the signatures of at least 30 per cent of workers in one or more factories. A committee would serve as a collective bargaining agent. Agreements signed by the committee are legal in the context of the new Act. The United States had threatened to withdraw its generalized system of preference (GSP) scheme if trade unions were not allowed in EPZs.

Currently workers, particularly women, have no opportunity to bargain for higher salaries or better benefits. Women garment workers typically start at 500 taka (US$8.40) per month and work up to 1,500 taka (US$16.80). Salary increases with job performance. Many companies manage to skirt the multitude of protections for workers defined by one law or another over the past 110 years. While the unions grow stronger, positive change in the garment industry is uncertain. On one hand, the BGMEA and unions do entertain the concept of improving worker feeding programmes in the interest of boosting productivity and pleasing foreign interests. On the other hand, some worry that the Bangladesh garment industry will decline significantly with the end of the Multifibre Arrangement (MFA) in 2005 and the new rules imposed under the WTO. The threat of lower profits could diminish the unions' ability to bargain successfully for better food programmes.

This information was compiled by Professor Golam Mowlah.

6.11 Simbi Roses

Thika District, Kenya

Type of enterprise: Simbi Roses, a rose flower company, sits on an 11-hectare farm located in Thika District, about 60 kilometres northeast of Nairobi. The farm was established in 1985 and grows only rose flowers, mainly for export.

Employees: 260 (including 220 workers plus supervisors and managers).

Food solution – key point: no-cost lunch, long break, improved sanitation and space made available for workers' vegetable plots.

Most of the workers at Simbi Roses, 90 per cent, live on the rose farm in modest stone houses. Employees work eight hours per day. Supervisors are entitled to two tea breaks and a lunch break. Workers have a single break from noon to 2:45 p.m. The main reason for such a long midday break is that the greenhouses get too warm and uncomfortable to work in during this time. The extended break provides workers with plenty of time to eat and rest.

Simbi Roses began to offer and finance lunch for workers in 1996. Many workers had complained of headaches and of being less productive in the afternoons; and management essentially responded by offering a free lunch. According to the farm manager, Mr. Jefferson K. Karue, many workers were apparently not eating anything during the lunch break. This was probably because they did not manage their finances well or they spent their money mostly on non-food items and family needs, and had very little for their own food. The manager and supervisors live on the farm with their families, but the other workers' families do not live on the farm, and this could also explain why these workers do not cook in their houses even with such a long lunch break.

Food solution

Simbi Roses contracted a private individual to prepare and serve a meal to the workers. Originally, two meal varieties were offered. Later employees settled on one local dish, called *githeri*, served daily, because it was their favourite and tended to be well prepared compared with the other dish. *Githeri* is made by cooking oil, onions, cabbage, maize and beans. The dish is purely vegetarian with the energy provided from the cooking oil and the maize, protein from beans and micronutrients from the onions, cabbage and the beans. After the main dish, the workers are served tea with milk and sugar. The maize and beans are cooked and eaten whole; thus the vitamins usually removed through de-hulling are available. Chances of developing hypertension, high cholesterol and Type 2 diabetes are minimized. The food has a low glycaemic index and high fibre content, so it helps eliminate cholesterol from the body. Beans are high in iron. The meal has little variety, however, which might limit some nutrients, as is discussed below.

Workers must provide their own bowl or plate and utensils, and they are responsible for keeping these clean. The lunch is open to all workers, including supervisors. On average, 180 people are served per day. This number includes nearly everyone working on any given day. The farm operates seven days a week; so of the 260 workers, some have days off and use this opportunity to travel and see their families. Also, some supervisors and a few of the workers who do not live on the farm return to their homes for lunch.

Fresh food is prepared daily since no food is usually left over. Food preparation is timed so that it is ready by the lunch break. The meal is cooked using firewood in a makeshift kitchen (a temporary shed made of iron sheets, open on one side). Employees eat in their houses or under a tree. Proper hygiene is difficult to maintain in the kitchen, due to its rough construction. However, Simbi Roses has now begun to build a simple, modern kitchen and all-purpose hall, where the workers can have their meals and also hold other social activities. To enhance healthy eating, the company has allowed the workers to plant kitchen gardens near their houses. Workers produce such vegetables as kale, cabbage, spinach, onions, tomatoes, capsicum (hot pepper) and coriander. This is mainly for household consumption, but some kitchen gardens do so well that some of the workers also generate income from them.

The company has no specific schedule for health programmes. However, people from the Ministry of Health are occasionally invited to talk to the employees about HIV/AIDS, sanitation and hygiene, while occupational labour officers give talks on safety at the workplace. The manager has interest in having a nutrition programme in place and is working towards introducing nutrition talks.

Possible disadvantages of food solution

Food safety doesn't appear to be a serious issue, yet the potential problem is being remedied nonetheless. The fact that workers must bring their own eating ware is inconvenient but perhaps practical given the circumstances. The new mess room will make lunch more comfortable. Having a place to wash and store utensils there would be useful. Some workers would like to see larger portions served; so this could be a point for improvement. Ironically, this "vegetarian" meal lacks many vegetables. The meal is largely grains and beans.

The maize and bean combination forms a complete protein, so this key element of the diet is satisfied. Cabbage is a good source of vitamins C and B6, potassium and calcium; onions add more vitamin C and minerals. Other leafy and root vegetables could supply vitamins A, B1, B2 and K, along with zinc and other minerals. The home gardens help here. Having more vegetables added to the regular dish would be helpful. One complaint among workers is this lack of vegetable choice; the other complaint is the portion size.

Costs and benefits to enterprise

Simbi Roses finances the meal service by paying a contractor 20 shillings (US$0.25) per lunch per person per day, seven days a week. This comes to approximately US$1,260 per month.

Mr. Karue said that he has not quantified any pay-offs realized by the company as a result of the food service; but he indicated that employee sick days have dropped and absenteeism is low, while productivity and staff morale have gone up. Simbi Roses enjoys a popular image compared with surrounding flower farms, mainly due to the existence of its meal service. As a result, Simbi Roses frequently experiences pressure from job seekers. In the case of absenteeism, the most common reasons are sickness from malaria and emergencies that involve relatives and family members. Afternoon headaches are a thing of the past now.

Government incentives

There are no government incentives in Kenya for serving a workplace meal.

Practical advice for implementation

Here we see a little effort that goes a long way. Simbi Roses manages to offer a somewhat nutritious lunch where there was no lunch before for only US$0.25 per worker. The company has essentially established a basic "army-like" field kitchen. The system works because the food is nutritious and workers enjoy it. Whether intentional or cultural, the chosen meal – beans, maize, onions and cabbage – provides a maximum amount of nutrients for a minimal price. Beans and maize can be stored easily, and together they form a complete protein with high iron content. So two health concerns – protein and iron deficiency – common in Africa are met. Cabbage and onions are durable and easy to grow, and they contain many nutrients. This is not the "better than nothing" food solution we saw in Ethiopia (see Chapter 4), in which employees pay for a meal that is not particularly nourishing.

This arrangement at Simbi Roses can work well in the informal sector, which is widespread across the African continent. Pay-offs to the company in morale, health and productivity ultimately translate into shillings, which can be invested in an even better food arrangement. The vegetable gardens are a nice touch and an excellent idea, costing the company nothing and benefiting employees hugely.

Union/employee perspective

According to the employees, the meal service is an excellent idea. Because they do not have to cook, they can get enough rest before resuming duty in the afternoon. This boosts their morale, helps them to stay alert and makes them more productive, they said. The food service also acts as a buffer for many of the workers. "Sometimes my budget is so stretched that I am not able to feed myself to the end of the month. So, I survive only on the meal provided by the company until my financial status improves again," said one middle-aged male worker. A young female employee said: "This meal is very helpful to new-comers. I survived only on this lunch during my first two weeks in employment until I received my first salary." Others said: "Some of us have so many needs that we find the meal helpful, because we divert what we save from not buying food for ourselves to other uses"; and "Others do not know how to manage their income and would starve if the meal was not available."

Naturally these comments reflect a low standard-of-living wage common through the developing world. Asked whether it would be fine to do away with the food service and be compensated through their salaries, only a few employees, among those with families, said they would not mind. The majority preferred to have the food service in place. The employees commended their employer for thinking of their welfare and were happy that the construction of a modern kitchen and eating facility was underway. They were happy with the length of their lunch break and did not need tea breaks. They asked, however, for the meal portion size to be increased, more vegetable varieties to be incorporated, and the general quality of the meal to be improved. A welfare committee presents workers' problems to the management in addition to looking after their welfare. They organize games (volleyball and football) and special Christmas parties funded by the company. Workers also have medical cover. There is no union.

This case study was prepared by Dr. Alice M. Mwangi.

6.12 Kenya Vehicle Manufacturers Ltd

Thika Town, Kenya

Type of enterprise: Kenya Vehicle Manufacturers Ltd. (KVM) started in 1974 as a vehicle assembling company. In 1994, the company diversified to include vehicle rehabilitation and the manufacturing of manually operated water pumps, huge tents, coke trolleys and bus bodies.

Employees: 230 to 240 (including 88 permanent and pensionable, 13 contracted, and over 100 piece-rate employees).

Food solution – key point: heavily subsidized lunch.

The majority of KVM workers reside within Thika Municipality, and over 90 per cent of them live two or three kilometres away from the factory. Employees work eight hours per day. Supervisors, managers and office staff are entitled to two tea breaks per day, served at their working location, and a lunch break. Workers have a single break of 35 minutes from 12.25 p.m. to 1 p.m. for lunch. We have decided that the food solution presented here best fits the category of "mess room", as in the preceding case study on Simbi, because what is described does not constitute a fully fledged canteen with a diversity of meal options.

The company began offering lunch to workers in 1979. There were three main reasons, according to the Administration and Human Resources Manager, Mr. B.N. Wabule. First was a lack of proximity to catering services, since KVM is relatively far removed from the town centre – 3.5 kilometres away. Secondly, the company wanted to ensure employees were served a decent and safe meal. Although it was possible for employees to obtain food from the female-operated mobile vendors and some food kiosks in the immediate neighbourhood, many KVM workers complained of stomach problems after eating this food and spent a lot of time in the health clinic, leading to loss of production time. Thirdly, the company wanted to save time, for workers only had 35 minutes for lunch. The canteen is a short walking distance from the factory floor.

Food solution

The food service consists of a modern kitchen and a dining area with two sections, the executive and the common canteens. Originally the food service was run by KVM itself. This proved too demanding. Instead of terminating the service, KVM contracted out to PEEJAY Caterers, a company formed by four former employees of the KVM food service. The meal comprises a main platter and a mug of milk tea, sweetened or unsweetened. One basic dish is served each day; this varies from day to day and includes: *ugali* (thick porridge from maize flour) with beef and cabbage mixed with carrots; *githeri* (mixture of maize, beans and cabbage) with beef; rice, cabbage, carrots and a beef/bean stew; and fried potatoes with beef and cabbage. Soup is included with the meal. In the executive canteen, there are fruit, soft drinks, chicken and fish.

Although the meal service is not compulsory, Mr. Wabule noted that about 99 per cent of the employees make use of the service and, on average, 235 employees are served daily. Usually only three or four workers per day come with their own packed lunch and do not make use of the lunch service, mainly due to medical reasons.

The food service utilizes a card system. Each employee has a meal card with his or her name on it, which they present before being served. The meal cards are left with the caterer, who makes a record of all the employees who have taken the meal on a daily basis. At the end of the month, the heavily subsidized meal cost is deducted from the employee's salary and paid to the caterers. Meals served in the common mess room cost 45 shillings per plate (US$0.57). The employee pays 10 shillings per plate (US$0.13), while the company pays 35 shillings. In the executive canteen, meals cost 120 shillings (US$1.52). Here the subsidy is not as great. The employee pays 100 shillings while the employer pays 20 shillings. Although nobody is restricted from eating at the executive canteen, only about 15 people make use of it daily.

Meals are fairly balanced in terms of food types, but no fruit is served in the common canteen. The portion sizes are large enough that a sedentary person eating them daily would easily gain excess weight and see a rise in his or her cholesterol levels from the beef. Most KVM employees, however, are engaged in heavy manual labour, requiring large amounts of energy. They remain in good health even with such large amounts of calories and beef intake. A quick observation of the workers as they went for lunch did not reveal any obvious obesity cases; quite a number were heavily built.

A special service is provided for employees who have been ill to the point of being hospitalized. In addition to the usual meal, they are also provided with a mug of milk and fruit at no additional costs. The management staff are very positive about the food service and think that it has been a success. The service has never faced any major near failures. It occasionally receives complaints on minor issues such as the thickness of the soup or the amount of milk in tea. Potable tap water is available, and the caterer thoroughly cleans utensils. The company nurse regularly inspects the kitchen for sanitation and hygiene. The company has no specific schedule for health programmes, but the Administration and Human Resources Manager indicated some interest in having such programmes in place.

Possible disadvantages of food solution

None apparent. Most of the employees perform heavy manual labour and are quite happy with the food portion sizes. Food safety doesn't appear to be a serious issue.

Costs and benefits to enterprise

According to Mr. Wabule, the company bears 80 per cent of the total cost of provision of lunch to its employees. This includes water, electricity and the food. For food alone, the company spends US$0.44 per employee per day, or a total of US$96.80 per day for employees using the common canteen. The company spends an additional US$0.25 per employee (US$3.75 per day) for employees in the executive canteen. This brings the total amount of money spent on employee food alone to US$2,410.00 per month.

While the pay-offs emanating from the food service could not be immediately quantified, Mr. Wabule noted that the company saves on production time. Absenteeism due to sickness is rare; employees are always in high spirits and have a protective attitude towards the enterprise. Ms. Nancy, the assistant to Mr. Wabule, says that workers have high morale and such a positive attitude that warning letters for lateness and other misconduct are rare – maybe a single case per year.

Government incentives

None.

Practical advice for implementation

Kenya Vehicle Manufacturers can offer a generous meal programme by minimizing kitchen costs. Companies of similar financial means might consider this approach. First, KVM decided to contract out the service. This saved the company administrative costs. Yet unlike the situation at K. Mohan, another company featured in this chapter, food is cooked daily on site. This cuts down on the risk of food-borne diseases from the transportation of food from a caterer's kitchen to the factory. The company's meal plan seems culturally appropriate too. In the Simbi case study, also from Kenya, we saw that employees don't mind eating the same lunch every day. At KVM, employees are offered no choice but get a little more diversity day to day. Clearly, preparing one kind of meal each day greatly reduces costs of preparation, fuel and cleaning.

Can this approach work anywhere? Workers from a different cultural background might request a choice, such as two or three meal options a day.

And if they don't have this choice, they might seek a meal elsewhere, which would undermine the meal programme. The decision to offer a simple meal at an inexpensive price over the offer of choice cannot be taken lightly.

Union/employee perspective

The workers belong to the Amalgamated Union of Kenya Metal Workers. Union officials are very happy with the food service. They have few complaints about the amount of money workers pay towards lunch. They appreciate what the company is doing but say that if it could also do away with the 10 shillings (US$0.13) meal fee, this would boost the workers even more. However, they say that the pay is reasonable. The officials also say that they have no complaints about the food quality. If workers are not happy about anything, there is always room to air their complaints. They will not advocate for the company to eliminate the food service and replace it with money because workers would otherwise have problems obtaining a decent meal. The union also agreed to the meal break length of 35 minutes. In many companies, employees work from 8 a.m. to 5 p.m. with an hour for lunch, for a total of eight hours of work. At KVM, workers finish work at 4:30 p.m., half an hour early to compensate for the shortened lunch break.

The employees like the meal service. They say the quality is good and exceeds what they pay for it. They also say that it boosts their morale, makes them more productive and saves time. "The meal service is very important for me," said one middle-aged male worker. "My family lives in the countryside while I live alone in town. After having my lunch here, I do not make a main meal in my house. I only take a snack in the evening, and am able to save some extra money to send to my family." A young male employee said: "Some of us take alcohol, and if we were given money in place of lunch, we would spend it on alcoholic drinks or even other non-food things and become weak and less productive."

The majority of the workers were happy with the meal quality and nobody complained about the portion sizes. A few, however, said that the vegetables were overcooked. They wanted more vegetable varieties and requested fruit to be served occasionally. They also requested more milk in the tea. This, however, raised fears among them that they might be asked to increase their financial contribution towards the lunch. A few felt that the lunch break was too short. Mr. Wabule had a specific comment: that nutrition and hygiene for workers in Kenya have not been given the prominence it deserves. There is need for nutrition programmes at the national level supported by government ministries and publicized through the media.

This case study was prepared by Dr. Alice M. Mwangi.

6.13 Agricultural workers' nutrition: Lessons from Uganda

One sad irony concerning workers' nutrition is that those who harvest the food are often those with the poorest access to food. Agricultural workers face numerous obstacles in many countries, rich and poor. In developing countries, new and hard-fought laws to protect workers in urban factories are seldom enforced in rural areas. Yet even in wealthy industrialized nations, with well-established health and safety regulations, farm workers often are faced with low-quality food and limited basic protections from exposure to weather, pesticides and herbicides (for their food and themselves). The reasons are partly logistic and partly social. It is difficult to transport meats and vegetables to rural areas, and it can be difficult to store food properly as well. Vast areas might be devoted to crops such as sugar cane, coffee or tea, which offer little in the way of local food for workers. Also, farm workers, particularly migrant harvesters, are at the bottom of the socio-economic ladder, often hired informally or illegally. Many are undocumented immigrants with few rights and limited knowledge of those rights. Work is often seasonal, further complicating efforts to establish collective bargaining agreements. In many countries, food harvesting was performed by slaves and then landless peasants; thus a tradition of oppression dates back centuries. The important task of harvesting food is often undervalued by growers, who rely on cheap and dispensable labour.

The harvesters' plight is also complicated by the fact that most live away from home in temporary and often dilapidated shelters. They might have no electricity, no running water and no means to store perishable food. They often are not allowed to bring their families to the fields, which could be hundreds of kilometres from their home. They frequently rely entirely on the landowner for food. Sometimes the landowner will pay the worker partially with food, such as sacks of corn meal and beans. This food then becomes the primary source of nutrition for months on end. Sometimes the food payment is totally inappropriate, with a most glaring example coming from South Africa where certain vineyards have paid workers partially with bottles of wine.

Background history

Uganda, like many countries, has its share of abuses and success stories concerning workers' nutrition. We are happy to report on the latter, which can serve as an example for other farming regions employing migrant workers. A short review of Uganda's recent history will help the reader appreciate

Uganda's latest efforts to improve workers' nutrition, spearheaded by the National Union of Plantation and Agricultural Workers.

Uganda was a British colony until 1962. One major objective of colonization was the exploitation of African raw materials (minerals and crops such as coffee, cotton, tea and sugar cane) and the creation of a market for industrial products from the colonizing countries. The colonial State concerned itself with the nature and character of production in the colonies, including Uganda, to ensure the supply of raw materials to European and other trading countries. Measures were therefore taken to secure the cheapest form of labour. As a cash economy was introduced, people increasingly worked for concerns that paid in cash, rather than by barter arrangements. Taxation was introduced in 1900 in the southern part of Uganda. A hut tax of 3 rupees a year was imposed on every male. The logic behind the tax was to compel the peasant to seek waged employment to pay the tax, which was only payable in cash. Taxation (hut and poll tax) was extended to the rest of Uganda as regions were incorporated into the colony. The other reason for taxation, naturally, was to raise revenue for the government.

Taxation alone was insufficient, in the absence of other measures, to force peasants into waged labour. Indeed when a labour shortage intensified, the response of the colonial government was to resort to forced labour. In 1905 the forced paid labour system, or *kasanvu* as it was known in Uganda, was established in Buganda (southern Uganda). Migrant workers came from Ugandan labour reserves in the north, from Kigezi and Ankole (southwest Uganda), and from the Belgian territories of Rwanda-Burundi, Congo and Tanganyika. The migrant labourers were men; women were expected to remain at home to cultivate food. The men walked hundreds of kilometres to and from employment centres, and lived under inhumane conditions. Employers were compelled to construct labour camps to accommodate the workers and provide food (a meagre dry ration of maize flour and beans) during the period of contracts. However, under the contract system, the workers' pay was based on a 30-day ticket, called *kipande*; and at the end of 30 days the work ticket could be denied if the employer felt the work had not been properly done. If denied, the worker would receive no cash or food ration.

The rise of trade unions

Because most workers were migrants, on 6- or 12-month contracts, they saw no value in subscribing to short-term union membership. Also, the employers (European and Asian expatriates) were hostile to any form of organized labour and threatened to withdraw free housing, food, medical treatment and other welfare facilities if workers joined a union. Under such conditions, it was very difficult to organize the workers into a trade union. However, by 1959, workers in the tea estates organized and formed a trade union called the National Union of Plantation and Agricultural Workers (NUPAWU), which spread rapidly to cover all the major tea estates and the two sugar plantations, Kakira and Lugazi (eastern Uganda). The union rallied the support of the workers to negotiate for better wages and a meal plan; the result was the conclusion of the Collective Bargaining Agreement (CBA) on terms and conditions of employment with employers in the sugar and tea industries. One of the provisions of the CBA was that "the employer shall provide food for the workers". Unfortunately, this part of the agreement was so general that it gave room for the management to provide the food of their choice.

Under the CBA, plantations began to serve porridge, or maize flour boiled in water, at the end of the day's tasks. Problems soon became evident and they remain widespread today. The flour is transported to working sites around the plantation, often in the same vehicles that transport fertilizers and agrochemicals. The maize and beans often sit for long periods in mouldy environments. The porridge is cooked in metal drums, often rusted. The water used for cooking is of questionable quality, frequently contaminated with fertilizer. Overworked cooks serve hordes of hungry and often angry workers not pleased with the food quality. Workers must provide their own cups or plates, and these are rarely clean. Workers either have no means to wash or no knowledge of the importance of washing fertilizers and chemical residues from their hands. The cooking grounds are outdoors and dirty. And there are no waste facilities, so cooking areas attract swarms of flies. The rate of absenteeism due to food-borne illness remains high. In the 1980s the CBA was extended to include lunch. Again, maize and beans became the sole meal for lunch.

The 1970s saw a near total collapse of the sugar industry under the Idi Amin regime. Uganda was producing nearly 150,000 tons of refined sugar annually during the 1960s; but during the 1980s the country was importing sugar. Local self-sufficiency became a major goal of the post-Amin governments, which rehabilitated the Kakira and Lugazi sugar estates. More war postponed production until the late 1980s. A third estate, called the Kinyara Sugar Works, began operation in the early 1990s.

The Kinyara Sugar Works

The Kinyara Sugar Works has set a very good example in feeding workers, which the NUPAWU is pressuring other employers to follow. Kinyara management provides a balanced diet to all workers. They have hired the services of a catering organization and have set up a canteen committee to oversee the quality and quantity of the food given to the workers. The meals consist of rice, potatoes, *posho* (maize-meal), meat, fish, beans and vegetables, which are alternated on a daily basis. Kinyara management has constructed a central kitchen, too, where all the cooking is done. For the field workers, food is transported in pickup trucks to the fields where sheds have been constructed. It is here that the workers are served food under hygienic conditions and in an organized manner.

The upfront costs to Kinyara to feed around 5,000 workers seem at first relatively high: about 1,500 shillings (US$1) per worker per day. Yet productivity has risen markedly. On the previous "porridge" diet at Kinyara, a cane harvester was cutting about 1.5 to 2 tons of cane per day, similar to the productivity rate at the Lugazi and Kakira estates. With the introduction of a healthier diet, productivity has shot up to 3 to 4 tons of cane per day per worker. The rates of absenteeism have dropped, as have the expenses for medical treatment.

Kinyara is government-owned and managed by Booker-Tate of the United Kingdom, whereas Kakira and Lugazi are government joint ventures with the Mehta and Madhvani families of India, respectively. In 1997, Booker-Tate recognized the NUPAWU as the trade union representing Kinyara workers. The NUPAWU negotiated for the same meal provision at the other two estates, yet Booker-Tate improved upon this. The management's stated goal for the improved feeding programme was to increase productivity, morale and safety to compete with the larger and better-established sugar-cane estates. And they certainly got this. The investment paid off.

Plantation owners increasingly are growing aware that nutrition is tied to productivity and that providing adequate calories to workers can help their operation remain competitive on a global level. One study of cutters and stackers on a South African sugar plantation revealed that workers expended on average over 3,100 kcal during working hours yet consumed only 1,300 kcal at work (Lambert, Cheevers and Coopoo, 1994). This led to a 3 per cent loss in body mass for some workers, and lower productivity. According to the NUPAWU, Uganda's Kakira plantation has initiated a feeding programme similar to Kinyara's well-balanced plan for a small subset of its workforce. The Lugazi plantation has established a food committee to study a meal programme. Lugazi did not respond to questions for this ILO case study.

In responding to questions for this ILO case study, Kakira management said that currently workers receive free meals of *posho* porridge with vegetables, the same meal every day. The 3,500 plantation workers have a 20-minute mid-morning meal break, during which they pick up their porridge from six satellite mess rooms. They eat in a sheltered, well-ventilated area with facilities with soap and water to wash in before meals. The mess halls are within easy walking distance from the fields. By mid-afternoon, after the day's work is done, workers return to their temporary quarters for a lunch and often eat outdoors. The quarters have full-time cooks who prepare food with proper equipment. Kakira is considering many improvements to the meal scheme, such as music at the mess halls and greater food variety. The company said it would undertake a study to understand the nutritional needs and concerns of the workers. Kakira is considering these changes in consultation with the union.

The NUPAWU is constantly demanding improvements in food quality and hygiene standards. Plantation and agricultural workplaces should be regularly inspected, by law, by the Ministry of Labour's Inspectorate Department. But this rarely happens. The NUPAWU is campaigning for ratification of the ILO Safety and Health in Agriculture Convention, 2001 (No. 184), with the hope that the working conditions for agricultural workers will improve.

This case study was prepared by Omara Amuko, International Union of Food (IUF) Health, Safety and Environment Coordinator.

6.14 Mess rooms summary

The reader might have noticed by now a continuum between food solutions. There's no solid line drawn between canteen and mess room. A mess room can be exceedingly basic. In Kenya we saw a tin shed serving decent food, to be eaten outside or back in dormitory-type housing. With more investment, the mess room can be a pleasant and relaxing shelter. Meals can be nutritious and heavily subsidized by the employer, or food can be basic with little or no subsidy. A range of possibilities exists, with some clearly more beneficial to employees. Chapter 3 closed with a chart illustrating this "workplace food solution continuum". Are mess rooms the poor person's canteen? They don't need to be. But if so, does it really matter? Mess rooms are an effective food solution for millions of workers in the informal sector or in small companies. We see that many aspects of mess room food programmes are easily transferable. A summary of the key elements in the case studies from this chapter follows.

MexMode

MexMode was the site of a union victory in which a strike over horrendous conditions led to a radically improved mess room that, in the end, helped boost company profits. The strike demonstrates the value employees place on food. The mess room is simply a room with tables and invited food vendors. Food is essentially fully subsidized. The positive: high morale, higher productivity. The negative: none.

Boncafé International

Boncafé encouraged employees to use kitchenettes. Employees cook, eat together and donate equipment. Boncafé's costs are minimal. The positive: employees have a place nearby to eat healthy food and relax. The negative: the kitchenettes could be better with minimal company investment in better equipment.

K. Mohan and Co.

On an NGO's recommendations, K. Mohan greatly improved its food service. The company provides a large room and a few basics, such as soap and water. Food is catered and cooked elsewhere. This can serve as a model for minimum standards for workers' nutrition for cash-strapped companies. The positive: employees now have a nutritious meal each day. The negative: none.

American Apparel

American Apparel took a "stacking" approach. The company started with a simple dining area with simple food, and added healthier foods and other benefits year by year. Morale rose along with the benefits, for the workers – minorities, many with limited English skills – who came to believe that the employer cared for them. The positive: high morale, better nutrition. The negative: none.

San Mateo County Municipality

Faced with a workforce largely on the road or spread across many facilities, San Mateo relies on health education and financial rewards so that employees can make the best meal choices. The positive: workers get some guidance. The negative: workers are still on their own to find healthy meals.

Russian-British Consulting Centre

This is a tiny company with several meal options. One option is a shared canteen with other companies, common in the Russian Federation. This is an efficient way in any country for a cluster of companies to pool resources to offer a single canteen for all their employees. The positive: a variety of low-cost dining options available. The negative: none.

Simbi Roses

Simbi had the most basic of arrangements, a man hired to cook the same meal each day for the employees. He cooks in a shed, and most workers eat outdoors. Meals are free and somewhat healthy, though. Construction is underway on a building with a kitchen and tables. The positive: free and reasonably healthy meals. The negative: none, now that Simbi is building a permanent kitchen.

Kenya Vehicle Manufacturers Ltd

This company responded to workers who became sick from street foods. The company maintains a low-cost dining facility where one type of meal is served each day. The cost to the company is low. The positive: food is nutritious, high in calories and safer than street food. The negative: none.

California

California is the only American state actively incorporating the national "five-a-day" fruit and vegetable programme into the workplace. A health taskforce offers business awards to encourage companies to improve workers' nutrition. One novel, inexpensive suggestion is to work with local vendors (coffee shops, lunch trucks) to serve healthier foods.

Bangladesh

Poor nutrition, including chronic anaemia, is greatly improved with subsidized or free workplace meal programmes. This, in turn, raises the country's productivity level. Good examples are hard to come by, but change is slowly coming as employers see that well-fed workers are better workers.

Uganda

Agricultural workers help provide food for the world but often go hungry themselves – a result of their low status in society, as well as the difficulty of feeding workers in remote locations. The Kinyara Sugar Works in Uganda has nearly doubled productivity by investing in a simple but nourishing meal plan that provides workers with food that is nutritious and safe from food-borne illnesses and agrochemicals.

7

REFRESHMENT FACILITIES AND LOCAL VENDORS

Photo: FAO/R. Faidutti

"I will not eat oysters. I want my food dead. Not sick, not wounded – dead."

Woody Allen

Key issues

Refreshments, food vans, local vendors

- This chapter presents inexpensive ideas for providing safe and healthy food.

- Employers can support local vendors to improve food quality. Street foods, for example, are notoriously insanitary. Employers can provide infrastructure to make food safer: ice, ice buckets, stainless steel trolleys or stalls, clean water, etc.

- Employers can persuade food van operators or shop owners to serve healthier food through financial incentives or the promise of regular customers.

- Refreshments, particularly during meetings, are often sweet and fatty foods, yet healthy alternatives abound. One healthy trend is free workplace fruit; another is healthy vending machines.

Pros of local vendors

- Working with a local vendor – either the owner of a stall, shop or restaurant – strengthens ties with the community and makes for smart business.

- Supporting local vendors is the most inexpensive food solution presented in this book. Merely providing a street vendor with access to clean water and a washroom will greatly improve food safety.

- Street foods, if properly handled, can be nutritious and inexpensive. Street vending makes significant contributions to the local economy. Recent efforts organized by the WHO and the FAO have markedly improved street market food safety.

- Farmers' markets cost a company next to nothing to arrange. They require little space. Employees benefit from inexpensive, fresh, local fruits and vegetables.

- These solutions can work well in the informal sector, which dominates the economies of countries throughout Africa and Southeast Asia.

- Vending machines can contain hot, nourishing food; and these machines can serve shift workers who work after the canteen or local stores have closed.

Cons of local vendors

- Workers who depend on local vending often have no place to eat their meal comfortably. Thus, even if the food is safe and nutritious (a big if), the break might not be relaxing. Relaxation is as important as nourishment.

- Street foods, if poorly handled, are a major source of food-borne illnesses. Employers must support the street vending infrastructure.

- Because construction workers have no canteen, mess hall or meal voucher, they often buy food on the street. The food is of questionable safety and nutrition. The workers also often have no clean place to eat.

Novel local vendor examples

- Hundreds of companies in Denmark participate in a free fruit programme that has been very popular with workers.

- Kaiser Permanente of Northern California has established weekly farmers' markets at several of its sites. These cost nothing to arrange and require little space. They are very popular with workers and the community, helping people reach the recommended "five-a-day" fruit and vegetable goal.

- South Africa significantly improved street foods safety through a carefully planned educational outreach programme, coupled with urban planning to ease crowding and improve waste collection and access to clean water.

Enterprises faced with limited resources can often take advantage of the surrounding neighbourhood to make the best of a situation. Street food vending is an instructive example: it is common around the globe; it offers inexpensive food for workers and a livelihood for the vendor. Yet the foremost concern with street vending is food safety. Hygiene conditions are often deplorable. Vendors often have no running water, no immediate place to relieve themselves, no place to wash hands and no place to store raw, perishable food. Companies with employees who depend on street vending for meals can step in to remedy the situation by offering water or an electricity hook-up. Likewise, factories in industrial parks can pool their resources to create a central area where many food vendors can set up a semi-permanent operation. The bottom line is that employers do not have to settle for poor local food options. Employers can work with local shop owners to improve food safety and quality with financial incentives or the promise of dedicated customers. Decent local vending is particularly important for construction workers. It is ironic that the workers who build our canteens have no canteens of their own. Construction workers rely almost entirely on packed lunches and mobile food vans, and they eat their meals in less than ideal conditions.

Within the confines of a company, employers can make small changes to improve a worker's access to nutritious food. Office meetings can have wholesome early morning and lunch foods instead of muffins, for example. Vending machines represent an exciting new area of nutrition. Traditionally, vending machines have been filled with candy, greasy snack foods and sugary drinks. The complaint among vending companies and their leasing customers has been that healthy foods simply don't sell and are left to spoil. Consumer tastes have been changing, though. Bottled water and juices in the United States marked the transition. No longer does soda pop dominate vending machines there. Japan has long been ahead of this trend with a fine selection of teas, hot and cold, without sugar. Pending approval, as of 2005, is California Senate Bill 74, which will require vending machines on state property to include at least 50 per cent healthy items. State property includes government buildings, state parks and roadside rest stops.

Vending machines these days can provide a variety of nourishing foods, even hot soups, yet occupy little space and cost little to businesses not large enough to operate a canteen. They are ideal for shiftworkers and night workers who toil after hours, when the canteen and local stores are closed. The topic itself would make for an interesting case study. Unfortunately, the major American and European vending machine companies failed to provide input despite repeated efforts to contact them. So this topic will not receive the fair treatment it deserves. Similarly, the topic of construction worker nutrition is also very important, yet information was hard to obtain. Section 7.5 of this chapter falls short of our intent to properly relay this great concern. We would like to revisit this topic in a future publication. Thus, this chapter offers only a few case studies and essays on local food solutions.

7.1   Kaiser Permanente of Northern California

Oakland, California, United States

Type of enterprise: Kaiser Permanente is the largest non-profit health plan in the United States, with headquarters in Oakland, California. Nationwide, the organization comprises 30 hospitals, 431 medical office buildings and nearly 148,000 employees and doctors in nine American states plus Washington, DC. Operating revenue for 2002 was US$22.5 billion. Kaiser Permanente of Northern California (KPNC) serves the northern half of California, above Fresno. (http://www.kaiserpermanente.org/)

Employees: 54,300.

Food solution – key point: on-site farmers' markets, along with healthier meeting foods and canteen changes.

Kaiser Permanente is in the health-care business, and the advice it gives to its clients (eat well and exercise) naturally applies to its workers. Kaiser Permanente estimates that obesity costs the organization US$220 million annually nationwide in additional health-care costs. In mid-2003 Kaiser Permanente of Northern California, one of nine regional company divisions, initiated a multi-dimensional programme called "We're Moving Together", to address the obesity issue and other health concerns. The programme has three components: physical activity and weight management; environmental changes to worksites and cafeterias; and a safety and injury reduction initiative. This case study will focus on changes regarding nutrition.

Food solution

Kaiser Permanente of Northern California maintains 12 medical centres and hospitals, and many medical office buildings. Three facilities – at Oakland, San Francisco and Richmond – have had success in providing employees with access to weekly on-site farmers' markets during working hours. A farmers' market is a temporary market where farmers sell products directly to consumers. The produce is often fresher than that found in supermarkets. The aim of KPNC's workplace farmers' market was to bring a healthy market to a population of a predictable size on a regular basis. One of the most common reasons that Californians gave for not eating fruits and vegetables was that they were "hard to get at work" – a reason cited by 61 per cent of survey respondents (California DOH, 2001). Weekly farmers' markets improve the nutrition of both workers and their families because food is often purchased for home consumption. Kaiser Permanente's farmers' markets have been quite popular. Seven new markets have opened as of early 2005, and as many as ten more may open by the end of 2005.

As a large employer and a prominent presence in the local communities, KPNC had to run through an extensive checklist before inviting farmers to its Oakland facility, the first location for its farmers' market. First, KPNC discussed the plan with the security and legal departments and with representatives from community and government relations, public affairs and human resources. The following requirements emerged: farmers must be able to set up stalls at no cost; the market would not compete with the cafeteria or coffee trolley; the market would not sell prepared or perishable goods; the market vendors would need their own insurance; the market would be scheduled on a day on which vendors (and their vehicles) would pose the least pressure on parking; vendors would clean up after themselves; and neighbourhood merchants would need to be supportive. The organization's role would be that of a facilitator with minimal financial obligation.

Next, KPNC contacted a local farmers' market association. (Dr. Preston Maring of KPNC, who initiated the markets, simply visited another farmers' market in downtown Oakland to gather information.) This was a crucial step, because expertise is needed in recruiting farmers to come to a non-traditional site during the week, when they would otherwise be tending their fields. The farmers' market association recruited a few growers, and KPNC decided to launch the new market in the spring. The Oakland market was soon popular with KPNC staff, patients and visitors to the hospital and medical facilities. The market features fruits, vegetables, breads and flowers. Kaiser Permanente of Northern California has since noticed that some patients schedule appointments on Fridays, the day of the market, just to be able to shop there. Other people from the neighbourhood also come. One local restaurant serves special omelettes for breakfast, which include foods from the market on Fridays. The market has provided a sense of community. The KPNC farmers' markets vary in size. They can fit on a pavement in front of the entrance to a building; not a lot of space is needed. They are conveniently located close to the building, so workers can easily access the markets during a break. The organization estimates that 650 people a week, or around two-thirds of the staff, visit the Oakland market. Some weeks register over 1,000 customers.

Other improvements in the area of nutrition at KPNC are worth mentioning. According to Project Manager, Anne Silk, a registered nurse, all facilities are making an effort to reduce or replace unhealthy foods at staff meetings with fruit, smaller muffins, bottled water, salads and healthier sandwiches. These foods come from local vendors. So far she and her

This page and opposite: Kaiser Permanente's farmers' markets occupy little space, offer fresh local fruits and vegetables throughout the year and are popular with workers and the local community.

colleagues have heard no grumbling about substituting fruit for salty snacks at catered lunches.

Changes in canteen options have been hard to achieve because of constraints with food vendors. Employees work in a variety of settings. The meal break, defined by California law, is at least 30 minutes. Some workers, such as those who staff service desks and interact directly with the public, have little flexibility and must coordinate with co-workers about when to take breaks. Other workers, such as medical professionals, are often pressed for time and do not take a full break. Still others are able to take breaks comfortably of 45 minutes to an hour, depending on their tasks and their managers. Night-shiftworkers in medical facilities sometimes need to make special meal arrangements during periods when the local canteen is closed. In general, though, the on-site canteen enables workers to grab a quick meal when time is short.

The KPNC Fresno facility is working with its food vendor to provide "heart healthful meals" based on guidelines established by the American Heart Association. These are mainly foods low in cholesterol and saturated fats, with an emphasis on larger servings of vegetables and meat substitutes, such as soya and other beans. The KPNC Walnut Creek facility now posts calorie information for most dishes. The Richmond facility displays signs with healthy ideas, such as ordering meals with gravy or high-calorie toppings on the side in a separate bowl or container. (Richmond also offers a popular cooking class that features healthy foods.) The KPNC Oakland facility is trying to reduce the portion sizes of canteen meals. The KPNC South Bay facility near San Jose benefits from the local Asian influence, with canteen dishes such as Vietnamese noodle soup with vegetables. The KPNC Petaluma facility attempted to offer more low-fat and low-sugar food options. The changes lasted only a few months before they were replaced with the original items. The vendor told Petaluma that the healthier items were not selling – an issue discussed further at the end of the case study. Vending machine changes have also been difficult, with the suppliers hesitant to stock healthier foods for fear they might not sell.

Possible disadvantages of food solution

The farmers' markets have been successful in encouraging workers to eat more fruit and vegetables. One possible disadvantage is that markets held on Friday don't help workers secure fresh produce for the following week. Many Americans shop for food once a week at the weekend, particularly single-parent and dual-worker families. A farmers' market on a Wednesday could enable workers to purchase leafy green vegetables and other produce that quickly lose freshness, a supplement to weekend purchases. One possible disadvantage of the canteen changes is that they might not go far enough to give the desired improvements, that is, lower weight and better blood pressure, blood glucose and cholesterol levels. Some employees in certain regions have access to some healthier foods, but it is not clear whether there is an incentive to make healthy choices.

Costs and benefits to enterprise

The programmes to date have incurred little cost. Most of the cost has been for incentives and prizes for walking teams (see below). Hanging signs in the cafeterias and posting messages on tables have had little cost associated with them. The farmers' market is essentially free.

There has been a significant increase in employee satisfaction from surveys taken after the Employee Wellness and Recognition Department launched its employee wellness campaign. There are no data yet available, however, on weight loss, lower cholesterol levels and other positive health markers.

Government incentives

No financial incentives in terms of tax breaks or subsidies are available for the aforementioned programmes.

Practical advice for implementation

A farmers' market can take care of itself once it is thoughtfully planned out. Most of California enjoys mild weather all the year round, which makes the market easy to sustain. There is no reason, however, why enterprises in colder climates could not host markets at least six months of the year. New York, Boston and other cold cities have farmers' markets from early April to late October. Even in the winter, some farmers can offer squash, apples, apple cider, breads, winter greens and greenhouse produce.

Employees have been very interested in participating in employee walks, wearing pedometers and competing individually or in teams for prizes. The organization would like to carry that success into the area of nutrition. The recommendation to eat healthier foods has been a hard sell. As seen in other case studies, the issue may be one of supply and demand. The Petaluma facility, where healthy food options didn't sell well and were subsequently removed from the menu, offers a pertinent example. The health coordinator there has recommended other facilities to advertise healthier items and educate the employees when introducing healthier food options. That is, create the demand and the food vendor will supply. As we saw in Canada's Husky canteen case study (Chapter 4), a health-conscious staff will choose healthy foods (and even healthy snacks) over less healthy options. The Richmond facility offers an interesting case to follow. The popular cooking class may lead employees to request healthier food options at lunch at the canteen. There appears to be very good communication among the many health coordinators, and each is willing to learn from the other. Kaiser Permanente of Northern California's contribution to employee nutrition is work in progress, which is a fine way to move forward.

Union/employee perspective

Kaiser Permanente of Northern California is a non-union site. All changes have been initiated and implemented by management, although worker suggestions are welcomed and often put into action.

7.2 Five-a-day: The fruit and vegetable movement

A preponderance of evidence now reveals that consuming fruits and vegetables can significantly reduce the risk of cardiovascular disease and certain cancers. According to the WHO Health Report, low fruit and vegetable intake is behind about 31 per cent of ischemic heart disease and 11 per cent of stroke worldwide. The WHO International Agency for Research on Cancer (IARC) estimates that fruit and vegetable consumption can prevent 20–30 per cent of upper gastrointestinal cancers and 5–12 per cent of all cancers worldwide (WHO, 2003c). Up to 2.7 million lives could be saved each year if fruit and vegetable consumption increased (WHO, 2003d, p. 3). The FAO and WHO recommend a minimum of 400 grams of fruit and vegetables per day, excluding potatoes and other starchy tubers. Most people worldwide eat only about 200 grams. Consuming at least 400 grams would help prevent chronic diseases and obesity, and also alleviate many micronutrient deficiencies in less developed countries (WHO/FAO, 2002). A "vegetarian" diet – by choice, culture or circumstance – will not necessarily have the adequate amount of fruits and vegetables. Poor populations subsisting on mostly starch or grains are at risk of numerous diseases and deficiencies. This is why health experts recommend eating a variety of fruits and vegetables.

How, then, can workers gain access to fruits and vegetables at the workplace? Many wealthier countries have a national programme promoting the consumption of fruits and vegetables. These have similar names, "five-a-day," "six-a-day," "*5 al dia*," etc. Some countries shoot high: France strives for ten servings a day. Hungary's programme is more realistic for its culture, a push for three a day. The Netherlands separates fruits and vegetables into a "2+2" programme. Finland doesn't consider servings, which can be ambiguous, and instead advises its citizens to eat 500 grams (half a kilo) of fruits and vegetables. Japan has a unique approach to good nutrition, which is more of a cultural attitude than an official programme: people there try to eat at least 30 different kinds of foodstuffs each day.

These "five-a-day" programmes are built through partnerships of government organizations (health, agriculture, consumer, education), NGOs (associations for the prevention of cancer, heart disease, diabetes, etc.) and industry (growers, importers, wholesalers, retailers). The programmes, with various levels of funding and presence from country to country, are based on science; and this includes nutrition, behaviour, communication, fund-raising and coalition-building skills. Representatives meet periodically at international symposiums organized in part by the WHO. The most recent was the Fourth "5-a-Day" International Symposium, in Christchurch, New Zealand, in August 2004. Few data are available about the success of various programmes.

In each of these fruit and vegetable programmes the target intervention group has not been workers per se, but rather schools, disadvantaged communities and the public at large. The Danish programme, as we will see in the next case study, is the one exception. As addressed in Chapter 3, not targeting workers is a greatly missed opportunity. When work consumes half of the waking hours for many workers during weekdays, and when there are no fruit or vegetables at the workplace, how can workers reach the "five-a-day" goal?

The definition of "vegetable" varies significantly between countries and regions. Largely this concerns the inclusion or exclusion of grains, beans and tubers. Consuming 400 grams of corn as the main vegetable, however, will not produce the desired effect of chronic disease and micronutrient deficiency reduction. Portion size and serving size are also ambiguous terms. Health experts, in designing local "five-a-day" programmes, need to consider this.

The FAO notes that 400 grams of fruits and vegetables per person per day equates to 146 kg per year. FAO data reveal that 173 kg per person per year is available, divided into 111.6 kg of vegetables and 61.4 kg of fruit (WHO, 2003d, p. 7). However, up to 33 per cent can be lost in distribution, reducing the amount to 115 kg, which is only 75 per cent of the desired level (WHO, 2003d, p. 7). So if the world is to eat more fruits and vegetables, more of these foods need to be produced, or better efficiencies are needed in distribution. Increasing production is quite feasible, according to the FAO, because, unlike animal husbandry, fruit and vegetable production is well adapted for small-scale production. Even in Japan, a highly industrialized country where land is scarce, it is not uncommon for city dwellers to purchase throughout the year basic green necessities – *daikon* (large white radish), *gobo* (burdock), *hakusai* (cabbage), cucumbers, green peppers, leeks, carrots, spinach, lotus root and much more – that are grown within a few kilometres of their homes. Developing countries may find new business opportunities to meet the increased fruit and vegetable demand from countries where there is not all-year-round production of vegetables locally, such as in the United States. It is hoped that small-scale production in developing countries would produce fruits and vegetables for local consumption among workers. Both farmers and workers should benefit from an abundance of inexpensive, local food, sold in bulk to internationally owned local companies.

But there is no guarantee that international market forces will be so kind. Many factors need to be established to secure equity, according to Dr. Carlos Monteiro of the University of São Paulo of the Fruit and Vegetable Promotion Initiative. This includes working with the private and public sectors and with NGOs in ushering a "nutritional transition" away from the famine stage (scarce, monotonous, cereal-based diets) and towards a more diverse diet, all the while striving to reduce poverty and malnutrition. In short, vegetables are not grown in poor regions familiar with hunger because they are not as filling as starch and grain, and cannot be stored for more than a few weeks.

Worldwide, the emphasis for the fruit and vegetable movement has been to raise production and distribution efficiencies (something the meat industries apparently have mastered), to educate communities and to feed school children. Health experts seem to recognize the importance of fruit and vegetables in the workplace, but any such reference is relegated to a casual suggestion, such as the following from the WHO *global strategy on diet, physical activity and health* (WHO, 2004b):

> Workplaces are important settings for health promotion and disease prevention. People need to be given the opportunity to make healthy choices in the workplace in order to reduce their exposure to risk. Further, the cost to employers of morbidity attributed to non-communicable diseases is increasing rapidly. Workplaces should make possible healthy food choices and support and encourage physical activity.

No suggestions are offered on how to provide workers with access to fruits and vegetables. More typical are well-thought and noteworthy programmes, such as the United States "five-a-day" initiative to ensure that school cafeteria menus include adequate choices of fruits and vegetables. Workers, naturally, are treated as adults and left to make their own choices (despite repeatedly demonstrating poor knowledge of nutrition) in obtaining healthy foods during work. There appears to be no reason why workplaces cannot assume a dominant role in the WHO/FAO agenda. Huge business opportunities exist for companies, at a national or local level, to purchase more fruits and vegetables for their workers just as schools are required to do. The Dole Fruit Company is diligently supporting the "five-a-day" efforts at schools. Other companies, including Dole, work with "five-a-day" in producing educational materials for consumers at supermarket chain stores. Clearly the missing player in the scheme is the millions of workplaces and millions of workers around the world.

7.3   Firmafrugt: Danish Workplace Fruit Initiative

Denmark is the only country with a well-established programme bringing the "five-a-day" fruit and vegetable concept into the workplace. In Denmark, this is actually a "six-a-day" programme, called "*6 om dagen*". For most countries, the fruit and vegetable promotion programmes are aimed at communities in the broadest sense. These programmes are educational outreach efforts to raise the awareness of the importance of fruit and vegetables in reducing the risk of chronic diseases. Occasionally, as in the United States, the programme is targeted towards under served "high-risk" groups, such as minorities. The concept of increasing fruit and vegetable intake at the workplace is not exotic; recommendations have certainly been made. The *WHO global strategy on diet, physical activity and health* (WHO, 2004b) mentions the importance of fruit and vegetables in the workplace at the end of the report. Denmark has taken the next logical step with its *firmafrugt* initiative, a well-conceived, organized and evaluated national programme to introduce free or low-cost fruits at work.

A Danish dietary survey in 1995 revealed that the average Dane consumed 280 grams of fruit and vegetables per day, far short of the FAO and WHO minimum recommendation of 400 grams. The amount was also essentially the same as it was in 1985, a reflection of no change despite public-awareness efforts on the topic during that period. In 1998 the Danish Veterinary and Food Agency teamed with the Danish Heart Association, the Danish Cancer Society and the National Board of Health to publish ambitious new recommendations for fruit and vegetable intake: 600 grams daily for anyone over the age of 10. With monies from the Ministry of Food, Fisheries and Agriculture and private funding, health experts launched a six-a-day fruit and vegetable research project. This would place the "6-a-day" programme on solid ground by identifying effective means for increasing sales and consumption of fruit and vegetables. Out of this research came three target areas: schools, workplaces (*firmafrugt*) and retail settings. The focus would be different from previous efforts of health education. Denmark wanted to increase the availability of and access to fruit and vegetables in these settings. Campaign activities were under way by 2000.

The following summary of the initial workplace effort is from a research paper by Robert Pederson of the Danish Cancer Society entitled, *6 a day Denmark: Increasing availability of and access to fruits and vegetables* (Pederson, 2004):

> Workplace fruit schemes cover a wide variety of schemes, ranging from extra fruit supplied to employees by canteens to private wholesale companies delivering ready to eat fruit in decorative baskets. Financing of schemes ranged from 100 per cent

employer paid schemes to 50/50 financing schemes paid for by individual employees. Fruit and vegetable intake was measured at five intervention and seven control worksites at baseline (n=283) and follow-up (n=248) using a modified 24-h recall instrument. The results showed a significant increase of 70 grams fruit per day for employees at intervention workplaces, concurrently male employees had a 50 per cent decrease in candy and sweet snacks.

Evaluation also showed that 96 per cent of the employees ate workplace fruit daily or nearly daily. Candy and sweet snacks were down by 22 grams per day, or 50 per cent. This translates into a 0.7 serving increase in fruit and vegetable consumption, positive news for the "6 om dagen" effort. The Danish Cancer Society in fact describes *firmafrugt* as one of its easiest and most effective interventions. The Pederson paper also described catering, a second aspect of *firmafrugt*:

> Five demonstration canteens worked with increasing the amount of fruit and vegetables served in canteens. Personnel and management were involved in defining the scope of activities and implementation, and canteen personnel worked closely with the project team. Intake was measured by weighing fruits and vegetables served minus waste at baseline, during intervention and at a one-year follow-up. Significant increases in fruit and vegetable intake were shown at all five demonstration canteens, on average 70 g/day/customer, and had increased to 95 g/day/customer at follow-up.

Businesses have since latched on to the *firmafrugt* project. Participation has climbed from 623 workplaces in 2001 to nearly 5,000 workplaces in 2003, and to over 9,200 in 2004 (Meyer, 2004). This represents 9 per cent of the Danish workforce. Currently private enterprises outnumber public ones by about 8 to 1. The participating enterprises are largely white-collar offices, but many factories are involved. The fruit itself is usually quite basic: apples, pears, oranges and seasonal fruits. Fruit and sometimes juice are served during breaks and at meetings. The fruit is simply displayed in baskets or in plain plastic bowls. This might be in a break room, boardroom, office entrance or canteen. Disposable towels are often available. Typically there is one piece of fruit available per employee per day, but some companies have a two-piece or unlimited policy. Fruit for shiftworkers is usually placed aside.

There is anecdotal evidence that the project attracts new employees, reduces turnover and promotes new business. Surveys show that: 97 per cent of workers consider *firmafrugt* a sign that the company cares about them; 85 per cent said the money couldn't be spent on anything better; and 85 per cent said they would miss the programme a lot if it were cancelled. When asked why they ate the fruit, employees said it's delicious (95 per cent), it's healthy (86 per cent), it's free (51 per cent), it makes them eat less candy

(47 per cent), or it provides a break (2 per cent) (Meyer, 2004). Employers see the programme as inexpensive and rewarding. The annual cost per employee is said to be about equal to the cost of one extra sick day per year per employee (Pederson, 2004, personal comment). Yet the price can vary from €0.25–0.75 (US$0.33–1.00) per piece of fruit, depending on the type of service – wholesale, drop-box schemes, decorative baskets, etc. Employers speculate that if fruit can balance blood sugar levels, this would lead to higher productivity, particularly later in the day. The programme is a nice addition to companies too small to offer a canteen. The 9 per cent of companies that feature *firmafrugt* also benefit from being trendy, a characteristic that could fade as more companies participate.

The fruit industry sees the programme as a new market. There are 40 new companies in operation in Denmark selling fruit to companies. Delivery varies according to the customer's wishes (and storing capacity). Fruit is often delivered daily or two to three times a week. Fruit might arrive in the original cartons or in decorative baskets. Trade unions have not yet been formally involved but remain supportive. In 2004 five trade unions participated in a think-tank for a *firmafrugt* campaign planned for 2005. The campaign will focus on public and blue-collar workplaces because workers in those sectors have lower fruit and vegetable intake on average compared with white-collar workers. This group includes the police, the retail trade, slaughterhouses, the fish and poultry industries and home helpers for the elderly. From the very beginning of the programme, the Women's Workers Union in particular has supported *firmafrugt* by participating in work group and public relations activities within its organization. For example, the union featured *firmafrugt* in its newsletters and magazines, and made it an agenda topic for various seminars and courses.

There are no apparent disadvantages to the workplace fruit concept. One possible concern could be waste, rotting fruit and messy workstations. Yet no complaints have surfaced. Another concern is devaluation, that is, workers would come to value fruit less because it is free or cheap. Just the opposite appears to be happening, however. Workplace fruit is an idea that nearly any enterprise can accommodate. Set-up costs are nil. Refrigeration or electricity is not needed. Local supermarkets or produce wholesalers can supply fruit in lieu of a formal supply system. Vegetables, too, can be introduced into the system. Market research shows that bite-size portions of vegetables – such as baby carrots, dried soya beans, dried wedges of root vegetables or oil-free popcorn – make for tasty and popular snacks.

7.4   Street foods and workers' nutrition

Street foods, as defined by the FAO, are ready-to-eat foods and beverages prepared and/or sold in streets or similar public areas. The FAO estimates that over two billion people worldwide eat street foods; and, not surprisingly, a good deal of them are workers grabbing a midday or evening meal.

Street food vending can be found in any country, and the system has many positive attributes. It is a source of employment for millions of men and women; and it is a source of inexpensive and, quite frequently, nutritious food. The negative sides of street food vending are the high risk of spreading food-borne illnesses, traffic congestion, rubbish and, occasionally, worker abuse. Food safety is a particular concern in all countries, rich and poor, whether the food comes from a hot-dog cart in New York City or a *som tam* (papaya salad) stall in Bangkok. The following pages concern street foods and programmes to improve this sector in emerging economies. The countries featured are singled out for the solutions they offer in improving the street food sector engaged in feeding large urban populations. Such solutions can significantly enhance workers' nutrition.

Countries that have loathed street food vending are coming to accept it. In reality, there is little choice for these countries because of the rapid growth of street food vending, fuelled in the past two decades by internal migration into city centres. In many countries, street food vending is far from a marginal enterprise. In Calcutta the street food trade yields a US$100 million profit annually; in Cotonou, Benin, the yearly turnover is US$20 million (Codjia, 2000). In Bangkok there are over 20,000 vendors (Dawson, Liamrangsi and Boccas, 1996). Similarly, consumers spend a significant proportion of their household budget on street foods: 25 to 30 per cent in Latin America, for example (Codjia, 2000). Street food vending flourishes because it fulfils a need. Thus, shutting down street food vending can be more trouble than improving it. This is not to say that improving street food vending is an easy task. Street food vending is both simple and complex. The simplicity is responsible for its proliferation: street food vendors need only a box to sell their food, not an expensive stall or van. The complexity lies partly in the economic and social changes behind the street food sector's growth and partly in the investment in education and infrastructure needed to improve its safety, all the while keeping street foods economically viable. Merely providing an infrastructure (water supply, drainage) often fails to accomplish a project's goal without providing education (toilet use and hand washing).

Street food vending varies slightly from region to region and culture to culture. In sub-Saharan Africa, street food vendors are predominantly women. The cost of setting up a vending business is low; cooking equipment

One of thousands of streer vendors in Jakarta meeting workers' daily needs (ILO/M. Reade Rounds).

often comes from the home. These women are able to employ traditional cooking skills and feed their children as well. Women are the primary street vendors in Viet Nam too. In India, women tend to sell traditional foods while men, who make up the majority, sell modern or urban dishes. In Mexico and Thailand, the variety of foods available from different vendors is dazzling; nearly any type of food can be purchased on the street. Similarly, steady customers vary from region to region too. Over three-quarters of the elementary school children in Ile-ife, Nigeria, buy two meals a day from street food vendors, and 96 per cent buy at least breakfast; the same scene is played out in many other African cities (Codjia, 2000). Low-wage workers represent the bulk of street food customers in sub-Saharan Africa, while white-collar and more affluent workers patronize street food stands in Latin America and parts of Asia.

One common thread for street food around the world is that it is largely an informal sector feeding informal sector workers. The informal sector is the main source of employment for the majority of workers in many parts of Africa and Asia. In South Africa, for example, workers in the informal sectors outnumber those in the formal sectors by over 20 to 1 (Chakravarty, 2001). Without the option of street foods, many workers would be hard pressed to find a solid meal at an affordable price. Street foods can be

Serving tea to customers in the Tigray region (ILO/A. Fiorente).

nutritious. In Calcutta, a well-rounded 1,000 kcal meal (with adequate protein, fat and carbohydrates) costs around US$0.25. Similarly in Bogor, Indonesia, for the same price, a worker can obtain approximately half of the daily recommended allowance for protein, iron and vitamins A and C. In Bangkok, street foods provide 40 per cent of total energy and 44 per cent of iron intake (Codjia, 2000).

Unfortunately, a bout of food poisoning from street food, which is not uncommon, nullifies any gains in the nutritional status of workers. Food poisoning from biological contaminants (bacteria, parasites) can knock a worker out of work for several days and, occasionally, lead to permanent disability. Also, chemical contaminates (metals, pesticides, illegal additives) can lead to neurological problems, cancer and other long-term health conditions. There is no estimate for the number of food poisonings from street vending, for they usually go unreported, but the WHO assumes it is huge, and estimates that over 70 per cent of diarrhoea is caused by contaminated food. One in three people worldwide suffers annually from a disease caused by microorganisms in food, and 1.8 million children die from severe food and waterborne diarrhoea (WHO, 2002c, p. 7). One example of chemical adulteration is an unhealthy yellow dye used instead of saffron in India, with no knowledge among vendors or customers that the dye is illegal. Illegal levels of saccharine often sweeten food there, too, again without knowledge of the consequences.

Street foods can become unsafe during primary production or transport, which introduces unsafe food into the market without inspection. Once inside a market or vending stall, food can become unsafe through improper handling, preparation or storage. Or vendors themselves can transfer harmful bacteria from their hands or utensils, often a result of a lack of resources for washing. Food can also become adulterated or misrepresented by unscrupulous distributors or undereducated vendors who do not understand food regulations. Unhealthy chemicals, such as pesticides or fumes from the streets, can enter the food at any stage in its production.

How then does a country maintain the positive attributes of street vending – easy accessibility, fast service, low cost, use of local foods, a source of nutrition, a source of livelihood and a source of social support for poor urban populations – while making the food safer? The FAO response, which began in earnest about 15 years ago, has been to make street food vending legitimate. Legitimizing street food vending enables health professionals to teach proper hygiene methods to vendors, who are largely poorly educated and often illiterate from rural regions. Raising the legal status of street food vending also encourages vendors to invest in safer equipment knowing they won't be hassled (and sometimes extorted) by the local police.

Cambodia: a woman carries a headload of street food (FAO/G. Bizzarri).

Malawi: roasted cassava is sold with roast meat (FAO/N. Mahunga).

The FAO has studied the street food sector in over 20 countries in Africa, Asia and Latin America, and has initiated or supported projects in about as many. These include Bolivia, Colombia, Côte d'Ivoire, Ecuador, Ghana, India, Lesotho, Mexico, Mozambique, Nigeria, Peru, Philippines, Senegal, South Africa, Thailand, Zaire and the region of the Caribbean and Central America. Data are available from the FAO on each of these projects. Each project involves such elements as: strategies for local authorities to address problems of street food regulations and control, waste collection, sewage, and spatial organization; training for public health inspectors and food producers; training for vendors; and the development of appropriate technological innovations (better stalls, for example) to be adapted by preparers and traders of street food at various stages of their operations (Codjia, 2000). The FAO has several success stories, although all these projects are aimed at the population at large and not workers specifically. Interestingly, FAO projects in the Philippines and Nigeria that use street foods for school feeding programmes can be adapted to feed workers in industrial parks or other high-density commercial districts.

The WHO maintains a slightly broader scope with its Healthy Marketplace projects, which cover street foods as well as food markets. The 2003 WHO publication with the NGO GTZ (Deutsche Gesellschaft für Technische Zusammenarbeit) entitled *Healthy marketplaces: Working towards ensuring the supply of safer food* (WHO EMRO, 2003) provides practical advice to initiate, implement and evaluate healthy marketplaces to improve access to safe and nutritious foods. The guide can be used in urban or rural settings. Governments and employers whose employees frequent marketplaces clearly have a vested interest in ensuring a healthy food supply. Pilot projects are under way in all the WHO regions; the guide referenced above reports on successes and challenges in healthy marketplaces established in Egypt, Suriname and Viet Nam. Related to this is the "PHAST food" movement (Participatory Hygiene and Sanitation Transformations). More information about this effort to promote good hygiene behaviour and improve sanitation is relayed in Chapter 11.

The WHO produced posters and similar educational materials that listed "ten golden rules for safe food preparation". These are:

1. Choose foods processed for safety

2. Cook food well

3. Eat cooked food immediately

4. Store cooked food safely

5. Reheat cooked food well or keep cold

6. Protect food from contact with insects, rats, other animals

7. Wash hands repeatedly

8. Avoid contact between raw and cooked foods

9. Keep all surfaces and utensils clean

10. Use safe water

However, the WHO wanted to make it even simpler than this for vendors to understand. The WHO condensed the ten golden rules into "five keys for safer food". These are described in a poster (available in 25 languages so far), which one can download at: www.who.int/foodsafety/publications/consumer/5keys/en/. Manuals for school canteens, home and street vending are available as well for health workers. These five keys are:

1. Keep clean (this includes hands, surfaces, utensils and food)

2. Separate raw and cooked (e.g. use separate containers and utensils)

3. Cook thoroughly (e.g. bring to boil, reheat)

4. Keep food at safe temperatures (e.g. above 60°C or below 5°C)

5. Use safe water and raw materials (e.g. pasteurized milk, watch for expiry date)

In 2003, at the 53rd Session of WHO Regional Committee for Africa, the WHO Regional Director for Africa stated that food-borne illness presents a major and continuing challenge to Africa as it adversely affects health, lowers economic productivity and, in several cases, results in death and disability. A report was presented noting that "well-structured national food safety programmes that are responsive to present and future needs and challenges in food safety should be of high priority to all governments; such programmes should include promotion and integration of preventive and scientific risk-based approaches to food safety systems". This report recommends that countries should establish coordinated enforceable food safety policies and regulations, and establish or reinforce participation in activities of the Codex Alimentarius Commission, a joint body of the WHO and the FAO. Information of the role of the Codex in street food safety is presented in Chapter 11.

The following three case studies are summaries of FAO evaluations of its projects in Calcutta, Bangkok and cities in South Africa. This is followed by a case study of the WHO's Healthy Marketplace project in the United Republic of Tanzania.

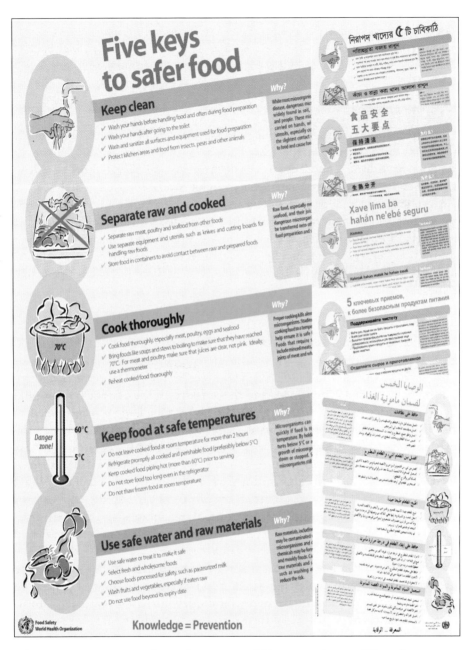

The WHO's Five Keys to Safer Food poster is available in more than 25 different languages.

7.4.1 Calcutta, India

The following is a summary of a case study by Indira Chakravarty and Colette Canet, presented in an article entitled "Street foods in Calcutta" from the journal Food, Nutrition and Agriculture, *published by the FAO in 1996. Appropriate updates have been added.*

Key findings

Street foods are widely popular among workers in Calcutta, particularly those in the informal sector who have no other food option. However, vendors have little knowledge of basic hygiene and illegal food additives, which jeopardize workers' nutrition. A pilot study revealed that both the Government and vendors are willing to improve the situation: vendors agree to zoning; unions agree to training; and the Government agrees to infrastructure improvements, such as more rubbish bins and potable water sources, as well as low-interest loans. Health experts improved hygiene in the four study sites with creative training. The "Calcutta model" is now spreading to nearby cities.

Background

Like many metropolises, Calcutta has experienced unprecedented growth in recent years. As workers continue to pour into the city, demand for basic services such as food and shelter far exceeds supply. Over-populated city centres have pushed many workers to the outskirts of the city and beyond, and long commutes to work have become the norm. People have been forced to change their schedules, tastes and attitudes towards eating. Thus we see the rise in street food vending, once viewed negatively as a lower-class phenomenon. Street foods have replaced many small restaurants because of their convenience. The food is inexpensive, and the taste is acceptable. Food stalls, sometimes no more elaborate than a box or bucket, spring up wherever people congregate, such as office centres, railway stations and marketplaces. As for marketplaces, vendors who once sold only raw foods now sell prepared foods in addition, capitalizing on the demand.

Street food vending provides income for many who would otherwise be unemployed. Entering into the street food vending business requires an investment of only a few rupees and a location, which are admittedly hard to find, as vendors are protective of their territory. Street foods are also a suitable source of nutrition, with many meals well balanced in their offerings of protein, fats, carbohydrates and calories. Despite the popularity and economic impact (over US$100 million a year), however, street foods have been barely tolerated by the city authorities, although this is changing.

The project

With funding and guidance from the FAO, the All India Institute of Hygiene and Public Health (AIIHPH) set out to improve the safety of street foods. The first step – which began in the early 1990s with cooperation from the Calcutta Municipal Corporation, the elected local government of Calcutta – was a survey to better understand the street food sector. The project, called "Improving Street Foods in Calcutta", largely entailed information gathering, although a small amount of training for vendors was performed. The study covered such issues as the legal aspects of street food vending; the safety of food preparation and handling; the socio-economic aspects affecting consumers and vendors; street food industry practices; and the environmental consequences of the activity.

The project involved four sites. The first was College Square and the area around Calcutta University and the Medical College Hospital. Customers were largely students and middle-class workers. The second site was the Sealdah area, which includes a large railway station, a college and shopping centres. Here the customers were largely commuters and low-wage workers. The third site was Dalhousie Square, which includes the Writers' Building, a central and congested area of about 150 square metres and 65 vendors. Here the customers were largely office workers and sightseers. The fourth site was the Gariahat shopping and residential area in southern Calcutta. Customers here were middle class and affluent. The project classified street foods into three groups: foods prepared in small factories and brought to street food stalls for sale; foods prepared at the vendor's home and brought to the stall; and foods prepared and sold at the stall.

Of the over 900 customers interviewed, all were employed. Their monthly salaries varied from 250 to 10,000 rupees (US$5 to US$200), from low- to middle-wage workers. Around 80 per cent were male, under age 48. The women customers had "dual careers," working inside and outside the home with no time to prepare lunch. For these women (and their husbands), street foods were the solution for midday meals and sometimes evening meals. Many customers lived far from Calcutta, commuting 20 to 100 kilometres each day, and meals were bought for the train ride home. In the Writers' Building area, about 75 per cent of the office workers bought food on the street five days a week. Over all, half the workers at the four sites bought street meals four or five days a week, and they had done this for years. They patronized different vendors and they ate on the spot. On average they spent 250 rupees (US$5) a month on street foods, which is as much as the monthly salary of the lowest-wage workers in the study. (The average meal is around 5 rupees (US$0.10), which means workers were buying on average 50 meals a month on the street.) A few workers spent upwards of 1,000 rupees (US$20) a month on street food, essentially obtaining 100 per cent of their total calories on the street.

Customers were conscious of their health, although they knew that street foods could be insanitary. They thought grilled, hot foods were the safest. Many meals were nutritious, providing 1,000 kcal and decent amounts of vegetables, fat and protein. Street foods were the least expensive means to obtain a meal outside the home. The selection was diverse, too, reflecting the many ethnic groups in Calcutta. Over 50 items were available for sale.

Over 300 vendors were interviewed, representing 30 per cent of the vendors in the project sites. All told, Calcutta has over 100,000 street food stalls and perhaps as high as 130,000. Half of the stalls are stationary; half are mobile. The stationary stalls employ over 100,000 workers, including the owners. In this study, all the stalls were permanent or semi-permanent. Of the interviewed vendors, 90 per cent were male, aged between 20 and 45. These men tended to sell foods with a cosmopolitan character, while women tended to sell traditional Bengali foods. Over 20 per cent of the vendors were illiterate, and the education level overall was low. Many vendors were commuters, carrying their wares on the train for 25 to 30 kilometres. They operated the stalls from 10 a.m. in the morning to 9 p.m. in the evening. They were unwilling to disclose their daily proceeds, but a conservative estimate placed their monthly profit at about 2,500 rupees (US$50) on average, much higher than the minimum wage. Vendor employees earned about 900 rupees (US$18) per month.

Food contamination was abundant. One concern was the toxic and synthetic dye called metanil yellow, long used in India as a saffron substitute and in fact illegal. Vendors did not know about regulations on metanil or any artificial colours. Unauthorized use of food additives, including metanil, was found in 30 of the 50 food samples collected. Many food samples also contained saccharin, which is only allowed in carbonated water at very low levels, below 100 ppm. Fermented foods such as lassi had high levels of microbiological contamination, even though the pH of this buttermilk drink normally hinders the growth of salmonella and other bacteria. The contamination occurred after processing, a result of poor storage and handling. E. coli was found in over half the food samples, another sign of improper handling and probably from faecal contamination. Unfermented dishes such as curries had pathogenic bacteria and larger parasites, probably from poor personal hygiene and prolonged holding. Water came from municipal sources and was of high quality but was subsequently contaminated in storage buckets and drums. Water for drinking, cooking and washing food, dishes and hands was contaminated in nearly half of the samples. (A separate study on water quality across the city had found that only 7 per cent of drinking-water samples around Calcutta were unsatisfactory and 88 per cent were excellent.)

Vendors in the study were unaware of food safety regulations and had no training in food handling. Calcutta maintains the authority to regulate, license and inspect food providers; but because the street food sector is not a legal entity, little is done to protect consumers. Vendors, however, were not adverse to regulation. Many were vocal about gaining legal recognition for the sector. Many indeed paid "protection" money to corrupt officials to stay in business. Some vendors had joined the Centre for Indian Trade Unions and the West Bengal Hawkers' Union in order to gain a unified voice.

Intervention: Part I

A symposium was held at the AIIHPH soon after the completion of the survey to assess the results and plan a course of action. The institute invited all the key players: street food vendors, the police department, the Government of West Bengal, the Calcutta Municipal Corporation, the Calcutta Metropolitan Development Authority, the Calcutta Metropolitan Water and Sanitation Authority, local universities and the FAO. Many recommendations were made, although only a few have been implemented ten years on.

Two elements of street food vending that were immediately clear to the symposium attendees were: (1) that the growth was unchecked and something needed to be done to control it; and (2) that because of the lack of jobs in the formal sector, municipal bodies could not eliminate or otherwise thwart street food sector activities merely in the name of maintaining health and order. That is, street food vending was too important not to improve. Training became the main component of Calcutta's street food policy. The AIIHPH developed training programmes for the vendors to improve hygiene, which were at first pilot programmes for a prolonged period but which are now being fully implemented. The training began in full in 2002 with 100 vendors, quickly followed by 2,000 more vendors divided into groups of 50. The programmes and materials were developed from the original study. Techniques include open-air lectures, exhibitions, street plays and video presentations. Vendors are instructed on the nature of food-borne illnesses; how to keep foods either cold (below 5°C) or hot (above 60°C); how to wash their hands, dishes and food, and how to use and store water; how to cook foods, separating raw and cooked foods during preparation; and why spitting spreads disease.

Calcutta police were also trained on how to monitor food stalls. Regulations were proposed. These include a system for licensing and rules for vending locations: only one side of the pavement will be allowed for vending; vending will not be allowed on carriageways, overpasses (flyovers) or where pedestrian traffic is constricted; and stalls must stay more than 15 metres away from busy bus stops. Vendors requested bins for waste disposal and more convenient access to potable water. Bolder plans include low-interest loans for vendors to invest in better vending equipment, such as kiosks or trolleys with stainless steel parts and canvas hoods to minimize bacterial growth. Three banks have made steps to accommodate such loans. Similarly, under the Government of India Scheme for Urban Microenterprises, vendors would be eligible for kiosks on condition they pay for them within five years.

Intervention: Part II

The original pilot studies have evolved into the Street Food Quality and Safety Programme. According to Professor Indira Chakravarty, AIIHPH Dean, two key measures have been taken to secure the sustainability of the programme: continuous training is being imparted to vendors, vendors' unions, consumers, police, municipality officers and other interested parties; and training manuals and other materials (posters, pamphlets, booklets and audio and video cassettes) have been developed and are being disseminated. Vendor unions have taken the initiative to develop a core group of trainers, provide training to vendors, make site visits and organize group meetings.

The "Calcutta model" has since spread to neighbouring Howrah and Burdwan, where initial studies have revealed a situation similar to that in Calcutta: that is, inexpensive and tasty food, good nutritional value, similar customer base, yet high levels of contamination and poor hygiene. An action plan has been developed with the following recommendations:

- preparation of list of vendors;

- identification of streets where hawking can be allowed;

- preparation of area-wise layout plan;

- proper coordination mechanism between municipality, police, vendors' union, vendors, etc. for overall improvement;

- provision of easy access to safe potable water;

- provision of proper waste disposal;

- provision of wastewater disposal;

- issuance of license/identity card to the vendors;

- regular analysis of food and water samples;

- health check-up of vendors;

- selling of food in properly designed kiosks; and

- regular programme on motivation and awareness generation among the regulatory bodies, vendors including vendors' unions (trainers) and consumers at all levels by training, education, communication and motivation.

And so, positive change has been incremental in eastern India.

7.4.2 Bangkok, Thailand

The following is a summary of a case study by Richard Dawson, Suang Liamrangsi and Franck Boccas, presented in an article entitled "Bangkok's street food project" from the journal Food, Nutrition and Agriculture, *published by the FAO in 1996. Appropriate updates have been added.*

Key findings

Health experts minimized the risk of food-borne illnesses from street foods by implementing a ten-point sanitary code of practice, largely applicable in most countries. Key to the strategy was the crafting of inexpensive solutions that vendors could implement themselves with limited resources, such as separating ice for human consumption and for food storage. This led to a slight compromise of the ten-point code of practice but yielded significant improvements nonetheless. Sanitation improvements led to more customers and higher profits for the vendors.

Background

Health experts began to study street foods in Bangkok in the early 1990s, during the same time frame as the preceding Calcutta case study. Bangkok was similar to Calcutta in that the street foods were plentiful, inexpensive, popular among workers, and often tasty and nutritious – and often laden with pathogens and toxic chemical substances. Yet while the Calcutta Government barely tolerated street foods and police harassment was not uncommon, the Bangkok Metropolitan Administration authorized and regulated street food vending through the city police and district public health officers. In the neighbouring city of Nonthaburi, the Environmental and Health Division of the local government had similar responsibilities. This legal recognition provided the foundation to improve the health and environmental risks from the street food sector.

The project

The Thai Department of Health (DOH) provides technical advice to local authorities concerning street foods. In 1994, after several years of study, the DOH teamed up with the FAO to conduct a pilot project in Bangkok and

Nonthaburi to improve the safety of street foods and their impact on the environment. Around the same time, the DOH had developed a ten-point sanitary code of practice for the street food sector to guide municipalities. The new study would examine the practicality of the code and, more important, determine a strategy for a sustainable programme for vendors to finance themselves without the need for subsidies. The DOH sanitary code, called the Code of Practice for Street Foods, is summarized here:

1. Vending units should be strong and easy to clean, and all food-preparation surfaces should always be clean and at least 60 cm above the ground.

2. Food and drinks should be protected from micro-organisms, insects, toxic chemical substances and dust by using suitable covers.

3. Ingredients, including seasonings, should be of a quality approved by the Food and Drug Administration.

4. Containers and spoons for condiments should be made of glass, stainless steel or white porcelain, and covers should always be used.

5. Ice for human consumption should be kept clean, never handled by hand, and never stored in containers with food, cans or other objects.

6. Utensils should be cleaned after each use, and they should be in good condition and made of a material that does not leach toxic substances into the food or drink.

7. Utensils should be washed in three steps in sinks at least 60 cm above the ground.

8. Utensils should be kept in a clean place at least 60 cm above the ground; bowls, dishes and glasses should be stored upside-down, and spoons, forks or chopsticks should be stored with the handles up.

9. Rubbish containers should be of a suitable size with covers and should be emptied and cleaned routinely.

10. Food handlers should be trained in food hygiene and focus on personal hygiene, food preparation, and cooks, especially, should always wear a clean white apron and keep hair covered during working periods.

Street foods constitute a significant part of the urban diet. A study conducted from 1991 to 1993 revealed that some 20,000 vendors serve over 200 types of street foods (Hutabarat, 1994). A wide variety of Thai, Chinese and Indian specialities was available 24 hours a day. Street foods contributed as much as 40 per cent of total energy intake, 39 per cent of protein intake and 44 per cent of iron intake (Hutabarat, 1994). For the new FAO/DOH study, five locations were chosen: four in Bangkok (Central Department Store, Dusit Zoo, Rachawat and Lad Prao Road) and one in Nonthaburi. The sites were chosen because they were visibly insanitary. Also, each area represented a different type of street food arrangement, such as daytime, evening, take-away or sit-down. Vendors were male and female, although men held the majority in the congested (high sale volume) areas of Central Department Store and Rachawat. The most profitable area was Central Department Store, where the vendors earned more than 2,000 baht (US$51.25) per day; the zoo was the least profitable area, where venders earned less than 500 baht (US$12.80), although still more than the minimum wage of 162 baht (US$4.15).

Regardless of income, volume or type of stall, no vendor was following the DOH codes. Washing and water use were the biggest concerns. Over 75 per cent of the vendors brought water from home or nearby public areas in plastic containers. Vendors used less than one litre of water per customer for cleaning and food preparation, a clear indication of a deficiency. Coliform bacteria (from human or animal intestines, a sign for poor hand washing) was found in over half the samples, and in early 90 per cent in some areas. Contamination of hands and utensils ranged from 18 per cent to 69 per cent, and was lowest in those

Photo ILO/M. Crozet

Photo ILO/M. Crozet

stalls with access to tap water. Partially treated wastewater was poured into ponds at the zoo, and untreated wastewater was dumped down public sewers. Foods and drinks were not covered to protect from dust or insects. Some seasonings were of low quality and not approved by the FDA. Ice for human consumption (in drinks) was usually kept in boxes with soft drinks and bottled water. Eating utensils were washed in a single bucket on the ground. Containers for condiments often did not have lids, nor did the rubbish bins. And so on with each of the ten points in the sanitary code.

Intervention: Part I

The first action carried out was mobilizing the vendors to attend half-day briefings on the street food project and code of practice. Briefings were organized locally. High-ranking officials took part in the briefing, including the mayor of Nonthaburi. A DOH officer provided an overview of basic hygiene and the technical justifications of the sanitary code. Vendors received aprons and head coverings with the DOH logo. The briefings led to oral agreements on a short-term work plan on corrective measures – in essence, to begin directly with food stall inspections to make recommendations on a case-by-case basis. The DOH understood that it could not enforce all ten points of the sanitary code immediately. The goal was to develop a plan that the vendors could afford and implement on their own, and this would serve as a model for the entire country. So the DOH identified four key areas for correction: the storage and handling of ice for human consumption; the storage and display of food; food handling; and the cleaning of utensils.

The ubiquitous problem of ice contamination proved to be the easiest correction to make. In Bangkok, cold drinks are served with crushed ice in a glass, cup or plastic bag. This ice came from an ice factory. Contamination occurs sometime during the transportation, crushing or storage. At the beginning of the project, vendors routinely stored ice for human consumption in boxes once (or still) holding dirty soft-drink bottles and food. And these boxes weren't washed. The concept of separating ice for serving and ice for storing was a simple concept to relay and administer. Vendors designated boxes that would be used only for ice for serving, and they used a clean cup or utensil to scoop the ice.

Food storage and display proved to be a more difficult correction. Pre-cooked ingredients (meats and seafood) and raw vegetables and raw sliced meat were kept at ambient temperatures without adequate covering. Raw foods were undercooked in soups, which were then topped with raw vegetables. Seasonings were largely exposed to dust, insects and other contaminants. Prepared meals sat exposed for hours. The raw papaya salad called *som tam* was particularly troublesome for the project staff. The ingredients – dried shrimp, raw crabs, raw vegetables and chillies – were crushed in a mortar and kept at ambient temperature. The staff recommended that raw foods (including vegetables to be eaten raw) should be thoroughly washed with potassium permanganate for disinfection; that pre-cooked meats be kept in an icebox; and that spices be kept in closed containers. They also hoped to eliminate raw crab from the *som tam* mix. All foods needed to be covered.

Keeping hot meals above the recommended 60°C seemed to be financially impossible; no vendor had the equipment for this. So vendors were instructed to reheat displayed food every two hours, which wasn't fully satisfactory but better than nothing. Similarly, hand washing was another ideal, but it wasn't practical. The solution was to have vendors use clean utensils to handle ready-to-eat food.

At all sites except for the zoo, corrective action progressed steadily over the first year, with many food stalls following most of the first nine codes. The Bangkok Metropolitan Administration provided rubbish bins and banners indicating that food safety improvements were being implemented. Vendors kept less food on display and more in cold storage, and placed a plastic covering over the display. Customers responded positively. Vendors at the Central Department Store site reported a 20 per cent increase in daily income. Other sites saw an increase in business but not as high as the Central

Department Store. The Dusit Zoo was a unique situation in which vendors were relatives of zoo employees who were allowed to sell food under a contract for one year, on a rotating basis with other zoo employee relatives. Because the business was temporary, the vendors probably did not want to make changes or investments in food safety.

Intervention: Part II

Mr. Suang Liamrangsi of the Bangkok Metropolitan Administration had collaborated with Dr. Biplab Nandi of the FAO Regional Office to strengthen the infrastructure of street food vending units in and around Bangkok. Despite progress, activities did not continue as planned for lack of adequate funding. In 2001, Mr. Liamrangsi began collaborating again with the FAO on strengthening the Quality of Bangkok Street Food and Food Centre Project. This was fully supported by the Bangkok Metropolitan Administration, and accordingly several initiatives were undertaken, such as: (1) holding a seminar on project policy for environment and sanitation officers in all the 50 districts of Bangkok; (2) conducting an orientation programme on the application of a new code of practice; and (3) providing apron and hair covers to food vendors in the demonstration areas. To generate interest among street food vendors, the city organized a contest called "Sanitary Street Food Vending Unit Design". Food vending units were organized into six categories. Vendors with the top designs were awarded cash and a certificate of merit.

The Bangkok Metropolitan Administration is keen to continuing its street food safety improvements. However, the novel plan successfully implemented in the mid-1990s in five areas has not really expanded. Mr. Liamrangsi and Dr. Nandi are both hoping for further collaboration between their organizations.

7.4.3 Gauteng Province, South Africa

The following is a summary of case studies presented in Improving street foods in South Africa *by J.H. Martins and L.E. Anelich, and* A strategy document to bring about proper coordination in the street food sector and consumer advocacy programmes *by Indira Chakravarty, published by the FAO in 2000 and 2001, respectively. Appropriate updates have been added.*

Key findings

In the Gauteng Province and other parts of South Africa, health experts demonstrated that knowledge of proper hygiene among street food vendors coupled with adequate infrastructure (nearby public washrooms, for example) improved food safety. Vendors were provided with health education and training. In 1997, the Codex Alimentarius Commission adopted a set of guidelines from the FAO experience in South Africa for the design of control measures for street food vending.

Background

The Government of South Africa set out to study and improve street food vending and found that the infrastructure in one province, Gauteng, already greatly contributed to a high level of hygiene and food safety. The project's objective was to improve street food quality across South Africa by providing street food vendors and food handlers with health education and training regarding safe food practices. The project had two parts: one was an assessment of food safety through meal sampling and testing; the other was a socio-economic study of the vendors and their customers. In Gauteng, a health team conducted face-to-face interviews with 200 vendors and 800 of their customers, and sampled prepared food from each of the vendors. Gauteng is the smallest of South Africa's nine provinces, but it is the most densely populated and is the country's economic powerhouse with three major cities, Johannesburg, Pretoria and Soweto.

The Government estimates that there are about 20,000 street vendors in the Durban metropolitan area, the largest concentration in the country, and about 7,000 sell prepared food. Other major cities also have thousands of food vendors. The South African population, about 40 million, spends over 2 billion rand (US$351 million) each year on food at restaurants and street stalls. The street food sector is not wholly unregulated. At the national level, 13 Acts can apply to the regulation of street food, and some local governments have food hygiene bylaws. Provincial food health control is the executive responsibility of the nine provincial health authorities. Many food vendors, however, operate without a licence.

The project

Of the 200 vendors randomly selected and interviewed in Gauteng province, 181 were female, 197 were black Africans and over half had completed secondary school. The majority (86 per cent) sold porridge and meat; and 98 per cent had a relatively clean floor surface, such as cement. Almost all vendors adhered to proper hygiene requirements regarding short and clean nails, hands free of sores, no smoking while working with food, and no coughing over food. Hand washing was common: 95 per cent of the vendors had access to a nearby toilet; 91 per cent had access to running water; and 92 per cent washed their hands after using the toilet. About half the vendors had their own water spigot, and 80 per cent had immediate access to water. Nearly 88 per cent used separate utensils for raw and cooked food.

The source of raw cooking materials was generally good, the study found, although the mode of transportation to the stall (walking or by trolley) was not optimal for keeping raw foods cold and safe from bacteria. Despite good hygiene practices, some 82 per cent of the vendors were not aware of a training programme for them and 66 per cent were not aware of the WHO's ten golden rules of street food preparation (or the WHO's new five keys to safer food).

The vendors' net monthly income averaged around 1,550 rand (US$272), compared with an average income of 1,900 rand for their customers. The customers were predominantly male, about 90 per cent, from all walks of life, married and single. On average they spent 250 rand (US$44) per month on street food. Most bought street foods five times a week, usually for lunch; and most were attracted by the low price and good taste. Over 97 per cent said the quality was good, and only 2 per cent reported getting sick from street food. To the health team's surprise and pleasure, the street foods sampled had relatively low levels of bacterial contamination, including no trace of salmonella. From this the team concluded that a "strong correlation can be seen regarding the high standard of hygiene practices observed by the vendors during preparation and serving of the foods and the relatively low microbiological counts and low incidences of pathogens tested for" (Martins and Anelich, 2000, p. 7).

Recommendations from the Gauteng study included:

- Funds to be allocated by the relevant authorities to build the necessary facilities and infrastructure to allow street vendors to operate in a proper, healthy environment, thereby contributing to the sale of safe foods.

- Street vendors to be required to pay a minimum fee, taking into account their financial constraints, for using space and facilities, as well as the proper maintenance of the infrastructure, once erected.

- Proper training to be given to the street vendors with regard to basic food hygiene at times on days suitable to them.

- Certain HACCP (Hazard Analysis and Critical Control Point) principles such as time and temperature control to be implemented accordingly.

- Negotiation between authorities and street vendors to be the preferred form of approach in all situations that may arise.

- Environmental Health Officers should not only act as enforcers of regulations by policing, but also as trainers, educators and helpers where necessary to assist the street vendors to become established.

- Government should crack down on particularly dangerous (and illegal) street foods sold in many settlements, such as raw milk and meats.

Merafong Local Municipality (formerly known as Carletonville) in Gauteng is one municipality working with street vendors to improve street food safety. Merafong considered the above recommendations in creating its seven-step initiative:

1. A steering committee was formed with representatives from a vendor union, the police force and local business, and the departments of health, town planning, engineering and traffic.

2. A socio-economic study was conducted to assess the number and location of food vendors and the hours of operation.

3. Land was identified for possible vending locations.

4. Vendors elected six representatives.

5. A set of by-laws was drafted for street food vending practices.

6. A "section 21" (non-profit) company was formed and is responsible to the local authorities for the land lease agreement, monthly license charges, location of vending stalls, flow of traffic and parking.

7. The city provided space for food stall storage, fresh water, latrines, rubbish collection and pavement restoration.

Vendors accepted the plan confident that it would lead to more sales and higher profits. No information is available about the outcome of this initiative.

Elsewhere across South Africa in collaboration with the FAO, the Government created a series of educational products to help vendors, food inspectors and consumers make the sale of street foods a safer and more profitable enterprise. One key document from the collaboration is the *Training manual for environmental health officers on safe handling practices for street foods*, compiled by Ali M.A. Kidiku for the FAO (FAO, 2001). A video shows vendors how to produce good, safe food that results in a boost in business in simple terms. The FAO also helped to reprint a series of training booklets that food inspectors throughout the country will use to educate street vendors. The South African experience is now used as a model for other regions. Many of the findings and recommendations were incorporated in the Codex standard entitled "Revised regional guidelines for the design of control measures for street-vended foods in Africa".

7.4.4 Dar es Salaam, Tanzania

The following is a summary of a case study by Gerald Moy in an article entitled "Healthy marketplaces: An approach for ensuring food safety and environmental health" from the journal Food Control *in December 2001.*

Background

At the request of the Ministry of Health of the United Republic of Tanzania, the WHO was invited to collaborate with municipal authorities in Dar es Salaam in the promotion of Healthy Marketplaces as a component of the Dar es Salaam Healthy City Project. The WHO organized a visit to Dar es Salaam in January 1997 and held extensive meetings with representatives of different organizations. These included national, regional and municipal government authorities; international, bilateral and non-governmental agencies; private sector and community groups; and other interested parties. The goal was to understand the roles of the various stakeholders in the initiative. As a result of these meetings, the WHO established broad-based support for the Dar es Salaam Healthy Marketplaces Project, providing the necessary consensus for such an inter-sectoral undertaking.

The project

The Buguruni Market in Dar es Salaam was chosen for a pilot study. The selection was based on its size, types of food sold, potential for collaboration among agencies and, most importantly, the enthusiasm of market participants. Buguruni Market serves 100,000 customers a day and sells a wide variety of foods, including fresh fruits and vegetables, meat and fish, and street-vended food. Live chickens are also available, with slaughtering and cleaning performed on-site. Other non-food products, such as household items and clothing, are also sold. The market had a single pit latrine and one standpipe for the entire market. Interruption of the water service was common and no large water storage facility existed at that time. There was also no central administration and maintenance, and no pest control. Food inspections were infrequent. Much of the market was constructed in an ad hoc manner by the vendors using scavenged materials. The land was owned and taxed by the Dar es Salaam City Commission. The vendors, 80 per cent female, belonged to the Wauza Mazao Buguruni Cooperative Society (WAMBUCO).

Intervention

After the initial assessment and selection of the Buguruni Market, the WHO and its partners organized a workshop for vendors and governmental and non-governmental organizations. The theme was the WHO's Healthy Market concept and the origin, prevention and control of food-borne hazards.

From the workshop emerged a group called the Buguruni Healthy Market Task Force (BHMTF), established by the Dar es Salaam City Commission with the following terms of reference. The task force would:

1.   Liaise with municipal health authorities in the overall development of a healthy marketplace, including: market administration (including food inspection and analytical service); water, sanitation and drainage (including toilets and hand-washing facilities); environmental sanitation (including solid and liquid waste management, and pest and noise control); training and education of food vendors; and education of consumers.

2.   Conduct Hazard Analysis Critical Control Point (HACCP) studies, under the supervision of a food safety adviser, and recommend appropriate intervention options for preventing or reducing identified hazards, including (a) good practices and norms in the marketplace; and (b) infrastructure design considerations.

3   Provide training and implementation of HACCP-based food safety interventions in the marketplace, including those that may arise at other stages of the food chain.

4.   Prepare a draft physical layout of the marketplace that ensures that sub-systems supporting food safety work together harmoniously and serve their respective functions. The physical layout should provide the best conditions possible for preventing contamination and for promoting adherence to good hygiene practices.

5.   Prepare and implement an annual plan of activities, including regular supervision.

6.   Evaluate at agreed intervals the progress and results of the task force.

Note that a further explanation of HACCP is available in Chapter 11. The BHMTF Plan of Action includes a full range of activities from infrastructure improvements to training and education of food handlers and consumers. During 1997 a number of activities were undertaken with the support of donors, including improvement in road access (supported by Plan International), construction of a solid waste storage bay (supported by the Japanese International Cooperation Agency) and construction of toilet and hand-washing facilities (WHO). Within the market, the BHMTF organized the collection and sorting of solid waste for subsequent disposal. As evidenced by improved handling of solid waste, activities within and outside the market have produced a synergism that has contributed significantly to the hygiene conditions in the market. Local resources have been mobilized for an education programme for market participants, consumers and other stakeholders to promote awareness that safe and nutritionally adequate food is the foundation of good health. Efforts are under way to promote direct community involvement and consultation to strengthen and sustain the Healthy Buguruni Market initiative. The BHMTF Plan of Action is implemented by the WAMBUCO Society, Ministry of Health and National Food Control Commission, the WHO, the Japanese International Cooperation Agency, and Plan International, among others.

Training of people in the Healthy Marketplaces concept, including the HACCP system, is a high priority. Healthy Marketplaces projects undertaken by the WHO have all included an initial mission to the city to promote an understanding of the long-term objectives and means for their attainment. In the course of these missions, questions related to food safety have given rise to the need for applied research. For example, many markets do not have access to cleaning products to sanitize surfaces and equipment. The WHO and its collaborating centres are working to find solutions for this and other problems.

While many cities have undertaken efforts to improve their market-places, such efforts have been isolated and not placed in the overall Healthy Marketplaces context, which has long-term objectives. For this reason, the establishment of a Healthy Marketplaces Task Force is viewed as an important first step in the rehabilitation of the marketplace. However, the preparation of and consensus for a comprehensive long-term master plan for the market-place is seen as the critical element for the purpose of evaluating a Healthy Marketplaces project. Subsequently, the introduction of basic marketplace infrastructure requirements, such as toilets, hand-washing facilities, solid and liquid waste removal, road access and drainage, may be used as indicators of progress. In addition, specific infrastructure needs, such as shaved ice for keeping fish and other seafood, may also mark progress in improving the safety and quality of food. Training of food producers, transporters, wholesalers, retailers and consumers in their roles and responsibilities for food safety is essential if real improvement in the safety and quality of food in the marketplace is to occur. Frequently, this will involve training people in the proper use of new infra-structure, such as washing their hands after using the toilet.

While the Healthy Marketplaces Network is still in its infancy, interest in the concept has been substantial with projects being implemented or planned in every WHO region. Because food-borne diseases, such as cholera, have been associated with street-vended foods sold in marketplaces, there is a growing awareness among market participants, government officials, the community and other interested par-ties that the essential role of Healthy Marketplaces is to provide safe and nutritious food which is, without question, one of the foundations for health. As market-places are increasingly recognized as one of the most important settings for health, it is likely that every city in the WHO Healthy Cities Programme will eventually have a Healthy Marketplaces component.

7.5 Construction sites: No canteen for those who build canteens

There are two tragic ironies concerning workers' nutrition. Farm workers, who harvest our food, often have the poorest access to a meal. And construction workers, who build our canteens, often have no place to eat. This section concerns the latter. Unlike case studies in this publication, which focus on individual companies, the following is an overview of how construction workers gain access to food at construction sites. In most countries there is no formal food arrangement at construction sites.

At least once a week, the *New York Times* will run a full-page advertisement for its own photography archive. Among the grainy black and white images of New York City are photographs of daring construction workers treacherously dining on I-beams hundreds of metres above the city. The images are certainly nostalgic and arresting. But when one thinks about this for a moment, the situation is really quite outrageous. This is analogous to an autoworker eating in a car he is assembling while dangerous drills and saws are running. Safety has improved dramatically at construction sites over the past century in the developed world. Yet this issue of how and where to eat remains surprisingly unsettled.

7.5.1 *United States*

In the United States, unions have chiselled out many rights for construction workers. Unionized sites nearly always have an established eating area, such as a trailer. This is written into the contract, for no national or local laws exist to provide for this basic necessity. The eating area is often part of a multi-purpose facility where workers change, store their lunches, wash their hands and face, and eat their lunches. Having a clean and separate eating area away from the construction site is important for several reasons. The first reason is to escape unpleasant weather – either hot, cold or rainy. A second reason is to escape the physical dangers of machines or falling objects. Another reason is to escape chemical pollutants associated with construction. Heavy metals such as lead easily can be ingested if special care is not taken. Respirators and clothes prevent lead from entering the body through the lungs and skin. Lead residue collects on clothes and hands, however, and can make its way onto food. Ingestion can lead to nausea and dizziness (which can be fatal at construction sites), as well as muscle weakness and insomnia. While the establishment of eating areas has been a profound improvement to construction sites, the quality ranges from smart to ramshackle. Furthermore, non-union sites usually have no special eating area.

Unions have also secured the workers' rights to water. The construction company must provide clean drinking water from a tap or in a protected cooler. Water is not guaranteed at non-union sites, which is a surprise because it is well known that heavy labour without adequate water intake can lead to heat exhaustion and dehydration. Workers at non-union sites often need to bring their own water supply. Workers usually have 30 minutes for a meal plus a few minutes before and after to wash and gear up. Yet what is not regulated, even at union sites, is what is available to eat. Workers are left to fend for themselves. There is no canteen and no certainty of a nearby restaurant. In the United States, many workers bring a packed lunch. These are usually hardy, high-calorie meals to help them through the working day; and the lunches often are packed in durable, insulated boxes, such as Igloo® coolers. The other meal option is to purchase street food, which can be a gamble.

Construction sites are notorious for a type of mobile food van called the "roach coach". As the name implies, the van maintains a less-than-desirable level of hygiene. The van offers drinks and sandwiches, both hot and cold. Vendors typically purchase the food wholesale, and they prepare sandwiches and the like at home for the next day's sale. The food is rarely healthy; processed ham or sausage sandwiches and soda pop are typical items for purchase, and their daily consumption can lead to health problems. The roach coach pulls up to the site during breakfast and lunch hours. This is an informal arrangement. Vendors learn of construction site locations through word of mouth. Foremen will sometimes tip off the vendors, for there is a mutual benefit in which a foreman needs to feed the workers and a vendor needs to sell the food.

The construction worker will eat this food on the street or bring it back to the trailer, if it exists. Food vans are often off-site; and sometimes, depending on the construction site, workers will need to cross highway traffic or traverse sloppy or danger site locations to access the food. Several construction workers interviewed for this book describe the food situation at construction sites as inhuman. They feel they are left scrounging for bad food to be eaten in a dirty, unpleasant environment – to which, to their chagrin, many workers grow accustomed.

Aside from a culinary inconvenience, the food situation at construction sites is plagued with more serious problems. One problem is the short-term health of employees. Diarrhoea or indigestion from bad street food is not uncommon, although no official figures exist because cases go unreported. Also, construction workers, who tend to be big men to begin with, are prone to obesity from a combination of their own dietary habits plus the high-calorie, high-fat fare available. This can lead to a lack of dexterity on the job. Many ladders are rated for under 115 kg (250 pounds) and heavy-duty ones for only 160 kg (345 pounds). A hefty construction worker with a tool belt and building material often exceeds this weight limit. Falls are the biggest killer in construction, and a lot of these falls are associated with ladder use, according to ongoing research projects by the National Institute for Occupational Safety and Health (NIOSH). As for long-term health, increasing rates of circulatory disease, cancers and diabetes are taking their toll on health insurance, disability and pension costs. Rates of health insurance in the United States, in particular, have risen so sharply in recent years that only about half of American construction workers have cover. Better diets can lower the risk of chronic diseases.

7.5.2 Europe

In Europe, labour laws concerning construction sites vary from country to country, even within the European Union. Construction workers are not necessarily better off than their American counterparts. According to the European Trade Union Confederation, workers' access to food at construction sites is not a top union concern. (Main concerns include wages, distribution of working time and non-unionized migrant workers.) Denmark has one of the best-regulated systems in which construction workers are provided with water and a clean place to eat. It is not uncommon in France for construction workers to have meal vouchers for restaurants. In several countries, water provision is compulsory only in summer and suggested during other seasons. Separate, clean eating areas are also not compulsory in most countries, and southern and eastern countries tend to be more lax in their recommendations.

7.5.3 Japan

In Asia, Japanese construction workers fare better than most. If meals are not provided at the site, these workers can get reasonably priced and healthy foods nearby. There are several reasons for this, some of which are explained in the next two case studies. Japan's dense population ensures that food shops are within walking distance of construction sites. Street foods for lunch are not common, but convenience stores are; and these stores sell boxed lunches. Food safety is quite good in Japan; and the traditional Japanese diet is among the healthiest in the world.

7.5.4 China

In China, food-safety inspectors are making plans to improve food quality at construction sites. In November 2004, Beijing inspectors conducted week-long visits to several sites to teach workers and managers basic food handling practices. This was in response to 14 separate food poisoning outbreaks in the Beijing area in 2004. These outbreaks result in dozens if not hundreds of workers being sick at once. One recent bad case was in Suzhou City in China's eastern Jiangsu Province in August 2003, when approximately 400 workers got sick from eating old, spoiled food (BBC, 2003). Throughout China the summer months are the worst for outbreaks because the heat spoils food quickly. But in Beijing particularly, the most common source of food poisoning is half-cooked beans. Because they are cooked quickly in huge cauldrons, they do not cook thoroughly. The Beijing Municipal Health Bureau reports success in reducing the number of nitrate poisonings in years past through worker education, and it hopes to duplicate this success with uncooked beans and other uncooked, non-refrigerated foods (Jing, 2004). The bureau has begun distributing 100,000 50-page booklets to workers and managers; there are over 1 million construction workers in Beijing alone, the bureau estimates (Jing, 2004).

Elsewhere in the developing world, construction workers are often migrant day labourers with few rights and few expectations about safety and nutrition. Food is served army-style from large kettles with little regard to food safety. Throughout Mexico and Central America, it is common to see workers eating street foods outdoors near construction sites with no means to wash before or after eating. Thus, access to food varies from region to region, but rarely is the situation ideal.

7.6 Onojo City junior high schools

Fukuoka, Japan

Type of enterprise: Onojo City is a suburb of Fukuoka, the fifth largest city in Japan. There are five public junior high schools in the city, which educate children ages 12 to 14.

Employees: over 150 (teachers, assistants, custodians, principals and vice-principals).

Food solution – key point: boxed lunch delivered regularly by local merchant.

Many junior high schools in Japan, such as those in Onojo City, are too small to maintain their own cafeteria. Elementary schools, on the other hand, have kitchens, which follow a government-regulated nutrition programme, regardless of the school size. Senior high schools are larger than junior high schools and have cafeterias. Some municipalities have built central kitchens that deliver lunches to all of the junior high schools in the community. This is not the case in Onojo City. Students are left with one option: they bring a boxed lunch from home, called an *o-bento* (see the following case study).

Teachers and other school workers, with no food available for sale on the premises, must fend for themselves. They are technically allowed to leave the school property during the lunch hour, which is between noon and 1 p.m. The practice is strongly frowned upon, however. Furthermore, some teachers have lunchtime duties, such as supervising students. The staff are essentially bound to the school. This leaves the staff with two meal options: bring an *o-bento* or order a lunch. Many employees find that making an *o-bento* in the morning can be troublesome. Often in Japanese culture, the wife or mother is expected to make an *o-bento* for the husband or child. Single men usually do not make an *o-bento* for lunch; and working mothers often do not have time to pack one for themselves.

Food solution

Many of the school employees opt to order a special *o-bento* lunch from a local merchant (*bento-ya*). This is slightly more advanced than ordering a sandwich or pizza, a common practice at workplaces in the United States. The school staff maintain an informal relationship with the *bento-ya*. Meals are delivered in boxes each day just before noon, and the boxes are picked up later in the afternoon. The meals are healthy, about as close as one can get to home-cooked. This is because the *bento-ya* is usually a local family operation serving just a few dozen workplaces, or a few hundred workers at most. One person at each school, usually the school secretary, telephones the *bento-ya* before school starts to learn about what specials are being offered that day. Usually there are only two or three options. Then the secretary collects orders from the staff and telephones the *bento-ya* again. No minimum order is required.

Meals range from about ¥500 to ¥1,000 (US$5–10). In classic *o-bento* style, each boxed lunch contains a large serving of rice, several different vegetables, pickles and a piece of fish, chicken, pork or beef. Beverages are not included, but all proper teachers' rooms are stocked with green tea and hot water. The food from the Onojo City *bento-ya* is usually local, except in the winter when fresh vegetables are scarce (although quite a few varieties are grown in local greenhouses). The arrangement is very convenient for teachers, who like many workers in Japan put in long hours. They do not need to pack a lunch in the morning, and they essentially have a meal waiting for them at noon. The staff eat at their desks in the teachers' room, except for those teachers assigned to supervision. These teachers simply bring the *o-bento* or a packed lunch and eat with the students.

Possible disadvantages of food solution

None apparent.

Costs and benefits to enterprise

None. The cost is borne entirely by the employee.

This is a food arrangement established by employees. The school (or the city) benefits somewhat from having less pressure to build a cafeteria or mess room.

Government incentives

None.

Practical advice for implementation

On the surface, the *bento-ya* service seems mundane. And for some Japanese workers it is. No one views the arrangement as a "worker benefit". Yet the service is special compared with options faced by workers around the world. For one thing, the food is fresh and healthy. This is not a highly processed pre-packaged lunch, nor is it a high-calorie fattening restaurant meal. The *bento-ya* service – at least how it is practised in Onojo City – provides a home-cooked meal nearly indistinguishable from an *o-bento* packed by mother. The quality is better than *o-bento* sold in convenience stores because it is made locally just an hour or so before delivery and not the previous night. Some supermarkets in Japan prepare *o-bento* just before lunch, and these are fresh. The *bento-ya* offers the extra convenience of delivery.

Although culturally unique to Japan, the *bento-ya* concept can benefit workers anywhere. In other countries there are local shops that deliver lunch. Few, however, deliver well-rounded healthy meals, such as the type that might be served at a fine canteen or restaurant. Delivery or take-away usually means fast and cheap, and fast and cheap usually means unhealthy. Take-away food is usually something one wouldn't want to eat every day. The *bento-ya* is a meal to be eaten daily. Companies cannot create a *bento-ya* system out of thin air. However, companies without canteens can work with local shops – either through a financial incentive or the promise of customers – to encourage shop owners to cook and deliver the type of food one can eat daily. American Apparel, featured in Chapter 6, comes close to this by instructing its caterer to supply healthier boxed lunches to its mess room. The bottom line is that a company doesn't have to settle for lousy food from local vendors. The promise of customers can influence what a local shop sells.

Union/employee perspective

While there is a teachers' union, it has no say in this meal arrangement. The *bento-ya* scheme is maintained by employees, and the scheme would have folded years ago if it weren't useful to employees.

7.7   Spotlight on Japan: The Japanese *o-bento* – Zen and the art of the packed lunch

The Japanese *o-bento* is a compartmentalized boxed lunch usually containing one large part rice, one part vegetable and one part fish, meat or egg. While many cultures have the concept of the lunch box, the Japanese boxed lunch is somewhat more. In a way, the *o-bento* represents a Japanese approach to food: convenient, fresh and balanced in terms of nutrition, colour, texture and shape, and appropriate to the occasion – season, event or place. The aesthetics are sometimes valued as much as taste. Children grow up with the *o-bento*, and many workers rely on it. Workers bring an *o-bento* from home (usually made by a wife or mother) or they purchase one from a multitude of shops. As a result of the *o-bento* tradition, most workers have access to nutritious foods during working hours. The *o-bento* and the Japanese diet in general have helped the Japanese people maintain ideal weight and health.

The *o-bento* has been a part of Japanese culture for at least 1,300 years. At first they were quite simple yet functional: rice or grain and vegetables wrapped in bamboo sheaths, which were thought to be antiseptic. Workers would carry these into the fields or worksites. The notion of hygiene has since remained integral to the *o-bento* design. Bamboo leaves soon gave way to thin wooden boxes, which workers would discard after one use. By the 16th century, even nobles were carrying *o-bento* during their business travels, and the concept of the decorative lacquer box evolved. Today, *o-bento* are sold in simple plastic containers or fancier wooden boxes.

Rice is the main *o-bento* ingredient. Sometimes it is the only ingredient, aside from a pickled plum (*umebushi*) in the centre and a sprinkling of sesame seeds. One common addition is *okazu* – a vegetable side dish. This adds to the nutritional value of the *o-bento*. This could include a mix of root vegetables, sea vegetables, fresh seasonal vegetables or pickled vegetables. Added to the rice and vegetables is a protein serving: grilled fish, fish cakes (*kamaboko*), eggs, chicken nuggets, beef strips or pork slices. All the food is bite-sized or else edible with chopsticks. No knife is needed.

Unlike workers in many parts of the world, nearly the entire Japanese workforce has convenient access to a decent lunch. Most large companies have canteens. For workers with no access to a canteen, *o-bento* are available everywhere in this densely populated country. In the preceding case study we read of junior high schools benefiting from a *bento-ya*, a small enterprise that makes *o-bento* boxes fresh to order, delivers them, and then picks up the lacquer boxes to reuse. Supermarkets, too, often offer good *o-bento* deals. The *o-bento* are made just before lunch from ingredients sold at the supermarket,

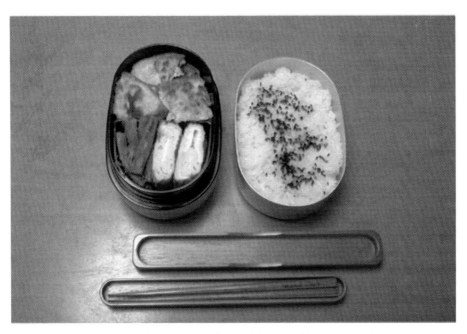

A typical Japanese o-bento *(lunch box) with rice, fish, vegetables and egg* (The Japan Forum).

such as fresh fish and vegetables. They range in price from ¥500–1,500 (US$5–15). Train stations sell *eki-ben*, derived from the Japanese words for station (*eki*) and *o-bento*. *Eki-ben* reflect the local cuisine – from the squid in Hokkaido *o-bento*, to the beef from Kobe, to chestnuts, burdock and mountain vegetables from other regions. *Eki-ben* range in price from ¥500–2,000, on average, depending on the food and attention to detail. The *eki-ben* are often healthy but mass-produced early in the morning. They are not always as fresh as the *bento-ya* lunches or, sometimes, the *o-bento* sold in supermarkets. A step below *eki-ben* in quality, but even more convenient and often cheaper, are *o-bento* from convenience stores. There seem to be convenience stores on every block in business districts. In fact, the proliferation of convenience stores in the last 20 years has brought mobile workers access to fast, healthy meals for lunch and dinner. *O-bento* are not inherently healthy, of course. Some contain greasy or fried food, salty foods, or Western foods such as processed sausages.

The lunch break in Japan is often 45 minutes to one hour. The cultural norm is to wait until the lunch hour to begin eating. Many companies have chimes to signal the beginning and end of the lunch period. Conditions may vary slightly from workplace to workplace. In the preceding case study, teachers at junior high schools have certain duties to perform during lunch, even though they are on a break. Companies with canteens sometimes have shorter lunch breaks, for management feels that workers do not need extra time to purchase a meal outside of the company. Workers in Japan are often obliged to perform certain tasks, so breaks (on paper) are no guarantee of an actual break.

Should workers venture outside the workplace for food, they have far more than *o-bento* to choose from. Many shops serving noodles do much of their business at lunch or in the early evening, serving the workforce who are working late. Some shops are simple shacks or trucks with few overheads, serving fast and inexpensive food. Food-borne illnesses from these types of establishments are a rarity. Some restaurants are set up particularly for workers and are open around the clock, such as the Yoshinoya chain. Workers, usually men, stop at Yoshinoya for *gyu-don*, big bowls of rice with beef slices and onions for as little as ¥280 (US$3). The meal lacks vegetables but is fine occasionally and certainly filling. (*Gyu-don* restaurants took a hit with the "mad cow" scare in 2003, and their future is uncertain.)

The bottom line is that Japanese workers are somewhat privileged in comparison with workers elsewhere. Street food is common throughout the world, but in Japan it is safer and more nutritious. Lunch boxes are common from country to country, but in Japan they are balanced meals. It is rare for a Japanese worker not to have convenient access to healthy food during working hours, if he or she chooses. Considering the end result – high productivity and the longest life spans in the world – companies and countries might be wise to follow the Japanese model ... and Japan might be wise to maintain it.

7.8 Healthy foods for meetings, seminars and catered events

Table 7.1 suggests ways to reduce saturated fat and calories when serving typical business meeting food. Often the calorie savings are significant. Choosing a smaller bagel, for example, cuts over 100 kcal; choosing a spring roll over an egg roll cuts 200 kcal. These foods can be purchased from local vendors. This table is adapted from recommendations presented in *Guidelines for offering healthful foods at meetings, seminars, and catered events* from the University of Minnesota School of Public Health. The target audience is American, but the recommendations cross many cultures.

Table 7.1 Ways to reduce saturated fats and calories in catered food

CHOOSE...	INSTEAD OF...
Beverages	
Bottled water (filtered, mineral, flavoured without sugar), teas, coffee or 100 per cent fruit and vegetable juices	Soda pop or fruit-flavoured drinks
Low-fat or skimmed milk	Whole milk or cream
Breakfasts	
Fresh fruit, dried fruits, unsweetened juices	Sweetened canned fruit and fruit drinks
Low-fat yoghurt (plain with fresh fruit)	Regular yoghurt (pre-sweetened)
Small bagels, smaller than 3.5 inches (9 cm)	Regular bagels, 4.5 inches (12 cm)
Small or mini-muffins, 2.5 inches (6.5 cm)	Regular muffins
Low-fat granola bars	Croissants, doughnuts, sweet rolls, pastries
Light margarine, low-fat cream cheese, natural jams or fruit spreads	Butter, regular cream cheese
Unsweetened or low-sugar cereals	Sweetened cereals
Wholegrain waffles, french toast	Regular (white flour) waffles or french toast
Lean ham or turkey bacon, vegetarian sausages or bacon substitutes	Bacon or sausage
Lunches or dinners	
Salads with dressings on the side	Salads with added dressing
Low-fat or fat-free dressings, flavourful vinegars or extra virgin olive oil	Regular salad dressing
Soups made with vegetable purée or skimmed milk	Soups made with cream or half-and-half
Pasta salads with low-fat dressing	Pasta salad with mayonnaise or cream dressing
Sandwiches on wholegrain breads	Sandwiches on croissants or white bread
Lean meats, skinless poultry, fish, tofu	High-fat and fried meats, bacon, poultry with skin, cold cuts, oil-packed fish

(contd...)

Table 7.1 Ways to reduce saturated fats and calories in catered food
(contd...)

CHOOSE...	INSTEAD OF...
Steamed vegetables	Vegetables fried or cooked in cream or butter
Wholegrain bread or rolls	Croissants or white bread
Margarine without trans fatty acids	Butter
Low-fat, low-calories desserts, such as fresh fruit, low-fat ice cream, low-fat frozen yoghurt, sherbet, sorbet, angel food cake with fruit topping	High-fat, high-calorie desserts, such as ice cream, cheese cake, pies, cream puffs and large slices of cake

Receptions

Cut fresh vegetables or "baby" vegetables served with low-fat dressing, salsa or tofu dip	Deep-fried vegetables
Cut fresh fruit	Fruit tarts, pie, cobblers
Grilled or broiled skinless chicken strips	Fried chicken, chicken with skin
Miniature meatballs from lean meat, turkey	Large meatballs made with fatty meat, or meatballs served in gravy or heavy sauces
Broiled or poached seafood	Deep-fried seafood, seafood in high-fat sauces
Mushroom caps with low-fat stuffing	Mushrooms with high-fat cheese or creamy stuffing
Miniature pizzas with mozzarella and vegetables	Large pizzas with pepperoni, Italian sausage or other high-fat meats
Vegetable spring rolls, fresh and not fried	Fried egg rolls
Small cubes of cheese, 0.75 inches (2 cm)	Large slices of cheese
Wholegrain, low-fat crackers	Regular crackers with trans fats
Low-fat, air-popped popcorn with no butter	Oil-popped popcorn or popcorn with butter
Baked or low-fat chips, pretzels	Regular chips
Dips made of salsa, hummus, or low-fat cottage cheese	Dips made of mayonnaise, sour cream, cream cheese or cheese sauce
Small slices of cake, 2 inches (5 cm)	Large slices of cake

7.9 Local vendors summary

Workers around the world who do not have a formal meal plan – a canteen, meal voucher or mess room – find themselves turning to local vendors for inexpensive morning, noon or evening meals. Street food vendors with trolleys or simple stands are a common source of inexpensive local food. Employers who have neither the space or budget to provide a dining area can work with local vendors to ensure that these meals are safe and nutritious. This could involve a small investment in local infrastructure. For example, businesses can pool their resources to provide clean water and toilets for street vendors near or within company grounds; employers in industrial parks can establish a common meal market among companies; or employers can work with local governments to raise the standard of hygiene for street vendors at a general, city-wide level. Without investment, employers can simply talk to local vendors to persuade them to serve healthier food options. Vendors will respond positively with the promise of dedicated customers sent their way.

Snacks at work often come from local vendors. This includes vending machines, fruit and food served at meetings. Employers can improve worker nutrition by making sure healthy snacks are available. A summary of key elements in case studies from this chapter follows.

Kaiser Permanente of Northern California

This chapter opened with a salute to fruit. Kaiser Permanente increased its employees' access to fresh fruit and vegetables by establishing farmers' markets. This required essentially no budget and only little space, just a strip on the street. What was necessary, however, was careful planning to find the farmers and to accommodate the needs and concerns of local businesses. The positive: helps workers reach the "five-a-day" fruit and vegetable goal. The negative: none.

Firmafrugt

Nations around the globe have created "five-a-day" or similar programmes to encourage fruit and vegetable consumption. Yet with breakfast taken quickly and with workplace lunch devoid of vegetables, it's hard to reach this goal. Denmark's *firmafrugt* programme offers free fruit to employees. The positive: inexpensive to administer, employees like it, reduces the dependency on snacking on junk food. The negative: none.

Street foods

Street foods are a major source of nutrition for hundreds of millions of workers, from those in the informal sectors of developing nations to unionized construction workers in industrialized countries. Food safety is the major concern. Vendors often have no knowledge of proper food handling and hygiene, and no resources to minimize the risk of food-borne contamination. Major efforts are underway by the WHO and the FAO with local governments to improve street foods. The positive: inexpensive and often nutritious food, source of local employment – particularly for women. The negative: high risk of food-borne illnesses.

Construction sites

The irony is that those who build canteens don't have canteens themselves. Construction workers in most countries have poor access to safe and healthy food. Many workers find that there is no place to store packed lunches, no clean place to eat, no place to wash before and after eating, and no healthy food, only street foods of questionable nutrition and safety. Unions have secured some benefits, such as meal trailers at unionized sites. The positive: unionized sites offer a clean place to eat, but good sites are rare. The negative: unhealthy foods increase obesity and chronic disease risk; contaminated foods make workers sick.

Onojo city junior high schools / o-bento

In Japan in junior high schools, teachers are obligated to remain on the school premises. Those in Onojo City in schools without canteens take advantage of local family shops that deliver healthy lunches every day. Teachers are daily customers; the shops deliver and collect lunch boxes. The Japanese lunch box concept, called o-bento, is generally very fresh, well balanced and convenient, available from o-bento shops, supermarkets and convenience stores. Workers throughout Japan are never far from a healthy meal during working hours.

Meetings, seminars and catered events

The workplace is filled with temptations, such as sugary and fatty snacks. Aside from fruit (see the *firmafrugt* case study), companies can substitute healthier snacks and meals for the typical, unhealthy sweets and goodies at meetings. Vending machines with healthy options, such as filtered water, are becoming increasingly popular too.

8

SOLUTIONS FOR FAMILIES

Photo: ILO/P. Deloche

"Food is our common ground, a universal experience·"

James Beard

Key issues

Low-cost shops, food vouchers, food provisions, dormitories

- Every meal provided to the worker at work benefits the family, for that is one less mouth to feed. This is especially true in the developing world.

- Low-cost shops provide workers with food and household staples. Food provisions include bulk grain distribution. Dormitories serve as shelters for migrant workers, particularly women. Food vouchers are discussed in Chapter 5.

Pros of family support

- Employers can distribute large sacks of rice, oats or other grain products several times a year. Grains are fairly easy to store. Whole grains or fortified grains can help reduce the nutritional deficiencies so common in poorer nations.

- Ensuring that children have nutrients to develop physically and mentally will provide for a productive future workforce, propelling nations out of their cycle of poverty. For children, iron and vitamin A deficiencies can result in learning disabilities, stunted growth and death, thus hampering economic development efforts.

- Low-cost shops exist in many parts of the world and can be a blessing to poor families. Companies can run these shops at a zero-profit margin for the sole benefit of workers and their families.

- One family solution in wealthier nations is the take-home meal concept, geared towards busy working parents. These meals are generally more nutritious and convenient than fast-food options that many families rely on several days a week.

- Properly run dormitories for young migrant workers, particularly women, can provide a haven from physical and sexual abuse, as well as a place to store food purchased in bulk and to cook and eat food in sanitary conditions.

- Bulk food distribution on top of salary is a feasible food solution for the informal sector, which dominates the economies of many parts of Africa and Southeast Asia.

Cons of family support

- Bulk food distribution is an added expense for a company with tight margins.

- Low-cost shops must not evolve into high-cost shops once workers come to depend on them – a common practice in company towns in years past.

Novel family examples

- Pfizer Canada is one of many companies with canteens offering take-home meals. The plan entails few costs above canteen maintenance. Meals are available for pick-up at the end of the working day, distributed from a vending booth.

- Unilab in the Philippines distributes 11 sacks of rice per year (and a special food package for the 12th month, Christmas). Each sack provides a family of four with enough rice for the month.

- Mashuda Shefali of Bangladesh has established dormitories for young women from the countryside working in Dhaka, predominantly in the garment industry. These save the women from the dangers of shantytowns. The women have access to clean water; can cook, eat and socialize in decency; and save money for their families back home.

Every meal provided to the worker at work benefits the family, for it means one less mouth to feed. This is especially true in the developing world. Employers can make additional efforts, however, to directly provide for an employee's family's nutritional needs. Bulk food distribution is one family solution. Employers can distribute large sacks of rice, oats or other grain products several times a year. Grains are fairly easy to store. Whole grains or fortified grains can help reduce the nutritional deficiencies so common in poorer nations. Iron deficiency affects up to 50 per cent of the world's population (Stoltzfus, 2001). It reduces the work capacity of entire populations, a serious hindrance to economic development. Common symptoms in adults include sluggishness, low immunity, low endurance, and a decrease in work productivity for mental and repetitive tasks (Haas and Brownlie, 2001). Conversely, adequate nourishment (through food fortification) can raise national productivity levels by 20 per cent (WHO, 2003a). For children, iron deficiency can result in learning disabilities, stunted growth and death, thus hampering economic development efforts in future generations. Iron fortified grains, donated by charitable organizations or governments and distributed by the employer to the employee, can reverse the downward spiral of poor nutrition and low productivity. Similarly, iodized salt distribution can reduce iodine deficiencies.

Low-cost shops exist in many parts of the world and can be a blessing to poor families. Companies can run these shops at a zero-profit margin for the sole benefit of workers and their families. Employers, with their good business connections, are often in a position to buy food at wholesale prices and incorporate its delivery into regular factory shipments. The low-cost shop concept in the past has been abused. Mining companies in the United States in the nineteenth and early twentieth centuries created a dependency on such shops for their employees, who became indebted to the company. Employers must create low-price shops to help workers, not handicap them.

One modern family solution in wealthier nations is the take-home meal concept. This is geared towards busy working parents. The concept is simple. The canteen prepares dinners for employees to take home at the end of the day. This requires very little extra resources for the canteen; dinners can be ordered in advanced or vended from a machine. One possible disadvantage is that the availability of take-home meals makes it easier for employees to work late. As we shall see in this chapter's first case study, take-home meals are increasingly commonplace.

Low-cost shops and food distribution centres are a family service. Thus, these family solutions address the ILO Workers with Family Responsibilities Convention, 1981 (No. 156). Article 5(b) states that employers should "develop or promote community services, public or private, such as child-care and family services and facilities". Take-home meals help all types of employees, even those without families. Yet the service can be of assistance to families in general and women in particular. This is because women in many cultures are expected to prepare food each night. In this regard, take-home meals can promote gender equality in the workplace by helping women earn a living by easing family responsibilities.

8.1　Pfizer Canada

Kirkland, Quebec, Canada

Type of enterprise: Pfizer Canada is the Canadian operation of New York-based Pfizer Inc., the world's largest pharmaceutical company. Pfizer's global revenue in 2003 was more than US$45 billion, with a net income of US$3.9 billion. (http://www.pfizer.ca, http://www.pfizer.com)

Employees: over 2,000.

Food solution – key point: inexpensive take-home dinners.

Pfizer Canada maintains a diverse workforce with many workers from households in which both parents work. In many industrialized countries, workers are increasingly pressed for time and find it difficult to prepare wholesome dinners after work. This is particularly true for female workers, who are often expected to prepare or otherwise purchase a meal for the family (although this has been changing in some countries, with men accepting cooking responsibilities). Increased commuting times makes the task of cooking even more difficult.

Fast-food establishments and supermarkets have responded to the demand for quick meals by providing family "take-home" or "take-away" meal options. Pfizer Canada is one of a growing number of companies also providing take-away meals for the family or individual. This type of workplace-based meal option offers two advantages: the food tends to be as healthy as the cafeteria lunch, which is usually nutritionally balanced; and the meal is ready for the employees when they leave. Employees purchasing a meal for home outside the company would otherwise need to pick it up from a shop, and this could easily add 30 minutes to the commute home.

Food solution

Pfizer Canada's take-away meal option is straightforward. Each day in the late afternoon two to four meal options are available from the cafeteria fully cooked, hot and packaged to take home. Meals include protein (meat, fish), starches (rice, potatoes, pasta) and vegetables. Often there is a vegetarian meal option. Meals cost CAN$3.50 (US$2.50) per individual serving, a price than hasn't been raised in the past eight years. Thus a family of four can eat for about US$10. Meals are prepared by the cafeteria staff after lunch and placed into dispensing machines, so the cost to Pfizer Canada aside from the meal subsidy is kept to a minimum. The meal programme is advantageous for working mothers, who often, in this society, have the task of cooking or otherwise acquiring meals for the family. However, Pfizer Canada does not keep track of which employees purchase these meals. Regular working hours are 9 a.m. to 5 p.m.

Possible disadvantages of food solution

There are no obvious disadvantages. It is said that "home-cooked" meals are healthier than take-away meals, but this assumes the mother or father knows how to cook a wholesome meal. The Pfizer Canada meals are prepared by professionals with an attention to nutrition, so they may very well be as nutritious or more nutritious than other meal options for workers. Some union representatives have argued that, in general, the availability of take-home meals and other conveniences makes it easier for employees to work late much in the same way that mobile phones can enslave instead of liberate. This has not been the case reported at Pfizer, though.

Costs and benefits to enterprise

The company pays the cost of the meal subsidy, which was not disclosed, as well as the cost of preparing a meal after lunch, said to be nominal.

Companies that offer simple yet unique benefits often top various "best place to work" awards, and Pfizer Canada is no exception. In 2003 Pfizer Canada was ranked as the 15th best company in Canada to work for by the *Report on Business* magazine, published by the Toronto *Globe and Mail* newspaper.

Government incentives

None.

Practical advice for implementation

For companies with a cafeteria, very few additional resources are needed to provide take-away meals. Pfizer Canada prepares many meals and makes them available in airtight individual servings via a dispensing machine. This way, the cafeteria staff do not need to be present late in the afternoon to serve customers after preparing these meals. Some companies offering take-away meals accept orders via company e-mail. Meals are prepared to order, and no

food is wasted. Other companies create evening meals from leftover lunch food. This, too, reduces cost.

Union/employee perspective

This is a non-union site. Employees apparently appreciate the service, for demand for take-away meals has not waned.

8.2   United Laboratories, Inc.

Manila, Philippines

Type of enterprise: United Laboratories, Inc.(Unilab), develops, manufactures and markets a wide range of prescription and consumer health products covering all major therapeutic categories. Many of these products are leading brands in the Philippines, Indonesia, Thailand, Malaysia, Singapore, Hong Kong (China), Viet Nam and Myanmar. Unilab has facilities throughout Southeast Asia. Its major manufacturing complex is in Manila. (http://www.unilab.com.ph)

Employees: over 3,000.

Food solution – key point: provision of 11 sacks of rice per year.

All employees at Unilab receive a meal subsidy for lunch, and those who work overtime receive a free meal. The company has several canteens, one for each compound. The main canteen serves 350 workers during two lunch shifts; another serves 450 over three lunch shifts. Workers have easy access to these canteens, and the staggered shifts reduce the crowd. While malnutrition is a concern in Manila, Unilab hires a dietician to ensure that the canteen meals are nutritionally balanced. The free sacks of rice are not meant to aid a malnourished Unilab workforce. This is a company perk.

Food solution

Unilab provides all regular employees with eleven 50-kg sacks of Sinandomeng rice throughout the year. This is a benefit above salary. The distribution of this wholegrain rice essentially provides a family of four with the most basic staple of Filipino cuisine. The rice is distributed from the 19th to the end of each month from January to November. (Unilab increased the distribution from ten sacks a few years ago.) In addition, in late December, all employees receive a Christmas basket full of goodies to share with their families. Workers carry home the sacks in their cars or on public transportation. At a shop, a 50-kg sack of rice would cost 900 to 1,000 Philippine pesos (US$16–18). For families on tight budgets, the free rice is a significant company benefit. Unilab saves money by buying the rice in bulk. Wholegrain rice (with the bran and germ) contains nutrients not found in "white" rice (the starchy endosperm only). These nutrients include the B and E family of vitamins, minerals and unsaturated fat. Wholegrain rice is also a complex carbohydrate, which takes longer to digest compared with simple carbohydrates (like white rice) and helps control excessive weight gain.

Employees with children younger than 5 years also receive one 400-gram can of powdered milk per month per qualified dependent. Unilab workers in other countries receive cash for rice.

Possible disadvantages of food solution

For workers at Unilab, there are no disadvantages. Workers who receive cash instead of rice, however, might be tempted to use that money for anything but rice, such as tobacco or gambling.

Costs and benefits to enterprise

Unilab spends a total of 2,570,000 pesos (US$45,885) per month for the rice benefit. Unilab's generous rice programme ensures that no employee goes hungry.

Practical advice for implementation

Unilab recommends that employers have a written policy on the entitlement, distribution, validity and options of the food distribution programme and that they make sure this policy is available to every employee. It was unclear why Unilab cannot distribute rice to workers in other countries. If rice distribution is a problem in a particular country despite funds being available, employers can consider issuing vouchers or coupons for rice. This would ensure that employees use the benefit to obtain only rice, as intended.

Union/employee perspective

Unilab is a non-unionized company. Instead there is an employees' council, which oversees welfare benefits.

8.3   Spotlight on the Russian Federation: Worker and family nutrition during and after the Union of Soviet Socialist Republics

The Russian Federation has undergone radical changes in the past ten years following the collapse of the Union of Soviet Socialist Republics (USSR), also known as the Soviet Union, and its adoption of a market economy – a change, in some ways, as sweeping as the overthrow of Russia's 300-year-old Romanov dynasty in 1917. The future remains uncertain, for the communist Government had kept such a strict control over political, economic and social institutions. Old knots are difficult to unravel. The economy today shows many positive signs: the Russian Federation ended 2003 with its fifth straight year of growth, averaging 6.5 per cent annually since the financial crisis of 1998. Real personal incomes have averaged annual increases over 12 per cent (8.8 per cent in 2002 and 14.5 per cent in 2003). And the Russian Federation has improved its international financial position since the 1998 financial crisis, with its foreign debt declining from 90 per cent of GDP to around 28 per cent (Goskomstat, 2003; World Fact Book, 2004a). Yet problems persist: the country's manufacturing base is dilapidated and must be modernized to achieve broad-based economic growth. The country also has a weak banking system, corruption, a business climate that discourages both domestic and foreign investors, and widespread distrust in institutions (IMF, 2004). The poor economy has been hard on families, many of whom struggle for decent meals.

The Russian Federation is massive, nearly 17 million square kilometres, with varied cultures and geological features, including tundra, forests and mild seaside climates. (This publication features only two case studies, both from Rostov-on-Don, and they make no attempt to begin to address this diversity.) Despite its size, much of the country lacks the proper conditions for agriculture, with poor soil and a climate that is either too cold or dry. The Russian Federation would have difficulty feeding its own people without stable trading ties with Ukraine and other members of the Commonwealth of Independent States.

In the heyday of the Soviet economy, in the late 1950s and early 1960s, Russian health (defined by infant mortality and life expectancy) was on par with Western Europe and the United States. Today, while female life expectancy remains at 72.1 years, male life expectancy has plummeted to 58.4 years (down from 64 in 1991) (WHO, 2003b). The Russian Federation has a firmly established, yet now underfunded, system of socialized medicine. Public health-care expenditure fell by over three-fifths to 2.8 per cent of the country's GDP from 1991 to 2000, compared with levels of 6 to 12 per cent in other developed nations (Ivanov and Suvorov, 2003). Although most of the population has access to free and basic medical care, the quality is low compared with Western standards. The system had begun to decline during the waning years of the Soviet Union, nearly bottomed out during the mid-1990s, and is only now recovering. Many factors have contributed to the population's health decline: inadequate nutrition and occasional food shortages; air and water pollution; smoking; alcoholism; and a lack of medical supplies or medicines to control infectious diseases, such as cholera and tuberculosis. Diphtheria, measles and other curable communicable diseases have reached epidemic levels not seen since the Bolshevik Revolution, and the rates of cancer and heart disease are the highest of any industrialized country (WHO, 2004c).

The interrelationships between under-nutrition, stress, low resistance and disease were particularly evident during the influenza epidemic during the winter of 1995–96, in which over one million people in Moscow alone were infected. Schools and businesses were shut down. Thus, just when the country was most economically vulnerable, workforce productivity sagged under the cycle of poor health, poor medical care and poor work performance. The rise in alcoholism, considered the country's most critical health problem after cardiovascular diseases and cancer, further reduced productivity. Traditionally rates of alcoholism have been high. A government health campaign in the mid-1980s sharply reduced alcohol consumption to around 7 litres of ethanol (pure alcohol) per capita, lower than some Western European countries. Eight litres will cause major medical problems, according the WHO. During the 1990s, however, the rates climbed steadily to nearly 11 litres in 1999 (WHO, 2004g) and continue to rise. Consumption of bootleg alcohol, which is common and dangerous, goes unreported.

Immediately after the collapse of the Soviet Union, workers' nutrition suffered. Workers' health was highly valued during the era of the Soviet Union, in principle, to maintain a high level of productivity. Up until the 1980s, Russia had a vast network of neighbourhood and work-site health clinics, with a ratio of medical professionals and clinics to patients far higher than in most countries. Workers were entitled to 18 days' holiday, a 70 per cent discount on health resorts, and a heavily subsidized factory meal. The All-Union Central Council of Trade Unions, with around 30 branches and an essentially mandatory membership requirement, monitored social benefit schemes. The trade union more or less followed the orders of the Government; its main function was to distribute workers' benefits. The workers' mentality was to work for society and not think about their health. The Ministry of Health would take care of health. Everyone had a role. This culture is deep-rooted.

About 85 per cent of the Soviet Union's 137 million workers in the mid-1980s were on state payrolls; the remaining workers were de facto state workers on farms and in independent activities. Workers were much like foot soldiers, and the army analogy describes workers' conditions well: hard work, inexpensive meals, discounted lodging, access to factory shops, medical coverage, free education and pensions, all of which came with no frills. Up to 90 per cent of the cost of lunch was covered by the company. This cost to the company was included in production and was not taxable. Lunch cost about 0.10 to 0.30 rubles compared with the average monthly wage for blue-collar workers of 195 rubles during the mid-1980s (United States Library of Congress, 1989). Each company had its own large canteen that usually operated 24 hours, in line with shiftworkers. Most workers had access to free mineral water; and those in "unhealthy" professions exposed to industrial hazards received free milk. Most companies also had low-priced shops, although the selection was very limited. Some factories, such as those in remote areas of Siberia and the Sakhalin Oblast (the far southeast), offered better benefits (lodging, commodities) and higher pay as a means to attract workers to such distant and desolate regions. Workers in light industries, such as textile and food processing, had lower pay and fewer benefits, although this was not common knowledge until the 1990s.

The workplace food quality on average was adequate but low in protein content. During the 1970s, the Soviet Union experienced food shortages, particularly meat; and by the end of the decade the government mandated food production at the workplace. This meant that factories of all types developed greenhouses and even pig farms. It was during this period of food shortages that Soviet productivity began to fall, with some workers drinking vodka during lunch and stealing production instruments and materials.

Many workers' benefits, including meal programmes, were largely cut with the collapse of the Soviet Union in 1991. Many workers in fact laboured without pay, let alone food. Many canteens were closed, a widespread trend that lasted until 2002. Around 50 per cent of Russian Federation factory canteens have been closed since 1994. The main reasons for closure have been the lingering economic crisis, company bankruptcy and the reduction of government nutrition subsidies. What communism set up in its creation of a culture of dependency on the Government, capitalism knocked down with a cruel reality of no care for no pay.

New canteens are opening today through company management initiatives. The trade unions are still too weak and overwhelmed with other issues (pay, working hours, safety) to petition strongly for canteens. The best meal programmes, not surprisingly, are at the most profitable companies. In the Rostov region, Dontabak, Atlantis-Pack, Rostselmash and UG-Rusi have well-managed and decent meals programmes. (These companies unfortunately declined to be the subjects of case studies in this book.) The agricultural machine factory Rostselmash, once with over 40,000 workers at several factories, was forced to lay off a great number of workers during the 1990s.

Now with a turnover of over 6 billion rubles (US$215 million), Rostselmash's Rostov workers enjoy subsidized meals that are about half the price (30 rubles/US$1), of similar quality meals in the city. Productivity, profitability and nutrition have worked in unison. That is to say, companies seem willing to offer better benefits to workers once profitability is established, a sign of resentment of runaway capitalism or the sweatshop mentality. And the workers' benefits have been a boon to profitability.

The majority of companies, particularly those in hard-hit rural regions, still have few workers' benefits in comparison with Soviet times. Life is not necessarily harder in modern Russia compared with the Soviet era, but for many workers it is less predictable. The pressing concerns for workers and unions today are consistent and decent pay, paid overtime or a cap on the 40-hour week, and safety. Many workers have taken to packing a filling yet unbalanced meal for lunch, such as bread with a little cured meat. Nutrition is not a major concern for many workers.

Yet nutrition in general, and workers' nutrition specifically, needs to be part of the national health agenda if the Russian Federation hopes to compete in the open market economy. This is beyond the scope of "before", "during" and "after" the Soviet Union. The toll of heart disease, cancer and alcoholism will continue to cripple productivity. Fundamental changes, not in government ideologies but rather in Russian diet and lifestyle (sausages and sour cream, little exercise, heavy smoking and heavy drinking, particularly among men), need to take place; and the workplace is a logical location to start. Better nutrition at work leading to better productivity leading to a better economy will break the cycle of poor health and working conditions that many Russians are now experiencing. Neighbouring Finland's North Karelia Project managed to change lifestyles for the better – with significant reductions in smoking, alcohol consumption and fatty foods, and increased consumption of vegetables, which many thought to be impossible in Finnish culture. To do the same in the Russian Federation will require both time and a similarly well-planned intervention programme suitable to the country's indomitable spirit. The anti-drinking campaigns, for example, however well intentioned, resulted in rapid bootlegging of homemade, low-quality alcohol.

The WHO, the World Bank, the United States Centers for Disease Control and Prevention and the United States Agency for International Development are working with Russian agencies to establish community-based health intervention programmes in several Russian cities. No programmes are scheduled for the workplace. However, the positive changes occurring in Rostov-on-Don, as documented in the following case study of a ball-bearing plant, is a sign that the Russian Federation may be turning the page to a bright, healthy, productive future.

8.4 10-BP (10th Bearing Plant)

Rostov-on-Don, Russian Federation

Type of enterprise: the company 10-BP is a machine-building plant, which has operated since 1959. The company mostly produces five general varieties of bearings, comprising 70 per cent of the company's total output. The company's customers are the largest automobile and tractor factories in the Russian Federation (KAMAZ, VAZ, UAZ, UralAZ) and in the Commonwealth of Independent States (BELAZ, Minsky). It also exports bearings to Ireland, Spain, Bulgaria, Poland and Finland. Commercial sales in 2003 were approximately US$19.5 million (at 29.1 rubles to the dollar).

Employees: 3,220 (2,580 industrial employees), down from 6,600 during the Soviet era.

Food solution – key point: low-cost grocery shops, subsidized canteens, and cafeterias.

The 10-BP company is one of the largest enterprises in the southern part of the country. The plant became a private enterprise in 1993. During the Soviet era, 10-BP had five canteens, three cafeterias (defined below), two shops and a confectionery outlet. Meals were subsidized by 90 per cent, and the foodstuffs in the shops were sold at a minimum mark-up. One of the canteens offered special dietary meals for workers with chronic diseases, such as stomach and liver problems. The menus were developed by a dietician. The plant had two shifts: a day shift from 07:00 to 15:30 hours, and a night shift from 15:30 to 24:00 hours. The canteens served both shifts, and around 80 per cent of the workers used the canteens. One other interesting feature was that workers in "unhealthy" professions – presumably those working with solvents and the like – received a free half litre of milk each day. About 35 per cent of the workers received milk.

Food solution

Workers have lost a few benefits over the years after the end of the Soviet Union. Today, only two canteens are left. They are located near the main workshops and can accommodate 100 people. The canteens, in this context, are places where workers can get a full meal. A confectionery outlet supplies the canteens with baked goods. In addition to this, there are two cafeterias and three grocery stores. The cafeterias serve lighter meals and snacks. The food is cooked in one kitchen and delivered to the canteens and cafeterias. All these facilities are well stocked and renovated, with air-conditioning and clean lavatories. A company sanitary inspector is hired to maintain a high level of hygiene and food quality. The foodstuffs for the canteens, cafeterias and shops are purchased by the special provision service of the plant.

At the three grocery shops, the cost of food is about 5 per cent lower than that in the city. Management had decided to keep this benefit from the Soviet era to supplement the nutrition of workers and their families. In fact, they added one more store. The stores sell typical Russian foods, such as dairy products, sausages and baked goods. The confectionery outlet produces high-quality and inexpensive bakery food (patties, pastries, buns, pies), which are cheaper than those in shops in the city. Most workers buy the bakery food for home.

There are still two shifts. The lunch break is 30 minutes, which is apparently enough time to eat because the eating areas are close to the work areas. Lunch is staggered from 10:30 to 13:00 hours, which minimizes long lines. The canteens are only open during the day shift. Only about 35 per cent of the employees (mostly shop workers) use the canteens. The canteen menu comprises six parts: cold dishes and snacks, soup, main dishes, bakery foods, drinks and garnishes. Within each part there is a choice of five or six dishes. Vegetables are available year round. Other than this, there is no special (or at least labelled) healthy menu. A set meal includes a salad, soup, meat (or fish) with garnish, a baked item and a drink. The average "real" cost is 67 rubles (US$2.30). The company subsidizes 40 per cent of the meal, bringing the price down to 40 rubles (US$1.40). The average monthly salary at the plant (40-hour weeks) in 2003 was 4,880 rubles (US$175). It may not be surprising that most employees bring a packed lunch, which is less expensive than purchasing a meal at work, even with the subsidy. Consider that 20 meals at 40 rubles equals 800 rubles a month, or about 16 per cent of the take-home pay. Workers in Western Europe or the United States, paying about US$7 a meal (US$140 a month) yet earning about US$4,000 a month, spend only 3.5 per cent of their pay on workplace meals.

Cafeteria food is not subsidized. There is a 15 per cent mark-up. However, some foods– that is, those made at the plant – are cheap. For example, a sandwich with salad and a drink is only 23 rubles (US$0.80). Workers can buy inexpensive baked goods too. There are tables to have lunch in the cafeteria, but many workers prefer to eat at their workplaces. Workers who do bring a packed lunch can keep it in a refrigerator during the day. They take lunch in rest areas equipped with kettles and dishes. Food prepared at home usually does not need to be reheated. During the working day, workers can take tea in the rest room. There are also coolers with free mineral water. Some workers, about 23 per cent, still receive a half litre of milk. This "privileged" nutrition programme is regulated by the labour legislation of the Russian Federation.

Possible disadvantages of food solution

There is no state subsidy for workers' nutrition, as in the Soviet era, only a subsidy from the company budget. There are also no longer any special healthy menus, and workers in the second shift lost access to the canteen. The company tries its best, however, to keep popular benefits, such as the grocery stores and confectionery outlet.

Costs and benefit to enterprise

Annually, the plant spends 360,000 rubles (US$12,900) for the canteen maintenance and the 40 per cent meal subsidy.

The company didn't mention the specific benefits of the grocery stores and meal programme. With the slight decline in benefits, one would expect an adverse outcome. Yet the Russian workers continue to take all changes in their stride, characteristic of the Russian people.

Government incentives

None.

Practical advice for implementation

Faced with an end of state subsidies after the break-up of the Soviet Union, 10-BP tried to salvage most of its nutrition-related subsidies. Some canteens were closed; subsidies were slashed. But workers still have some options. The on-site confectionery, selling baked goods nearly at cost and supplying the canteen, seems to be an excellent idea for companies in similar straits. The confectionery outlet essentially covers its own operating costs. It doesn't cost 10-BP much to maintain, yet it is a popular benefit for workers and their families. The grocery stores, too, provide basic foods at a low cost. Slashing benefits was no doubt painful for 10-BP. The company slashed what could be considered "fluff" – the very high subsidy, special menus and multiple canteens – and left the core benefits. The staggered lunch times are a practical way to reduce lunch queues, particularly for a situation where around 1,000 employees vie for only 200 seats.

Simple shops like the ones at 10-BP require few overheads. Only a few employees are needed. Companies who wish to supplement worker nutrition should consider such shops. The company can decide the types of food to be sold. And depending on the company's resources and business connections, grocery items can be bought at a discount and incorporated into daily company deliveries. These savings should be passed on to the worker. That is, the company should not see the shops as profit-making. Tempting workers with the convenience of a nearby grocery and then charging a higher price for this convenience would only impose greater financial hardship on the workers; and this could come back to haunt the company in the form of worker resentment, low morale and lower productivity.

Union/employee perspective

The financial subsidy for workers' nutrition is controlled by the trade union organization. The trade union has also secured an 80 per cent subsidy for workers and their families at sanitariums and health resorts, a popular benefit.

8.5 Dormitories for female garment workers in Bangladesh

Nari Uddug Kendra (Centre for Women's Initiatives)

Bangladesh has undergone rapid change in the last 25 years as its citizens from rural areas pour into Dhaka in search of newly created jobs in the garment industry, as well as for other economic opportunities. The plight of these workers is well documented in Chapter 6 in a case study entitled "Turning the page on poor workers' nutrition". The following case study is about a dormitory project in Bangladesh for female migrant workers, started by Ms. Mashuda Khatun Shefali.

According to the Bangladesh Garment Manufacturers and Exporters Association (BGMEA), the export-oriented garment industry in Bangladesh has grown from US$866 million in 1991 to US$5.5 billion in 2004, an average annual growth rate of 16.24 per cent, making it by far the country's largest export sector (BGMEA, 2004). The number of garment factories has also grown substantially, from 573 factories in 1984 to more than 3,000 today, employing over 1.5 million workers, 90 per cent of whom are women (Reddy, 2002). Associated industries employ another 10 million workers, according to the BGMEA.

Housing shortages and cultural norms

Most garment factories are situated in and around Dhaka, the capital. An influx of workers has brought about a massive housing shortage. Abuse by landlords is rampant, and millions of workers live in shanty towns with no electricity and unreliable access to clean water. The housing shortage takes a particularly heavy toll on female workers, who are often young, illiterate and naive. They are often taken advantage of, and they endure physical and verbal abuse. More than 80 per cent of the women are below age 20 and more than 75 per cent are single, according to a 1991 report by the Bangladesh Institute of Development Studies (Reddy, 2002).

Mashuda Khatun Shefali, a human rights activist, first started working with female garment workers in the 1980s through Friday evening literacy classes. She quickly learned of these women's immediate needs for safe and affordable housing. The conservative society frowns upon women living alone. Many landlords will not rent to them, labelling them as women with loose morals. In slum areas, an 2.5-by-3m bamboo and tin hut rents for about US$22 a month, an entire monthly salary for a garment worker. Women must share huts with three or four other workers. Conditions are insanitary. (There is a dirt floor.) And there is no safe way to store food purchased in bulk.

Shefali created Nari Uddug Kendra (NUK), or the Centre for Women's Initiatives, and opened her first female dormitory for 150 workers in 1991. The British High Commission financed the project; and Shefali was awarded an Ashoka Fellowship, which further supported the project. NUK now operates four dormitories (which NUK calls hostels) in four different garment areas. All are within walking distance to where the women work. There is space for 350 residents; rent is approximately US$3.65 per month. These rents are now subsidized by 50 per cent.

New housing with space for storage and cooking

The dormitories have evolved over the years. At first, NUK implemented communal dining, but the women did not like it. The intent was to provide balanced meals. This cost around US$10 a month, which the women couldn't afford. Also, many women preferred the freedom to cook by themselves or in a small group. This desire to cook quickly led to shortages of stove space, and some women couldn't eat until midnight. More stoves were eventually added. Meals include vegetables, lentils and rice and occasionally chicken and fish. Nari Uddug Kendra provides free health education to the women, and this includes cooking and nutrition lessons, and it also works with employers to provide better food and dining services at work.

The dormitories are multi-floor buildings in middle-class, residential neighbourhoods – far safer than the shanty towns. To convince the landlords and neighbours that the female workers are morally upright, the dormitories maintain strict visiting rules. There is a watchman and an iron gate that is closed at 11 p.m. The safety and cleanliness of the dormitories allows the women to buy food in bulk for a discount and store it. These women place "security" as the top advantage of the dormitories over the slums, above "low cost" and "convenience to work" (Reddy, 2002).

Ongoing struggles

NUK's two biggest problems are funding and a culture that places a multitude of restrictions on women. Concerning the latter, female workers are expected to be chaste and to assume traditional roles of maintaining a household. Many in the society frown upon the fact that the factory workers are learning to read, opening bank accounts and taking other steps towards independence. Workers and Shefali herself are sometimes harassed for challenging cultural norms. Yet the women workers do not see themselves as pioneers; they merely want to maximize their safety and savings so that they can send money home and return there themselves.

The living arrangements in the dormitories are not ideal. The rooms are cramped. The women sleep in bunk beds. There are around ten women per toilet and bath. However, this is a vast improvement over the shanty towns. NUK cannot afford many luxuries aside from a television and fans. Securing funding is a constant struggle. The rent paid by workers to NUK is not enough to cover the cost of renovations and rent paid by NUK to landlords and developers.

On a positive note, NUK is well known in Bangladesh. The Government included NUK's model for dormitories in its position paper at the 1996 United Nations Habitat Conference in Istanbul. Garment factories, while suspicious of NUK's intentions early on, have come to see safe dormitories as a means to keep workers healthier and happier and thus more productive. Factory owners are now considering creating or managing decent dormitories. The Bangladesh Government has not established many dormitories. The Government sees itself more as a facilitator for private sector and NGO initiatives. Change has been slow but positive. The BGMEA has signed an agreement with NUK to develop housing and health facilities, and will provide support by negotiating for low-interest building loans and discounted government land.

8.6   Solutions for families summary

In research for this chapter on family solutions, three key areas were identified: helping families vulnerable to malnutrition; helping migrant workers, particularly young women; and helping busy working parents. For example, distributing sacks of fortified grains at work, while not an inexpensive proposition, can have far-reaching effects. Sacks can be distributed to workers throughout the year. Grains fortified with iron can sharply reduce the incidence of anaemia that plagues much of the developing world. Rice with vitamin A can reduce this deficiency in children, which helps support a healthy future workforce. Companies with some funds but unable to establish a canteen or mess room might consider purchasing fortified grains in bulk.

The farmers' market concept, featured in Chapter 7, is a family solution that requires virtually no budget to maintain. This is one of those win-win situations in which farmers are happy to have customers and to have rent-free stalls; and employees are happy to have quick and convenient access to fresh fruits and vegetables at work. Most produce is purchased for the family. A summary of key elements in case studies from the present chapter follows.

Pfizer Canada

The take-home meal plan is a new trend; and companies such as Pfizer with such plans are topping the "best place to work" awards and coming across as progressive. Employees can order a meal in the afternoon and pick it up later. Few kitchen employees are needed to work extended hours. The meal option is particularly helpful for working parents too busy to cook a proper meal and tempted to purchase take-away on the way home. Take-away from work is cheaper, healthier and faster. The positive: little extra cost to canteen; popular perk. The negative: none.

United Laboratories Inc.

At Unilab management ensures that the workers and their family have the most basic of Filipino staples, rice. These workers themselves have, at the minimum, modestly paying jobs and are not at great risk for malnutrition or hunger. The rice is more a social benefit than a necessity. Workers receive a sack of rice each month from January to November, and a food basket in December. The positive: a popular perk; improves workers' health. The negative: none.

10-BP

Companies with a little space and some financial resources can establish a company store or bakery, as relayed in the BP-10 case study. Costs can be kept low because the shop does not need to return a profit. Workers pick up inexpensive foods for their families. The positive: low-cost, convenient foods for workers. The negative: none.

Nari Uddug Kendra

Dormitories, such as the four created by this organization in Bangladesh, provide young women with shelter from the elements, as well as protection from male predators. Young women pour into metropolitan areas from rural areas seeking employment in the garment and other low-wage industries. Many end up in shanty towns. Many are taken advantage of by unscrupulous employers and landlords. A properly run dormitory can be a haven for these women. Regarding nutrition, the dormitories should contain kitchens where the women can prepare decent meals in the evening. Women workers can save money by buying food staples in bulk. Money saved can be sent back home to their families.

9

CLEAN DRINKING WATER

Photo: Tai Yang Enterprise Co. Ltd

"A little water is a sea to an ant."

Afghan proverb

Key issues

Clean drinking water

- Access to a regular supply of safe water is a basic human right, recognized by the United Nations, Article 12 of the International Covenant on Economic, Social and Cultural Rights.

- At least 2.4 billion people lack access to basic sanitation, of which 1.1 billion have no source of clean drinking water, such as protected springs and wells.

- An estimated 2.2 million people die every year from diarrhoeal diseases (including cholera) associated with inadequate water supply, sanitation and hygiene. In Bangladesh alone, 35 to 77 million out of a total of 125 million people are at risk of drinking arsenic-contaminated water.

- There are no specific guidelines for water at the workplace, other than the fact that employers in many countries must provide some form of potable water.

- Water (hydration) needs naturally increase in warmer climates and in situations of hard manual labour.

- Most industrialized countries have safe water supplies. Tap water is generally healthy. Bottled water at the workplace, although common and often preferred by workers, is largely a benefit and not a necessity, except at certain remote sites.

- Chlorination is an effective water purifier.

Pros of water provision

- A properly hydrated workforce is more productive.

- Water is healthier than soft drinks and coffee. Drinking several glasses of water a day aids in digestion and healthy weight maintenance.

- Clean water can be used for tea as well.

Cons of water provision

- Few, aside from expense to company.

- Bottled water requires planning for delivery, storage, bottle changes and collection. Spills from sloppy maintenance can cause accidents.

- Vending machines with water in lieu of (free) clean tap water places the cost burden on employees.

Novel water provision examples

- Tai Yang in Cambodia installed an advanced water filtration system. Initial costs were high, but the solution was far cheaper and safer than relying on water delivery by truck. (The local water supply is contaminated.) Tai Yang saved costs by relying on expertise from its parent company in Taiwan, China.

- Confection et Emballages in Haiti installed numerous water coolers that quickly paid for themselves as workers' productivity rose.

- The Russian-British Consulting Centre in Rostov-on-Don (Chapter 6) installed an inexpensive filter on the spigot in its kitchenette, reducing bottled water cost by nearly 90 per cent.

- Water coolers at Glaxo Wellcome Manufacturing (Chapter 4) and water promotion led to a sharp decline in the consumption of sugary drinks.

Humans can survive for several weeks without food but scarcely a few days without water. Access to a regular supply of safe water is a basic human right, recognized by the United Nations. Article 12 of the International Covenant on Economic, Social and Cultural Rights recognizes "the right of everyone to the enjoyment of the highest attainable standard of physical and mental health". In 2000, the United Nations Committee on Economic, Social and Cultural Rights adopted a General Comment on the right to health that interprets this to include access to safe drinking water. In 2002, the committee further recognized that water itself was an independent right. Thus, fresh water is a legal entitlement protected internationally, not simply a commodity or service provided on a charitable basis.

Nevertheless, at least 2.4 billion people lack access to basic sanitation, of which 1.1 billion have no source of clean drinking water, such as protected springs and wells (WHO, 2000b). As a result, according to WHO figures, 2.2 million people die every year from diarrhoeal diseases (including cholera) associated with inadequate water supply, sanitation and hygiene (WHO, 2004d). The majority are children in developing countries. Over 200 million people are infected with schistosomiasis (WHO, 2004e); and in Bangladesh alone, 35 to 77 million people out of a total of 125 million are at risk of drinking arsenic-contaminated water (WHO, 2004f).

In the United Nations Millennium Declaration, delivered at the close of the Millennium Summit of the United Nations in 2001, over a hundred heads of state and government pledged to "reduce by half the proportion of people without sustainable access to safe drinking water". The declaration reconfirmed the central role of water and sanitation in sustainable development and poverty alleviation. The WHO has a set of guidelines for governments to provide clean drinking water and proper elimination of wastewater. In 1982, the WHO shifted its focus from "international standards" to "guidelines" for drinking water quality. The main reason for not promoting international standards is the advantage of a risk-benefit approach (quantitative or qualitative) to the establishment of national standards and regulations. The idea is that application of the guidelines to different countries should take account of the socio-cultural, environmental and economic circumstances particular to those countries. The text of most of the guidelines and information on their updating are available on the Internet at: www.who.int/water_sanitation_health/GDWQ/index.html.

There are no specific guidelines for water at the workplace, other than the fact that employers in many countries must provide some form of potable water. Large factories or companies, particularly in remote areas, can essentially follow the WHO guidelines. One obvious method to improve water quality would be for those companies that pollute the waterways to stop, if only for the safety of their own workers. As we read in the McMurdo Station case study from Antarctica, management there opted to build a sea water desalination plant to provide potable water, acting in many ways like an independent municipality. Indeed, some companies are installing sophisticated filtering systems to please employees or to address serious concerns about the local water supply. Because of the relative safety of the modern water supply in many countries, providing bottled or filtered water at the workplace is usually a benefit and is not required by law. Increasingly, workers are drinking more water because hydration is a top concern of many diets. Aside from simply relying on the local water supply, employers have several water solutions to choose from, such as large bottles, small bottles, advanced filters and simply filters.

9.1   The office water cooler culture

In the developed world, clean drinking water is rarely a concern. Occasionally waterborne disease outbreaks occur, particularly after a heavy rain when storm drainage systems are taxed. Most municipalities in most countries with developed or emerging economies do a fine job at providing safe drinking water treated through chlorination. The desire to drink bottled water is largely a matter of taste, not health. Up to half the bottled water sold around the world is actually re-treated municipal tap water, according to the International Bottled Water Association. Labelled as "purified" or "filtered", this water does not need to meet any standard of purification beyond that of ordinary tap water. Bottled water in most countries is regulated as a food, unlike tap water; and in the United States and many other countries, bottled water is allowed to contain levels of biological and other contaminants not permissible in tap water.

Most water made available at the workplace is ordinary tap water or filtered water. Water fountains (drinking fountains) dispense tap water. Water coolers are either filtered water or spring water. Smaller bottles from vending machines are usually spring water, mineral water or sparkling water.

Spring water comes from underground water that flows naturally to the surface, not open surface sources like lakes and reservoirs. Well water is water that comes from aquifers. (Artesian wells refer to confined aquifers under pressure that, once tapped, naturally flow upwards with water without pumping.) Distilled water is pure H_2O condensed from steam, which is thought to be healthier yet no studies support such claims. Mineral water is spring water or well water that contains at least 250 parts per million of dissolved minerals. Sparkling water is water with natural carbon dioxide, which often needs to be removed during the purification process and added again so that the water contains the same amount of carbon dioxide it had at its source. These types of bottled water are safer than tap water only by virtue of having less or no chlorine. They are not necessarily free of bacteria or metals. Bottled water is filtered through a variety of means: distillation, carbon filtering, reverse osmosis, ozone, ultraviolet radiation, or combinations of these. Each method has its benefits and limitations, which includes expense. Carbon filters remove organics (bacteria and organic chemicals, such as pesticides) but not metals. Reverse osmosis removes metals but is a bulky system. Ultraviolet and ozone treatments kill bacteria but are expensive.

Chlorine is an inexpensive and effective cleaner, a favourite of municipalities, but it contributes to tap water's foul taste; and the chemical can combine with other molecules to create cancer-causing agents. Chlorine's by-products, namely trihalomethanes such as chloroform, are probable human carcinogens when present in high levels, causing possible long-term cancers in a few people. Trihalomethanes form when chlorine reacts with organic molecules in water, such as from leaves. The benefits of chlorination far out-weigh the risks, however. Before chlorination, tens of millions of people died annually worldwide from cholera and other waterborne diseases. After Peru relaxed chlorination treatment in 1991, a cholera outbreak struck (the first in the Americas in nearly a century) and over 15,000 people died (Wanjek, 2003, p. 153). The problem in Peru is only now getting under control. For mass consumption, chlorination is widely heralded as one of the greatest public health achievements of the twentieth century.

The office water cooler is a fixture in many countries. The tradition seems to have begun in the western part of the United States about 100 years ago when many homes and buildings did not have a reliable water supply. Arrowhead Springs was one of the first providers, delivering five-gallon glass jugs of spring water by horse and wagon. (European workplaces have long had drinking fountains, spigots and smaller bottles of water. Asia and parts of the Middle East and Africa traditionally have boiled water for tea.) Today, many office buildings and their pipes are old, and water can have high concentrations of iron or lead from the pipes. The levels are still usually considered safe, and, in fact, the water wouldn't be allowed to flow by law if it weren't safe. It is the perceived risk and taste preference that allows the water cooler culture to live on. Water coolers have evolved into a place where workers come to socialize and even gossip. Water coolers serve as a source of nourishment and relaxation.

Demand for bottled or otherwise filtered water for the workplace is growing, according to market research from Nestlé. In the United States, water coolers with spring water are the most common sources of non-tap drinking water. In Europe, office water coolers comprise less than 10 per cent of the bottled water market, but this niche has been growing and is expected to continue to grow significantly in the coming years with marketing planned

Street vendor on the coastal road in Beirut (ILO/P. Deloche).

by Nestlé and Danone, according to Zenith International, a drinks consultancy (Zenith International, 2001). Great Britain has the most water coolers in Europe, over a half million, according to Zenith International. Water coolers are growing in popularity in the Middle East as well. Offices account for over 60 per cent of bulk bottle water sales in Bahrain, Cyprus, Kuwait and Oman. Israel had 120,000 units in 1998, and Saudi Arabia, Lebanon and Bahrain each had over 25,000 (Zenith International, 1999).

By volume, the United States is the largest consumer of bottled water, purchasing over 24.2 billion litres in 2003, nearly a 250 per cent increase from 1993 (IBWA, 2004). (Most of the increase has been in home consumption and vending machines, not in the workplace.) Mexico, Brazil, China and Italy complete the top five water consumers by country and by volume, according to the Beverage Marketing Corporation. Per capita, Italy leads the market, with each resident drinking on average over 180 litres per year, or about a half litre a day. Italy is followed by Mexico, France, the United Arab Emirates and Luxembourg (IBWA, 2004). The United States is 13th on the list, behind most of Western Europe, at 85 litres per year per capita. No data could be obtained that differentiates home and office bottled water consumption. Similarly, no surveys were available that describe employee preference for water.

The water cooler bottles are usually 5 gallons or 19 or 20 litres in PET plastic containers. These usually sit inverted on top of the water cooler, although some workplaces or individual employees attach simple hand pumps to the bottles to dispense the water. Water coolers have their advantages: namely, employees like them. The water is usually fresh and cold. The product is usually spring water, which is perceived to be of higher quality than filtered tap water. Water coolers have many limitations too. For one, the full bottles are heavy, about 20 kilograms. Workers can hurt themselves changing bottles, or water can leak onto the floor, causing an accident. Storing full and empty bottles can be problematic. And some companies have security concerns, complicating delivery and collection.

9.2   Portable, potable water and bottle-less solutions

Within the past decade, the demand for smaller containers of non-carbonated bottled water has taken off. These containers are half-litre or litre size. As we saw in the United Kingdom Ministry of Defence case study (Chapter 4), soldiers prefer to carry bottled water (which isn't light!) instead of tablets to purify untreated water. During operations in Iraqi and Kuwait, British soldiers were carrying and drinking 6 litres of bottled water a day, which translated to a shipment of nearly 800,000 bottles (234 one-ton pallet loads) per week. Smaller bottles are typically sold in vending machines. One advantage of small bottles in vending machines is that they can offer variety, that is, spring, filtered or distilled water with flavours. It is not feasible to dispense mineral water or sparkling water from a water cooler. One disadvantage compared with water coolers, from the worker's point of view, is that consumption of smaller bottles transfers the cost from the employer to the employee. According to the International Bottled Water Association, water in small bottles – from vending machines and shops – outsold the big jugs for offices and homes in the United States for the first time in 2003.

Another office water trend is "bottle-less" or point-of-service systems. These can be broken down into three general types. The largest and most expensive are immense filtration systems built into the building infrastructure. Some newer buildings have such systems, and they can be particularly useful for enterprises in remote regions that need to tap into their own water supply. Mid-size point-of-service systems are essentially durable, high-quality filtration systems packed into a stylish dispenser about as large as a water cooler. These coolers filter tap water right at the dispenser. The system relies on several filtering techniques, the most common of which is the reverse osmosis filter. Such systems offer many advantages. Tap water is filtered, so no deliveries are necessary. Companies do not need to order, store, change and return bottles either. Initial costs can be high but long-term use will see a return on investment. Point-of-service systems are cutting into the office and home market because of their perceived convenience. According to the United States water company Culligan, "big" bottles of water cost an office of 16 workers around US$30 a week, as opposed to US$30 a month for a point-of-service system.

A more "watered-down" version of the point-of-service system is the use of a simple tap filter or filtered pitcher, which is common in homes. The following case study describes a small enterprise in the Russian Federation that installed a tap filter in its kitchen, which slashed drinking-water costs by 90 per cent.

9.3   Russian-British Consulting Centre

Rostov-on-Don, Russian Federation

Type of enterprise: the Russian-British Consulting Centre (RBCC) serves as a technical aid programme of the Know-How Fund that provides independent consulting support to the business community, local authorities, companies of various ownership forms and private entrepreneurs (see the full case study in Chapter 6).

Employees: 12.

Food solution – key point: spigot filter instead of bottled water.

Water solution

The RBCC is a small company of modest means. The company keeps a kitchenette stocked with coffee, tea and milk. The centre was buying bottled water for its employees at a cost of about 600 rubles (US$20) a month. In 2004 the company installed a countertop water filter system on the kitchen spigot, which provides water of equally high quality at a fraction of the cost of bottled water. A hose is attached to the spigot, which directs water through a filter cartridge to clean water for drinking or making coffee and tea. The filter system is designed to easily detach, if desired, to allow regular tap water to flow to wash dishes.

The initial cost for the filter system was 900 rubles (US$30). The filter cartridges are about 450 rubles (US$15) and two are needed per year, for a total cost of 900 rubles (US$30). The system improves the taste of the water and filters lead, chlorine and some microbes, all of which are of concern to employees. The system is also easy to maintain and eliminates the need for storage space for bottled water.

Possible disadvantages of water solution

None, really. Someone must remember to change the filter. Initial costs can be high for some companies, but the savings are large.

Costs and benefits to enterprise

An annual price reduction from 7,200 rubles (US$240) to 1,800 rubles (US$60) for the first year and, most likely, 900 rubles (US$30) for subsequent years.

RBCC installed a commercial filter on the spigot in its kitchen area, which saves this small enterprise about 90 per cent on its bottled water bill.

Practical advice for implementation

Most companies, large and small, can install these commercially available filter systems and save up to 90 per cent on their bottled water bill. The solution seems particularly well suited to small companies. Large companies would need to remember to change filters throughout the building. A small company, like RBCC, however, needs only to remember to change one filter. Filters can be bought in bulk at a saving and stored indefinitely. The use of spigot filters, called the point-of-use system, can also offer many other benefits: waste reduction (no bottles), storage reduction, no delivery and fewer ordering hassles, and no need to lift heavy bottles onto a water cooler.

9.4 Tai Yang Enterprise Co. Ltd

Phnom Penh, Cambodia

Type of enterprise: Tai Yang is a garment factory in one of the three factory zones in Phnom Penh. It is owned by Tai Nan Enterprises, which has its head office in Taiwan, China.

Employees: 3,700 (over 95 per cent women).

Food solution – key point: advanced water filtration system.

Water solution

The region surrounding Phnom Penh in Cambodia has a chronic problem with poor drinking water. Tai Yang's water supply comes directly from the Preak Tnot River without being treated by a municipal treatment facility. Tai Yang operates a water pump station at the river, 7 kilometres from its factories. In the past, Tai Yang has used this untreated water for all its water needs: drinking, cooking, bathing, washing and industrial use. Drinking water was also trucked in at great expense. Not surprisingly, workers got sick from consuming the dirty water. The situation was unlikely to change because the Government had no plan (or no budget) to construct a water treatment plant.

Tai Yang teamed up with engineers from Taiwan, China, to install and operate its own water filtration system. Most materials and technical assistance came from Taiwan, China. This is a multi-stage filtration system in which water passes through a sand filter, an activated carbon filter, a micron membrane to remove particulates and then a reverse-osmosis process. The filtration produces clean drinking water, both hot and cold. Workers are free to drink as much water as they like whenever they like, although they cannot take the water home. Some workers fill up small bottles of water for personal consumption. Water dispensers are ordinary drinking fountains.

Each of the facility's buildings has its own filtration system. Filters must be changed once a week. Local experts and Taiwanese engineers maintain the system. The system is expensive, but so too are the alternatives. Some factories in the region receive potable water by truck, which is stored in tanks. Not only is this costly, but the water is not guaranteed to be safe. Contamination often occurs either at the source or in transit.

Possible disadvantages of water solution

None.

Costs and benefits to enterprise

The system cost US$150,000. Upkeep is US$700 a week. Filters need changing once a week, which is included in upkeep costs.

Productivity rose as sickness fell. Tai Yang saves on water storage costs and medicine to treat waterborne illnesses. Workers are in good health and morale is high.

Practical advice for implementation

This is an extreme example of "do it yourself". Several factors led to the implementation of a water filtration system at Tai Yang. There was international support, worker and union complaints and a realization that the local government wasn't going to improve water quality anytime soon. Other enterprises that receive large shipments of potable water, for lack of municipal resources, can benefit from advanced filtration systems. Initial investment is high, but the system in the long run is less expensive than water delivery. There is a threshold that determines profitability. Smaller companies needing fewer litres of potable water a day might find it cheaper to continue with water delivery. Tai Yan, with its almost 4,000 workers (a small town), did not have this luxury.

The water in Phnom Penh is untreated, so a simple spigot filter similar to the one used in the Russian RBCC case study will not do. An advanced system was required. Many factories in Southeast Asia, Bangladesh and large parts of Africa also have poor-quality drinking water. The set-up cost for a filtration system, US$150,000, seems daunting. Tai Yang benefited from its parent company in Taiwan, China, a technologically advanced nation. Other enterprises without the financial means for water investment might consider alternative sources of technical and financial support. In the garment industry, the wealthier manufacturers and retailers that profit from lower-wage labour in developing nations might also donate money or technology as a sign of goodwill. Nike's code of conduct was successfully adopted in Viet Nam and led to improvements in workers' access to proper meals and clean water (see Tae Kwang Vina, Chapter 4). Poor water is such a widespread concern that any agency interested in improving health and productivity should consider workplace-based water filtration systems.

Of course, the people around Phnom Penh, not just the factories, suffer from water contamination. With its filtration system now up and running,

Tai Yang might consider allowing workers to take a few litres of water home each day. It is unclear how much more this would cost the company.

Union/employee perspective

The demand for better drinking water was not entirely home grown. In 1999, Cambodia and the United States entered into a three-year Trade Agreement on Textile and Apparel. The agreement offered up to an 18 per cent annual increase in Cambodia's export entitlements to the United States provided the Cambodian Government supported "the implementation of a programme to improve working conditions in the textile and apparel sector, including internationally recognised core labour standards, through the application of Cambodian labour law" (Article 10B, US-Cambodia Textile Agreement). Clean water was part of the deal. Cambodia's garment industry came under the watchful eye of international scrutiny. The union at Tai Yang capitalized on this international support and worked with Tai Yang management to build its own treatment facility. The union and workers are proud of their efforts.

Faced with a contaminated local water supply, Tai Yang installed its own water filtration system, which gives employees convenient and unlimited access to clean, cool water.

9.5 National Aeronautics and Space Administration Goddard Space Flight Center

Greenbelt, Maryland, United States

Type of enterprise: the National Aeronautics and Space Administration (NASA) Goddard Space Flight Center (GSFC) is one of the United States space agency's ten research centres, situated a few miles from the Washington, DC, NASA headquarters. The centre builds and operates satellites, including the Hubble Space Telescope, for space science and earth science research. The centre also conducts significant amounts of research about the earth, the solar system and the cosmos. Workers are a mix of engineers, scientists, blue-collar workers and support staff. (http://www.gsfc.nasa.gov)

Employees: over 10,000.

Food solution – key point: water cooler clubs.

Water solution

The United States Federal Government will not provide water coolers for its workers at most facilities under most circumstances. Federal regulations require only the provision of safe drinking water, and all government facilities have an ample supply of water fountains and, usually, kitchens with sinks. The justification for not providing water coolers is that federal facilities operate on taxpayers' money and that taxes should not be used for luxury items. The Government will not pay for coffee, tea, doughnuts, sandwiches and many other fixtures of private company offices. The one exception at GSFC is for employees working in trailers with no running water; they are supplied with water coolers.

Although the tap water at GSFC is checked daily for excessive lead, rust or other possible hazards, and although the water is consistently found to be safe, many employees prefer bottled water. Their decision is based on other taste preferences or general distrust. (Neighbouring Washington, DC, has had a long, infamous history of water contamination.) The NASA Goddard facility is spread out over many square kilometres and comprises scores of buildings. Most buildings have vending machines that offer non-carbonated bottled water at a price of about US$1.00 for 0.5 litres. Drinking more than one bottle a day can quickly get expensive.

Throughout GSFC, workers informally and independently form water cooler clubs (as well as coffee clubs). The concept is quite simple. The most common approach is a system in which 10 to 20 workers in a certain department or building wing pool their money to purchase 5-gallon (19-litre) bottles of water. The cost is around US$5 at discounted wholesalers. Five gallons of water from the vending machine would cost US$38. Purchasing techniques vary but essentially rely on one worker with a pick-up truck or large car buying five or ten or more bottles at a time at a nearby wholesaler. Thus, ten workers each put in US$5 a piece for ten bottles of water. These workers are then free to drink as much water as they please; there is no quota. Other workers wanting a glass of water are requested to leave US$0.25 in a jar next to the water cooler. Where does the money for the water cooler itself come from? This isn't discussed. Some are purchased with office budget or project budget money, as if it were a computer or carton of paper. Prices for water coolers vary widely, from US$50 to US$200 depending on durability and features such as hot and cold taps.

Possible disadvantages of water solution

It's the typical problem of the commons. People who don't pay for the water try to get a glass here and there for free. Normally folks remain civil, but occasionally loud verbal arguments arise. Purchasing is certainly not trouble free. Having the water delivered would be far more convenient; but this is difficult at GSFC, particularly with the increased security after 11 September 2001. Personal deliveries for the most part are no longer allowed on base. The delivery could come through a professional service such as UPS or FedEx, but this would increase the price of the water. Water is delivered to GSFC for those in trailers without running water. Management orders this water, though, through a special procedure unavailable to other workers.

Costs to enterprise

The centre pays nothing.

Practical advice for implementation

Water clubs are a way for employees to save some money on bottled water where employers are not willing to accommodate a request for water coolers. Most organizations do not have as strict security as GSFC, and delivery would be more convenient. Purchasing a spigot filter, as seen in the preceding RBCC case study, is an option for GSFC in light of its security issues. However, the kitchen areas at GSFC are heavily trafficked, and sinks are used to wash dishes and to fill up jugs to water plants. All those people connecting and disconnecting a filter could lead to problems.

9.6 Confection et Emballages

Port-au-Prince, Haiti

Type of enterprise: Confection et Emballages is a garment factory in Haiti, the subject of an ILO project called "Improving working conditions and productivity in the garment industry in Haiti". The following is a report from 2003 on its water programme. Confection et Emballages unfortunately burned down during the Haitian riots of 2004. The lesson remains applicable, though.

Employees: 300.

Food solution – key point: water coolers.

Water solution

Workers at Confection et Emballages worked in hot premises most of the year. The hot climate, together with the heat produced by the intensive lighting required for the special type of production, had a negative impact on the quality of the work environment. The buildings were not originally constructed to facilitate natural ventilation. Structural works to address these deficiencies were considered too costly by the management, and improved mechanical ventilation only partially contributed to alleviate the problem.

In search of low-cost, effective solutions, and following participation in an ILO training programme on "Work Improvement in Small Enterprises" (WISE), the management opened a mess room to allow workers to relax in a more comfortable environment during lunch breaks. It installed five new water coolers in addition to the two already in place. Seven water coolers served a workforce of 300 workers, one for every 40–45 workers, not an ideal ratio but certainly an improvement on the previous situation. Higher availability of water coolers in proximity to individual workplaces made their use very popular, and the management was in the process of introducing more of them to fully meet the demand.

Possible disadvantages of water solution

None.

Costs and benefits to enterprise

Each water cooler is rented at about US$10 per month, while each tank of

After participating in a WISE course the company made many improvements, including provision of drinking water for workers (ILO/C. Loiselle).

water (5 gallons, or 19 litres) costs little more than US$1.00. For each cooler, two water tanks are required each day, for a total of 14 water tanks at a total cost of about US$14.

In the view of Sabrina St-Rémy, Production Planning and Control Manager, this cost was largely compensated by returns in performance by the workforce. Lack of water and consequent dehydration not only had serious effects on the health of the workers but also significantly lowered the level of attention and efficiency at work.

Practical advice for implementation

This was a simple, inexpensive solution in lieu of proper ventilation. Both were needed, but clean drinking water is always a positive.

Union/employee perspective

None.

9.7 Clean drinking water summary

Water coolers and bottle-less solutions

In developed nations the public water system is generally safe to drink. Water treatment facilities usually use chlorine to kill harmful bacteria and other pathogens in the water supply; and chlorination is largely considered one of the greatest public health achievements of the twentieth century. Thus, bottled and filtered water is a benefit, not a necessity, at workplaces with a municipal water supply. Many workers do not like the taste of chlorinated water, however. (Chlorine remains in the system to kill pathogens beyond the treatment facility.) And this dislike might discourage water consumption. Water coolers are standard in American offices and are gaining popularity elsewhere. Concerns for employers include delivery, storage and changing heavy bottles. Bottle-less solutions are filtration systems that remove chlorine and other chemicals from tap water. Concerns for employers include the initial expense and ongoing filter costs.

Russian-British Consulting Centre

This small office installed a commercial filter on the spigot in its kitchenette. The filtered water is 90 per cent cheaper than bottled water. The positive: simple solution for small offices. The negative: the filter needs to be changed often if a kitchen has many users.

Tai Yang Enterprise Co. Ltd

Tai Yang in Phnom Penh could not rely on the local water supply. The water quality is poor and workers who drink it often get sick. The company trucked in potable water at great expense, but the water sometimes became contaminated during shipment. With the technical assistance of its parent company in Taiwan, China, the company installed a multi-stage filtration system in which water passes through a sand filter, an activated carbon filter, a micron membrane to remove particulates and then a reverse-osmosis process. The positive: clean, tasty water; no sick employees. The negative: expensive to set up; complicated to maintain; need experts on hand.

NASA Goddard Space Flight Center

This facility, like other government workplaces, cannot pay for bottled water for employees if potable, municipal water is available. Employees in many offices and buildings form "water clubs" to purchase 19-litre bottles for water coolers. The positive: employees drink more water. The negative: people who do not pay and try to sneak a glass of water from time to time, leading to arguments.

Confection et Emballages

This garment factory in Port-au-Prince installed five new water coolers, bringing the total to seven, to serve a workforce of 300 workers. The factory was hot and workers' water needs were great. The coolers were very popular. The positive: gains seen in productivity. The negative: not enough coolers for 300 workers, but a good start.

PART III

RESOURCES FOR UNIONS, EMPLOYERS AND GOVERNMENTS

10   A CHECKLIST FOR ENTERPRISE DECISION-MAKING

This publication has identified several factors that employers need to consider when developing meal options for their employees.

Number of workers

The larger the workforce, the greater the economic justification and reward in offering a formal meal plan.

Budget for meal plan

As depicted in figures 3.2 and 3.3 at the end of Chapter 3, a variety of food solutions exists depending on an employer's budget.

Space available for facility

Businesses in crowded urban settings might have difficulty allocating space for a dining area. When space is limited or too costly, meal vouchers can be a viable alternative to a canteen or mess room.

Length of break

Unlike the 8-hour day and 40-hour week, time allocation for meal breaks often is not regulated. Short meal breaks, 30 minutes or less, make it difficult to obtain meals beyond the company grounds. Long queues and limited seating at the canteen cut into meal breaks. Workers in warm climates need extra time to rest to avoid heat exhaustion.

Proximity/accessibility of meal plan

Related to break length, the locations of facilities must be chosen to ease accessibility. One canteen at the edge of the company grounds doesn't help employees on the other side unless they have convenient access to the canteen.

Similarly, workers in industrial settings wearing protective materials need time and space to change and wash.

Food safety
Employers must remain diligent about proper food handling and hygiene, or run the risk of making hundreds of workers ill with one meal. Food must be free from workplace chemical residue and served in a clean area.

Food security
Malnutrition often occurs when people have limited access to healthy foods, a result of economics (food unaffordable), distribution (food variety unavailable in markets), natural calamity (drought, infestation), education (poor understanding of nutrition or food preparation) or war. Employers have the opportunity to offer the types of healthy foods that employees might not have access to, such as fresh fruits and vegetables.

Workforce dietary/health concerns
Workers around the world have different dietary concerns. In industrialized countries, obesity and chronic diseases are more of a nutritional concern than macro- and micronutrient deficiencies. In many developing nations, the reverse is true. Meal plans should address these dietary concerns.

Education
Employees who are educated about proper nutrition and then offered access to healthy foods will be more likely to eat them, compared with workers who receive no education.

Workforce gender
In many developing countries, a case can be made that women have different dietary needs from men and that these needs often aren't met. Iron deficiency and anaemia are more common among women, for example. Women of child-bearing age need micronutrients such as folate (folic acid) before pregnancy, to ensure the health of their children.

Special needs
Companies, particularly multinationals, must remain aware of cultural norms, such as food restrictions on religious grounds.

Here is how these factors apply to food solutions presented in this publication.

10.1 Canteens

The 1988 ILO publication *Canteens and food services in industry: A manual* (Brown, 1988) provides basic instructions on how to operate a canteen. Canteens are businesses within businesses, and no simple checklist can adequately prepare an employer to establish one. There are a few factors to consider, however, when planning a canteen. Workers will not patronize a poorly run canteen, resulting in a failed costly investment for the company.

- Is there space for a facility?

- Is the space large enough to accommodate the expected number of workers? For fewer than 25 workers, the dining area should be 18.5 m² plus approximately 0.6 m² for each additional person.

- Do other options exist for workers, such as kitchenettes, recreational areas or nearby restaurants, to compensate for a shortage of space?

- Is there infrastructure to provide clean water for cooking, washing and drinking?

- Is there a budget for building and equipment maintenance, cleaning, pest control and stocking the lavatories with soap, etc.?

- Is there space for fuel, food and rubbish storage? Is it secure?

- Is there easy access for food delivery and rubbish collection?

- Is there a dedicated canteen staff trained in hygiene and food handling?

- Have the local authorities been contacted to instruct on health and food safety regulations, and other legal issues?

- Is there a professional catering service available, and can the caterer offer healthy foods at reasonable prices?

- Do the food choices address the nutritional needs of the workers?

- Does the menu accommodate special dietary needs arising from gender (and pregnancy), religion, culture or health?

- Is the meal plan available to all employees associated with the enterprise, including those on contract (including cleaning staff), working temporarily or working part time?

- Is there a budget to subsidize meals?

- Have the menu and pricing been reviewed by employees or their unions?

- Can the canteen accommodate night workers? If not, has the employer considered where and what workers will eat when the canteen is closed?

- Do workers have convenient access to the canteen by foot or bus?

- Is there a cloakroom or hooks for coats and umbrellas?

- Is there enough time for workers to travel to the canteen, get food, pay for food, find a seat, eat and return to work within the time allotted for the break?

- Is there a place to change clothes and wash?

- Is the canteen ventilated and does it protect workers from the weather?

- Does the canteen have windows, lighting, and other factors to make for a pleasant dining experience?

- Does the canteen serve a dual purpose? If so, tables and chairs must be moveable.

- Is the kitchen an easily cleaned, impermeable, non-slip surface?

- Would you and your boss eat here?

10.2 Vouchers

Food and meal vouchers are predominantly used at established stores and eateries working within the formal sector, adhering to health code regulations. Food safety is less of a concern. The key concerns are time, availability and affordability. One of the charms of the voucher system is the ease of use. The employer need not be concerned about the details of operating a canteen or contracting the service to a caterer. So the checklist is less extensive.

- Does the country have an established voucher system?

- Has the employer researched the benefits that each voucher provider has to offer?

- Will workers benefit from a meal voucher or food voucher? Meal vouchers serve those cultures that value midday meals and which have affordable restaurants. Food vouchers extend the social benefit to workers' families.

- Do workers have safe and convenient access to local shops?

- Do workers have access to shops during inclement weather?

- Do workers have enough time to visit a local shop, eat and return to work in the allotted meal break time?

- Are there affordable food options for the employee?

- Are there a variety of shops to suit a variety of tastes?

- Are there healthy food options suitable for daily consumption?

- Is the employer willing to offer employees information about nutrition so that they can make wise decisions about what types of food are best for them?

- Can local shops accommodate special dietary needs arising from gender (and pregnancy), religion, culture or health?

- Are vouchers available to all employees associated with the enterprise, including those on contract, working temporarily or working part time?

- Can the voucher accommodate night workers? If not, has the employer considered where and what night workers will eat?

- Is the face value of the meal voucher enough to match the price of a meal, assuming that no change will be given?

- Is the employer willing to subsidize at least half the meal price?

- Is the employer willing to abide by the strict rules of voucher use, as defined by law from country to country?

- Would you and your boss patronize the local shops?

10.3 Mess rooms

Eating areas, recreational areas and mess rooms require less of an investment compared with a canteen. They are easier to create and maintain because, by the definition used in this publication, little or no cooking is performed in the mess room. Food for sale or distribution is catered. Nevertheless, care is needed in planning to ensure these areas remain a decent place for workers to eat and relax. Many of the factors that apply to canteens apply here. Mess rooms, being large, are often located in a designated building, taking up an entire floor. Workers buy food at the mess room or bring it in. However, eating areas and recreational areas can be tiny, pleasant spaces with just a few chairs and tables tucked here or there. Often these are located within the building of a group of workers. Workers bring food into these areas.

- Is there a legal requirement to provide a mess room depending on the size of the workforce?

- Is there enough space? Mess rooms require as much space as canteens. For fewer than 25 workers, the dining area should be 18.5 m² plus about 0.6 m² for each additional person.

- Does the mess room design allow for easy cleaning, with impermeable, non-slip floors and moveable tables and chairs?

- Is there a budget for building maintenance, cleaning, pest control and stocking the lavatories with soap?

- If the mess room is to offer foods prepared by a caterer outside the workplace, is there easy access for food delivery and rubbish collection?

- For eating and recreational areas, is there regular rubbish removal?

- Is there a place to safely store food, if necessary?

- Are there appliances or facilities to help (the caterer) keep cold foods cold and hot foods hot?

- Have the local authorities been contacted to instruct on health and food safety regulations and other legal issues?

- Do workers have convenient access to the mess room by foot or bus?

- Is there enough time for workers to travel to the dining area, pay for food, find a seat, eat and return to work within the time allotted for the break?

- Is there a cloakroom or hooks for coats and umbrellas?

- Is there a place to change clothes and wash?

- Is there a way for workers to heat their own food?

- Is there clean drinking water?

- Is the mess room ventilated and does it protect workers from the weather?

- Does the mess room have windows, lighting and other factors to make for a pleasant dining experience?

- Can the dining areas accommodate night workers? If not, has the employer considered where and what workers will eat when the room is closed?

- Does the food provided address the nutritional needs of the workers? Has the employer considered offering healthy foods, such as vitamin-supplemented foods for workers facing chronic malnutrition or foods that help prevent obesity and chronic diseases?

- Does the food provided accommodate special dietary needs arising from gender (and pregnancy), religion, culture or health?

- Is the meal plan available to all employees associated with the enterprise, including those on contract (including cleaning staff), working temporarily or working part time?

- Is there a budget to subsidize meals?

- Would you and your boss eat here?

10.4 Kitchenettes

These small rooms provide a space for employees to store food (in a refrigerator, if necessary), to heat food and to wash their plates and utensils. Some kitchenettes are large enough to accommodate a table. If the kitchenette can't hold a table, workers need an eating area or recreational area to eat. Eating at one's desk or workstation should be avoided, because this can damage equipment and dirty the work area; and it is usually not relaxing, providing no rest or stress relief. Often it is the workers' responsibility to keep kitchenettes clean, leading to occasional confrontations when they are left dirty.

- Is there adequate power supply for appliances?

- Is a cleaner or maid available once a week or so to clean?

- Is there daily removal of rubbish?

- Is there a clean water supply for cooking and drinking?

- Is there a spigot and sink with soap for washing?

- Is there a cupboard or drawers for storing cooking utensils, plates, etc.?

- Is there a box or refrigerator to store food safely?

- Is there a fire extinguisher?

- Is there adequate ventilation to remove smoke and odours?

- Is there a pleasant place nearby to eat? Eating at the desk or workstation is not desirable.

- Would you and your boss use the kitchenette?

10.5 Mobile refreshment facilities

This publication did not present case studies on company-commissioned mobile food vans and food trolleys. Trolleys are common in office buildings, particularly in Asia. These are simple carts pushed about from floor to floor, room to room, carrying snacks and meals for sale. The main concern is food safety.

- Are hot foods served hot, above 60°C?

- Is food never kept at room temperature for more than two hours?

- Are there healthy food options?

- Can the trolley roll over carpeting and easily move about?

- Can the trolley move from floor to floor, if necessary?

- Does the trolley or van attendant avoid touching food directly?

- Do trolley and van attendants have access to lavatories with soap and water?

- Do workers have access to a washroom before eating?

- Do workers have towels or other supplies to keep work areas clean?

- Would you and your boss purchase food from the vans or trolleys?

10.6 Vending machines

Vending machines are sometimes owned or rented by the employer. Sometimes a second party pays the employer for the business opportunity of placing vending machines within crowded company grounds. Most of the time, vending machines provide snacks and drinks, and they are often a source of unhealthy foods. Sometimes vending machines offer sandwiches or soups to complement other meal plans.

- Is there adequate power supply?

- Are vending machines properly maintained and in working order?

- Are the vending machines properly secured to prevent tipping?

- Are old foods regularly replaced if they don't sell?

- Are there healthy food options?

- Are there healthy drink options?

- Do workers, particularly those on night shifts, have 24-hour access to the vending machines?

- Can the vending machines provide options for morning, midday and evening meals?

- Is there a dining area or relaxing area to eat vended food?

- Are emergency contact numbers posted on the machines in case of malfunction or food poisoning?

- Do the vending machines provide change and accept a variety of coins and paper money?

10.7 Local vendors

This category of local vendors applies broadly to all meal options outside the company walls. Food variety, accessibility, nutrition and food safety are the main concerns. If an enterprise relies on local vendors, these concerns must be addressed.

- Do workers have enough time to visit a local vendor, eat and return to work in the allotted meal break time?

- Do workers have safe and convenient access to local vendors?

- Do employees have access to food and a pleasant place to eat during inclement weather?

- Are there affordable food options for the employee?

- Are there healthy food options suitable for daily consumption?

- Are there a variety of vendors to suit a variety of tastes?

- Do local vendors understand proper hygiene and food handling?

- Do local vendors have access to washrooms?

- Do local vendors have the ability to keep food at safe temperatures?

- Is the employer willing to help the local vendor with hygiene and food safety needs?

- Would you and your boss patronize the local vendors?

10.8 Options for different types of organization

Micro enterprises

Micro enterprises are owner-managed organizations with approximately one to five employees. One appropriate food solution is the kitchenette. Here, employees can store packed meals in a small refrigerator or chest. They can warm food in a microwave or on a hotplate. A small dining area will enable workers to leave their work areas for a little stress relief. If space is limited, the owner can provide a folding table and chairs to be stowed away before and after the meal break. In lieu of offering a spot to cook and eat, employers with modest finances can make an informal arrangement for meal reimbursements at local shops. A fruit basket is an inexpensive, welcomed perk. In the absence of finances, electricity or fuel, owners can set aside a clean and relaxing eating area for employees, sheltered from unpleasant weather. Food should be stored in a chest to protect it from heat, chemicals or other workplace hazards. Clean water to wash hands and drink is a necessity.

Small enterprises

Small enterprises are owner-managed organizations with approximately five to 25 employees. The kitchenette can be an appropriate solution. With modest financial resources, the employer can purchase or facilitate a few appliances in the kitchen area, such as a microwave and refrigerator. Employers with a larger budget can consider meal vouchers or subsidizing healthy, catered food from a local vendor, delivered daily and served in a dining area. Owners with no budget or space must still remember the basics: a clean spot to store food, clean water, a relaxing place to eat or adequate time allowance for the employee to leave the workplace for a meal. Owners can invite local vendors to the workplace to sell food. In such a situation, vendors can benefit from access to water and storage facilities; workers have the convenience of having food brought to them. Owners can also talk to local shop owners and encourage them to sell healthy meals with the promise of "sending" the shopkeeper customers.

Medium-sized enterprises

Medium-sized enterprises have approximately 25 to 100 employees, too few for a canteen to be viable. Meal vouchers and mess rooms are appropriate. Employers can stagger meal breaks so that workers have more room to cook and eat comfortably in the kitchen and dining areas. Employers can consider subsidizing catered food. In developing nations, this can be done inexpensively by hiring a cook to provide a single meal each day. Employers should remain aware of their workers' needs and provide fortified foods or supplements for workers suffering from micronutrient deficiencies, which are common in such countries. Employers with modest budgets can provide bulk food distribution, such as grains, for the workers' families.

Large enterprises

Employers with more than 100 employees should consider meal vouchers or mess rooms. Canteens can also be a viable solution at sites with 100 employees or more, or at remote sites where no other dining option is available. Large enterprises are more likely to have the space and resources to: invite local vendors on site, establish farmers' markets, bargain with local caterers, distribute foods to workers' families or work with a local university in monitoring workers' nutritional needs.

Informal sector

Much of what applies to micro and small enterprises also applies to the informal sector. Street foods provide a major source of nourishment for workers in this sector. Employers can work with vendors to make street foods safer by offering clean water, ice, storage containers or utensils – even if they are stamped with the employer's logo. (A 1999 symposium on the informal sector organized by the ILO and the International Confederation of Free Trade Unions categorized this sector as encompassing: (a) owner-employers of micro enterprises, which employ a few paid workers, with or without apprentices; (b) own-account workers, who own and operate one-person businesses, who work alone or with the help of unpaid workers, generally family members and apprentices; and (c) dependent workers, paid or unpaid, including wage workers in micro enterprises, unpaid family workers, apprentices, contract labour, homeworkers and paid domestic workers.)

11 INTERNATIONAL STANDARDS, POLICIES AND PROGRAMMES

Nutrition, food security, and food and water safety have long been a concern for the World Health Organization, the Food and Agriculture Organization, the World Bank and related United Nation agencies. Workers' wellbeing, in turn, has long been the domain of the International Labour Organization. For example, the ILO Weekly Rest (Industry) Convention, 1921 (No. 14), and later, the Weekly Rest (Commerce and Offices) Convention, 1957 (No. 106), establish a minimum period of weekly rest for workers – that is, at least 24 hours, and preferably 36 hours, per seven-day period. The Welfare Facilities Recommendation, 1956 (No. 102), is the ILO's strongest statement on eating conditions across sectors. The proposed Consolidated Maritime Labour Convention makes provisions for food preparation and meal conditions for seafarers.

While there are no international standards regarding workers' nutrition, a multitude of programmes and documents have been developed in recent years that can help guide governments and employers on this important topic. These are listed below, followed by a short summary of each of them.

International Labour Organization
Welfare Facilities Recommendation, 1956 (No. 102)
J. Brown: *Canteens and food services in industry: A manual*, 1988
ILO SOLVE (Stress, Tobacco, Alcohol & drugs, HIV/AIDS, Violence) Programme
Consolidated Maritime Labour Convention (draft)

Global perspective
WHO: *Global Strategy for Food Safety*, 2002
WHO: *Global Strategy on Diet, Physical Activity and Health*, 2004
United Nations: *5th Report on the World Nutrition Situation: Nutrition for improved development outcomes*, 2004
WHO/World Bank: *Food policy options: Preventing and controlling nutrition related non-communicable diseases*, 2002

Nutrition

WHO/FAO: *Diet, nutrition and the prevention of chronic diseases*, 2002
WHO/FAO: *Preparation and use of food-based dietary guidelines*, 1996
USAID/UNICEF/WHO: *Nutrition essentials: A guide for program managers*, 1999
WHO/UNICEF/UNA: *Iron deficiency anaemia: Assessment, prevention and control. A guide for programme managers*, 2001

Food quality and safety

Public Sector Food Procurement Initiative (PSFPI) (England)
Codex Alimentarius
Hazard Analysis and Critical Control Point (HACCP) system for food safety
Participatory Hygiene and Sanitation Transformations (PHAST) Initiative
WHO: *Guidelines for drinking-water quality*, 2004
FAO: *The economics of food safety in developing countries*, 2003
FAO: *Training manual for environmental health officers on safe handling practices for street foods*, 2001

11.1 International Labour Organization

Box 11.1 reproduces extracts of the ILO's Welfare Facilities Recommendation, 1956 (No. 102).

11.1   Welfare Facilities Recommendation, 1956 (No. 102) (extracts)

The General Conference of the International Labour Organization,

Having been convened at Geneva by the Governing Body of the International Labour Office, and having met in its Thirty-ninth Session on 6 June 1956, and

Having decided upon the adoption of certain proposals with regard to welfare facilities for workers, which is the fifth item on the agenda of the session, and

Having determined that these proposals shall take the form of a Recommendation,

adopts this twenty-sixth day of June of the year one thousand nine hundred and fifty-six, the following Recommendation, which may be cited as the Welfare Facilities Recommendation, 1956:

Whereas it is desirable to define certain principles and establish certain standards concerning the following welfare facilities for workers:

(a) feeding facilities in or near the undertaking;

(b) rest facilities in or near the undertaking and recreation facilities excluding holiday facilities; and

(c) transportation facilities to and from work where ordinary public transport is inadequate or impracticable,

The Conference recommends that the following provisions should be applied as fully and as rapidly as national conditions allow, by voluntary, governmental or other appropriate action, and that each Member should report to the International Labour Office as requested by the Governing Body concerning the measures taken to give effect thereto.

I. Scope

1. This Recommendation applies to manual and non-manual workers employed in public or private undertakings, excluding workers in agriculture and sea transport.

2. In any case in which it is doubtful whether an undertaking is one to which this Recommendation applies, the question should be settled either by the competent authority after consultation with the organizations of employers and workers concerned, or in accordance with the law or practice of the country.

II. Methods of Implementation

3. Having regard to the variety of welfare facilities and of national practices in making provision for them, the facilities specified in this Recommendation may be provided by means of public or voluntary action:

(a) through laws and regulations, or

(b) in any other manner approved by the competent authority after consultation with employers' and workers' organizations, or

(c) by virtue of collective agreement or as otherwise agreed upon by the employers and workers concerned.

III. Feeding Facilities

A. Canteens

4. Canteens providing appropriate meals should be set up and operated in or near undertakings where this is desirable, having regard to the number of workers employed by the undertaking, the demand for and prospective use of the facilities, the non-availability of other appropriate facilities for obtaining meals and any other relevant conditions and circumstances.

5. If canteens are provided by virtue of national laws or regulations, the competent authority should be empowered to require the setting up and operation of canteens in or near undertakings where more than a specified minimum number of workers is employed or where this is desirable for any other reason determined by the competent authority.

6. If canteens are the responsibility of works committees established by national laws or regulations, this responsibility should be exercised in undertakings where the setting up and operation of such canteens are desirable.

7. If canteens are provided by virtue of collective agreement or in any other manner except as indicated in Paragraphs 5 and 6, the arrangements so arrived at should apply to undertakings where this is desirable for any reason as determined by agreement between the employers and workers concerned.

8. The competent authority or some other appropriate body should make suitable arrangements to give information, advice and guidance to individual undertakings with respect to technical questions involved in the setting up and operation of canteens.

9.
(1) Where adequate publications are not already in existence, the competent authority or some other appropriate body should prepare and publish detailed information, suggestions and guidance, adapted to the special conditions in the country concerned, on methods of setting up and operating canteens.

(2) Such information should include suggestions on:

(a) location of the canteens in relation to the various buildings or departments of the undertakings concerned;
(b) establishment of joint canteens for several undertakings in so far as is appropriate;
(c) accommodation in canteens: standards of space, lighting, heating, temperature and ventilation;
(d) layout of canteens: dining room or rooms, service area, kitchen, dishwashing area, storage, administration office, and lockers and washroom for canteen personnel;

(e) equipment, furnishing and decoration of canteens: equipment for the preparation and cooking of food, refrigeration, storage and washing up; types of fuel for cooking; types of tables and chairs in the dining room or rooms; scheme of painting and decoration;

(f) types of meals provided: standard menu, standard menu with options, à la carte; dietetic menus where medically prescribed; special menus for workers in unhealthy occupations; breakfast, midday meal or other meals for shift workers;

(g) standard of nutrition: nutritional values of foodstuffs, planned menus and balanced diets;

(h) types of service in the canteen: hatch or counter service, cafeteria, and table service; personnel needed for each type of service;

(i) standards of hygiene in the kitchen and dining rooms;

(j) financial questions: initial capital outlay for construction, equipment and furnishing, continuing overheads and maintenance expenses, food and personnel costs, accounts, prices charged for meals.

B. Buffets and Trolleys

10.

(1) In undertakings where it is not practicable to set up canteens providing appropriate meals, and in other undertakings where such canteens already exist, buffets or trolleys should be provided, where necessary and practicable, for the sale to the workers of packed meals or snacks and tea, coffee, milk and other beverages. Trolleys should not, however, be introduced into workplaces in which dangerous or harmful processes make it undesirable that workers should partake of food and drink there.

(2) Some of these facilities should be made available not only during the midday or mid-shift interval but also during the recognized rest pauses and breaks.

C. Mess Rooms and Other Suitable Rooms

11.

(1) In undertakings where it is not practicable to set up canteens providing appropriate meals, and, where necessary, in other undertakings where such canteens already exist, mess room facilities should be provided, where practicable and appropriate, for individual workers to prepare or heat and take meals provided by themselves.

(2) The facilities so provided should include at least:

(a) a room in which provision suited to the climate is made for relieving discomfort from cold or heat;

(b) adequate ventilation and lighting;
(c) suitable tables and seating facilities in sufficient numbers;
(d) appropriate appliances for heating food and beverages;
(e) an adequate supply of wholesome drinking water.

D. Mobile Canteens

12. In undertakings in which workers are dispersed over wide work areas, it is desirable, where practicable and necessary, and where other satisfactory facilities are not available, to provide mobile canteens for the sale of appropriate meals to the worker.

E. Other Facilities

13. Special consideration should be given to providing shift workers with facilities for obtaining adequate meals and beverages at appropriate times.

14. In localities where there are insufficient facilities for purchasing appropriate food, beverages and meals, measures should be taken to provide workers with such facilities.

F. Use of Facilities

15. The workers should in no case be compelled, except as required by national laws and regulations for reasons of health, to use any of the feeding facilities provided.

11.1.1 Canteens and food services in industry: A manual

This 1998 ILO publication, by Joanna Brown, contains information about how to organize, manage and finance a canteen; as well as advice on mess rooms, refreshment facilities, local vendors and low-cost shops.

11.1.2 ILO SOLVE Programme

SOLVE is ILO's interactive educational programme designed to assist in the development of policy and action to address stress, alcohol and drugs, violence (both physical and psychological), HIV/AIDS and tobacco, which all lead to health-related problems for the worker and lower productivity for the enterprise or organization. Along with nutritional deficiency, they represent a major cause of accidents, fatal injuries, disease and absenteeism at work in both industrialized and developing countries. The programme focuses on prevention in translating concepts into policies and policies into action at the national and enterprise levels.

The programme addresses the fact that work-related stress affects at least 40 million workers in 15 Member States in the European Union, a cost of at least €20 billion (US$27 billion) annually. Absenteeism is two to three times higher among drug and alcohol abusers than for other workers. Nearly 1,000 workers are murdered on the job every year in the United States, and workplace homicide is the leading cause of death at work for women and the second leading cause for men, after traffic accidents. HIV/AIDS causes enormous, still largely unquantified, human and economic cost; productivity in South Africa could decline by 50 per cent in the next ten years at a result of HIV/AIDS. The use of or exposure to tobacco products has become the largest cause of preventable death worldwide, and smokers account for 50 per cent more working days lost than non-smokers. Complementing the information delineated in this publication, the ILO also hopes to raise the prominence of workers' nutrition by folding this concern into SOLVE's five existing areas. One relevant topic is shift work and night work, which adds to work-related stress as well as nutritional disorders.[1]

11.1.3 Draft Consolidated Maritime Labour Convention

This document, now in draft form, will be discussed, revised further and is expected to be adopted at an International Maritime Conference in February 2006. As the title implies, the ILO's various maritime Conventions are in the process of being consolidated into a single instrument. The draft Convention makes specific provisions regarding kitchens, dining areas, food handling, catering and qualifications for ships' cooks. The purpose is to ensure that seafarers have access to high-quality food and drinking water provided under regulated hygienic conditions. Meals should take account of differing cultural, religious and gastronomic backgrounds; and seafarers living on board a ship should be provided with food free of charge during the period of engagement. In addition, the International Labour Conference is scheduled to adopt the Recommendation on Work in the Fishing Sector in June 2005. For the maritime Convention, refer to: http://www.ilo.org/public/english/standards/relm/maritime/.

---

[1] The following texts have been excerpted in large part from the respective programme descriptions.

11.2 Global perspective

11.2.1 WHO: Global Strategy for Food Safety

Food-borne diseases take a major toll on health. Millions of people fall ill and many die as a result of eating unsafe food. The 53rd World Health Assembly, in resolution WHA53.15, requested the WHO Director-General to put in place a global strategy for surveillance of food-borne diseases and to initiate a range of other activities on food safety and health. The WHO organized a strategy planning meeting on food safety in Geneva, February 2001. Following further consultation with member states, the WHO drew up a global food safety strategy, including surveillance, as outlined in this document. The WHO *Global Strategy for Food Safety* is available in Arabic, Chinese, English, French, Russian and Spanish. Refer to: http://www.who.int/foodsafety/publications/general/global_strategy/en/.

11.2.2 WHO: Global Strategy on Diet, Physical Activity and Health

A few largely preventable risk factors account for most of the world's disease burden. Chronic diseases – including cardiovascular conditions, diabetes, stroke, cancers and respiratory diseases – account for 59 per cent of the 57 million deaths annually, and 46 per cent of the global disease burden. This reflects a significant change in diet habits and physical activity levels worldwide as a result of industrialization, urbanization, economic development and increasing food market globalization. Recognizing this, the WHO is adopting a broad-ranging approach and has begun to formulate a Global Strategy on Diet, Physical Activity and Health, under a May 2002 mandate from the World Health Assembly (WHA). This population-wide, prevention-based strategy is being developed through extensive consultation and was presented to the World Health Assembly in May 2004. The overall goal of the strategy is to improve public health through healthy eating and physical activity. The text of the final resolution, WHA57.17 and the annexed *Global Strategy on Diet, Physical Activity and Health* is available in Arabic, Chinese, English, French, Russian and Spanish. Refer to: http://www.who.int/ dietphysicalactivity/en/.

11.2.3 United Nations: Fifth Report on the World Nutrition Situation: Nutrition for improved development outcomes

This report, published in March 2004, is the result of a partnership between a task force convened by the Standing Committee on Nutrition and the many

United Nations and other agencies that provided access to data and expertise. The *Fifth Report on the World Nutrition Situation* continues the tradition of reporting on trends in nutrition throughout the life cycle and of challenging the nutrition community. But instead of asking the question "How is nutrition affected by global changes?", it asks the question more proactively: "How can a nutrition perspective accelerate the attainment of a comprehensive set of development goals?" Inspired by the commitments made at the Millennium Summit of the United Nations in September 2000, translated into a series of Millennium Development Goals (MDGs), the report makes the case that the role of nutrition in development goes far beyond providing an indicator of progress towards the MDGs. The report is available at: http://www.unsystem.org/scn/ Publications/html/RWNS.html. The Millennium Development Goals are listed at http://www.un.org/ millenniumgoals/.

11.2.4 WHO/World Bank: Food policy options: Preventing and controlling nutrition related non-communicable diseases

This is a report of a WHO and World Bank consultation from November 2002. Although diet structure and activity throughout the developing world have shifted drastically over the past several decades, little is known about effective policies to influence the supply and demand for food to control the undesirable effects of those shifts, such as obesity, heart disease and cancer. Two questions specifically need to be addressed: 1) are the traditional policy levers for crops and livestock still important and feasible options, considering the latest developments in processing, distribution and marketing?, and 2) what research should be done in the process of formulating an "action agenda" over the longer term? The answer to the first question concerns "traditional" versus "new policy levers", and includes: a) recognition of the limitations of conventional food policies; b) demanding truth in advertising; c) harnessing the influence of supermarkets and multinational corporations; d) choosing realistic options to shift demand; e) addressing internal infrastructure; and f) using schools for targeted intervention.

The second question concerns the necessary research for an "action agenda". There is a major need for longitudinal research to follow individuals and households in the way the China Health and Nutrition Survey does. Currently, few studies allow linkage of prices, diet and health outcomes in any systematic manner that considers the timing of the changes. Details of the recommended research are outlined in the text, which is available at: http://www1.worldbank.org/hnp/publication.asp.

11.3 Nutrition

11.3.1 WHO/FAO: Diet, nutrition and the prevention of chronic diseases

This report of a Joint WHO/FAO Expert Consultation reviews the evidence on the effects of diet and nutrition on chronic diseases and makes recommendations for public health policies and strategies that encompass societal, behavioural and ecological dimensions. Although the primary aim of the consultation was to set targets related to diet and nutrition, the importance of physical activity was also emphasized. The consultation considered diet in the context of the macroeconomic implications of public health recommendations on agriculture, and the global supply and demand for fresh and processed foodstuffs. In setting out ways to decrease the burden of chronic diseases such as obesity, Type 2 diabetes, cardiovascular diseases (including hypertension and stroke), cancer, dental diseases and osteoporosis, this report proposes that nutrition should be placed at the forefront of public health policies and programmes.

This report will be of interest to policy-makers and public health professionals alike, in a wide range of disciplines including nutrition, general medicine and gerontology. It shows how, at the population level, diet and exercise throughout the life course can reduce the threat of a global epidemic of chronic diseases. The 150-page document is available at:
http://www.who.int/ dietphysicalactivity/publications/trs916/en/ or
http://www.fao.org/DOCREP/005/AC911E/ac911e00.htm

11.3.2 WHO/FAO: Preparation and use of food-based dietary guidelines

Food-based dietary guidelines were among the priority considerations at the International Conference on Nutrition, convened by the FAO and the WHO in Rome in 1992. *Preparation and use of food-based dietary guidelines* is a report of a joint FAO/WHO consultation in Nicosia, Cyprus. The document was published in 1996 and is available at: http://www.fao.org/DOCREP/ x0243e/x0243e00.htm. The overall purpose of the consultation was to establish the scientific basis for developing and using food-based dietary guidelines to improve the food consumption patterns and nutritional wellbeing of individuals and populations. Such guidelines are needed in virtually all countries given the role that food consumption and dietary practices play in nutrition-related disorders, whether of deficiency or excess. Formerly, most national dietary guidelines were nutrient-based and their use met with only moderate success. This report demonstrates how national authorities can change the traditional focus from nutrients to locally available foods.

The report includes a summary of dietary assessment methodologies – national food supply data, household food consumption data and individual consumption data – which are appropriate for drawing up and monitoring the use and impact of dietary guidelines. For the latter, five methods are presented: food records, 24-hour dietary recall, food frequency questionnaires, diet histories and food habit questionnaires. Methods of analysis and computation of nutrient intakes including computer software are described, as is the method of presentation of data on consumption of particular foods and food groups.

11.3.3 *USAID/UNICEF/WHO:* Nutrition essentials: A guide for program managers

This 1999 nutrition guide from USAID, UNICEF and WHO, revised in 2004, is available at: http://www.basics.org/publications/abs/abs_nutrition.html. The comprehensive guide was developed to help programme managers integrate nutrition with other health services and to strengthen nutrition in ongoing primary health-care programmes. The guide can be used to refer to current protocols and guidelines; learn the technical reasoning behind a decision to focus on certain nutrition behaviours; find checklists or ideas for checklists that can be adapted locally for programme planning and evaluation; research new ideas about how to solve common problems; and serve as a training aid for designing a curriculum or making overheads and handouts. Health managers who work at the district level may benefit particularly from this resource. So too may employers looking to combat iron, iodine and vitamin A deficiencies among workers. Major topics covered include: (1) priority nutrition interventions; (2) planning nutrition interventions in the district; (3) technical guidelines for integrating nutrition in health services; (4) forming community partnerships; (5) communications activities for improving nutrition; (6) supporting nutrition interventions; and (7) nutrition protocols.

11.3.4 *WHO/UNICEF/UNA:* Iron deficiency anaemia: Assessment, prevention and control. A guide for programme managers

Published in 2001, *Iron deficiency anaemia: Assessment, prevention and control. A guide for programme managers* is a collaboration between WHO, UNICEF and the United Nations University. This document deals primarily with indicators for monitoring interventions to combat iron deficiency, including iron deficiency anaemia (IDA), but it also reviews the current methods of assessing and preventing iron deficiency in the light of recent significant scientific advances. Criteria for defining IDA, and the severity of anaemia based on prevalence estimates, are provided. Approaches to obtaining dietary information, and guidance in designing national iron deficiency prevention programmes, are presented. Strategies for preventing iron deficiency through food-based approaches, i.e. dietary improvement or modification and fortification, and a schedule for using iron supplements to control iron deficiency and to treat mild to moderate iron deficiency anaemia, are discussed. For each strategy, desirable actions are outlined and criteria are suggested for assessment of the intervention. Attention is given to micronutrient complementarities in programme implementation, e.g., the particularly close link between the improvement of iron status and that of vitamin A. Finally, this document recommends action-oriented research on the control of iron deficiency, providing guidance in undertaking feasibility studies on iron fortification in most countries. An English version is available at: http://www.who.int/nut/publications.htm.

11.4 Food safety

11.4.1 Public Sector Food Procurement Initiative (England)

The public sector in England spends £1.8 billion (US$3.4 billion) on food and catering services. The Government wants to use this buying power to help deliver the aims of the Government's Sustainable Farming and Food Strategy (SFFS) in England – that is, to deliver a world-class sustainable farming and food sector that contributes to a better environment and healthier and prosperous communities. The Public Sector Food Procurement Initiative's five priority objectives are to: raise production and process standards; increase tenders from small and local producers; increase consumption of healthy and nutritious food; reduce adverse environmental impacts of production and supply; and increase capacity of small and local suppliers to meet demand. The benefits include: more sustainable British rural local economies; more competitive small and medium-sized suppliers; improved animal welfare; healthier and better performing students and workforce; a more sustainable environment; savings from minimizing waste; reduced hospital stays and greater choice for ethnic and religious groups. Additional information is available at: http://www.defra.gov.uk/farm/sustain/procurement/.

11.4.2 Codex Alimentarius

The Codex Alimentarius Commission was established in 1963 as a subsidiary body of the FAO and the WHO, with 165 member countries. It was established to formulate internationally accepted food safety standards to protect consumer health and ensure fair trade practices. The Codex Alimentarius Commission is the only international forum that brings together scientists, technical experts, government regulators, and international consumer and industry organizations. The Commission has succeeded in:

- defining general principles of food hygiene, protecting the food chain from primary production to the final consumer;

- establishing internationally recognized standards and guidelines for international food trade, valued at US$300 billion a year;

- setting rules for the safe use of food additives and establishing guidelines for proper labelling.

- setting maximum residue limits in food for over 3,200 pesticides;

- evaluating more than 1,005 food additives;

- clarifying the definition of organic food to prevent misleading claims about food quality or production methods;

- setting up 30 specialized committees – composed of top government health professionals, scientists and representatives of the food and agriculture sectors – to provide the ongoing scientific basis for Codex standards.

The Codex texts are used by governments as part of their national food safety requirements. They are also used by commercial partners in specifying the grade and quality of consignments in international trade. Codex is highly relevant to street foods, providing protection for the hundreds of millions of workers in both the formal and informal sectors served by (or working in) the informal sector of street food vending. In 1995, the Codex Alimentarius Commission adopted a recommended code of practice for the preparation and sale of street foods in Latin America and the Caribbean. In 1997, the Commission adopted a second set of guidelines, this time from South Africa, for the design of control measures for street food vending. Together these guidelines form the basis for regional codes of practice, to be adapted by each country and enforced by local authorities. In addition, in 1999 the Commission published its revised and amended *General principles of food hygiene* (available at: http://www.fao.rog/docrep/w6419e/w6419e00.htm), which included new ideas reflected in the Hazard Analysis and Critical Control Point (HACCP) system. This document is relevant both to workplace catering and street food vending. The FAO notes, however, that the HACCP system is too advanced to apply to street foods in poorer countries.

Key Codex standards relevant to workers' nutrition:

- Preparation and Sale of Street Foods (Latin America and the Caribbean), Ref. No. CAC/RCP 43; 1995 (revised in 2001).

- Design of Control Measures for Street-Vended Foods in Africa, Ref. No. CAC/GL 22; 1997 (revised in 1999).

- General Principles of Food Hygiene, Ref. No. CAC/RCP 1; 1969 (revised in 1997, amended in 1999).

- General Standard for Contaminants and Toxins in Foods, Ref. No. CODEX STAN 193; 1995 (revised in 1997, amended in 2001).

The 35th Session of the Codex Committee on Food Hygiene in 2003 discussed finalizing the *Guidelines on the application of HACCP in small and/or less developed businesses*. The FAO and the WHO are preparing a manual on this issue and are setting up a meeting to implement this (as of early 2005). For more information on Codex, refer to: http://www.codexalimentarius.net. Note: unofficial web sites using similar Internet addresses exist.

11.4.3 Hazard Analysis Critical Control Point (HACCP) system for food safety

The HACCP concept provides a systematic approach to identify and assess hazards and risks associated with the manufacture, distribution and use of a food product. The HACCP system has seven key elements: identification of hazards and assessment of severity; determination of critical control points required to control identified hazards; specification of critical limits that indicate whether an operation is under control at a particular critical control point; establishment and implementation of monitoring systems; execution of corrective actions when critical limits are not met; verification of the system; and record keeping. Critical control points refer to foods, locations, practices or raw materials where a control can be implemented. A critical limit is the point where a measured value (e.g. bacteria count) or practice becomes unacceptable. By means of an instructive example it is worth noting that, through HACCP, experts identified that water contamination in Calcutta street foods (see Chapter 7) was occurring as a result of poor storage, not poor point sources or transport methods.

The system originated in the United States in the 1990s (United States Food and Drug Administration and United States Department of Agriculture), where it is a mandated practice for meat, poultry, seafood, juice and other food industries. While few deny the usefulness of the HACCP concept, some health experts argue that the system is too thorough, complex and expensive to improve street foods in poorer nations. For example, FAO food projects reflect HACCP principles, but these agencies do not recommend full-blown HACCP systems for all street foods and marketplaces. The foundation of risk reduction in poorer nations is basic hygiene improvement. One project that does rely on the HACCP system is the WHO's Healthy Marketplace. (See Chapter 7 for a case study.) In such a marketplace, HACCP is used to identify all the major health hazards and to establish priorities for action once a problem arises. For a "Healthy Marketplace", HACCP is a tool for education and training, and it offers a logical framework to capture best practices and transfer them through the market's food distribution system. More information is available at: http://vm.cfsan.fda.gov/~lrd/haccp.html and http://haccpalliance.org/.

See also *Strategies for implementing HACCP in small and/or less developed businesses, Report of a WHO consultation*, The Hague, 16–19 June 1999, at: http://www.who.int/foodsafety/publications/fs_management/haccp_small-bus/en/.

11.4.4 Participatory Hygiene and Sanitation Transformations (PHAST) Initiative

Participatory Hygiene and Sanitation Transformations (PHAST) is an innovative approach designed to promote hygiene behaviours, sanitation improvements and community management of water and sanitation facilities using specifically developed participatory techniques. The *Participatory hygiene and sanitation transformations: A new approach to working with communities* document (WHO, 1996) describes the underlying principles of the approach, the development of the specific participatory tools, and the results of the field tests done in four African countries. The document includes: (1) the principles which underlie the approach; (2) how the methodology was developed at workshops in the African region; (3) the impact that PHAST made on communities and extension workers that were part of the field test, and the lessons learned during the field test; and (4) how the approach can be adopted more widely and what the enabling factors for this are. The document is available at: http://www.who.int/water_sanitation_health/hygiene/envsan/phast/en/.

11.4.5 WHO: Guidelines for drinking-water quality

These guidelines are the international reference point for standard setting and drinking-water safety. The guidelines are supported by other publications explaining how they were derived and intended to assist in implementing safe water activities. The first and second editions of the *Guidelines for drinking-water quality* (WHO, 2004h) were used by developing and developed countries worldwide as the basis for regulation and standard setting to ensure the safety of drinking water. They recognized the priority that should be given to ensuring microbial safety and provided guideline values for a large number of chemical hazards. The third edition of the guidelines has been comprehensively updated to take account of developments in risk assessment and risk management since the second edition. It describes a "framework for safe drinking-water" and discusses the roles and responsibilities of different stakeholders, including the complementary roles of national regulators, suppliers, communities and independent "surveillance" agencies.

Developments in this edition of the guidelines include significantly expanded guidance on ensuring the microbial safety of drinking water – in particular through comprehensive system-specific "water safety plans". Information on many chemicals has been revised to account for new scientific information, and information on chemicals not previously considered has been included. For the first time, reviews of many waterborne pathogens are provided. Recognizing the need for different tools and approaches in supporting large and community supplies, this edition continues to describe the principal characteristics of the approaches to each. New sections deal with the application of the *Guidelines* to specific circumstances, such as emergencies and disasters, large buildings, packaged/bottled water, travellers, desalination systems, food production and processing, and water safety on ships and in aviation.

The third edition of the guidelines is available at: http://www.who.int/ water_sanitation_health/dwq/gdwq3/en/. Downloadable training materials on drinking water quality are available at: http://www.who.int/water_sanitation_ health/dwq/dwqtraining/en/. These training materials cover a wide range of topics and include 23 sessions – both presentations and practical sessions. Each presentation in the materials includes a session plan, a background paper and overhead transparencies. Each practical session provides guidance as to how such sessions might be delivered and the materials required.

11.4.6 FAO: The economics of food safety in developing countries

The economics of food safety in developing countries, FAO ESA Working Paper No. 03-19 (2003), authored by Spencer Henson, aims to provide an overview of issues associated with the economics of food safety in developing countries. It is intended to highlight the major questions and concerns associated with an economic analysis of food safety issues, both generally and specifically in a developing country context. Thus, it provides an overview of these issues and highlights key references for readers who wish to explore these issues in greater depth.

The paper provides a basic overview of what is meant by food safety, highlighting the main hazards potentially associated with food. It assesses the burden imposed on developing countries, both in terms of rates of human morbidity and premature mortality and the economic and social costs imposed on developing societies. In so doing, the paucity of data on the magnitude of food-borne illness in developing countries is highlighted. The ways in which markets may fail to provide for an appropriate level of food safety, and thus the case for government regulation, are then discussed. Much of the remainder of the paper explores attempts by developing country governments to enhance their capacity in strategic areas in some depth in terms of the key elements of food safety capacity and analysis. It concludes by suggesting positive ways forward through which the capacity of developing countries to manage food safety, both for the protection of their domestic populations and promotion of trade in agricultural and food products, can be enhanced. The paper is available at: http://www.fao.org/es/esa/.

11.4.7 FAO: Training manual for environmental health officers on safe handling practices for street foods

This FAO manual of 2001 was prepared as a guide for environmental health officers on how to plan and implement a training programme for street food vendors and food handlers. It covers briefly the problems of food-borne diseases, socio-economic implications and the need to carry out a situation analysis of their respective working areas. It specifically targets food vendors, and the emphasis of the training modules is on sources of micro-organisms such as bacteria and viruses that cause food-borne disease, what these organisms require to grow and routes of contamination. The manual also covers prevention of food-borne diseases through food, personal and environmental hygiene practices. The manual was prepared for the FAO by the Government of South Africa, and this and similar documents concerning street food safety are available at: http://www.doh.gov.za/department/ foodcontrol/streetfood.

11.5 Health education

11.5.1 The Ottawa Charter

The first International Conference on Health Promotion met in Ottawa in November 1986 and created a Charter. The Charter defines health promotion as the process of enabling people to increase control over, and to improve, their health. To reach a state of complete physical, mental and social wellbeing, an individual or group must be able to identify and to realize aspirations, to satisfy needs and to change or cope with the environment. Health is seen as a resource for everyday life, not the objective of living. It is a positive concept emphasizing social and personal resources, as well as physical capacities. Therefore, health promotion is not just the responsibility of the health sector, but goes beyond healthy lifestyles to wellbeing. The fundamental conditions and resources for health are: peace, shelter, education, food, income, a stable ecosystem, sustainable resources, social justice and equity. The Ottawa Charter identified three basic strategies for health promotion: advocate, enable and mediate. It identified five priority action areas: build healthy public policy, create supportive environments, strengthen community actions, develop personal skills and reorient health services. The full text is available at: http://www.euro.who.int/AboutWHO/Policy/20010827_2.

11.5.2 The Jakarta Declaration

The Jakarta Declaration on Leading Health Promotion into the 21st Century comes from the Fourth International Conference on Health Promotion, held in 1997, a decade after the Ottawa Charter. The Declaration states that health promotion is a valuable investment and that health is a basic human right and essential for social and economic development. Poverty, above all, is the greatest threat to health. The Declaration also states there is clear evidence that: comprehensive approaches to health development are the most effective; particular settings (such as the workplace) offer practical opportunities for the implementation of comprehensive strategies; participation is essential to sustain efforts; and health learning fosters participation. Most important for health educators, the Declaration establishes five priorities for health promotion: (1) promote social responsibility for health; (2) increase investments for health development; (3) consolidate and expand partnerships for health; (4) increase community capacity and empower the individual; and (5) secure an infrastructure for health promotion. The full text of the Jakarta Declaration is available in 15 languages at: http://www.who.int/hpr/ncp/jakarta.conference.shtml.

12   CONCLUSIONS

In researching material for this publication, we had the goodwill of NGOs, employers and trade unions, and other groups and people concerned for workers' welfare. Many agreed that the topic of workers' nutrition was very important. Yet almost across the board, workplace nutrition was not a top concern for them. Many took nutrition for granted; others had more pressing issues to deal with. In the workplace, the main concerns seem to be safety, wages and job security. Nutrition programmes to combat chronic diseases, obesity or malnutrition around the world are largely aimed at elementary schools and the community at large, not the workplace.

Most large companies in the industrialized world have meal programmes as a matter of course. There's the company canteen. The attitude is that if workers don't like the food there, then they are free to bring a packed lunch or buy a meal elsewhere. Many countries and companies still subscribe to the post-war notion of "fattening up" the workforce; the objective is to provide an abundance of food, but not necessarily healthy food. Smaller companies might have a table or back room where workers can eat. Very little thought or investment is given to the subject. Workers are treated as adults, and they are expected to fend for themselves in securing a meal. And they are given, on average, around 30 minutes to do so. In developing countries, workplace meals are a luxury. Vast numbers of workers are employed in the informal sector, and many work straight through the day with few breaks and no meal. Some workers keep snacks in their pockets to tide them over until the evening meal at home. The trouble is that even their evening meal might not be all that nutritious.

Our argument is that good nutrition is the foundation of workplace productivity, safety, wages, job security – concerns shared by governments, employers, trade unions and workers. Iron deficiency, for example, affects up to half the world's population, predominantly in the developing world (Stoltzfus, 2001). Low iron levels are associated with weakness, sluggishness and lack of coordination. Ensuring that workers have enough iron (or calories, in general) will lead to greater productivity and reduce accidents. This in turn leads to higher profits for the company, leading to higher wages and better job security. Too many nations are deep in a cycle of poverty and malnutrition. Children lack the key nutrients to develop physically and mentally. Their capacity to work as adults is hindered. They remain poor, and their country remains poor, for a starved population results in starved productivity and stagnation. Reversing this cycle requires nutritious workplace meals or bulk distribution of fortified grains and foodstuffs, which enable workers to stay healthy, to work better, to feed their families, to raise healthy children and to ensure a future generation of healthy workers.

In industrialized countries, one of the highest business costs is health care. Sick days, long-term absences and the general drain on productivity due to circulatory disease or obesity, to name just a few problems, cut into a company's bottom line. Again, proper nutrition can help here. Studies have shown that obese workers are twice as likely as fit workers to miss work (Wolf and Colditz, 1998). Obesity also results in a loss of dexterity and compromises job safety. The incidence of chronic diseases and obesity can be significantly reduced through diet and exercise (WHO/FAO, 2002). The WHO and national health institutes are articulate and unambiguous on how to reduce these risks through diet: fewer sugars, fewer simple carbohydrates, fewer saturated fats, fewer calories, more complex carbohydrates, more unsaturated fats and more fruits and vegetables. A canteen with unhealthy meal options or, in general, poor access to healthy food during the working day fuels the epidemic of chronic disease.

Enterprises are hurting themselves in not offering better meal options. Governments around the world have initiated "five-a-day" fruit and vegetable campaigns. Yet so many workers are faced with nearly the exact opposite of these recommendations. The most common dishes in many canteens and local eating establishments are fried and fatty foods (burgers, sausages), simple carbohydrates (white bread, thin-cut fried potatoes) and essentially no vegetables aside from garnishes. Vending machines compound the issue with unhealthy snacks and drinks. What if the workplace were the locale for nutrition intervention, as some schools are? Aside from providing the very nutrients for productivity, meals at work shared with co-workers provide a sense of camaraderie, increase morale and reduce stress.

Decent meals with adequate rest are fundamental to a healthy workplace. Yet in producing this publication, we have found that workplace nutrition is largely a missed opportunity. Consider these basic facts: most adults work; most are "captive" at work for at least eight hours a day, five days a week; most need to eat during working hours; and most workers at any given enterprise share similar health concerns, such as iron deficiency, calorie deficiency or excessive weight gain. For health practitioners, workers are the ideal target population. The workplace is the locale for easy intervention. This is illustrated in the case study on K. Mohan and Co. in Bangalore (Chapter 6). Health experts identified malnutrition among garment workers at K. Mohan and worked with the company to provide daily, free midday meals with iron supplementation. For K. Mohan, this was a small investment that may yield large returns. K. Mohan is one of only a small percentage of companies in poorer regions of the world that has taken steps to provide a decent meal to employees. Elsewhere meals are meagre or altogether lacking.

Workers' nutrition need not be a costly investment. Governments and employers can implement a multitude of measures to improve workers' access to food and rest during working hours. Here is a summary of some of those presented in this publication.

12.1 Governments

Governments can provide the infrastructure and legal framework for workers' nutrition efforts to be implemented. They must first understand that nutrition is a wise national investment; and the workplace for adults, like the school canteen for children, is the logical place to offer safer and healthier meal options, coupled with health education. One example of government intervention is India's Factories Act of 1948, which requires, as a minimum, a canteen in companies of a particular size. In Brazil, the meal voucher law specifies protein and calorie content. Singapore offers grants to companies to promote workplace health. There is no government, however, that requires all employers to offer a healthy meal programme. Access to healthy food (and, conversely, protection from unsafe and unhealthy food and eating arrangements) is as essential as workplace protection from chemicals or noise. Government rules and financial incentives can provide this protection and level the playing field for companies. A few specific recommendations follow.

12.1.1 Tax incentives

Enterprises need financial incentives to offer decent meal plans to their employees. Governments can help here with tax breaks. Tax reductions are common for canteens. In many countries, canteen equipment and food is tax exempt. As we saw in Chapter 5, the voucher system also needs tax burden relief in order to flourish. The near elimination of tax incentives in the United Kingdom has crushed the government-regulated meal voucher system. Conversely, the voucher system is popular in Brazil, France and other countries where, because of tax relief, companies can subsidize half or all of the voucher ticket value. Vouchers have been shown to build a strong restaurant and food sector, ultimately increasing tax revenue. No government wants to subsidize poor nutrition; this is counterproductive to the goal of building a strong workforce. Governments can be selective in the types of canteens or meal programmes that receive tax credits, giving preferential treatment to healthy meal plans.

12.1.2 Health promotion

Many countries promote health, exercise and diet. Programmes are usually aimed at elementary schools, disadvantaged urban populations or the nation as a whole. Few health-promotion programmes in the area of nutrition target the workplace. The ubiquitous "five-a-day" fruit and vegetable programmes are a pertinent example. Only Denmark brings such a programme to the workplace with its *firmafrugt* (fruit at work) programme. The Danish Government found that the population understood that eating fruits and vegetables was healthy; this wasn't enough to change eating habits, though. The problem might seem obvious. Eat five a day... okay, but when? Breakfast for many workers in industrialized countries is rushed. Orange juice or a banana might offer the first serving. During the working day, many workers have no access to fruit and vegetables. So in the evening, to meet the government recommendations, one must have four or five servings. Most people, as to be expected, have one or two servings. Through the workplace, governments have the opportunity to make sure workers have the healthy foods that the WHO, FAO and all the health experts recommend.

Singapore and Canada deserve mention with their programmes to promote workplace health and nutrition. Many other countries concentrate solely on education or exercise. Singapore and Canada, and most recently the state of California in the United States, have designed programmes targeting the workplace canteen so that workers have access to the foods they know they're supposed to eat. Singapore also provides grants to promote workplace wellness.

12.1.3 Laws on break times

Few countries regulate times of meal breaks, in the way that the eight-hour working day is a standard. By mandating a minimum meal break time, governments can send a positive message to employers and workers that midday meals and rest are productive. Laws put all businesses on an equal footing, so managers and employees will feel less pressure to skip lunch or to eat a quick lunch at a workstation to remain competitive.

12.1.4 Laws on meal provision

Employers must be encouraged, if not required, to provide some food solution, which is a workers' right as basic as rest, water or occupational safety. Clearly company finances, size and location must be taken into account. When a canteen or voucher plan is not economically feasible, employers must consider rudimentary mess rooms, cupboards or refrigeration to store packed lunches, or storage or water facilities for street vendors. That is, employers should not have the freedom to offer no meal arrangement.

12.1.5 Street foods

In many countries in Asia, Africa and Latin America, street foods are a predominant source of nutrition for workers. Governments must take a leading role in ensuring the safety of street foods. The two factors that determine the level of food safety are infrastructure and vendors' knowledge of hygiene and food handling. The two factors cannot be divorced. Vendors need access to clean water, lavatories and washrooms; and they must be educated about proper food handling. Understanding that one must wash one's hands means little if there is no means to wash them.

A first step for governments in this regard is to provide some form of legal recognition of street foods. This may be resented by restaurant and shop owners because they compete with street food vendors. Vendors have few overheads, and so the food tends to be cheaper. However, vendors exist in great numbers because they are filling a niche, an underserved population of low-wage workers who cannot afford to eat at restaurants and who have no access to a company canteen. With legal recognition established, vendors will be more willing to make investments in street vending – that is, investments in better equipment and education. Understanding the number and location of vendors (by virtue of licensing them) enables a government to move forward with education and other improvements.

The next step is to provide structure to the chaotic world of vending. This is done primarily through zoning. Restricting vendors from certain street corners or overpasses will ease car- and foot-traffic concerns. Concessions must be made, however, to ensure vendors can set up their stalls at locations where people congregate. These decisions should be reached through dialogue with organizations of street vendors and others affected. Once legal vending locations are established, governments can move forward with infrastructure improvements. Street food vendors need access to public lavatories with soap and water. Vendors also need a clean water supply to cook and wash. To reduce the number of rodents and insects, governments must also provide regular rubbish collection. The expense of these infrastructure improvements for cash-strapped municipalities can be daunting. However, governments need not take on the full economic burden. Educational materials on hygiene and food handling are available from the WHO, the FAO and other health organizations. Local businesses whose workers patronize the street food vendors have a vested interest in making street foods safe. These businesses can provide materials to the vendors, such as food containers and aprons with the sponsoring company's logo. The goal is to make street food vending safety self-sustaining. Low-interest or zero-interest loans for vendors can enable them to buy better equipment, such as carts with a three-tier basin for washing dishes and with stainless steel surfaces to reduce bacterial growth.

12.2 Employers

Employers must come to an understanding that proper nutrition equates to higher productivity. Nutrition is a wise company investment. In industrialized nations, employers must understand that merely providing a meal programme or access to food can be counterproductive if that food is not healthy. In developing nations, employers must understand that good nutrition will make for a stronger, better-equipped workforce that, in the long run, will make their company and country more competitive and more attractive to investors.

12.2.1 Access to meals and rest

Access to proper food and rest is a major concern. The length of the meal break is important; it must fit the employer's chosen food solution(s). For example, if the company has no canteen or dining area, the employee will need to venture outside the company for a meal; and 30 minutes is not enough time to travel to a neighbouring shop, order food, eat, pay and return. Thirty minutes might be adequate if there is a local canteen where workers can purchase a meal and find a seat swiftly. Time is relative. Once the proper time is allocated, employers must provide healthy food options at a reasonable price. Through canteens and mess rooms, employers can control the cost and quality of food. Workers in poorer nations might have micronutrient deficiencies. These can be remedied through well-considered food provision. Workers in wealthier nations might be at risk of excessive weight gain or chronic disease. These concerns can also be addressed through food provision. Stocking the canteen or mess room with foods that don't meet workers' dietary requirements will ultimately lead to a weakened workforce. Thus, access is relative too.

If a company does not have a formal meal plan, then it must provide workers with a means of buying a nutritious meal or storing a home-made meal safely. In Chapter 7 we saw how construction companies fall short of this goal. There are no canteens on construction sites; there is often no place to safely store food brought from home; and often the only access to food is street vendors of questionable integrity or knowledge of food safety. When budgets or space limitations do not allow for the creation of a canteen or mess room, businesses might consider kitchenettes with refrigerators or cupboards to store food. Accompanying such kitchenettes should be a clean and pleasant place to eat away from workstations and protected from the weather: something as simple as a table and chairs.

12.2.2 Local vendors

If workers have no food choice other than local restaurant or street foods, then employers must work with local business and vendors to ensure high-quality and safe meals that can be eaten each day with no short-term or long-term ill-health consequences. Employers can work with restaurants in suggesting low-cost daily specials or adding healthy items to the menu. An employer's bargaining chip with the restaurant owner is the promise of a steady flow of customers or the incentive of financial assistance. Many workers around the world cannot afford to eat at a restaurant every day. Employers can compensate by issuing meal vouchers. Or, if workers visit street food vendors, employers can make small infrastructure investments (potable water, soap, storage) to ensure the quality of this food.

Employers can invite local vendors into the company grounds. This will cost the employer nothing or next to nothing. Vendors will have the benefit of a steady customer base and, it is hoped, use of a washroom. Employers can even help the vendors with proper food transport and storage, further minimizing the risk of food-borne diseases. Companies in industrial areas can pool their resources with other employers to create a central area of street food vending. Employees benefit from the convenience; vendors benefit from customers, leading to more profit and more investment in safety; and employers benefit from a better-nourished workforce able to eat and rest comfortably in 30 minutes or so.

12.2.3 Health education

Employers who want their employees to stay healthy must educate them about proper diet and hygiene. In several case studies presented in Chapter 4, we saw how education was key in motivating employees to eat the healthy foods offered to them at the canteen. Conversely, we also saw how a lack of education led to employees rejecting healthy canteen changes to the extent that the contracted caterer wouldn't offer healthier selections because they didn't sell. Health education includes seminars, cooking demonstrations, newsletters and informative posters and placards near and around the canteen or mess room.

12.2.4 Monetary incentives

When education fails, money can help. In the case study on Singapore's Glaxo Wellcome Manufacturing, we saw how workers loaded up at the salad bar because, with a subsidy, salads were essentially free. In the Dole case study, we saw how the heavy subsidy on only healthy foods made eating unhealthy foods an unpopular option. At Husky, sugar-free and herbal teas were free. Employers operating canteens or mess rooms usually subsidize meals, but employers can be selective and offer greater discounts on the healthiest menu options. In developing countries, meals or meal tokens are better than cash, because cash can be lost, stolen, gambled or used for tobacco or alcohol.

12.2.5 Families

In some cultures, the male wage earner eats first, leaving less food for the children and mother. Feeding the worker will leave more food for the family. And healthy children grow up to be healthy and more productive workers. Employers can help combat hunger at home through the distribution of fortified grains or rice, or other staples. The employer can save money by buying such supplies in bulk, often with established business connections and shipping and storage capability. Employers can also help workers' families through the creation of low-cost food shops. These shops should not be created to return a profit but rather just cover overhead costs to guarantee the lowest prices for the customers.

12.2.6 Water

Access to a regular supply of safe water is a basic human right, recognized by the United Nations. There are no specific guidelines for water at the workplace, other than the fact that employers in many countries must provide some form of potable water. Because of the relative safety of modern water supplies in the industrialized world, providing bottled or filtered water at the workplace is usually a benefit and is not required by law. Some companies in developing nations, however, are installing sophisticated filtering systems to address serious concerns about the local water supply.

12.3 Workers and trade unions

Workers must remain diligent in protecting their right to safe food, water and rest at work. Similarly, they must come to understand the value of a proper meal and rest during working hours to reduce stress, stay sharp on the job and to remain healthy.

12.3.1 Trade unions

Local, national and international trade unions and workers' organizations can secure break lengths and meal programmes in collective bargaining agreements. In Mexico, the food was so bad at one garment factory that workers went on strike over this and other concerns. The food solution did not cost the company much money; essentially the employer invited five local vendors to sell meals in the company mess room, and the company covered most of the cost of the meals. In Austria, the union-initiated "fair eating" movement takes eating healthily to the next level: where the canteen food is produced through fair and sustainable business practices around the world, with a preference given to local products.

Global trade unions can get involved in social and environmental issues, such as the need for fortified foods, clean water and proper sanitation. These unions can attempt to establish standards for industries particularly plagued by poor access to proper meals, such as construction and food harvesting.

12.3.2 Workers' committees

Workers can petition employers for improvements in a non-threatening way by volunteering to lead the search for solutions. Workers at Singapore's Glaxo Wellcome Manufacturing, frustrated with a bland canteen and no local shops for meals, petitioned the company for funds to make changes. The company gladly obliged, and the workers created a new canteen to their liking. Elsewhere in Singapore, workers brought in their own appliances but used company space and electricity to cook healthy meals during the working day.

12.4 Concluding comments

The twentieth century saw remarkable progress in workers' rights and, subsequently, business productivity. The battle is far from over, particularly in developing and emerging economies; but in much of the industrialized world, the workplace has become safer. Dangers once omnipresent are slowly fading from the workplace landscape. Many company owners have resisted changes, citing concerns over the expense of safety regulations. Yet as workers and their unions petition for safer workplaces, and as national and international laws equal the playing field and force all to play by the same rules, safety improvements will translate into economic gains.

Occupational safety and health have been a key area of concern for the ILO since its inception in 1919. So too has been this notion of level playing-fields. "The failure of any nation to adopt humane conditions of labour is an obstacle in the way of other nations which desire to improve the conditions in their own countries", states the Preamble to the ILO Constitution. In the global economy, it becomes increasingly important that workers everywhere are treated fairly so that businesses are not encouraged to set up shop where laws are lax and labour (and life) come cheap. Safety regulations are one element of international workplace equality. Workers' nutrition is another element that has progressed along with improvements in safety and health. The notion of workers eating gruel from a tin cup seems antiquated in many countries, but unfortunately not all.

This publication has:

- defined key elements of proper nutrition;

- demonstrated the link between poor nutrition and poor national output;

- demonstrated the link between good nutrition and high productivity;

- described how unhealthy foods can lead to obesity and chronic diseases (largely affecting industrialized countries, but a growing concern in emerging economies);

- described macro- and micronutrient deficiencies (largely affecting developing nations but not absent from the industrialized world);

- listed relevant laws, regulations and guides; and

- provided examples of a variety of food solutions, some expensive and others available at no cost to enterprises.

In the low-cost regime, we saw how farmers' markets can provide workers with fruit and vegetables; how small investments in infrastructure can make street foods safer for workers; and how a basic meal in many developing countries will cost the employer only a few cents per employee per day, or around US$50 annually. In the Russian Federation we learned how meal subsidies, once standard during the Soviet era, vanished with the emergence of free markets but are slowly returning as businesses become more profitable. In the high-cost regime, we saw impressive canteens with subsidized healthy foods.

The solutions presented in this publication have, in turn:

- boosted employee morale and productivity;

- reduced the number of accidents and sick days;

- saved on long-term costs of health care;

- promoted the good name of the employer; and/or

- increased national GDP or tax revenue.

If, as a business owner, you had one bundle of money to spend, what would be the relative gain or merit of spending it on health care, meal solutions, education, retirement funds, vacation plans or another social benefit?

We could find no direct answer to this question – no scientific review or cost-benefit analysis looking at the actual and perceived value of such benefits. But we can leave the reader with this one thought: without a foundation of good workplace nutrition, many other hard-fought benefits become meaningless. A good medical plan will be pushed to the limit if workers are sick from poor nutrition. Retirement benefits are not useful if the worker dies of a stroke or heart attack by the retirement age. Job security is impossible to guarantee when sick workers and malnourished children crush national productivity and investment. Governments, employers, workers and their organizations together must capitalize on the opportunity to use the workplace as a platform to promote nutrition in order to reap the rewards that this so clearly yields: health, safety, productivity, economic growth and a civil society. We look forward to the day when having access to a decent meal during working hours with adequate rest is the obvious choice to reach our common goals.

MACRONUTRIENTS. PROTEINS, FATS AND CARBOHYDRATES

Macronutrients are broadly defined as those food components present in the diet in quantities of one gram or more. They include proteins, carbohydrates, fats and oils, most dietary fibre and also alcohol and water (WHO, 1998, p. 55). Macronutrients are sometimes referred to as energy-giving foods.

Proteins

Proteins are needed for the growth and maintenance of muscle, bone, skin and organs, and for the synthesis of key enzymes, hormones and antibodies. Proteins are made from combinations of 20 amino acids, which are chemical chains comprising the elements carbon, hydrogen, oxygen and nitrogen. Of these 20, eight are considered "essential" and must be present in the diet because they cannot be synthesized by the body from precursors. These essential amino acids are isoleucine, leucine, lysine, methionine, phenylalanine, threonine, tryptophan and valine. Histidine is sometimes characterized as essential or semi-essential, because adults generally produce adequate amounts but children do not. Similarly, arginine is considered essential during times of stress when the body cannot produce enough of this amino acid. Aside from serving the role of being a protein building block, amino acids individually may help also with specific body functions. For example, lysine may help the body absorb and conserve calcium; arginine supplies nitric oxide, which the body uses to dilate the arteries during exercise to increase blood flow.

Proteins from animal sources are mostly "complete" or "high-quality" proteins, meaning they contain all of the essential amino acids. Vegetable proteins lack one or more essential amino acids and are referred to as "incomplete" or "low-quality" proteins. A vegetarian diet can supply all the essential amino acids provided one combines complementary vegetable proteins, such as those from rice and beans, for example. Lysine and tryptophan, however, are hard to obtain in a vegetarian diet and special care (i.e. supplementation) may be needed to ensure proper nutrition. Soya beans and soya products, such as tofu, contain all the essential amino acids but some amino acids are in low abundance, and therefore soya is not considered a high-quality protein.

No upper limit of protein intake has been set, but data suggest that excessive protein consumption can adversely affect the kidneys. Such symptoms are frequently seen in those individuals on so-called all-protein (low-carbohydrate) diets. Health experts in many countries recommend a daily intake for adults of 0.8 grams of protein per kilogram of body weight (WHO, 1998, p. 59). Diets largely composed of cereals and legumes with some animal products (meat, eggs or milk) are sufficient enough to supply this amount. Diets chiefly composed of low-quality proteins, however, need to provide 0.9 grams of protein per kilogram of body weight for proper nutrition. The risk of protein energy malnutrition is high in regions where diarrhoea is prevalent. Once diarrhoea is treated, workers should be given extra energy, proteins and also vitamins and minerals to regain weight and nutrients lost during the diarrhoea episode. Here, health experts recommend increasing the protein intake by 10 per cent. Protein needs during convalescence increase by 20–40 per cent (WHO, 1998, p. 59). Although bodybuilders claim the need for protein supplementation to increase body muscle mass, healthy workers in heavy industry (e.g., mining or forestry) do not require additional protein.

A deficiency in just one essential amino acid will result in a decrease in protein synthesis and may lead to mental retardation or stunted growth among children or a loss of muscle mass among adults. Severe protein deficiency takes on two forms: kwashiorkor, characterized by oedema (fluid build-up in tissues) due to poor protein quality; and marasmus, a wasting syndrome due to inadequate protein and total energy intake. Protein deficiencies are rare in developed countries but still of great concern in developing countries. Excessive nitrogen in the urine is often a sign of protein deficiency, a result of the catabolism of lean body mass and visceral proteins in order to provide the essential amino acids lacking in the diet.

The WHO suggests that 8–15 per cent of total energy consumption should come from protein, with the range depending on whether one is eating high- or low-quality protein or in convalescence (WHO, 1998, p. 59). Of this, 10–25 per cent of dietary protein should be of animal origin. Virtually all unprocessed foods contain protein, even foods thought of as carbohydrates, such as rice and wheat. Animal products are considered to provide the highest quality, highest "biological value" protein. These products naturally include: beef, pork, lamb, game, fowl, fish, some insects, dairy products and eggs.

Legumes – particularly soya beans and other beans, chickpeas, split peas and lentils – are considered very good sources of vegetable protein, as are nuts and some seeds. Potatoes are high in protein quality but low in quantity; cereals and leafy vegetables are low in protein quality but complement legumes. Whey protein (commercially available in powder form) is a high-quality, relatively inexpensive protein source with a long shelf life suitable for warm climates and remote work locations where meat products may be hard to secure or store. Whey is the watery part of milk that separates from curds in the process of cheese making.

Fats

Fats and oils, although often maligned, are vital for proper nutrition. Colloquially, fats are solid at room temperature while oils are liquid, but in this discussion, the word "fat" will apply to both fats and oils.

Fats provide essential fatty acids, which are not made by the body and must be obtained from food. These fatty acids are the raw materials that help regulate blood pressure, blood clotting, inflammation, and other body functions. Fat is also necessary for healthy skin and hair and for the transport of the fat-soluble vitamins A, D, E and K. Fats serve as energy reserves, stored in the adipose tissue (fat cells) that helps cushion and insulate the body. The body first burns carbohydrates during physical exertion. After about 20 minutes of intense exertion, the body depends on fat for calories.

Fats belong to a class of chemicals called lipids. Dietary fats consist of a chain of carbon atoms (numbering 12 to 20) with hydrogen and oxygen attachments at various positions and degrees of saturation along the chain. The metabolic rate of a fat depends on the number and arrangement of these atoms. A saturated fat has a maximum number of hydrogen atoms along its carbon chain. This type of fat is more readily stored in adipose tissue as a long-term fuel reserve because it provides a higher energy yield compared with an unsaturated fat. A monounsaturated fat (with one double bond on the carbon chain and thus fewer hydrogen atoms) is preferentially used for energy more quickly than saturated fat.

Dietary fats are broadly classified as saturated (solid at room temperature) and unsaturated (liquid at room temperature). Unsaturated fats include mono-unsaturated fats and polyunsaturated fats (containing two or more double bonds). Hydrogenated oils and trans fatty acids are unsaturated fats that absorb hydrogen during cooking or processing, which increases their level of saturation.

Whether from plant or animal sources, fats contain more than twice the number of calories as equal measures of carbohydrates or proteins. On average, fats contain 9 kcal per gram. Experts recommend that adults derive at least 15 per cent of their energy from fats and oils and that women of child-bearing age consume at least 20 per cent (WHO, 1998, p. 59). Certain fats are healthier than others, however, and the key to proper nutrition is the proper balance of unsaturated fatty acids. Active, non-obese adults may derive up to 35 per cent of their energy from fat, and sedentary adults may consume up to 30 per cent as long as no more than 10 per cent of the energy intake is from saturated fats. In general, the need for fat increases during times of protein malnutrition and decreases in the presence of dietary disease, such as coronary disease and obesity. A minimum requirement for dietary (unsaturated) fat is 10 per cent of the energy intake (WHO, 1998, p. 60).

Saturated fats are largely considered unhealthy and their consumption should be kept to a minimum. These fats are the primary dietary cause of high blood levels of low-density lipoprotein, or LDL, the so-called "bad cholesterol" (as opposed to "good cholesterol", HDL, high-density lipoprotein). Cholesterol is another type of lipid. The higher the level of LDL in the body, the greater the risk of a heart attack. Although the precise reason remains unclear, many scientists say the following scenario is at play. Cholesterol, itself an important substance for good health, will build up in the walls of the arteries when present in excessive amounts in the blood. Cholesterol may cause the arteries to harden, making them less flexible and more vulnerable to plaque build-up and narrowing, which hinders blood flow. An optimal LDL blood level is below 100 mg/dL, while a high and potentially harmful level is above 160 mg/dL (NHLBI, 2001). Saturated fats with lauric, myristic, palmatic acids, particularly, raise blood LDL levels.

Saturated fats are often but not exclusively associated with high-cholesterol foods. Sources of saturated fat include most animal products, particularly butter, cheese, whole milk, ice cream, organ meats, fatty cuts of beef and pork and some shellfish. Coconut, palm and palm-kernel oils are also high in saturated fats. Health experts recommend avoiding or sharply limiting food products with more than 20 per cent saturated fat. The dietary requirement of fatty acids can be met entirely through the consumption of unsaturated fats. However, saturated fats in small amounts can be healthy if the sources (e.g., meat or cheese) provide other beneficial nutrients. Red palm oil, specifically, is an excellent source of vitamins A and E (in the form of carotenoids and tocopherols) and serves as a nutritious, low-priced oil for populations chronically deficient in these vitamins.

Unsaturated fats help regulate a healthy LDL/HDL ratio. Poly-unsaturated fats lower LDL levels while monounsaturated fats increase HDL levels. Polyunsaturated fats, depending on their level of saturation, contain the essential fatty acids omega-3 and omega-6. (The number depends on the location of certain chemical bonds along the carbon chain.) Linoleic acid is a key form of omega-6, and linolenic acid is a key form of omega-3; and both form yet other important fatty acids. There is great debate over the importance and proper ratio of these fatty acids in the diet. Omega-3, also written as n-3 or ω–3, is associated with lower cardiovascular mortality (Cernea, Hancu and Raz, 2003). A primary source for omega-3 is marine food. Vegetable oils in general are rich in omega-6. The recommended ratio of linoleic ω–6 acid to linolenic ω–3 acid ranges from 10:1 to 5:1, with the narrowing ratio indicative of growing knowledge about how ω–3 and the fatty acids it creates, EPA and DHA, may improve cardiovascular health (WHO, 1998, p. 60). Western diets often have an undesirable ratio of 40:1.

Sources of omega-6 polyunsaturated fats include the oils of sunflower, safflower, corn and soya bean. Sources of omega-3 include flaxseed and flaxseed oil, walnuts and walnut oil, oily fish such as salmon, mackerel, herring, sild, pilchard, sardine and anchovy, cod liver oil, and whale and seal blubber. The ratio of ω–6 to ω–3 in corn, soya bean, canola (rapeseed) and flax oils is 45:1, 10:1, 3:1 and 0.3:1 respectively. Monounsaturated food sources include nuts and nut oils (such as peanut oil), olives and olive oil, avocados, canola oil and, to some extent, meat and butter.

Although considered healthy, unsaturated fats do have their limit. Like saturated fats, they are high-caloric, energy-dense foods. High intake of any kind of fat can contribute to an increased risk of obesity, cardiovascular disease, cancer, diabetes, arthritis and gall bladder disease (A.D.A.M., 2004). Also, high intake of ω–6 polyunsaturated fats has been found to promote certain types of cancer, suggesting that tumours require polyunsaturated fats for growth (Micozzi, 1992).

Broadly speaking, consumption of fats that are solid at room temperature (e.g., lard, butter and vegetable shortening) are more likely to result in excessive weight gain and coronary heart disease compared with the consumption of liquid fats. Exceptions to this rule include, on one side, "solid" and "healthy" marine animal fat and, on the other side, liquid palm and coconut oils. Of recent concern is the ubiquity of so-called "trans" fats and hydrogenated oils in processed foods. Trans fats are trans fatty acids that form when vegetable oil hardens, a process called hydrogenation. According to food manufacturers, consumers often find foods with trans fats to be tastier than products with no fat or healthier fats. Trans fats can also prolong the shelf life of food products. Trans fatty acids are commonly found in fried foods, most margarines, processed foods and commercial baked goods such as crackers, biscuits and doughnuts.

Trans fats have been shown to not only raise blood levels of LDL, the bad cholesterol, but also lower levels of HDL, the good cholesterol (Mensink et al., 2003). Thus, reducing – if not eliminating – trans fatty acids from the diet lowers the risk of coronary heart disease (Expert Panel, 1995). Labels on food products in many countries delineate the amount of saturated, monounsaturated and polyunsaturated fats contained within the food. Trans fatty acids, long disguised as unsaturated fats, may soon appear as a separate listing on labels. The United States will include trans fat information on food labels from 2006.

Regarding obesity, fats can quickly add up in the daily calorie count. Fifty-five grams of fat contribute about 500 kcal (55 grams x 9 kcal/gram), which would be 20 per cent of a 2500-kcal diet. A 125-gram hamburger patty contains about 22 grams of fat, most of which is saturated fat. Reduction of fat in the diet by 10 per cent translates to a reduction of about 3 kilograms in body weight over two months (Mokdad et al., 2001).

Carbohydrates

Carbohydrates are the main source of energy in most diets. In fact, the primary function of carbohydrates is to provide energy for the body, especially the brain and the nervous system. This varied macronutrient takes the form of sugars, oligosaccharides, starches and fibre, all related by their simple molecular structure of carbon tied to water molecules. The body breaks down carbohydrates into glucose – like a pellet of fuel which cells use to perform their many functions.

There appears to be no absolute daily carbohydrate requirement, for the human body can derive energy from fat and protein if necessary. The WHO recommends that at least 10 per cent of energy intake should come from carbohydrates (about 50 grams) to prevent severe ketosis, a condition in which the blood becomes abnormally acidic from ketones, the by-product of burning fat for fuel instead of glucose. A diet consisting primarily of carbo-hydrates, on the other hand, may cheat the body of valuable nutrients found in proteins and fats. Health experts recommend that between 50 and 70 per cent of one's energy intake be derived from carbohydrates (WHO, 1998). As with fats, however, a proper balance of certain types of carbohydrates can prevent chronic diseases such as obesity, cancer and cardiovascular disease.

Sugars are simple carbohydrates, those most easily digested and quickly converted to glucose for fuel. Common sugars are sucrose, also called saccharose, primarily derived from sugar cane and sugar beets; fructose, from fruits and honey; and lactose, from milk. Fructose is a monosaccharide; and sucrose and other sugars are disaccharides, containing two sugar "units". Sucrose, for example, is a combination of fructose and glucose. The consumption of simple sugars throughout the day – particularly sucrose and high-fructose corn syrup, as found in soft drinks – adds calories to the diet but few nutrients. Sugar also increases the risk of tooth decay in the absence of routine oral hygiene practices (Konig and Navia, 1995). Moderate intake of sugars, however, can make food more palatable. And the slight relationship between sugar consumption and obesity is offset by an inverse relationship between sugar and fat intake (Gibney et al., 1995). Also, hyperactivity in children appears to be not associated with sugar intake, as commonly believed (A.D.A.M., 2004). Thus there are no specific recommendations yet for limiting natural sugars.

Oligosaccharides are complex carbohydrates comprising three to ten sugars. Common oligosaccharides such as raffinose and stachyose are found in legumes. Starches and fibres are polysaccharides – large chains of often hundreds of monosaccharides molecules. These too are complex carbohydrates. Common starches are amylose, found in rice and wheat, and amylopectin, found in potatoes, corn and tapioca. Dietary fibres such as cellulose are polysaccharides in which the monosaccharides cannot be broken apart by digestive enzymes. However, in the large bowel, intestinal bacteria ferment fibre to produce important fatty acids (some of which may prevent certain cancers, such as colon cancer), measurable amounts of energy, and methane gas.

Complex carbohydrates take longer to digest and are preferred over simple carbohydrates for weight maintenance and the control of diabetes, an emerging pandemic. The reason is complex, but a simplified scenario follows. The presence of glucose in the bloodstream released in digestion triggers the pancreas to produce insulin. Insulin, like a key to a gate, enables the "pellets" of glucose fuel to enter into cells. The hallmark of Type 2 diabetes is insulin resistance, when muscle and other cells no longer allow insulin molecules to attach and enable the transfer of glucose. With nowhere to go, glucose builds up in the bloodstream, leading to hyperglycaemia, or high blood glucose. To compensate, the pancreas produces more insulin. The cells sense this flood of insulin and become even more resistant, resulting in a vicious cycle. Some scientists believe that the ubiquity of simple carbohydrates in the diet – from sugary food, soft drinks and processed foods, which break apart complex carbohydrates into their simpler components – strains the pancreas and leads to insulin resistance (A.D.A.M., 2004).

Because complex carbohydrates take longer to digest, their component glucose molecules are released more slowly into the bloodstream, compared with the rush of glucose from simple carbohydrates. The pancreas in turn generates insulin at a slower rate, and cells can readily absorb the glucose fuel before it builds up in the bloodstream. Exercise, too, appears to prompt cells to absorb glucose. The glycaemic index, often a scale of 1 to 100, is a measure of how quickly a carbohydrate will raise blood glucose levels. Simple sugars have a high glycaemic index, as do potatoes and white bread. Baking raises the glycaemic index of breads, particularly white and "non-whole wheat" breads. Brown rice, wholegrain breads, pastas, pulses and legumes have a lower glycaemic index and should be consumed as the main source of carbohydrates.

Slower digestion also provides a feeling of fullness, curbing hunger in between meals. This limits the need for snacking, a major cause of weight gain. Dietary fibre contributes to a feeling of fullness, provides calories that will not be stored as body fat, aids in food elimination from the body, and thus is seen as beneficial in preventing obesity (Duncan, Bacon and Weinsier, 1983). Most recommendations for adults specify an intake of at least 20 grams of fibre daily, which translates to about 10 grams per 1,000 kcal, although twice this amount can be easily tolerated (WHO, 1998, p. 64). Dietary fibre is either water-soluble or -insoluble. Water-insoluble fibre, such as cellulose, is predominantly found in fruits and vegetables, often in the skin and stems. Water-soluble fibre, such as pectin and gum, is found in oats, barley, legumes and the flesh of fruit. Water-soluble fibre in particular seems to reduce the risk of colon cancer (Le Marchand et al., 1997). One drawback is that fibre interferes with the absorption of nutrients, particularly minerals. Thus, requirements for protein and minerals need to be adjusted accordingly in the presence of a high-fibre diet.

Despite the growing popularity of so-called "low-carb" and high-protein diets to promote weight loss in developed countries, particularly the United States, most societies have eaten a diet based on carbohydrates for the past several millennia with no apparent side effect of obesity. Unlike many animals, humans do not effectively convert carbohydrates into fat and store this for energy during times of famine. Up to 97 per cent of "extra" ingested fat may be stored as body fat, whereas only around 70 per cent of "extra" ingested carbohydrates are available, for the very process of fat conversion burns carbohydrates. Thus, calorie for calorie, fats (particularly saturated fats) have a greater tendency to lead to weight gain than carbohydrates (particularly complex carbohydrates) do. Also, alcohol, by inhibiting lipid oxidation, indirectly favours the storage of dietary fats (Jequier, 2002).

In summary, with regard to macronutrients and the prevention of chronic diseases, experts recommend that healthy adults choose a diet with a calorific intake of roughly 50–70 per cent carbohydrates (predominantly complex carbohydrates), 15–30 per cent fat (predominantly unsaturated fats) and 8–15 per cent protein (with some animal protein). Saturated fats increase the risk of some cancers, cardiovascular disease and obesity and obesity-related diseases, while a proper balance of unsaturated fats reduces these risks. Excessive amounts of simple carbohydrates increase the risk of weight gain and may be associated with diabetes, while complex carbohydrates and fibre reduce these risks and may prevent certain cancers.

MICRONUTRIENTS. VITAMINS, MINERALS AND OTHER NUTRIENTS

Micronutrients are vitamins and minerals that are essential, often in minute quantities, for proper growth and metabolism. The discovery and subsequent in-depth study of their role and importance in the diet is considered one of the greatest public health achievements of the twentieth century. Micronutrient deficiencies are cited as causing or exacerbating a host of mental and physical diseases, including infectious diseases. A diversified diet will help prevent micronutrient malnutrition. Food fortification and supplementation are also useful approaches.

Despite steady gains through the twentieth century in the field of nutrition, more than 1 billion people are ill or disabled as a result of a micronutrient deficiency, and over 2 billion more people are at risk (WHO, 1998, p. 66). That's half the world's population. As with diseases associated with macronutrients – e.g., cardiovascular disease, diabetes, cancer or obesity – micronutrient-related diseases cut across class, age and gender in both developing and industrialized countries. Examples of illnesses and conditions brought about by a micronutrient deficiency include mental retardation, depression, dementia, low work capacity, chronic fatigue, blindness and loss of bone and muscle strength.

These conditions, many of which are reversible, directly affect the near-term health of employees and the quality of work they perform. Thus, an adequate supply of micronutrients for the workforce is paramount. Of pressing concern is iron deficiency anaemia, which is estimated to affect over 2 billion people (Stoltzfus, 2001). Anaemia as well as more mild levels of iron deficiency decreases physical work capacity and work productivity in repetitive tasks, yet it can be inexpensively remedied. This and other micronutrient deficiencies are explained in further detail below.

Vitamins

Vitamins are organic chemicals found in plants and animals that are essential for human growth and health maintenance. There are more than a dozen known vitamins, and the most important are detailed here. A varied diet can supply these vitamins naturally, but supplementation is recommended for those individuals lacking vitamins as a result of famine, war, harsh climate or poor eating habits.

Vitamin A, or retinol, is best known for its role in vision. Night blindness and xerophthalmia, a drying up of the mucous membranes of the eyes, are early signs of a vitamin A deficiency. Vitamin A also plays an important role in the control of gene expression and in the creation of epithelial cells, such as skin, lung and intestinal tissue. This fat-soluble vitamin is stored in the liver. Deficiencies are of particular concern in children, who have not developed adequate vitamin A stores. Worldwide, 100 to 140 million children are vitamin A deficient; 250,000 to 500,000 become blind every year; and half of these children die within 12 months of losing their sight (WHO, 2003e). While adults need less vitamin A than children, a case can be made that, in certain scenarios, feeding an employee at work may leave more food at home for a child.

Vitamin A is found in meat, egg yolk, liver and fish liver oils, and is often added to dairy products. Beta-carotene is a provitamin that the human body converts to vitamin A; and this is found in red, orange and yellow fruits and vegetables and in dark, leafy green vegetables. Colour intensity is not an indication of β–carotene content, although carrots do have high levels of this provitamin. Approximately 6 µg β–carotene is nutritionally equivalent to 1 µg retinol. The recommended dietary intake is 2,100–3,000 µg β–carotene or 350–500 µg retinol per 1,000 kcal (WHO, 1998, p. 70). Low-fat and vegetarian diets reduce vitamin A bioavailability by limiting absorption, so additional vitamin A may be needed. Conversely, dietary fat, protein and vitamin E enhance β–carotene utilization. Some studies suggest that vitamin A is associated with a reduced risk of cardiovascular disease and cancers of the colon, lung and stomach (Halliwell, 2000), although β–carotene supplements have led to increased lung cancer risk among smokers (Alpha-Tocopherol, 1994).

Vitamin B_1, or thiamine, is necessary for the health of the heart and nervous system. This is a water-soluble vitamin that passes through the body quickly. The half-life is 15 days, which means the body needs a constant supply. Thiamine is found in pork, legumes, yeast and wholegrain products. White breads, white flour and pastas are often fortified with thiamine along with two other water-soluble vitamins, riboflavin and niacin (B_2 and B_3). The minimum recommend daily allowance is 0.5 mg per 1,000 kcal. Pregnant and lactating women require 0.6–0.7 mg per 1,000 kcal. Thiamin deficiency, now uncommon outside of severe famine, is sometimes seen among alcoholics. A deficiency can lead to wet beriberi, a cardiovascular disorder, and dry beriberi, or neuropathy, a nervous system disorder. Symptoms include weakness and confusion.

Vitamin B_2, or riboflavin, is necessary for a variety of metabolic processes and is utilized in energy production via the respiratory chain. Riboflavin is present in most edible plants and animals. Particularly good sources include eggs, liver, broccoli, whole grains and fortified grains. The minimum recommended daily allowance is 0.6 mg per 1,000 kcal; lactating and pregnant women require slightly more. Deficiency in this water-soluble vitamin can lead to ariboflavinosis, characterized by weakness, sore throat and swelling of blood and other fluids in the throat region (pharyngeal and oral mucous membranes).

Vitamin B_3, or niacin, provides the building blocks for enzymes used for intercellular respiration and energy production. Like riboflavin, niacin is a water-soluble vitamin present is most edible plants and animals. Particularly good sources include seeds, leafy green vegetables, fish, liver, whole wheat and legumes. The minimum recommend daily allowance is 6 mg per 1,000 kcal; lactating and pregnant women require slightly more. The classic niacin deficiency disease is pellagra, characterized by skin inflammation, dementia and diarrhoea. Rare in industrialized nations, pellagra is seen among populations with diets predominantly comprising corn or sorghum, as in parts of Africa, China and India.

Vitamin B_6 refers to a family of three chemicals, pyridoxine, pyridoxal and pyridoxamine. These are largely used in the body by the muscles to help release glucose from glycogen. These versatile chemicals are used also in over 100 different enzyme reactions. Vitamin B_6 may play a role in immune system responsiveness and glucose homeostasis. Food sources include bananas, whole grains, eggs, poultry, fish and pork. The recommended daily requirement is 0.6 to 1.0 mg per 1,000 kcal. Because of its role in amino acid metabolism, vitamin B_6 requirements increase for high-protein diets. Food processing greatly diminishes vitamin B_6 availability, and many therapeutic drugs can interfere with its uptake. A severe vitamin B_6 deficiency may cause seizures, anaemia and inflammation of the skin and tongue.

Vitamin B_9, or folate (folic acid), is necessary for nucleotide and amino acid metabolism. Along with the other water-soluble B vitamins, folate is now added to breads and cereals in many countries. The human body absorbs folic acid in fortified foods more efficiently than naturally-occurring folate. Particularly good natural sources include dark green vegetables, avocados, chickpeas and lentils. Folic acid decreases the risk for fetal neural tube defects, defects of the baby's brain (anencephaly) or spine (spina bifida). Women of child-bearing years are recommended to consume at least 400 µg of folic acid daily. For men, 150 µg per 1,000 kcal appears sufficient. Low folate levels are associated with cardiovascular disease, although it remains unclear whether supplementation reverses the disease.

Vitamin B_{12}, or cobalamin, is necessary for fatty acid and amino acid breakdown, the synthesis of red blood cells, and the maintenance of the nervous system. Unlike other water-soluble vitamins, B_{12} is stored in the liver, secreted in the bile, and reabsorbed. The daily requirement is low, about 2 µg (and 2.2 µg and 2.6 µg for pregnant and lactating women, respectively). Vitamin B_{12} is found only in animal products. Algae such as nori and spirulina do not contain human bioavailable forms of B_{12}. Sources of abundant B_{12} include clams, oysters and organ meats. Egg yolks, fish and poultry contain high amounts. Long-term strict vegetarians who avoid eggs and dairy products must take supplementation. Symptoms of deficiency may take up to 20 years to develop. These include neuropathy, depression, dementia and poor attention span. Other symptoms are sore tongue and anaemia, similar to a folic acid deficiency.

Vitamin C, or ascorbic acid, improves iron absorption, plays a key role in the immune system and in the conversion of cholesterol to bile acids, and is needed for the synthesis of neurotransmitters and certain hormones. Also, vitamin C is an antioxidant and may help in the prevention of cataracts, certain cancers, cardiovascular disease and other degenerative diseases. Superior food sources are citrus fruits and juices, berries, melons, "bell" peppers of any colour, tomatoes and leafy green vegetables. Vitamin C is easily destroyed by heat and food processing; the best sources are raw foods. The recommended intake of 30 mg per 1,000 kcal exceeds the true vitamin C requirement but takes into account the added benefit of increased iron absorption. Iron deficiency, far more so than vitamin C deficiency, is a serious problem worldwide. The telltale disease of vitamin C deficiency is scurvy, characterized by swollen and bleeding gums, loose teeth, hemorrhaging, poor wound healing, weakness and fatigue. Megadoses of vitamin C, from 1,500 to 2,000 mg, often cause diarrhoea, abdominal cramps, nausea and, possibly, kidney stones.

Vitamin D refers to a family of chemicals that regulate calcium absorption and utilization. Vitamin D_3, or cholecalciferol, found naturally in foods, is most readily utilized by the body, although vitamin D_2, derived from plants, can also be beneficial. Both are fat soluble, like vitamin A, and are stored in body fat. Good sources include fatty fish such as salmon and mackerel, fish liver oil and certain egg yolks. Milk only contains significant levels of vitamin D when fortified. The body can manufacture adequate amounts of vitamin D_3 when oils in the skin are exposed to ultraviolet light from the sun. The amount of sunshine needed varies widely, however, depending on skin colour, exposure, and latitude (angle of ultraviolet beam). Darker skin is less efficient at absorbing ultraviolet light compared with fair skin. As such, the recommended intake of vitamin D varies, set at approximately 5 µg a day for young and middle-aged adults and 10 µg a day for seniors. Because vitamin D is stored, doses from food greater than 200 µg may be toxic. Pantothenic acid, a B-complex vitamin sometimes referred to as vitamin B_5, is necessary for the biological synthesis of vitamin D. Deficiency may cause rickets (in children), muscle weakness and osteomalacia, or softening of the bones, in adults.

Vitamin E represents a group of fat-soluble chemicals that serve as anti-oxidants, preventing the oxidation of unsaturated fatty acids. Vitamin E aids in membrane stability and protects cellular structures from damage caused by free oxygen radicals. Some studies have shown that vitamin E reduces the risk of certain cancers, cardiovascular disease and cataracts. The recommended daily intake is 3.5 to 5 mg of d-α-tocopherol, a form of vitamin E, per 1,000 kcal. The daily requirements increase with higher intake of unsaturated fat, approximately 0.4 mg of d-α-tocopherol per gram polyunsaturated fatty acid. Animal products and most fruits and vegetables are poor sources of vitamin E. Good sources include seeds, nuts, whole grains and wheatgerm, and certain vegetable oils, such as safflower and corn. Vitamin E deficiency is rare, and few side effects from high doses are known.

Vitamin K is essential for blood clotting. Although a fat-soluble vitamin, less than a few days' worth of intake is stored in the liver and the bone, so it must be replenished. Dark, leafy green vegetables are an excellent source of vitamin K, along with fermented soya foods such as *natto* (fermented soya bean). Other good sources include kiwi fruit, egg yolk, dairy products, liver and canola (rapeseed) and olive oils. The recommended intake is 75–125 µg a day, often provided by a single serving of dark green vegetables. One form of vitamin K can be produced in significant amounts by bacteria in the intestines, but diet must be the main source of vitamin K.

Minerals

Minerals and trace elements, in relation to human health, are inorganic chemicals essential for growth and fitness. Of particular public health importance are calcium, fluoride, iodine, iron, sodium and zinc. A varied diet can supply most minerals and trace elements naturally, but supplementation may be needed for fluoride and, depending on the location, certain chemicals not abundant in the soil (e.g., selenium) and thus not present in the local food supply.

Calcium is an essential component of bone and a regulator of muscle and nervous system activity. Calcium is the most common mineral in the body, and 99 per cent of the body's calcium is stored in bone and teeth. Key calcium food sources include dairy products, tofu and other soya products, other legumes such as beans and peas, sesame seeds, sardines and fish with edible bones, and leafy green vegetables such as broccoli, kale and pak choi. Calcium deficiency is associated with osteoporosis and thus hip fractures, high blood pressure and colon cancer. Early in life, bones readily absorb calcium. The process peaks at about age 25. Later in life, very little calcium is absorbed into the bones; and calcium requirements from day to day not met by the diet result in a weakening of the bones, as calcium is leeched. The situation is similar to a bank account, where one must store as much calcium as possible early on to "spend" during retirement. Calcium supplements are not unanimously recommended, for increased calcium intake results in poor absorption of iron and zinc. Nor is there a blanket recommendation for calcium intake, for many factors – age, gender, diet, physical activity and perhaps genetics – determine one's true requirement. For example, acidic foods such as soda pop and high-protein diets (particularly animal protein) leech calcium from the bones. People in industrialized nations with such diets require nearly twice as much calcium as those who consume mostly vegetables and grains. The WHO recommends a range of 250 to 400 mg of calcium per 1,000 kcal, assuming the recommending protein intake of 8–15 per cent of total calories.

Fluorine, absorbed by the body in the form of fluoride, significantly decreases the prevalence of tooth decay; and the fluoridation of public drinking water is considered one of the great public health achievements of the twentieth century. More recently, scientists have learned that fluoride also plays a role in bone growth and fracture healing. Most foods contain very little fluoride. Good sources include sea vegetables and other sea foods and green tea, which absorbs fluorine from the soil more efficiently than other plants do. Many parts of the world must rely on fluoride added to the drinking water supply. The suggested dietary goal is 0.7 mg per 1,000 kcal. Excessive fluoride intake (over 3 mg per day) can cause mottling on tooth enamel.

Iodine is essential for thyroid hormone synthesis and cell differentiation. The classic iodine deficiency disease is goitre, characterized by a swollen thyroid and difficulty in breathing and swallowing. An iodine deficiency in children or during fetal development can lead to cretinism and mental retardation. Mild iodine deficiency can cause apathy. Iodine deficiency is increasingly rare but still affects populations far from the sea, such as Central Asia and Switzerland, where the soil (and thus local food products) are low in iodine. Sea vegetables and other sea foods are iodine-rich. Table salt fortified with iodine has eliminated iodine deficiency in many parts of the world. The recommended daily intake is 75 µg per 1,000 kcal, with the requirement of pregnant women slightly higher.

Iron, as a constituent of haemoglobin, is needed to carry oxygen in red blood cells. Iron is also a key element in many enzymatic reactions. Even a slight reduction of blood iron (haemoglobin concentration of below 110 g/l) is associated with delayed learning and behaviour changes in children (Grantham-McGregor and Ani, 2001). Anaemia, a condition marked by low concentrations of haemoglobin, often results in adults in sluggishness, low endurance, and decreases in physical work capacity and work productivity for repetitive tasks (Haas and Brownlie, 2001). Modest falls in iron levels also increase absorption of toxic metals, such as cadmium and lead. An estimated 2 billion people worldwide have or express symptoms of iron deficiency, constituting a public health emergency (WHO, 1998, p. 76). Women are at greater risk of iron deficiency due to blood loss during menstruation. Anaemia in general can be remedied through the provision of iron-rich or iron-fortified foods. The daily recommended iron intake varies, however, because the bioavailability of iron from foods varies from 1 to 45 per cent. Vitamin C and animal foods enhance iron absorption; fibre, tannins (found in tea), phytates (found in grains) and polyphenols (found in coffee and red wine) reduce it. Recommendations are provided in consideration of very low (<5 per cent), low (5–10 per cent), intermediate (11–18 per cent) and high (>19 per cent) bioavailability. Corresponding intake levels are 20, 11, 5.5 and 3.5 mg per 1,000 kcal. The type of iron more easily absorbed is haem-iron. Sources include clams, oysters, organ meats, beef, pork, poultry, fish and fortified grains. Fortification of wheat or maize flour, salt and soy sauce has been shown to be successful in regions where the natural diet is low in bioavailable iron.

Sodium helps regulate water distribution, blood pressure and the body's acid-base balance. Many foods and even water have sodium, but the most familiar source is common salt, sodium chloride, $NaCl$. The sodium cation, Na^+, works in concert with potassium, K^+, in regulating the flow of water and some other chemicals in and out of our cells. A 1:1 ratio of potassium and sodium along with equal or more amounts of calcium help maintain optimal blood pressure. The natural sodium content in foods is enough to meet the minimum requirement, approximately 500 mg per day. The WHO considers a healthy level to be between 1,000 and 2,000 mg. (Note that 2 g of sodium is 5 g of salt, or less than a teaspoon.) Processed, canned and restaurant foods are often high in sodium, even though they might not taste overtly salty. High sodium levels, however, are associated with increased risk of cerebrovascular stroke (Perry and Beevers, 1992) and high blood pressure (Law, Frost and Wald, 1991). The kidneys excrete excess sodium through the urinary tract and recycle sodium when in short supply. Sodium deficiency is rare, occasionally seen among athletes after persistent sweating and too much sodium-free water.

Zinc has recently been seen to be crucial for a healthy immune system, for linear growth, and in supporting neural activity and memory. Like iron, however, its level of absorption can vary greatly. Zinc is involved in at least 60 different enzyme reactions, including the RNA polymerases. (RNA acts as an intermediary, carrying genetic information from the DNA to the location of protein synthesis.) Meat and fish are naturally abundant in zinc, along with wheat germ. The zinc in milk is not well absorbed, due to its calcium content, which lowers the bioavailability. Most plants are low in zinc, and vegetable protein (high in phytic acid) lowers zinc's bioavailability. The substitution of vegetable protein for animal protein is a leading cause of zinc deficiency. Coffee, with its polyphenols, and fibre also reduces zinc bioavailability. For diets with high (20 per cent) and low (10 per cent) bioavailability, the recommended intake is 6 mg and 10 mg of zinc per 1,000 kcal, respectively.

Other essential minerals include boron, copper, chromium, magnesium, manganese, molybdenum, nickel, phosphorus, potassium and selenium.

Other nutrients

Simple fortification or dietary supplementation in pill form, although exceedingly beneficial in some circumstances, cannot be viewed as a panacea. Food is more than a container of macronutrients, vitamins and minerals that can be isolated in a laboratory and injected directly into the bloodstream. Attaining nutrients through food instead of supplementation is largely seen as a superior means of meeting nutritional requirements. This may be due to the fact that little is still known about other components in the foods we eat, particularly carotenoids, bioflavonoids, salicytates, and phytoestrogens. Also, a class of chemicals called antioxidants appears to reduce the risk of age-related diseases by helping repair cellular and DNA damage caused by free radicals. Free radicals, natural by-products of breathing and actually needed for the immune system, are highly reactive molecules or single atoms that will "steal" electrons from DNA and other molecules unless "neutralized" by an antioxidant.

Carotenoids include lycopene, which is found in tomatoes and watermelon. This compound may lower the risk of certain cancers (Hwang and Bowen, 2002). Two others, lutein and zeaxanthin, present in dark, leafy green vegetables, are concentrated in the retina and may help protect vision as we age (Mozaffarieh, Sacu and Wedrich, 2003). There are over 500 plant carotenoids, with many appearing to have some significant role in health. Many bioflavonoids are antioxidants and may reduce the risk of cardiovascular disease and cancer. Phytoestrogens, which include flavonoids, may reduce the effects brought by menopause and may be beneficial in preventing breast and prostate cancer (Sarkar and Li, 2003). Antioxidants transcend nutritional classification and include vitamins (A, C, E, β–carotene), minerals (selenium) and many bioflavonoids. Diets rich in fruits and vegetables supply an abundance of all the types of compounds mentioned above.

Water is considered a macronutrient, and the need for fluid is met through both food and beverages. Water is more important for short-term survival than food, and under most conditions humans would die if deprived of water for more than a couple of days. The human body is approximately 60 per cent water, and an adequate intake of water is needed to balance water lost through breath, sweat and urine. Water can be an important source of iron, iodine, fluoride, calcium, copper and many trace elements. Water is protected as a human right under international law. (Access to water enjoys explicit protection under the 1979 Convention on the Elimination of all Forms of Discrimination against Women and the 1989 Convention on the Rights of the Child.) The recommended intake of drinking water varies widely, for most foods contain water, and some, particularly fruits, are up to 90 per cent water. Also, requirements vary according to climate and physical activity. Of greater concern is water quality in the prevention of communicable and food-borne diseases, as discussed in Chapter 9.

Alcohol provides some essential minerals and compounds in certain populations, such as amino acids from fermented cacti and thiamine from traditional African beer. And there is evidence that moderate amounts of ethanol may reduce the incidence of coronary heart disease, increase levels of HDL and reduce stress. However, it is unwise to promote alcohol for its health benefits because the risk of alcohol abuse and its related ill social, physical and mental health effects is too great.

BIBLIOGRAPHY

A.D.A.M. Medical Encyclopedia. 2004. *Fat*, available online: http://www.nlm.nih.gov/medlineplus/ency/article/002468.htm [Nov. 2004].

Alpha-Tocopherol, Beta Carotene Cancer Prevention Study Group. 1994. "The effect of vitamin E and beta carotene on the incidence of lung cancer and other cancers in male smokers", *New England Journal of Medicine*, Vol. 330, No. 15, pp. 1029–1035.

American Dietetic Association. 1997. "New study proves significant Medicare savings with medical nutrition therapy", press release, 19 Mar.

——. 2003. "Memo to working Americans: 'Desktop dining' trend demands new office eating etiquette", press release, 30 Sep.

Arcand, J. 2001. *Undernourishment and economic growth: The efficiency cost of hunger*, FAO Economic and Social Development Paper 147 (Rome, FAO).

Australian Department of Health and Ageing. 2004. *Diabetes statistics*, available online: http://www.healthinsite.gov.au/topics/Diabetes_Statistics [Nov. 2004].

Australian Institute of Health and Welfare. 2002. *Diabetes: Australian Facts 2002*, AIHW Cat. No. CVD 20, Diabetes Series No. 3 (Canberra).

Australian National Health and Medical Research Council (NHMRC). 2000. *Nutrition in Aboriginal and Torres Strait Islander peoples*, information paper (Canberra).

Backman, D.; Carman, J. 2004. *Fruits and vegetables and physical activity at the worksite: Business leaders and working women speak out on access and environment* (Sacramento, CA, California Department of Health Services).

Baer, L.; Hausman, H. 2003. "USDA's fruit and vegetable pilot program reveals school environments that include fruits and vegetables generate increased consumption among students", press release, Produce For Better Health Foundation, 31 Mar.

Bangladesh Garment Manufacturers and Exporters Association (BGMEA). 2004. *Garment export data*, available online: http://www.bgmea.com/data.htm [Nov. 2004].

Bazzano, L. et al. 2003. "Dietary fiber intake and reduced risk of coronary heart disease in US men and women: The National Health and Nutrition Examination Survey I Epidemiologic Follow-up Study", *Archives of Internal Medicine*, Vol. 163, No. 16, pp. 1897–1904.

BBC. 2003. "Mass food poisoning hits China workers", *BBC Online*, 24 Aug., available online: http://news.bbc.co.uk/2/low/asia-pacific/3177319.stm [Nov. 2004].

Benson, L. et al. 2003. "Ancient maize from Chacoan great houses: Where was it grown?", *Proceedings of the National Academy of Sciences*, Vol. 100, No. 22, pp. 13111–13115.

Better Health Channel. 2004. *Aboriginal diet and nutrition*, available online: http://www.betterhealth.vic.gov.au/bhcv2/bhcarticles.nsf/pages/Aboriginal_diet_and_nutrition [Nov. 2004].

Brown, J. 1988. *Canteens and food services in industry: A manual* (ILO, Geneva).

California Department of Health Services (DOH). 2001. *California Dietary Practices Survey*, unpublished 2001 preliminary data (Sacramento, CA).

——. 2003a. *California Behavioral Risk Factor Survey*, 2002 data, Survey Research Group, Cancer Surveillance Section (Sacramento, CA).

——. 2003b. *The economic burden of physical inactivity, overweight and obesity in California*, unpublished report, Cancer Prevention and Nutrition Section, and Epidemiology and Health Promotion Section (Sacramento, CA).

Cameron, A. 2003. *Health economic evaluation of diet and physical activity interventions for the prevention of non-communicable diseases*, unpublished report.

——. et al. 2003. "Overweight and obesity in Australia: The 1999–2000 Australian Diabetes, Obesity and Lifestyle Study (AusDiab)", *Medical Journal of Australia*, Vol. 178, No. 9, pp. 427–432.

Cernea, S.; Hancu, N.; Raz, I. 2003. "Diet and coronary heart disease in diabetes", *Acta Diabetol*, Vol. 40, Suppl. 2, pp. S389–400.

Chakravarty, I. 2001. *A strategy document to bring about proper coordination in the street food sector and consumer advocacy programmes (FAO, TCP-SAF-8924 (A))* (Pretoria, FAO).

Codex Alimentarius Commission. 1999. *General principles of food hygiene* (Rome).

——. 2003. *Report of the Thirty-fifth Session of the Codex Committee on Food Hygiene* (Washington, DC).

Codjia, G. 2000. *FAO technical support for improvement within the street food sector* (Pretoria, South Africa Department of Health).

Cowan, D. 1998. "Power to the healthy", in *Employee health and productivity*, as cited in the *Guide to nutrition promotion in the workplace*, p. 8 (Toronto, Ontario Public Health Association, 2002).

Dawson, R.; Liamrangsi, S.; Boccas, F. 1996. "Bangkok's street food project", *Food, Nutrition and Agriculture*, No. 17–18, pp. 38–44.

Deloitte and Touche. 1997. *Industrial Society Catering Survey* (London).

Deurenberg-Yap, M. et al. 2000. "The paradox of low body mass index and high body fat percentage among Chinese, Malays and Indians in Singapore", *International Journal of Obesity and Related Metabolic Disorders*, Vol. 24, No. 8, pp. 1011–1017.

DiSogra, L.; Taccone, F. 2003. *5 A Day for Better Health Program (USA)*, presented at Food and Vegetable Promotion Initiative, World Health Organization, Geneva, 25–27 Aug.

Duncan, K.; Bacon, J.; Weinsier, R. 1983. "The effects of high and low energy density diets on satiety, energy intake, and eating time of obese and non-obese subjects", *American Journal of Clinical Nutrition*, Vol. 37, No. 5, pp. 763–767.

Eurest. 2004. *Eurest Lunchtime Report 2004* (Uxbridge, United Kingdom, Compass Group).

Eurodiet Project. 2003. "Toward public health nutrition strategies in the European Union to implement food based dietary guidelines and to enhance healthier lifestyles", *Public Health Nutrition*, Vol. 4, No. 2A, pp. 307–324.

Eurostaf. 2001. *La restauration commerciale – perspectives stratégiques et financières* (Paris).

Expert Panel on Trans Fatty Acids and Coronary Heart Disease. 1995. "Trans fatty acids and coronary heart disease risk. Report of the expert panel on trans fatty acids and coronary heart disease", *American Journal of Clinical Nutrition*, Vol. 62, No. 3, pp. 655S–708S.

Finkelstein, E.; Fiebelkorn, I.; Wang, G. 2004. "State-level estimates of annual medical expenditures attributable to obesity", *Obesity Research*, Vol. 12, No. 1, pp. 18–24.

Flegal, K. et al. 2002. "Prevalence and trends in obesity among US adults, 1999–2000", *Journal of the American Medical Association*, Vol. 288, No. 14, pp. 1723–1727.

Flynn, A. 2003. "No time for lunch", Public and Commercial Services Union press release, 26 July.

Food and Agriculture Organization (FAO). 1966. *Nutrition and working efficiency*, Basic Study No. 5 (Rome).

——. 1971. *Report of the FAO/ILO/WHO Expert Consultation on Workers' Feeding, 10–15 May* (Rome).

——. 1976. *The feeding of workers in developing countries*, Food and Nutrition Paper No. 6 (Rome).

——. 1998. *Rural women and food security: Current situation and perspectives* (Rome).

——. 2001. *Training manual for environmental health officers on safe handling practices for street foods* (Rome), available online: http://www.doh.gov.za/department/foodcontrol/streetfood/03.pdf

Galenson, W.; Pyatt, G. 1964. *The quality of labour and economic development in certain countries*, ILO Studies and Reports, New Series, No. 68 (Geneva).

Gibney, M. et al. 1995. "Consumption of sugars", *American Journal of Clinical Nutrition*, Vol. 62, No. 1S, pp. 178S–194S.

Global Alliance for Workers and Communities (GA). 2003a. *An appraisal report on the improvement of nutritional aspects (canteen food, hygiene, water) and reduction of iron deficiency anaemia (IDA) in workers at their workplace.*

——. 2003b. *Developing health care programmes in associated factories*, white paper (Department of Community Health, St John's Medical College and Global Alliance).

Goskomstat. 2003. *Federal State Statistics Service*, available online: http://www.gks.ru [July 2004].

Grantham-McGregor, S.; Ani, C. 2001. "A review of studies on the effect of iron deficiency on cognitive development in children", *Journal of Nutrition*, Vol. 131, No. 2S-II, pp. 649S–668S.

Haas, J.; Brownlie, T. 2001. "Iron deficiency and reduced work capacity: A critical review of the research to determine a causal relationship", *Journal of Nutrition*, Vol. 131, No. 2S-II, pp. 576S–590S.

Halliwell, B. 2000. "The antioxidant paradox", *The Lancet*, Vol. 355, pp. 1179–1180.

Henson, S. 2003. *The economics of food safety in developing countries*, FAO ESA Working Paper No. 03-19 (Rome, FAO Agricultural and Development Economics Division).

Hogan, P.; Dall, T.; Nikolov, P. 2003. "Economic costs of diabetes in the United States in 2002", *Diabetes Care*, Vol. 26, No. 3, pp. 917–932.

Horton, S. 1999. "Opportunities for investments in nutrition in low-income Asia", *Asian Development Review*, Vol. 17, No. 1-2, pp. 246–273.

Hossains, M. 1989. "Food security, agriculture and the economy: The next 25 years", in Bangladesh Planning Commission: *Food strategies in Bangladesh: Medium and long-term perspectives* (Dhaka, The University Press Ltd.).

Hungary Ministry of Health (MoH). 2003. *Johan Béla National Programme for the Decade of Health* (Budapest).

Hutabarat, L. 1994. *Street foods in Bangkok: The nutritional contribution and the contaminants content of street foods* (Rome, FAO).

Hwang, E.; Bowen, P. 2002. "Can the consumption of tomatoes or lycopene reduce cancer risk?", *Integrative Cancer Therapy*, Vol. 1, No. 2, pp. 121–132.

Institut de Coopération Sociale Internationale (ICOSI). 2004. *Meal vouchers – A tool serving the interests of the social pact in Europe* (Paris).

Institute of Nutrition and Food Science (INFS). 1997. *National Nutrition Survey of Bangladesh 1995/96* (Dhaka, Dhaka University).

——. 1998. *Socio-economic and nutritional status of selected garment workers of Bangladesh, 1995/97* (Dhaka, Dhaka University).

International Bottled Water Association (IBWA). 2004. *The 2003 stats: Solid gains put bottled water in No. 2 spot*, fact sheet from the IBWA, based on Beverage Marketing Corporation data (Alexandria, VA).

International Labour Office (ILO). 1946. *Nutrition in industry* (Montreal).

——. 2003. *Safety in numbers: Pointers for a global safety culture at work* (Geneva).

International Monetary Fund (IMF). 2004. "Concluding statement of the IMF mission to the Russian Federation (in the context of the 2004 Article IV consultation)", 24 June (Moscow).

Ivanov, V.; Suvorov, A. 2003. *Why has life expectancy in Russia fallen so dramatically in the past decade?* (Moscow, Institute of Economic Forecasting).

Jequier, E. 2002. "Pathways to obesity", *International Journal of Obesity and Related Metabolic Disorders*, Vol. 26, Suppl. 2, pp. S12–17.

Jing, L. 2004. "Beijing authorities strengthen food safety", *China Daily* website, 3 Nov., available: http://www.chinadaily.com.cn/english/doc/2004-11/03/content_388104.htm [Nov. 2004].

Jones, T.; Eaton, C. 1994. "Cost–benefit analysis of walking to prevent coronary heart disease", *Archives of Family Medicine*, Vol. 3, No. 8, pp. 703–710.

Kiefer, I. et al. 1998. "Obesity in Austria: Epidemiologic and social medicine aspects", *Acta Med Austriaca*, Vol. 25, No. 4–5, pp. 126–128.

Konig, K.; Navia, J. 1995. "Nutritional role of sugars in oral health", *American Journal of Clinical Nutrition*, Vol. 62, Suppl. 1, pp. 275S–282S.

Kumanyika, S. et al. 2002. "Obesity prevention: the case for action", *International Journal of Obesity*, Vol. 26, No. 3, pp. 425–436.

Lambert, M.; Cheevers, E.; Coopoo, Y. 1994. "Relationship between energy expenditure and productivity of sugar cane cutters and stackers", *Occupational Medicine*, Vol. 44, No. 4, pp. 190–194.

Law, M.; Frost, C.; Wald, N. 1991. "By how much does dietary salt reduction lower blood pressure? I – Analysis of data from trials of salt reduction", *British Medical Journal*, Vol. 302, No. 6780, pp. 819–824.

Le Marchand, L. et al. 1997. "Dietary fibre and colorectal cancer risk", *Epidemiology*, Vol. 8, No. 6, pp. 658–665.

Leeder, S. et al. 2002. "The economic consequences of non-communicable diseases, with special reference to cardiovascular disease", draft prepared for World Bank Symposium for Chronic Disease, 16 Sep.

Lewin Group. 1998. *The cost of covering medical nutrition therapy services under TRICARE: Benefits costs, cost avoidance and savings*, final report for the United States Department of Defense, Health Affairs (Washington, DC).

Liu, J. et al. 2002. "The economic burden of coronary heart disease in the UK", *Heart*, Vol. 88, No. 6, pp. 597–603.

Lyons, W.; Moller, C. 2002. "Britain becoming a SAD place to work as lunch breaks become a distant memory", *The Scotsman*, 2 July.

Martins, J.H.; Anelich, L.E. 2000. *Improving street foods in South Africa*, conducted for the FAO, TCP/SAF/8924(A) (Pretoria, FAO).

Mazzon, J.A. 2001. *Programa de alimentação do trabalhador: 25 anos de contribuições ao desenvolvimento do Brasil* (São Paulo, Fundação Instituto de Administração, Universidade de São Paulo).

McAulay, V. et al. 2001. "Acute hypoglycemia in humans causes attentional dysfunction while nonverbal intelligence is preserved", *Diabetes Care*, Vol. 24, No. 10, pp. 1745–1750.

Measham, A.; Chatterjee, M. 1999. *Wasting away – The crisis of malnutrition in India* (Washington, DC, World Bank).

Mensink, R. et al. 2003. "Effects of dietary fatty acids and carbohydrates on the ratio of serum total to HDL cholesterol and on serum lipids and apolipoproteins: A meta-analysis of 60 controlled trials", *American Journal of Clinical Nutrition*, Vol. 77, No. 5, pp. 1146–1155.

Meyer, M. 2004. *Workplace Fruit Programme*, presented at the 4th International 5 A Day Symposium, Christchurch, 10 Aug.

Micozzi, M. 1992. *Macronutrients: Investigating their role in cancer* (New York, Marcel Decker).

Mokdad, A. et al. 2001. "The continuing epidemics of obesity and diabetes in the United States", *Journal of the American Medical Association*, Vol. 286, No. 10, pp. 1195–1200.

Mowlah, G. 2004. *Report on workers' nutrition in Bangladesh* (Dhaka, Institute of Nutrition and Food Sciences, University of Dhaka).

Mozaffarieh, M.; Sacu, S.; Wedrich, A. 2003. 'The role of the carotenoids, lutein and zeaxanthin, in protecting against age-related macular degeneration: A review based on controversial evidence", *Nutrition Journal*, Vol. 2, No. 1, available online: http://www.nutritionj.com/content/2/1/20.

Navarro, A., et al. 2003. "Characterization of meat consumption and risk of colorectal cancer in Cordoba, Argentina", *Nutrition*, Vol. 19, No. 1, pp. 7–10.

National Heart, Lung and Blood Institute. 2001. *High blood cholesterol: What you need to know*, fact sheet, NIH Publication No. 01-3290 (Bethesda, MD).

——. 2002. *Morbidity and mortality: 2002 chart book on cardiovascular, lung, and blood diseases* (Bethesda, MD).

Nutrition Resource Centre. 2002. *Guide to nutrition promotion in the workplace* (Toronto, Ontario Public Health Association).

Ogden, C. et al. 2002. "Prevalence and trends in overweight among US children and adolescents, 1999–2000", *Journal of the American Medical Association*, Vol. 288, No. 14, pp. 1728–1732.

Ontario Ministry of Health and Long-Term Care. 2004. *Diabetes: Strategies for prevention*, available online:http://www.health.gov.on.ca/english/public/pub/ministry_reports/diabetes/diabetes.html [Nov. 2004].

Pan American Health Organization (PAHO). 2003. *Situación de la seguridad alimentaria nutricional en Guatemala: 1991–2002* (Guatemala, Sistema de Naciones Unidas de Guatemala).

Pederson, R. 2004. *6 a day Denmark: Increasing availability of and access to fruit and vegetables* (Copenhagen, Danish Cancer Society).

Pereira, M. et al. 2005. "Fast-food habits, weight gain, and insulin resistance (the CARDIA study): 15-year prospective analysis", *The Lancet*, Vol. 365, No. 9453, pp. 36–42.

Perry, I.; Beevers, D. 1992. "Salt intake and stroke: A possible direct effect", *Journal of Human Hypertension Issues*, Vol. 6, No. 1, pp. 23–25.

Peugeot. 2004. "Le site PSA Peugeot Citroën de Rennes développe, en partenariat avec Previade-Mutouest et Sodexho, un programme de prévention santé par l'alimentation pour ses collaborateurs", PSA Peugeot Citroën press kit, June.

Pietinen, P. et al. 2001. "Nutrition and cardiovascular disease in Finland since the early 1970s: A success story", *Journal of Nutrition, Health and Aging*, Vol. 5, No. 3, pp. 150–154.

Popkin, B. et al. 2001. "Trends in diet, nutritional status, and diet-related non-communicable diseases in China and India: The economic costs of the nutrition transition", *Nutrition Review*, Vol. 59, No. 12, pp. 379–90.

Reddy, A. 2002. "Creating safe space and new opportunities for women workers", *Changemakers Journal*, Jan., available online: http://www.changemakers.net/journal/02january/reddy.cfm [Jan.2002].

Ross, J.; Horton, S. 1998. *Economic consequences of iron deficiency* (Ottawa, The Micronutrient Initiative).

Sarkar, F.; Li, Y. 2003. "Soy isoflavones and cancer prevention", *Cancer Investigation*, Vol. 21, No. 5, pp. 44–57.

Saskatchewan Department of Health. 2001. *Public health/population health services in Saskatchewan* (Saskatchewan, Regina).

Singapore Ministry of Health. 1999. *National Health Survey 1998* (Singapore, Epidemiology and Disease Control Division).

Singapore Ministry of Manpower. 2003. *Labour Force Survey 2003*, Nov. (Singapore).

Singapore Ministry of Trade and Industry. 2004. *Main Indicators of the Singapore Economy* (Singapore, Singapore Department of Statistics).

Spurgeon, A. 2003. *Working time: Its impact on safety and health* (Geneva, ILO).

Statistik Austria. 2004. *Statistik Austria*, available online: http://www.statistik.at/index_englisch.shtml [Nov. 2004].

Stephenson, J. et al. 2000. *The costs of illness attributable to physical inactivity in Australia, A preliminary study*, prepared for the Commonwealth Department of Health and Aged Care and the Australian Sports Commission (Canberra).

Stoltzfus, R. 2001. "Defining iron-deficiency anemia in public health terms: A time for reflection", *Journal of Nutrition*, Vol. 131, No. 2S-II, pp. 565S–567S.

Thompson, D. et al. 1998. "Estimated economic costs of obesity to U.S. business", *American Journal of Health Promotion*, Vol. 13, No. 2, pp. 120–127.

Trinkl, A. 1999. "Health plays a crucial role in California labor market, according to UCSF researchers", University of California, San Francisco, press release, 7 Aug.

Ulmer, H. et al. 2001. "Recent trends and socio-demographic distribution of cardiovascular risk factors: Results from two population surveys in the Austrian WHO CINDI demonstration area", *Wien Klin Wochenschr*, Vol. 113, No. 15–16, pp. 573–579.

United Nations. 2003. *Romania Common Country Assessment 2003* (Bucharest, United Nations System in Romania).

——. 2004. *Fifth Report on the World Nutrition Situation: Nutrition for improved development outcomes*, United Nations System Standing Committee on Nutrition, Mar. (New York).

United States Code. 2000. "Basic 40-hour workweek; work schedules; regulations", Title 5, 6101(a)(3)(F) (Washington, DC, Office of the Law Division Counsel).

United States Department of Health and Human Services (US DHHS). 1996. *Enhancing health in the Head Start workplace: A training guide* (Washington, DC, US DHHS Head Start Bureau).

United States Library of Congress. 1989. *Soviet Union: A country study*, available online: http://www.country-data.com/frd/cs/sutoc.html [Nov. 2004].

USAID/UNICEF/WHO. 1999. *Nutrition essentials: A guide for program managers* (Washington, DC, BASICS).

Veloso, I.; Santana, V. 2002. "Impacto nutricional do programa de alimentação do trabalhador no Brasil (Impact of the worker food programme in Brazil)", *Revista Panamericana de Salud Publica*, Vol. 11, No. 1, pp. 24–31.

Verdejo, G.; Bortman, M. 2000. "Argentina: Health situation analysis and trends, 1986–1995", *Epidemiological Bulletin*, Vol. 21, No. 1, pp. 7–10.

Viswanath, V. 2002. "The world of corporate catering", *The Hindu Business Line*, 22 June, available online: http://www.blonnet.com/canvas/2002/06/22/stories/2002062200010100.htm.

Wang, G.; Dietz, W. 2002. "Economic burden of obesity in youths aged 6 to 17 years: 1979–1999", *Pediatrics*, Vol. 109, No. 5, p. E81, available online: http://pediatrics.aappublications.org/cgi/content/full/109/5/e81.

Wanjek, C. 2003. *Bad medicine – Misconceptions and misuses revealed, from distance healing to vitamin O* (New York, Wiley and Sons).

Wolf, A.; Colditz, G. 1998. "Current estimates of the economic cost of obesity in the United States", *Obesity Research*, Vol. 6, No. 2, pp. 97–106.

World Bank. 2000. *Bangladesh: Breaking the malnutrition barrier* (Dhaka, University Press Limited).

——/Indian Institute of Management. 2003. *Nike in Vietnam: The Tae Kwang Vina factory*, Empowerment Case Studies Series (Washington, DC, World Bank).

World Fact Book. 2004a. *Russia*, available online: http://www.cia.gov/cia/publications/factbook/geos/rs.html [Nov. 2004].

——. 2004b. *Lebanon*, available online: http://www.cia.gov/cia/publications/factbook/geos/le.html [Nov. 2004].

World Health Organization (WHO). 1996. *Participatory hygiene and sanitation transformations: A new approach to working with communities* (Geneva).

——. 1999. *Strategies for implementing HACCP in small and/or less developed businesses*, report of a WHO consultation (The Hague).

——. 2000a. *Global database on child growth and malnutrition: Forecast of trends*, WHO/NHD/00.3 (Geneva).

——. 2000b. *Global water supply and sanitation assessment 2000 report* (Geneva, WHO/New York United Nations Children's Fund).

——. 2002a. *The World Health Report 2002: Reducing risks, promoting healthy life* (Geneva).

——. 2002b. *The cost of diabetes*, fact sheet No. 236, available online: http://www.who.int/mediacentre/factsheets/fs236/en/ [Nov. 2004].

——. 2002c. *Global Strategy for Food Safety: Safer food for better health* (Geneva).

——. 2003a. *Battling iron deficiency anaemia*, available online: http://www.who.int/nut/ida.htm [Nov. 2004].

——. 2003b. *The World Health Report 2003: Shaping the future* (Geneva).

——. 2003c. *Fruit, vegetables and NCD disease prevention*, WHO fact sheet, Sep. (Geneva).

——. 2003d. *WHO fruit and vegetable promotion initiative*, report of the meeting, Geneva, 25–27 Aug. 2003 (Geneva).

——. 2003e. *Micronutrient deficiencies – Combating vitamin A deficiency*, available online: http://www.who.int/nut/vad.htm [Nov. 2004].

——. 2004a. *Obesity and overweight*, available online: http://www.who.int/dietphysicalactivity/publications/facts/obesity/en/ [Nov. 2004].

——. 2004b. *Global Strategy on Diet, Physical Activity and Health*, annex of World Health Assembly Resolution WHA57.17, paragraph 62, 22 May (Geneva).

——. 2004c. *Russian Federation*, available online: http://www.who.int/countries/rus/en/ [Nov. 2004].

——. 2004d. *Water-related diseases, Diarrhoea*, available online: http://www.who.int/water_sanitation_health/diseases/diarrhoea/en/ [Nov. 2004].

——. 2004e. *Water-related diseases, Schistosomiasis*, available online: http://www.who.int/water_sanitation_health/diseases/schisto/en/ [Nov. 2004].

——. 2004f. *Water-related diseases, Arsenicosis*, available online: http://www.who.int/water_sanitation_health/diseases/arsenicosis/en/ [Nov. 2004].

——. 2004g. *Global alcohol database, adult per capita consumption*, available online at: http://www3.who.int/whosis/menu.cfm+path=whosis,alcohol&language=english. [Jan. 2005].

——. 2004h. *Guidelines for drinking-water quality* (Geneva).

—— Expert Consultation. 2004. "Appropriate body-mass index for Asian populations and its implications for policy and intervention strategies", *The Lancet*, Vol. 363, No. 9403, pp. 157–163.

——/FAO. 1998. *Preparation and use of food-based dietary guidelines*, report of a joint FAO/WHO consultation, WHO Technical Report Series No. 880 (Geneva).

——/——. 2002. *Diet, nutrition and the prevention of chronic diseases*, report of a joint WHO/FAO expert consultation, WHO Technical Report Series 916 (Geneva).

—— Regional Office for the Eastern Mediterranean (WHO EMRO). 2003. *Healthy marketplaces: Working towards ensuring the supply of safer food*, document WHO-WM/FCS/005/E/G/11.03/1000 (Cairo).

—— Regional Office for Europe (WHO ROE). 1998. *Highlights on health in Austria* (Copenhagen).

—— ——. 1999. *Highlights on health in Romania* (Copenhagen).

—— Regional Office for the Western Pacific (WHO ROWP). 2003. *Health care decision-making in the Western Pacific Region: Diabetes and the care continuum in the Pacific Island countries* (Manila).

——/UNICEF/UNA. 2001. *Iron deficiency anaemia: Assessment, prevention and control. A guide for programme managers*, Document WHO/NHD/01.3 (Geneva, WHO).

——/World Bank. 2002. *Food policy options: Preventing and controlling nutrition related non-communicable diseases*, HNP Discussion Paper (Washington, DC, World Bank).

Zenith International. 1999. "Water explosion in Middle East", press release, 5 Aug.

——. 2001. "One million water coolers in Western Europe", press release, 6 Sep.

INDEX

Note: Page numbers in **bold** refer to shaded boxes and tables; those in *italic* refer to figures and the Appendices.